LOOKING FOR OLD ON[T]
TWO CENTURIES OF LANDSCA[.]

Every year, thousands of people drive along southern Ontario's country roads, past its farmyards, and through its hamlets. In *Looking for Old Ontario*, Thomas McIlwraith shows us how to `read' familiar countryside landmarks as chapters in a rich historical narrative. Drawing on thirty years of field work and archival research, the author reflects on and interprets two hundred years of interaction between the land and its inhabitants.

Looking for Old Ontario guides the traveller through the vernacular landscape of the province, to look in a new way at barns and fences, jails and post offices, inns and mills, canals and railways, roadsides, cemeteries, and much, much more. To McIlwraith's trained eye, even the most ordinary features of the cultural landscape can communicate social meaning. He shows us how to date a house. He explains the popularity of brick in the province. He notes the economical use and reuse of materials and ponders their meaning. He helps us look with fresh eyes at `the unexceptional, the ordinary, the vernacular,' for it is there, he believes, that we may uncover the character of those who have built and rebuilt old Ontario.

McIlwraith's careful sleuthing and his contemplative style differentiate his work from manuals or handbooks. And, since landscape interpretation is a highly visual subject, *Looking for Old Ontario* is illustrated extensively with photographs, drawings, and maps. This book will be useful to general readers anywhere who are interested in recognizing the broader meanings of their communities' heritage, as well as to students of geography, history, and planning.

THOMAS F. McILWRAITH is an associate professor of geography at Erindale College, University of Toronto.

THOMAS F. McILWRAITH

Looking for Old Ontario

TWO CENTURIES OF LANDSCAPE CHANGE

UNIVERSITY OF TORONTO PRESS
Toronto Buffalo London

ISBN 0–8020–0708–2 (cloth)
ISBN 0–8020–7658–0 (paper)

Printed on acid-free paper

Canadian Cataloguing in Publication Data

McIlwraith, Thomas Forsyth, 1941–
  Looking for old Ontario : two centuries of landscape change

  Includes bibliographical references and index.
  ISBN 0–8020–0708–2 (bound) ISBN 0–8020–7658–0 (pbk.)

  1. Human geography – Ontario, Southern. 2. Landscape –
  Ontario, Southern – History. 3. Buildings – Ontario,
  Southern – History. 4. Ontario, Southern – Historical
  geography. I. Title.

  GF512.06M32 1997   304.2'09713   C96–931861–8

University of Toronto Press acknowledges
the assistance to its publishing program of the
Canada Council and the Ontario Arts Council.

This book has been published with the help of a grant from the
Humanities and Social Sciences Federation of Canada,
using funds provided by the
Social Sciences and Humanities Research Council of Canada.

For my wife, Duane,
and our boys, Tad and Gavin

Contents

Illustrations

NOTE: Survey township and county names are used in captions for locational purposes; administrative changes have made some of these place names obsolete.

Preface

I cannot remember a time when I have not been looking at Ontario. Studying the land is what geographers do, and I was doing geography instinctively long before I was aware of the possibility of pursuing a career in it. Historical geography, and then the idea of cultural landscape, came to my attention during my graduate student years, and now, some three decades later, I am still keen to apply these aspects of the field to finding out about the land of Ontario.

Learning about Ontario has been a joyous experience for me, enriched by comments and insights from a host of colleagues and friends. Among those who have helped me to understand Ontario are Tommy Adamson, Tony Adamson, Christopher Andreae, John Blumenson, Martyn Bowden, Heather Broadbent, Mary Brunet, Gordon Cochrane, Russ Cooper, Dorothy Duncan, Peter Ennals, Mary Lou Evans, Ron Farquhar, David Fayle, Janet Fayle, Gunter Gad, George Grant, Peter Haggett, David Hanna, Grant Head, Tom Hill, Steve Hoelscher, Deryck Holdsworth, Cecil Houston, Lorne Joyce, Martha Kidd, Ralph Krueger, David Lambden, Jim Lemon, Bob Macaulay, David McClung, James McClure, Ken Macpherson, B. Madill, Mary Manning, M. Maxwell, Ian Montagnes, Tim Orpwood, Brian Osborne, Steven Otto, Wallace Oughtred, Deight Potts, Ted Relph, Douglas Richardson, Bob Sandusky, Oliver Seiler, Gerry Shain, Seamus Smyth, Neilson Stark, Rob Summerby-Murray, James Talman, Chester Teeple, Bill Thomson, Chris Tossel, Bill Towns, Herbert Walker, John Warkentin, Bill Westfall, Faye Whitfield, Gordon Winder, David Wood, Graeme Wynn, and Wilbur Zelinsky.

Scores of householders, shopkeepers, millers, and entrepreneurs throughout southern Ontario have fielded my inquiries, and I salute them for their grace and attention at every turn. I remember the annual, week-long field camps with third-year undergraduates from Erindale: at Lafontaine, Paisley, Peterborough, Hay Bay, Turkey Point, Mattawa, Campbellford, and the Pinery. The students were out on the back roads and village streets of heartland Ontario, in the barns and the farm kitchens too, always sketching, questioning, and challenging me to think about what we were seeing. I feel as though I have walked or driven most of the roads between the southern Great Lakes and the Precambrian Shield with these groups, and I know that I have taken thousands of photographs of this photogenic region. I remember also ten enriching years as a member and chairman of the Local Architectural Conservation Advisory Committee of the City of Mississauga and the stimulating discussions and outings made possible as a result. More than a few developers and administrators were puzzled by our zeal, but what a tremendous learning experience we had.

Special thanks go to Don Evoy for his drawings, to Byron Moldofsky and Jane Davey for the maps, and to John Mezaks and Leon Warmski for guiding me enthusiastically through the Archives of Ontario. The Ontario Arts Council, the Social Sciences Federation of Canada, and the Department of Geography at the University of Toronto have been generous. At the University of Toronto Press, Gerry Hallowell has encouraged me with good humour and profound insight. John Parry, Darlene Zeleney, and Rob Ferguson have put their experienced mark on text, layout, and design.

To my family, who never stopped believing that a book might eventually emerge from all those expeditions through the countryside, here it is. I dedicate it to you.

TFM
Mississauga

LOOKING FOR OLD ONTARIO

1

Acknowledging landscape

Ontario's landscape is filled with evidence of its history. From Windsor to Cornwall, from Niagara to the edge of the Precambrian Shield, the hopes and achievements of tens of thousands of men and women are written on its fields, roads, houses, villages, and much more. This book is a reflection and interpretation of the way the land reveals those lives. It offers direction for reading the story and demonstrates the rich rewards of such an enterprise.

The cultural landscape of Ontario is the product of innumerable, often anonymous stage hands, toiling over two centuries and creating the sets for a slow, powerful drama (Figure 1.1). Surveyors scored the land, and generations have inscribed it with a barn here, a tombstone there, a line of trees somewhere else. Not a household has failed to leave its mark. Many Ontarians in the 1990s are dedicated heritage conservationists, committed to maintaining the vitality of those signatures, often faded, some almost erased, and to giving future generations a chance to make their own entries in continuity with those who have gone before. All residents of the province are beneficiaries of this rich heritage.

In 1965 I took a photograph of a field of pumpkins in front of a weathered farmstead in Hastings County (Figure 1.2). At the time it was simply a pretty view, but I have frequently returned to that picture, and each time I do so I see something more. An old shed in the background has chimneys. Had it been a dwelling at one time? The front door of the house looks thoroughly uninviting. Was it not the main entrance? The house stands on higher ground than do the other buildings. Why do so many farmhouses occupy such sites? And why do the pumpkins occupy what I shall for ever call (betraying my urban roots) the `front lawn'?

Many people have looked at Ontario's landscape without really seeing it, or have been bored by what they saw. Charles Dickens, writing in 1842, found Ontario very flat and `bare of scenic interest'; the *Canadian Illustrated News* a few years later described it as `tame and domestic.'[1] An 1894 tourist guide bluntly stated that between Smiths Falls and Perth `the country is unattractive.'[2] John Kenneth Galbraith called his childhood area, west of St Thomas,

Figure I.I THE STAGE. People, animals, and buildings come together on a rural road, participants in the Ontario story. Campbellton, Elgin County, c. 1900.

in the 1920s 'an uninteresting country.'[3] A Manitoban used words such as 'sober,' 'stable,' and 'serene' to describe his adopted province in the 1960s.[4] A British colleague of mine once spoke of 'beautiful monotony' after spending a day driving up and down the straight roads near Lindsay.

Figure I.2 PUMPKIN FIELD. Hastings County, 1965.

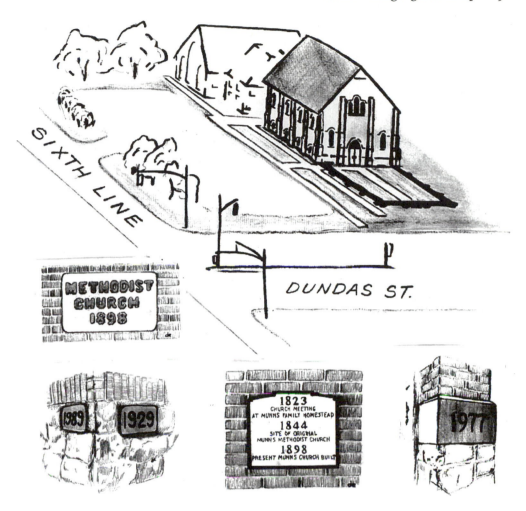

Figure 1.3 DATING. Six different dates are recorded on this church site, only three of them linked to visible structures. The congregation was founded in 1823; the first sanctuary was built in 1844, the present sanctuary in 1898, and the manse in 1929. The sanctuary was moved back (for road widening) in 1977, placing its front wall on the rear line of foundation stones, leaving the ghost of the former position visible in front until new landscaping obliterated those foundation stones in 1991. The parish hall was built in 1989. Freehand sketching is a useful and enjoyable supplement to the photographic record. Munn's United Church, Dundas Street, Halton County.

Despite its apparent openness, however, the land only reluctantly answers our questions. How few of us are prepared to agree that `a house is infinitely communicative, and tells many things besides the figure of its master's income.´⁵ A date on a church seems straightforward enough, but how does one deal with a site plastered with dates (Figure 1.3)? To read a landscape is to interpret it and to reflect on it, and bring it to life. Time and again I have been struck by this vitality – an empty church becomes a house, or a barn timber becomes a fence post. The rumpled countryside is a marvellous place that Ontarians have inhabited and continually reinvented. It may be ambiguous and perplexing, but surely not dull.

To appreciate a living landscape we must also draw on the written record, from such sources as biography and legislative studies, to understand long-gone events. Surveyors' instructions help us understand the geometry of fields; architectural history and church history give clues as to the presence, so often, of a gothic-shaped window above the farmhouse door. Far more still has worn beyond recognition. How many of us would pause to wonder whether the crushed stone spread along a country road was once a fieldstone wall, built perhaps in the 1860s and broken into road metal in the 1920s? Yet we learn from official reports and personal recollections that this pattern was repeated countless times. It stirs up more questions: about building materials, fencing, roads, industrialization, and recycling, and how everything intertwines in the landscape. There is the risk, of course, of reading too much from the current scene. We should not assume, for example, that front lawns of palatial farm-houses commonly supported croquet pitches, just because of one or two en-gravings in illustrated atlases from the 1870s. But landscape analysts who disregard the written record are as culpable as those historians who overlook visual clues.[6]

This book is part of the broader study of Ontario history, archaeology, and geography. It is, moreover, a regional study, not local. By comparing what we see in widely scattered parts of southern Ontario we may be able to discern underlying truths about those who lived throughout the region, not just in a particular village or township. Consider the broad, straggly fences, zigzag cedar rails in some areas and the pine stumps or rocks or hawthorn bushes in others. Despite differences in looks and material, each testifies to people who had land and resources to spare but lacked the extra labour needed to make a neat, manufactured product. Also, all the fences are orderly, straight lines, true to the universal influence of the land survey and private property. Their builders recognized that such fencelines would be part of their world for the long term.

The more one understands connections, and the more one is prepared to look at the land critically, the more quickly the notion that the countryside of southern Ontario lacks interest may be put to rest. Too rarely has the land itself taken the spotlight. It is my intention here to enrich the understanding of rural and small-town southern Ontario by adding a landscape perspective.

An example

The Smith-Armstrong farm occupies forty hectares (about one hundred acres) of gravelly, outwash plain facing Highway 10 just below Caledon Mountain,

Figure 1.4 SMITH-ARMSTRONG FARM, 1971. A public road is the closest vantage-point for most observers most of the time. Hurontario Street, Chinguacousy Township, Peel County.

a distinctive ridge about twenty km northwest of Brampton (Figure 1.4). I have known the property by sight for fully forty years but have never met its inhabitants or, indeed, been closer to it than the roadside. Ours has been an odd sort of relationship, but very much the type of involvement most of us are likely to have with any landscape.

The house of patterned brick is the centrepiece. Its pretentiousness and decorative detail suggest that here dwells (or dwelt) a wealthy person, keen to show off and be in the vanguard of change. It is very different from the modern bungalows and split-level houses in nearby subdivisions. The vertical lines would suggest to an experienced observer that it was built in the last quarter of the nineteenth century. The tower, in the Italianate style, could date back as early as 1855 if it adorned a public building, but here it is more probably copied from elsewhere – possibly Brampton or Toronto – and may be decades younger.

The chimneys are a distraction, being asymmetrically placed; a balanced façade is more common, and this exception on such a handsome building calls out for explanation. The roadside viewing point, however, offers the observer none.

Imposing as the house is, the silo and trees are taller still, and one barn is massive. Together they diminish the stature of the house. Fences and treelines articulate the farm plan: straight edges and right angles reflect a grid-system of lots and roadlines that has endured since before the first settlers arrived. The woodlot barely visible in the background closes the view, its remote position suiting its low-intensity use.

The Smith-Armstrong farm is a functioning unit with a consciously designed layout. In economic terms, the fields are raw-material sites, the barn a refinery, and the house an office. Socially, the house is a dwelling and the occupants' means of announcing their prosperity to those passing on the road. Why is it not closer to the road? One answer is that a central location was convenient; from there the farmer could reach every field and still have reasonable access to town and market. Another is that it also permitted family members to gaze across their domain, reinforcing practicality with aesthetic and emotional pleasure.

Thirty years ago an avenue of trees, probably maple or basswood, stood along the farm lane. Only the stumps remain – relics of a century-old decision to plant saplings and establish a grand entrance up to the house and of a more recent decision to open up the scene once again. The stumps help us appreciate change. In a similar way, the mix of wooden and metal barns announces the spread of industrial products, and instinct tells us that corrugated steel sheeting is newer, and perhaps more durable or less in need of maintenance, than wood.

The big barn is a teaser. The gable roof suggests that it was built before 1880, for after that barns usually carried hipped roofs. Yet this one stands atop a cement block foundation, and blocks were not manufactured before 1900. Prior to Confederation, barns were built to store export wheat and needed no foundations. Smith could have been one of thousands of farmers who lifted his old barn up onto new stables after livestock were introduced with mixed farming in the 1870s and 1880s. But in those years a stable would have been built of stone, not concrete block. Is it not odd that a prosperous farmer, living in an imposing house, seems to have been twenty years or more late in building a stable or to have constructed the superstructure in an obsolete design? Or is the barn, far larger than most built in the era of wheat, the same age as the blocks, but simply not of the usual profile?

Questions about the barn invite closer examination of the house. Could it be older than the last quarter of the nineteenth century? Maybe the upper-storey windows on either side of the tower were added, providing more light upstairs than the more common central-gable window. A central window was perhaps concealed, if the tower is not original. The basic house plan was widespread before 1840, but patterned brick common only after 1860. Possibly the tower was built into the front of an older house, the entire place wrapped in a veneer of matching brick, and the upper-storey windows punched through the roof.

This sort of construction, step by step, has been common in Ontario. The pace of renewal was so variable that one can often see back to several pasts at one time. Today's scene is made up of accumulated decisions. Only the latest layer of brick or paint is supposed to show, but here or there a chip or crack uncovers an earlier finish. Southern Ontario offers a countryside of alterations, not originals.

A biography of the Smith-Armstrong farm will probably never be written, but we are well along in preparing our own. Much of it is speculative, and to go further would require closer inspection. One might wander through barns or along field lines, or reminisce in farm kitchens – many owners are delighted when someone shows interest in the old place. Charles Buck was a recipient of such hospitality back before 1930: 'Housewives were sometimes disturbed at their tasks and farmers stopped their horses, for the most part cheerfully, to show their houses and to answer questions concerning them.'[7] The barnyard or attic interview might well be supplemented by documents – crucial, for the passage of time and changes in ownership cloud facts or embellish them with hearsay. But oral and written evidence is a bonus. The structures will speak reliably, if we know the language.

Local heritage conservationists have prepared an architectural and historical description of the Smith-Armstrong house.[8] They date the house to 1861, rather earlier than my estimate, but support for the theory of a cultured owner. Indeed, John Smith's ambitions carried him through a lifetime of public service, culminating with his representing Peel in the provincial legislature between 1892 and 1908. The report is silent, however, on the possibility that the tower and brick were added. Nor does it comment on the odd positioning of the chimneys.

The Smith-Armstrong farm has never stopped changing. The stumps dis-appeared between 1971 and 1978, and saplings are growing up in a new layout focused on a large roadside signboard announcing that the site is used for breeding racehorses. Great long, low stables, built in the 1970s and 1980s, stretch through the background, replacing the barns seen in Figure 1.4. The house, now truly an office, stands in overly splendid isolation. All the nearby trees are gone, and the space, once cosy and refuge-like, has taken on a vastness that is almost Albertan. In a 1988 print, artist Carole Black retrieved the personality she felt had been lost by placing the house in a grove.[9] Black is one of a dozen or more artists helping Ontarians cope with their changing landscape. Yet the task of farm making, or more generally of using land effectively, is not finished, and never will be.

Outline of this study

We step forward to interpret the land with perhaps more bravado than sea-soning. Yet we ought also to set out with the expectation that a feeling for what the landscape is all about will develop and that one question will lead to another. People who have achieved this state have been called human environmentalists, revellers in what has been described as the 'holistic, par-ticularistic, peripatetic, qualitative, sensual, and ultimately, idiosyncratic and deeply emotional' essence of the land.[10] And there is no end to that revelry, for much remains poorly understood despite years of fieldwork by hundreds of explorers. Few activities are as open to revision as is reading a cultural landscape.

Figure 1.5 COUNTIES OF SOUTHERN ONTARIO, 1961.

The vastness of Ontario is daunting, and I have chosen to focus largely on the open countryside of farms and towns south of Muskoka and Haliburton, commonly known as `southern Ontario´ and comprising barely one-tenth of the area of the province in the 1990s. (See the map in Figure 1.5; I generally name counties or major towns when referring to places.) City landscapes are inspired by more than the Ontario countryside, and that must be someone else´s story. For now, the rural scene invites our attention, without delay. Much in southern Ontario has passed beyond recognition, and still more has disappeared under city sprawl. More than sixty years ago Charles Buck, a pioneer in rural studies, wrote: `Had a study of this subject been begun about twenty or thirty years earlier, the task would have been easier.´[11] His is a timeless lament.

It is quite proper to speak of the landscape as a text, and to think in terms of `reading´ a landscape, in this broad sense. In this introductory chapter, I write about why one should even consider looking at the land in this way and offer a sample reading at the roadside. But becoming adept at reading landscape requires more than walking a country road, and in part I (chapters 2–5) I consider matters that will help us along the way – Ontarians´ attitudes towards their surroundings; Ontario´s history; the provincial system of land survey and place naming; and the technologies and resources used to build Ontario.

Part II examines individual features, starting with houses. They are everywhere, thrusting boldly forward of barns in the countryside and roughly lined up along tree-shaded streets in the towns. They are excellent subjects for demonstrating the sequence of architectural styles, the progress of making additions, and the consistency of vernacular behaviour (chapter 6). The decorative urge – gingerbread trim and the like – is merrily displayed on thousands of Ontario houses (chapter 7). Churches and schools, barns, fences, industrial buildings, and gravestones are the subjects of chapters 8 to 12. These structures are rather less versatile in their signalling, if only because there are fewer of them, yet each offers further insight into the look of Ontario. I work in lesser bits and pieces of the landscape at appropriate moments, hoping thereby to enrich our understanding of what is already familiar.

The clustering of individual elements of a landscape is the subject of chapters 13 to 16, which make up part III. Farms, country roadsides, systems of roads and railways, and streetscapes in the towns all are groupings for contemplation, and the variety of arrangements is vast. Yet there is regularity. Farm layouts are remarkably similar throughout southern Ontario. So too are villages, strung out as droplets of dew on the screen of country roads. Manufacturing clusters take on familiar layouts at water-power sites, and retail buildings do likewise along a town's main street. All these combinations make cultural statements not possible by individual structures.

In the final two chapters, in part IV, I ask: where, and when, is old Ontario? It would seem that every place in Ontario ought to exude something that could be called 'Ontarioness,' but does it? Parts of the Ontario side of the Ottawa River look like Quebec; parts of the Quebec side look like Ontario. Niagara-on-the-Lake has a New England feeling. And to say that Ontario began with the Constitutional Act in 1791, or the first Loyalists arriving in 1784, or the fall of Quebec in 1759, or Champlain's pass through in 1615 only affirms that time limits, similarly, are imprecise. Again and again the physical boundaries have been reshaped by human initiative, and slow, inconspicuous processes extend the life of Ontario from a period of two centuries to far back into the past and indefinitely into the future. This is a book about decay and new life, a theme that has caught the attention of the heritage conservation movement late in the twentieth century.

I contemplated preparing a reference map of all the places named in the text – there are hundreds, many of them obscure – and listing them in the index. But I have decided not to do so, partly out of consideration for privacy, but also because of my landscape approach. I am talking about familiar things, not particular ones, and a precise list is contrary to my aims. I want readers to see a house or fence generically, as an expression of ordinary people responding to ordinary needs, and to notice that these responses repeat themselves from place to place. Imagine yourself driving a back road north of Woodstock, noticing a brick farmhouse, and saying: 'That looks like grandmother's house on the Bay of Quinte,' and then finding that I talk about such houses with an example from near Beaverton. Landscape reading involves making connections, and I encourage readers to insert their own images, wherever those may be. Be part of discovering southern Ontario as the interconnected place it truly is.

PART I
BUILDING OLD ONTARIO

2

The evolving vernacular

`Palimpsest´ means `rubbed again.´ It is a label applied to ancient parchments that have been written on again and again but imperfectly erased between successive uses. What a fine way to describe southern Ontario´s landscape, including its buildings, repeatedly altered but always showing what went before.

Most people limit their aesthetic awareness to a few famous buildings and beauty spots, and then only when away on holiday. And most of us are inclined to praise only those structures that stand unchanged and to invest money to restore others, `denatured,´ to the way they looked when new.[1] Alterations made long ago to old buildings could be forgiven even if new alterations – since, say, 1900 – could not. In Ontario´s perfect heritage town, Niagara-on-the-Lake, an apology for visible changes appears in a walking-tour pamphlet. In another Niagara book, the pen-and-ink artist chooses to suppress alterations so as to avoid `violating the reader´s sensibility.´[2] Western society does not embrace the palimpsest principle easily.

Streetscapes and rural lands everywhere in Ontario exhibit layers of life, one generation after another, yet this capability is seldom appreciated. Rather, town streets and the open countryside are too commonly seen only as unwelcome interventions in our impatience to get somewhere else. Says one jaded commentator: `Fast motoring transformed our view of the countryside between towns and farmsteads from that of a pleasant and interesting space . . . to that of a barrier separating the settlements, to be conquered or at least endured.´[3] Car passengers who sleep the miles away end up viewing the world as a number of discrete spots; they have a weak sense of the connectedness of places. Intimacy has been lost, and disdain, if not outright contempt, prevails. Children whine, `Are we there yet?´

Driving between towns does not have to be an endurance test, however. Zipping along a superhighway presents the landscape at a different scale from puttering along a country road, but it is landscape none the less. Travelling along Highway 401 can be like scanning a text for its tone, general patterns, and worthiness for fuller examination. Buses give an elevated prespective, and trains provide comparative, close-up views of villages and towns in rapid succession. Commercial aircraft offer low-elevation, oblique views during take-off and landing, and higher elevations bring into focus broad patterns of the survey and landforms. Private light planes leave no place free from bird's-eye scrutiny.

One can appreciate the evolved landscape from these distant vantage points, but think how much more one may discover by getting directly onto the land, walking. Walking permits intimate contact with places, and it provides the chance for pondering all the little things that add up to the lived-in world, and at a suitably deliberate pace. Walking is our best hope for increasing awareness of the human landscape that surrounds and embraces us.

Historical geographers, preservationists, and others in recent decades have begun tackling the intriguing questions that emerge from daily experience in a world of interconnected spaces and times. Do not ordinary buildings tell us as much about ourselves and our forebears as architect-designed ones? How does one date altered structures? Can one argue that it is unethical to put a veneer wall over an existing building? How private is private property if we can gaze at it as we walk or drive by or fly over it and owners consciously show off their premises to those passing by? Beginning in the 1960s, throngs of landscape enthusiasts have given creative support to the stirring thought that 'the land spreads tremendous, a palimpsest, the people's own manuscript, their handmade history book.'[4] We shall affirm those words and phrases in numerous instances throughout this book.

High art and vernacular

Far too often, the exceptional obscures our awareness of the unexceptional, the ordinary, the vernacular. Ontario has had perhaps fifty octagonal buildings among hundreds of thousands of rectangular ones, yet this minuscule fraction has been the focus of unrelenting curiosity (Figure 2.1).[5] Phrenologist (some might say 'crackpot') Orson Fowler argued that the wide angles prevented one from being cornered by the devil.[6] Eric Arthur is rather more pragmatic, speaking disdainfully of 'quaint octagonal houses ... definitely freakish and inconvenient in plan, with kite-shaped rooms and awkwardly placed stairs and fire places.'[7] He believes an urge to be different produced 'these quite innocent monuments.'

The covered bridge at West Montrose, north of Waterloo, has aroused a similar response. Tourists relate its lore, agree that the historical plaque makes it a legitimate attraction, and give it an entry in *The Canadian Book of the Road*.[8] Dozens of covered bridges continue in use in New England, and thousands of settlers migrated from there to Ontario during the nineteenth century, so it is proper to ask whether the bridge is an oddity or the sole survivor of many. The fact is that the New England migration to Ontario was

Figure 2.1 OCTAGONAL HOUSE. Inexperienced observers easily focus on the unusual features of the landscape, rather than the ordinary ones. Chinguacousy Township, Peel County.

over before the covered bridge became common, and no more than ten were ever built here. West Montrose's seems to be an oddity, and its preservation, as with any artefact, may overplay its importance in the landscape. But the appeal of covered bridges persists, and in 1991 the city of Guelph covered a modern footbridge crossing the Speed River.

Unique structures are usually designed by members of an architectural elite who have chosen to make the Grand Tour in preference to exploring the ordinary byways. These buildings, set above the mainstream of ordinary life, are identified as high art. Court-houses are in this category. Octagonal houses and covered bridges are, without question, unusual, but rather closer in spirit to the humdrum buildings of ordinary people. We speak of commonplace structures as vernacular. They reflect the way people leading uneventful lives coped day by day. The octagonal house and the covered truss bridge are peculiar in form, but certainly the local materials used – timber and brick – brand them, too, as vernacular structures.

We know little about how the vernacular landscape comes about, is lived in, and then evolves to something different. Lamented one scholar of the English landscape, 'We need a theory of building history which will explain the medieval preference for impermanent building, the emergence of permanent vernacular building in the fifteenth century, its extension and the successive rebuildings of vernacular houses from the late sixteenth to the early eighteenth century, and the replacement of vernacular by ''polite'' or ''pattern book'' architecture from the mid-eighteenth century.'[9] Ontario has passed through these stages in more rapid succession, but such concerns inform this book too.

People entering the raw Ontario forest during the nineteenth century had no choice but to start out with simple buildings, using local materials only slightly refined. Their log houses resembled the folk art of pre-industrial peoples, but it is, I believe, more appropriate to say that these rude structures were muzzled versions of the domestic popular and high-art forms familiar to their occupants. This tension between what was known and what was attainable set the tone of vernacular Ontario throughout the nineteenth century.

The settler's aim was to catch up with established conventions. The quest was assisted by dozens of books extolling the virtues of country life and offering house plans and farmyard layouts.[10] Gradually barns and farm-building groupings, and then houses, came to reflect the developing farming system. Decorative detail and imported materials carried the landscape to new levels of popular expression. Mass production and mail-order shopping, even for full buildings, became commonplace in the twentieth century.

The neoclassical architectural style illustrates this struggle for identity (Figure 2.2). Taking the customs house of 1784 in Dublin, Ireland, as the model (and it was an English model, despite its location), the best copies in old Ontario were vestigial, and mostly filtered through the United States. In one instance, pilasters (false columns) and a fan-shaped transom window above the door gave the Davy house (1819) a touch of class that elevated a plain, functional dwelling beyond normal expectations; side wings were likewise a stylistic treatment for the back kitchen and woodshed and faintly echoed the Dublin exemplar. Decades passed before the means existed in Ontario for the full fashion to be replicated in public buildings. By the time Kingston's city hall was completed in 1843 the neoclassical era was virtually past.

Ordinary citizens, still scrambling to catch up with fashion, cheerfully superimposed newly popular gothic details on what existed before. Mixtures of designs challenged the purity that made the match between Dublin and Kingston so striking (Figure 2.3). Unwittingly the residents of southern Ontario were establishing an identity for their province. By mid-century, Ontario vernacular eclecticism was taking hold – a distinctive blend of high-art elements given the common touch. It persists to this day.

Age and alteration

Dating a vernacular building is one of the most satisfying field experiences. All landscape observers have this urge, but it is easy to be misled. It is altogether too tempting to apply the date of a stylish doorway or chimney stack to the entire structure, without paying sufficient attention to the full building and its setting. The date of occupancy, even the era, of almost every farmhouse

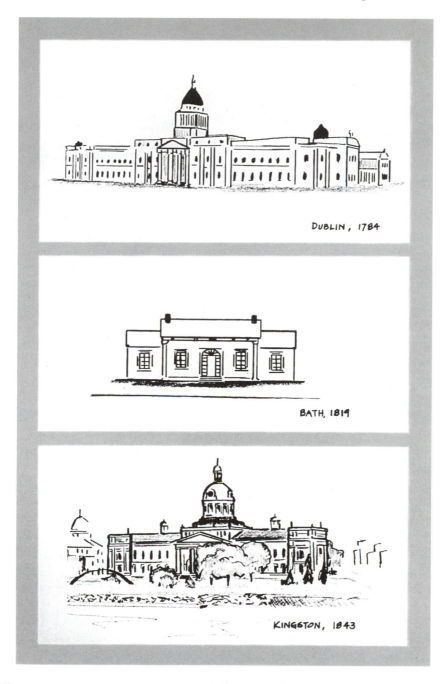

DUBLIN, 1784

BATH, 1819

KINGSTON, 1843

Figure 2.2 THE NEOCLASSICAL STYLE. Dilution and renewal occur when foreign building styles find their way into unrefined settings. Dublin's custom house and Kingston's city hall are sixty years different in age yet very similar. The Davy house (middle), near Kingston, is only a faint shadow of each of them.

Figure 2.3 GOTHICIZING THE CLASSICAL. St Andrews Roman Catholic (1840) attempted to suppress its American Greek-temple roots with gothic (pointed) windows rather too tall for the wall. Oakville, Halton County.

in southern Ontario has become obscured with use and adaptation. Recognizing the true decade or quarter-century can be a noteworthy accomplishment. On the rare occasion when an exact date is known, it can be used to verify or reconsider the estimate.

As buildings age, the will to arrest the process increases. The following passage dates from 1853, when Ontario was still a pioneer place: 'The old church has serviced its generation too well and honorably to have the venerableness of its old age marred by the upstart refinements of modern times.'[11] For many of those concerned with design, purity is sacred and alteration sacrilege. 'We have no right whatever to touch them,' wrote British architect and critic John Ruskin in 1851. 'They are not ours. They belong partly to those who built them, and partly to all the generations of mankind who are to follow us.'[12] The same sentiment appears in an Ontario context more than a century later: 'The very worst enemies of elderly architecture are affluence and fire, and it is sometimes difficult to decide which of them does the greater damage.'[13]

It is fair to say that most citizens are not stirred by such matters, however. They are more likely to identify with the laconic recollections of a resident of Bruce County: 'There was an old log house, and then the people built a frame house. Well then we added a piece onto it, and bricked it, and tore down the old house and built a woodshed.'[14] Change was an essential part of life, and practical considerations held sway over nostalgia. There was little feeling that a woodshed belonged to the story of humankind.

As surely as a sequence of pristine buildings demonstrates stages in design and construction history, the processes linking one stage to another are evident in individual buildings that have been altered. In Alton, for example, the ghost of a first, small workshop in dressed stone shows through the enlarged façade of rough, unfinished stone.[15] Here is the expression of a successful entrepreneur, starting out on a modest scale and then growing. Altered buildings give continuity to the countryside.

The passage of time itself is the greatest cause of changes and makes dating each specific event difficult. If a window frame rots because of a damaged drainpipe, both are likely to be replaced with whatever material and design are currently available and serviceable, regardless of how well they match the rest of the structure. The past in today's landscape is a statement of changes blatant and subtle, year by year and layer upon layer.

Time and again landscapes recount the basic choice between the structure, rejuvenated and functional but architecturally impure, and the unchanged, decaying hulk, about to be demolished and replaced with something completely new. Old buildings that look current and useful are simply occupying the next step in a steady process of revitalization which has kept them going over several generations. Restoration and excessive alteration tend to conceal this natural evolution.

Alteration frequently involves the reuse of old structural materials in new

Figure 2.4 TIMBERS REUSED. The long, horizontal barn beam once was a plate, positioned beneath the eaves of another building; rafters were seated in the notches. This barn was made from three smaller buildings, dismantled and rearranged into the present form before 1900. Elora Road, south of Paisley, Bruce County.

arrangements. Barns, being what we would call `unfinished' on the inside, openly display the process of recycling (Figure 2.4). Timbers continued to be used over again in new construction for generations after more modern procedures could have been adopted. In due course, they became the source material from which lighter products – planks and boards – were sawn. We read of a corpse `coffined in a casket improvised from troughs removed for that purpose from the roof of a house.'[16] Timber salvaged from the fairground pavilion in Paisley, dismantled in 1929, was sawn into lumber and reused in the new frame pavilion.[17] A log house demolished in the 1950s was sawn into

Figure 2.5 WALL MATERIAL AND STRUCTURE. Eight-inch, hand-cut spikes, nailed to an inner board wall and laid in mortar every five or six layers, tie the brick veneer to the structure. The arched window-heads do not match the square-topped sash and may be replacements to carry a brick wall; they suggest that the brick was added later. Cargill, Bruce Country.

Figure 2.6 POPULARITY OF BRICK SUSTAINED. Asphalt rolls curl and crack in a most unbricklike way and have inappropriate joints. Note same material used to simulate stone, next door. Fergus, Wellington County.

2,000 metres of well seasoned, sound boards up to two-thirds of a metre wide, `enough to frame several bungalows.´[18]

Of all alterations, one of the most common and deceptive is veneering – bricking over a framed house, or placing boards over logs, or applying any one of many non-structural wrappers such as stucco or aluminum panels at some date well after the basic construction (Figure 2.5, on page 23). The Bruce County quotation five paragraphs back contains the important remark, `and bricked it,´ mentioned in such an offhand manner as to suggest that the episode was far from unusual.

Brick veneer is one of the most common ways of altering Ontario buildings, wrapping up log, wood-framed, and even solid brick buildings. Boards cover logs, stucco covers plank, vinyl sheeting covers square timbers; there is hardly any limit.[19] The variety of wall coverings increased as society matured. Aspiring residents seeking something more tasteful than logs turned to patterned brick, tooled stone, and milled lumber. Others concealed the unmatching portions of a house built in stages by wrapping up the enlarged structure in a uniform layer of brick or stucco. By 1881, it was estimated that more than half of the rural houses south of a line from Goderich to Lake Simcoe to Kingston and Brockville were `first class´: that is brick, stone, or good frame. Many such structures concealed much more modest beginnings. The most vernacular parts of rural Ontario in the 1990s are those townships, near the southerly edge of the Precambrian Shield, that reported fewer than one first-class house in three in 1881.[20]

Veneering is consistent with making improvements by small steps, but rarely has it been studied in the context of the development of a landscape. Perhaps it is the fact that a veneer is so all-embracing that it too easily gives its age to the age of the building it covers. If it is part of the original construction – as finished boards over rough boards, for instance – the date may not be questioned. But a veneer from another era than that of the building can be jarring, even if added for upkeep and modernness. Asphalt sheeting that simulates brick is such a case (Figure 2.6).[21] It adds to the vernacular mixture that is basic to Ontario's identity.

Veneers are more than merely cosmetic, though they can certainly be that too. Paint is a sort of veneer and also serves as a preservative. 'Roughcast' is a coarse plaster made of lime and gravel; it used to be placed over logs or boards to protect as well as to give the durable look of stone – if not examined too closely. Brick is an insulator and requires little maintenance, two reasons that continue to make it a popular veneer. It may be placed over stucco or roughcast. Aluminum and vinyl are modern veneers that maintain the look of a wooden building without the labour of repainting every few years; they too may cover earlier veneers (Figure 2.7). Many log houses have stood for more than a century, unnoticed and preserved, layered over successively with boards, bricks, asphalt, and aluminum.

Even the best veneer eventually shows its superficiality. Whitewash and paint fade. Stucco and roughcast chip or crack or shrink to show the ghosts of closed-in windows or doors.[22] Rust stains appear on iron panels, and corner covers fall off aluminum panels. A zigzag crack in brick, caused by inadequate footing, is a sure sign of veneering, especially in combination with deeply recessed window frames.

Late in the twentieth century it has become fashionable to take some or all of the layers off again. Observers must distinguish between original original and regained original. Sandblasted brick, like bread with the crust removed, is easily detected; nail holes left after boards have been removed are almost impossible to see. Owners can peel back from vinyl, through asbestos shingle, brick, and stucco, to log, for instance, stopping at whatever stage suits personal tastes. There may be a strong urge to go all the way back to log for the full pioneer effect. Reusing the stripped boards or bricks in a new building of nineteenth-century lines pushes truth to the limit.

There has always been a tendency to make a building seem more than it really is – to 'dress it up.' As early as 1838, Anna Jameson described how the family home in Fenelon Falls had stucco pointed to resemble stone, 'to make a log house pretty.'[23] It was not a unique episode (Figure 2.8). The 1827 court-house in London has its brick covered in stucco and marked out as stone

Figure 2.7 REVENEERING. In 1975 this house was given aluminum siding (top),
concealing the patterned brick exterior (bottom), which was
probably a veneer of the 1870s over wood siding. The architectural detail of the
doorway, the shallow pitch of the roof, and the locale all suggest that the
house dates from the 1840s. Hurontario Street, north of Brampton,
Peel County.

blocks. Christ Church in Vittoria, an Anglican building of the 1840s, has its
board siding lined out in similar fashion, again to look like stone.[24] Many
roughcast houses have been given this treatment, and concrete blocks are
`rusticated´ (cast with a stonelike finish) for the same effect. Church, crown,
Upper Canada´s premier literary family, and many anonymous `little´ people
could not countenance being seen in inferior materials.

  A showy front is another common form of deception. In the 1830s, the front
of the Anglican church in Belleville was red brick, but the other walls were
wood, `coloured red to make up the deficiency of the costlier material.´[25] The

Figure 2.8 DECEPTIONS. Not satisfied merely to apply lathing straps and stucco to protect (and conceal) a log wall, many owners marked out the stucco to resemble stone blocks, adding grandeur. Puslinch Township, Wellington County.

soft patina of hand-made brick cannot be replicated in wood, however, and sensitive parishioners must have prayed that no one would check the sides or rear wall. Mixtures of solid and veneered brick also catered to the illusion of soundness while reducing expense. In a part of Ontario where stone and wood were the familiar building materials of the nineteenth century, a brick front must have seemed exotic (Figure 2.9).

It has been argued that disguises and deceptions are immoral, perhaps even dishonest.[26] The introduction of 'mathematical tiles' that looked like eighteenth-century British bricks doubtless gave some respectability to veneers,[27] yet heritage supporters were indignant when a public figure reported that he 'once aluminumed a house.'[28] That was naughty. But is refacing a building a sin? Surely every structure is a true product of its time and circumstances and deserves to be accepted at face value in the landscape. Early in the settlement age, roughcast was being used to mimic stone; using vinyl today to ape wood is no different. Log-like rounded boards, painted brown or creosoted, are applied to frame houses. Chances are that somewhere this material has been put over real logs!

Over-construction

Ontario settlers regularly used far more material than necessary when putting up buildings. Over-construction is a vernacular trait, a sign of people using unfamiliar techniques and substances. It was security for those who doubted their capabilities as builders, though bulk alone did not ensure survival.[29] Faulty structures did fall down.

Over-construction made sense when sawmills were scarce and labour dear. Round logs are cheaper to produce than squared timbers, and squared timbers in turn are less expensive than sawn planks or boards. Piling up logs in the configuration of a barn or house made immediate use of one of the byproducts of clearing land. In another sense, it was a way to stockpile and season materials for the longer-term construction project – a respectable, framed house. No one knows how many times a family watched with satisfaction as the primitive shelter was dismantled and the round logs were squared up and fitted together as a timber framework. Other logs may have been drawn off for sawing into planks, or taken to a sash-and-door works for further refinement. Sometimes two stages show in a single piece: the plank with broad-axe marks on one side and a sawblade imprint on the other.

Stripping away of the excess of over-construction is a high-art characteristic and was undertaken only with experience. A barn built with lumber requires 20 per cent less wood than one using square timbers to enclose the same space. Concrete walls two-thirds the thickness of brick or stone are just as strong.[30] By the later nineteenth century, mass production and the spread of trained architects were speeding the decline of over-construction. So did the

Figure 2.9 'SHOWING OFF' ON THE FRONT. Brick front and stone sides. Here the front has been painted, but not the corner bricks on the side, a further twist to the supposed invisibility of side walls. Napanee, Lennox and Addington County.

perception that buildings were not, as some believed, expected to last indefinitely. No nineteenth-century Ontarian would have taken seriously Ruskin's assertion of 1851 that 'when we build, let us think that we build for ever.'[31] In place of fitted timbers, milled lumber nailed together became normal. It is also far less durable, and in recent decades it has become necessary for the province to establish building codes to ensure that even minimum standards are met.

Excessive tolerances persisted in the building arts in rural Ontario through to the early twentieth century. As a result, the vast majority of rural structures deteriorate slowly, and opportunities for seeing back from the 1990s into the nineteenth century are many. They are almost certainly better than the chances of looking back from the year 2100 and recognizing buildings put up in the late twentieth century.

For the builders of old Ontario alteration – recycling, veneering, and dressing up the front – and over-construction were aspects of moving forward by small steps. People had the habit of doing whatever they could initially in order to get by, with every intention of making refinements later. These are the conservative displays of a progressive society. A dictum of domestic building in the United States – `the sensible has again and again been sacrificed to the sentimental' – has seldom applied to Ontario.[32]

Public and private spaces

We take it for granted that we may savour countryside vistas for our own, personal pleasure. Consider these lines from Ralph Waldo Emerson: `The charming landscape which I saw this morning is indubitably made up of some twenty or thirty farms. Miller owns this field, Locke that, and Manning the woodland beyond. But none of them owns the landscape. There is a property in the horizon which no man has but he whose eyes can integrate all the parts, that is, the poet. This is the best part of these men's farms, yet to this their warranty-deeds give no title.'[33]

We live within our landscape. We traverse it along thousands of miles of public rights-of-way: provincial highways, gravelled township roads, village streets, and lanes running behind business blocks. Our eyes wander freely across the faces of buildings or planted fields, along fence lines or mill dams, and out to woodlots at the horizon. Cattle-crossing signs, railway overpasses, and pedestrian crosswalks bind opposite sides of the road together, strengthening our sensation of being in the land and part of its daily pulse. Shops, parking lots, hotels, churches, cemeteries, and farm auctions routinely welcome strangers onto private property, offering further vantage points.

Outward-looking houses stare back at us.[34] `The home's interior unfolds out of use onto its façade.'[35] The position of windows and doors indicates where rooms are, the roof pitch gives an idea of the importance of upstairs space, and overall balance reflects the orderliness and self-confidence of the dweller (Figure 2.10). Façades tell much, but not all; knowledge of the room layout of the Rainham house, for example, and a few dozen others like it nearby has added substantially to our understanding of Mennonite social history.[36] Floor-plans may reveal common functional roots for many houses in a district or give a clue to when distinctive, published pattern-book styles became available, sweeping aside the vernacular ones.[37]

The predictive value of house fronts is relatively greater, the more advanced the society.[38] Charles Buck found that inside detail of Ontario housing in the 1930s was quite easy to anticipate from outside appearance.[39] Cityfolks who buy century-old houses today increase the transparency of their intentions by blocking up windows, moving doors, and inserting skylights to suit their suburban way of life. Heritage conservationists are alarmed at this activity, simply because so many of homeowners' private decisions do become so obvious to outsiders.

Being in the countryside or on a village street puts one deeply inside the total landscape, even without setting foot inside a house. Fences enclose fields but do not conceal them, and the fence structure shows all but the under-

Figure 2.10 PUBLIC AND PRIVATE. Houses with two front doors are rare in Ontario. This feature gives outward expression to distinctive characteristics of the Pennsylvania culture of which it is a part and hints at a different arrangement of internal space from that found in one-door houses. This six-bay house, with its low-pitched roof, dates from before 1810 and is one of the oldest buildings standing in Ontario. Rainham Centre, Haldimand County.

ground portion of the post. Decaying barns, with their siding peeling off to reveal their skeletons, are like buildings turned inside-out. So much is revealed; so little truly hidden. The challenge is to become Emerson's poet, able to read Ontario convincingly despite having only incidental opportunity to disappear into its most private spaces.

3
Natural and human history

Southern Ontario surely has one of the most placid histories of any place of its size the world over. It is practically inert geologically, and its glacial deposits were laid down only with glacial speed. The martyrdom of Jesuit missionaries in Huronia in 1649, the rebellion of 1837, and the feuding Donnelly families of Lucan in the 1870s are rare aberrations in a peaceful process of social change. The last (and almost only) domestic war hero, Sir Isaac Brock, fell in the War of 1812. City fires, the occasional tornado, and Hurricane Hazel in October 1954 are events only slightly more memorable. It is hard to imagine becoming excited about such a stable, orderly place, yet it is the very soundness of its roots that has allowed Ontario both to prosper and to maintain the visibility of what has gone before. This overview of southern Ontario's history draws heavily on elements from all eras, visible in the 1990s, to carry the message.

Natural history

It has been said that in 1800 a squirrel could run and jump from tree to tree from Cornwall to Windsor without ever touching the ground. Ontario's forest was that continuous, and the streams were that small. Maple and beech predominated in the upland areas, elm and cedar in the wetter spots. White pine grew everywhere, with thick stands in the sand plains south of Brantford and near Lake Scugog. Southwest from the London area, small natural prairies occasionally occurred, fringed with white oak. As farm makers punched out their little clearings during the nineteenth century, the amount of forest edge lengthened, and sumach, berry bushes, and poison ivy spread unchecked.

Every Ontario barn is a gallery of the Great Lakes mixed forest. Settlers learned by experience the special properties of each species: strength, elasticity, workability, durability, and beauty. Oak or red pine was for heavy frames, and spruce or hemlock for light; tamarack, white cedar, and elm made good floor joists; ash and birch were whittled into pegs for holding the frame together; cedar was riven into roof shingles. Elsewhere on the farm, pitch pine was used in pumps, and hemlock for such rough work as lathing. Fence rails were red or white cedar, posts locust or ash, and furniture maple or walnut.[1] Hickory nuts and maple sap made those trees popular in the living state as well as cut down.

Southern Ontario is good farming country. Hardwood forests produce light soils, workable with the rudimentary tools of a pioneering society. The heavier soils of wetland areas could not be exploited as quickly but proved to be rich and tractable in due course. Sandy soils, loams, and clays all occur, and alkalinity varies widely. The climate becomes gradually more moderate as one moves from the Ottawa River valley southwestward through to the Detroit River but is nowhere severe. `Southern Ontario´ is an agricultural definition and is best described as varying widely yet offering everywhere a decent living, even to inexperienced husbandmen.

Water-supply has always been adequate. The first settlers in every region drew it from surface streams, but as they cut down the forests soil washed into the channels and muddied the sparkling waters. The upper layer of soil lost much of its ability to store water, and streamflow became irregular from season to season. In response, residents dug wells, tapping into prodigious supplies of groundwater. It is everywhere, and divining has been a safe avocation in Ontario! A hand pump became the hallmark of every farm building site, and the broad open fields allowed the wind to whip along, making wind-pumps possible. All this change occurred within the lifetime of children born in the backwoods. Electric motors now do the job invisibly.

All but the tiniest rivulets have been used for their waterpower. Direct gearing from a paddle-wheel or turbine produced mechanical energy that could be used on the site. In the twentieth century, production of hydro-electric energy and development of cheap transmission have allowed industrial development anywhere in the province. Ontario´s streams have always been used more for power than transportation, and the dams have frequently served also as bridges. Freshwater salmon migrations were disrupted.

Southern Ontario has only mundane minerals. None induced floods of immigrants, as did gold in California in 1849, for instance. Rather, it was bog iron, recovered near Long Point in the 1820s, and an iron-ore deposit exploited at Marmora in the same decade from which Ontario grew. Both sources helped supply small-scale blacksmiths during the farm-making age. Petroleum was first pumped in Lambton County in the 1860s, and natural gas along the Lake Erie shore came somewhat later; again, both have been of limited scope. Salt mines at Goderich and Windsor round out the list.

Limestone, sandstone, granites, and clay have been of great significance in the evolution of Ontario. Dolomite limestone is the caprock of the Niagara Escarpment and found underfoot for miles back from the front wall of the ridge. It makes fine cornerstones (Figure 3.1). More lies in the Kingston area, and limestone plains extend across the Kawartha-Trent region and eastward

Figure 3.1 LIMESTONE. The biggest blocks are used for cornerstones, sills, and window-headers and were probably quarried. Smaller pieces of irregular size and shape are used in less vulnerable places; many may be surface debris of glacial origin. Marine fossils are common. Near Inglewood, Peel County.

Figure 3.2 SANDSTONE is easily worked, making it popular for decorating showy public structures. Grey sandstone, Michigan Central Railway station, 1883, Niagara Falls. See also Figure 8.24, for pink sandstone.

from Ottawa. Limestone from a quarry is a creamy-white colour that darkens with exposure. Pieces that have lain on the surface for centuries are dappled grey, distinctive pitted by rainwater, including acid rain in recent years. Decorative marbles (recrystallized limestone) are scattered throughout eastern Ontario.

Sandstone is a softer, layered rock, easy to carve (Figure 3.2). A pink variety has been shipped widely from the Forks of the Credit River and used for public buildings, among them the main legislative building at Queen's Park.[2] In eastern Ontario, grey sandstone blocks cut to the size of bricks are common, laid up as one does a brick wall.

Granites are Ontario's oldest rocks, formed under pressure and heat a billion years ago. In southern Ontario they occur as scattered boulders carried by glaciers, more than 8,000 years ago, from the Precambrian Shield mass to which they belong. In any one place granites come in all shades – brown, pink, metallic blue-grey – and many sparkle with minerals (Figure 3.3). When heated, they may be split to produce flat building faces.

Clay – the raw material for bricks – is widespread. Brick construction in old Ontario predominates in a belt from Cobourg through to Lake Huron and

Figure 3.3 GRANITE. Fieldstone easily produces old Ontario's most riotously colourful structures. School, 1874. Puslinch Township, Wellington County.

southward to Brantford and London. In the Toronto region, and from Waterloo north and west, brick and brick veneer made up more than half the housing stock in 1931.[3] Through the Bay of Quinte and eastward, stone construction predominates. Southwest of Chatham, brick is similarly scarce, and its use is restricted to barn foundations and tile underdrainage of the flat, stone-free floor of glacial Lake Warren – Essex and Kent counties today. Shales, too, have been burned to make bricks. Much more shale has been used directly for the foundations of barns and houses. Flat blocks were easily quarried from minor stream beds exposed by erosion during the process of clearing land (Figure 3.4).

The most common of all minerals in southern Ontario is gravel, or glacial till, as it may be generally known. Ranging in size down from rocks to stones to pebbles to sand to dust, tills are the fractured debris scraped from bedrock by glaciations and deposited irregularly over the surface. Tills have been thrown up as moraines or eskers (linear features) or in clusters of drumlins (small, egg-shaped hills). Others occur as smooth, fan-shaped features, where melting water has washed them out and sorted the particles by size. Many more deposits are mixed up, however, and industrialists have crushed and sorted them before use. Tills produce well-drained roadbeds and are the reason that life in Ontario has rarely been impeded by flooding.

It all adds up to a comfortable physical setting, if not spectacular. Niagara Falls is Ontario's most alluring treasure, and the benchmark against which

Figure 3.4 RIVER SHALE, found throughout southern Ontario, made ideal
foundation stones. Sawmill Creek, Mississauga.

the province's landscape has come to be judged. The Oak Ridges moraine
and the Rideau Lakes are bland in comparison, and no one pauses to admire
the drained site of Lake Wawanosh in Lambton County. Yet each ravine,
beachfront, and glacial moraine, each crisp autumn morning, each running
stream has been more useful than threatening. In Ontario, inexperienced
settlers could make mistakes and survive, and they took to it with little risk.

Human history

Native Ontarians – the Huron and their allies – built with wood, grass, and
earth. Their longhouses and hearths were constantly being renewed according
to age-old construction techniques and, as a result, were simultaneously ageless and new. Following the decline of the Huron after 1649, replacement
ceased. Iroquoian peoples passed through southern Ontario from time to time
but did not settle permanently, and gradually all but archaeological evidence
of Native occupation vanished. Among the last signs must have been the
cornfields, reverting to scrubland and, by the later eighteenth century, to climax
forest.

Today, only the spectacular petroglyphs and burial mounds near Peterborough, and occasional gravestones in Christian cemeteries, tell of life before

Figure 3.5 FIRST NATIONS communities have left few prehistoric signs on the landscape. This gravemarker recognizes the life of Mondoron, `Chief of the Wyandotts and Hurons´ (1808–1880). His adopted Western surname is far more prominent than his birthname, and the marker is indistinguishable from others in the cemetery. On the Detroit River at Amherstburg, Essex County.

European settlement (Figure 3.5).[4] Provisions in the Ontario Heritage Act, 1974, and the Environmental Assessment Act, 1977, have made citizens conscious of more pre-European burial and village sites than ever before. These places do not show in the landscape except under the closest scrutiny, and out of respect and concern to avoid damage, archaeologists and First Nations leaders clearly aim to keep it that way. As a result, First Nations roots simply do not show.

Figure 3.6 THE LOYALIST ERA. A `foreign´ house, thrust on a raw landscape before 1800. Fairfield House, built 1793. Amherstview, Lennox and Addington County.

During the 1780s, some 7,000 refugees from the American Revolutionary War – United Empire Loyalists (UELs) – took up this vacant land. They, too, built with local materials, but not out of choice. Loyalists give the impression of never having been pioneers, and they rejected log shanties and stump-strewn fields with all possible haste. UELs are remembered today by their grand houses and churches in such places as Niagara-on-the-Lake, Amherst-burg, and Adolphustown (Figure 3.6). No more than two or three hundred of these substantial buildings survive. They look much as they did originally, and all are anchors in the cultural landscape. Many sport commemorative plaques, and the group is celebrated well out of proportion to its numbers.

For every UEL in Upper Canada (as Ontario was called between 1791 and 1841) there were in the 1810s twenty other Americans who came because this was the next best land on the way west. For these opportunists, British au-thority was less important than cheap farmland. They better filled the image of storybook pioneers, chopping trees and building log cabins. The landscapes of the more prosperous among them must have blended in with those of the Loyalists. In contrast, the settings of the poorer newcomers would have re-sembled the farmlands of the non-agricultural immigrants from the British Isles, who first came in substantial numbers between 1828 and 1832.

The land was organized for sale in rectangular parcels, clearly visible today.[5] But little of the gridwork of fields and roads would have been discernible before 1840, despite a population of half a million. Instead, a visitor would see irregular clearings and rough tracks wiggling among stumps.[6] The only fences were within farms, to keep animals out of crops or gardens; boundary-line fences were not necessary until clearings spread out to touch each other. Settlement was scattered because of large grants to the UELs, sometimes several thousand hectares per family. Even ordinary settlers acquired lots far larger than they could manage. The degree of progress varied enormously from one district to another, but overall no more than 4 or 5 per cent of the forest cover had been cleared into farms in this first half-century. Old Ontario remained forest bound, virtually out of sight from the world at large.[7]

1830s to 1890s

Gradually Ontario was transformed from deep forest to rural countryside. Wherever forest clearing occurred, overland run-off increased, scouring channels in the loose soil. Heavy subsurface clays and bedrock shales became exposed, available for burning into bricks. Railway builders cut through the undulating land seeking level alignments after 1850 and uncovered vast deposits of glacial gravels. This finding led to construction of well-drained, gravelled roads, replacing rutty earth roads that were impassable in wet weather. Settlers cut down trees as a normal part of getting ahead; neither they nor the enthusiastic lumber barons could leave this great resource of building material and fuel alone.[8] They had removed fully three-quarters of it by the 1890s, with hardly a thought given to renewal.[9]

The results of `working up by one's bootstraps' began to show after 1840: `Elora is going ahead, and no mistake. Bricks, stone, mortar, hodmen, carpenters, shavings, shingles, lumber and scaffolding are the most familiar sights, while saw-grating, hammer-rapping, trowel-ringing, plane-scraping and ``raising'' shouts are the most familiar sounds.'[10] Wheat exports stimulated rapid expansion of farmland and trade, and by the 1850s unbroken lines of farms stretched back from the lakefront along township roads. Barns proliferated, and port elevators were set up in strategic points such as Goderich and Prescott. Both kinds of building were framed and planked with the output of hundreds of water-powered sawmills. A few large lakefront flour mills undertook commercial work, and hundreds more ground small quantities for neighbourhood needs. The Welland (1830), Rideau (1832), and St Lawrence (1848) canals scratched the land and stimulated harbour development and boatworks.

Progress was measured by tearing apart, building afresh, and adding on. The log house was `an extempore affair . . . and by-and-by is pulled down.'[11] Moss chinking and leather hinges were replaced by sawn boards and iron fittings. A few people tried stone, but most did as in Wellington County, where at mid-century there were `extensive piles of frame buildings.'[12] Hand-cast bricks set Ontario's course towards becoming the brick province by the 1890s. Two rooms became four, and the loft expanded into a useful upper storey. Pointed windows, slender towers, and scrolling and spidery ironwork trim transformed purely functional houses into busy assemblages of mixed architectural pedigree (Figure 3.7). Houses were adapted for commercial or institutional functions, and distinctive new buildings evolved for specialized needs.

Southern Ontario's population passed one million in the 1850s and reached twice that number by 1891. The number of houses rose from 146,000 in 1851 to more than 350,000 in 1881.[13] People who once travelled to fulfill their calling – land surveyors, clergymen, millers, gravecarvers, brickmakers, and judges among them – settled down in local neighbourhoods as population density rose. New settlement in the old townships such as Augusta (inland from Brockville) in the 1840s was taking place on divided lots, producing a landscape of mixed age.[14] Such was the case throughout the first two or three tiers of townships back from Lake Erie and Lake Ontario. In contrast, the Huron-Bruce area was the last to be settled, in the 1860s, and with a haste that may explain the relatively high degree of homogeneity of its built landscape.[15] Other settlers tried the Precambrian Shield, and more than a trickle took off for the American Midwest.

Farmed acreage reached its peak about 1890, but concern for disappearance of the forests was being widely expressed much earlier. As far back as 1824 William Lyon Mackenzie had written with despair of 'venerable' oaks being cut on Burlington Bay.[16] A generation later residents sought to purchase islands in Rice Lake to preserve their beauty.[17] As farm clearings merged into one another, the call for fenceline shade trees grew louder.[18] During the 1860s, clearing had advanced into the Bruce peninsula, Muskoka, Haliburton, and Renfrew – poor, rocky areas beyond the limits of reasonable farming. Most of this land should never have been put into farm, and almost immediately it began reverting to bush (Figure 3.8). In established areas, too, trees started making a comeback. By 1890 country schools regularly held Arbor Day plantings, and lines of Norway spruce began to appear along farm lanes a decade later.

The soil was exploited for commercial gain with scant concern for sustained yield, and Ontarians may consider themselves fortunate that American wheat drove them out of that export market by the 1870s. The switch to mixed farming served the growing urban population (25 per cent lived in cities in 1891) and reduced the farmer's risk, and pasturing animals manured the starving fields. Ten acres was a typical field size in Victorian Ontario, and each field had to be fenced to accommodate newly established rotations of crops and livestock. Miles of cedar-rail fencing was drawn from land drained for expanded farming. Pigs took over the first log house, and the wheat barn was raised on a stone foundation stable.

Mixed farming was labour-intensive. Even with maturing children and

Figure 3.7 DOMESTIC EXUBERANCE. Massive town houses, built in the late nineteenth century and encrusted with decoration, announced to the passing world the achievements of their occupants. Highway 2, Gananoque, Leeds County.

Figure 3.8 BROKEN DREAMS lie strewn across the province, the result of inadequate soil or of changes in techniques or markets. Saugeen Township, Bruce Country.

grandchildren, plus the assistance of machines, families were frequently pressed beyond their capabilities. For a few decades tenant workers and their families provided additional pairs of hands. Commonly they lived in the family farmhouse, in quarters above the kitchen wing. Tenant farm-hands were the first to go when rural depopulation took hold in the 1890s.

Engravings from the 1870s show manicured country roads passing through prosperous vistas.[19] Each crossroads hamlet was a little service centre, with a school, several churches, a store, and a smithy or harness shop. In town, brick business blocks sprang up on main street, each labelled with the name of the leading local family that built it. Large church buildings and fancy town houses became common too. The first railways were built during the 1850s. Along with all-weather roads, gravelled with glacial tills uncovered during railway construction, they laced Ontario together and permitted daily delivery of hay and dairy products to towns and cities. Larger farms and bigger factories emerged from among undifferentiated family-scale operations.

Ontarians revelled in their own successes and imagined that the sky was the limit. Farmers began to use cash, even to pay off their road-building duties – so-called statute labour. Neighbourhood businesses, such as sash and door production, put manufactured consumer goods within reach of local residents.

Sir John A. Macdonald's protectionist National Policy (1879) encouraged local initiative, but it also invited investors to seek ever-bigger markets. This process undermined local self-sufficiency. Mergers, as in the railway industry in the

1880s, diminished the critical element of pride in a locally managed enterprise. Local businesses were falling by the wayside as Canada moved towards mass consumer activity during the 1890s.

1890s to 1940s

In the next half-century the momentum of growth shifted from the countryside to the towns and cities. From the sameness of villages and dirt roads emerged a system of major and minor highways and major and minor urban centres. For those go-ahead parts, Ontario was a very modern place about 1900. At no other time were the buildings so young or their condition so good. It was the era of the Good Roads movement, the Eaton's catalogue, and the Carnegie library; places such as Chesley milled prairie wheat en route to overseas markets. We know that industrialization was good for Hamilton and Toronto, but so it was too for countryside places (Figure 3.9) such as the Grand River valley.[20] But there were backwaters too. The area north of London, for example, was described as 'a desolation of decayed and empty farmhouses,'[21] and that between Toronto and the Quebec boundary as 'richer in ruined houses than any other country but Ireland.'[22]

The rural population of the province fell below 50 per cent of the total about 1908. Young men and women left the land for city jobs and were replaced by machinery that increased the productivity of those who remained. Veterans returning after the First World War and intending to resume life on the farm

Figure 3.9 INDUSTRIALIZATION. By the end of the nineteenth century, factory and retail jobs were steadily drawing people off the farms and into the towns. Campbellford, on the Trent River, Northumberland County.

found that mechanization had rendered 100 acres unrealistically small. Often several unconnected farm lots were merged under a single family working out of the old home. In the farming heartland, from the Grand River westward, new sheds indicated new specialties such as vegetables and flue-cured tobacco, but mixed farming still prevailed. Elsewhere, to be modern meant renovation rather than building anew.

Throughout the province countryside assets were underused. Barns stood empty, rooms once noisy with the laughter of farm-hand children were dusty and quiet, and redundant churches lined weedy roadsides. The older generation retired to town. Even fields disappeared as reforestation programs took root after the First World War. Plantations started then, and mature today, may be identified by decaying fences running through the trees. One element that experienced more use was the paved highway, and winter snow ploughing cleared the way for the widespread introduction of automobiles.

Rural Ontario was largely bypassed in the interwar years but still was not very far away for the thousands of townspeople born or raised on the farm. Many were grateful for the opportunity to reclaim family haunts and relative self-sufficiency during the Great Depression of the 1930s.

The arts community found in rural Ontario a place to rediscover their country. Homer Watson painted in the Grand River valley in the 1880s, and Stephen Leacock wrote whimsically about small towns just before 1914. Architect Eric Arthur, local historian Charles Buck, artists A.J. Casson, Thoreau MacDonald, and C.W. Jefferys, and photographer C.P. Meredith are among those who heard the call.[23] Along with a few naturalists, they stole through the quiescent 1930s countryside. Within twenty years, a new public would begin to discover the wonders of this gentle place, and a renaissance would be under way.

1940s and onward

The automobile reintroduced Ontarians to the countryside, and electricity, available on every farm lot by 1950, opened to city folks the prospect of living there instead of in suburban developments such as Don Mills. The Sunday drive and the family picnic revealed a world of peaceful views and pleasant old buildings. Landowners severed vacant roadside parcels for the newcomers who dreamed of building the latest split-level bungalow with breezeway and three-car garage. Entire farms were consumed by subdivisions, extending the boundaries of once-compact towns such as St Thomas and Oshawa. Unlike their country predecessors, built step by step over generations, these new houses were off-the-shelf models built and sold by professional agents. The only part not completed when occupants took up residence was the payment, stretched out over a twenty-five–year mortgage.

The village general store succumbed to a drive-in plaza on the new bypass road around a town miles away. Intersections were enlarged to serve more

Figure 3.10 THE CROSSROADS. Ideal corner locations of the horse-drawn era (top) became liabilities in the automobile age. Relocation back from the corner between 1965 (middle) and 1981 (bottom). Caledon village, Peel County.

Figure 3.11 REPRODUCTIONS. New materials in old configurations help us cling to the past in comfort. Harsh, unweathered brick, the absence of barns and mature trees, and failure to align with the rectangular land survey are clues that this is a late-twentieth-century copy. Caledon Township, Peel County, 1977.

traffic, leaving the corner sites, once so popular, vulnerable (Figure 3.10). Upstairs along main-street business blocks, dusty windows and broken blinds told of small-town tenants moved to high-rise apartments and rental town houses at the fringes of the Golden Horseshoe. The survival of main street was in doubt.[24] Fleets of yellow buses radiating out from consolidated schools every afternoon at four related the same story. The branch-line railway, once the key to survival, later the path of escape to the city, became a bare gravel strip. Few sights are more forlorn than the vacant patch at the centre of a small Ontario town that has lost its railway.

Automobiles have created their own landscape: traffic signals, muffler shops, parking lots, and car dealerships, to name a few examples. Oakville's Ford Motor plant and its modern office building, opened in 1948, stand where once Halton County's orchards and market gardens flourished. Limited-access highways occupy some ten hectares of land for every kilometre of route. Gas bars and wreckers' yards weakly concealed behind opaque fences are universal.

The car's most profound legacy is suburban Ontario. Suburbia has been the second great transformation, as dramatic in its effects as deforestation was in an earlier century. Cars turned farmland into streetsides, too often now over-

Figure 3.12 CHANGE ENDURES. The Gibraltar Point lighthouse (1806), a factory chimney of the 1890s, downtown office skyscrapers of the 1960s, and CN Tower (1976) each reach for the sky in different arrangements, for different reasons. Verticalness is the one constant. Note the historical plaque mounted on the lighthouse. Looking north from Toronto Island, 1982.

whelmed by garage doors with houses tacked on behind.[25] For a while in the
1970s, by-laws controlling roadside sprawl around cities seemed to be having
some effect. But despite the Planning Acts of 1949 and 1980, the Environmental Assessment Act, 1977, and the Heritage Act, 1974, roadside straggle
is more visible than ever. Rural subdivisions, highway service strips, and
country industrial parks are everywhere. In 1993, a provincial commission
again tackled this problem, recommending that the boundaries between towns
and countryside once more be sharpened.[26]

Rural degeneracy has been arrested by urbane reuse. Restored country
schools, cedar-rail fences, forebay barns, and small-town business blocks are
fashionable. If there was no fine old Ontario patterned-brick farmhouse on
one´s ideal site for a country home, a reproduction could always be built (Figure
3.11). This thoroughly modern version of the age-old fashion of architectural
revival has produced a spatter of new old houses in the countryside. Aspects
of the site and materials help the alert eye to spot them, but as time passes
the deception will become more and more inconspicuous.

The world continues to erode and rejuvenate in the 1990s. A few years ago
we worried about the Dutch elm disease; today concern is for a disease that
threatens maple trees. The landscape anticipates – by way of signboards announcing subdivisions, or by a six-lane bridge occupied by a four-lane roadway.
But expectation of change has always been with us. Wooden blocks set into
an 1890 house wall anticipated a porch, and perhaps it will still be attached
some day. A church tower anticipates a steeple, and rails laid in a bridge deck
in Petrolia awaited a streetcar line never built.[27]

Change shows best in prosperous societies. There the incentive, including
the decision to remember the past, flourishes amid structures already durably
built (Figure 3.12). As long as people respond to their opportunities at different
rates, the landscape will continue to be filled with an endless variety of features
worn and pristine, new, used, and altered. Especially in a spread-out, rural
setting, the earlier layers – boundaries, groves, slopes – show through and
enrich the overall message of change. That is the prospect for the 1990s, as
it has been in Ontario for every era over the past two centuries.

4

Surveys and place names

A metal pole stands at the intersection of two gravel roads in Osprey Township, in a remote area southward from Georgian Bay (Figure 4.1). Bolted to it are two bent and rusted metal signs, at right angles to each other, one reading `SIDE RD. 20´ and the other `CON. 4.´ This labelling marks the passage of a land surveyor and introduces the passing motorist to the system of recording the land. Rural folks know the code so well that it is of minor importance that the sign has become almost illegible. But city people, out for a country drive, occasionally stray through Osprey, and for them the labelling is almost certainly puzzling. In this chapter I describe the land survey and examine the ways in which Ontarians named the places in their province.

The township survey

The rectangular system

`Side Road 20´ and `Concession 4´ are, to the uninformed motorist, merely road names. In fact, they communicate far more, being the survey-system references identifying individual blocks of farmland. This designation is based on simple Euclidean geometry, and it permitted orderly allocation of vacant land to swarms of land-hungry immigrants during the pre-Confederation era.

`CON.´ refers to the concession, a strip of land one or two farms wide and running from one edge of a township to the other (Figure 4.2). On the sign, this abbreviation specifies the `concession road´ running along the length of one side – in this case, the fourth concession. `SIDE RD.´ (or `S.R.´) identifies the road crossing the concession at right angles to the concession road (and hence often called a cross road). `20´ tells us that the side road lies along the edge of the twentieth farm lot in the concession of, in Osprey's case, thirty-five farm lots.[1] Each combination of township name, concession number (often in roman numerals), and lot number specifies a unique parcel of land in Ontario. This standard unit of 100 acres (about forty hectares) is approximately square, and a back-line strip of woodland, visible from a slightly elevated

Figure 4.1 SIGNS OF THE LAND DIVISION. Labelling on roadsigns in rural Ontario brings the survey system to our attention. The Toronto *Star* and *Star Weekly* erected roadsigns throughout rural Ontario about 1950, showing the newspaper´s perception of its zone of influence at that time. Osprey Township, Grey County.

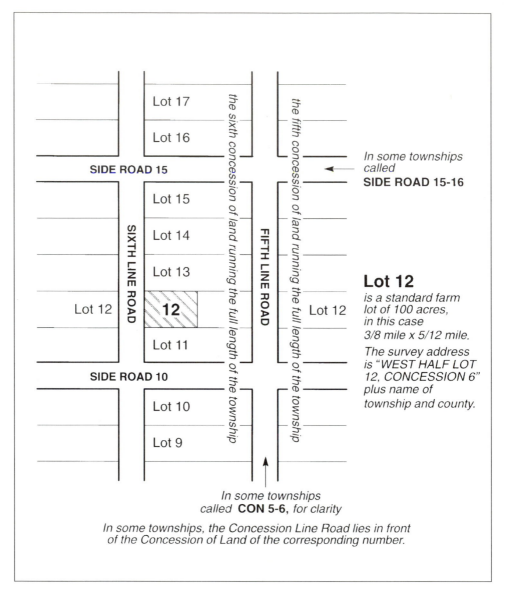

Figure 4.2 THE ONTARIO LOT DIVISION.

crossroads corner, should be sufficient for one to identify the bounds of an entire farm lot (Figure 4.3).

The township survey bears the stamp of the late-eighteenth-century Enlightenment, when symmetry and order were the rule. It is a large step away from medieval irregularity and anticipates the section and range system laid out along meridians in the Canadian west later in the nineteenth century. Ontario's layout frequently failed to meet expectations, however. Corners were

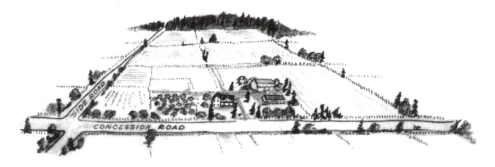

Figure 4.3 100 ACRES. The basic farm lot is somewhat deeper than it is wide.

supposed to be square, but throughout York County from St Clair Avenue northward, for example, they are seventy-four degrees. A protractor laid on the sidewalk blocks at the corner of Montgomery Avenue and Yonge Street in north Toronto shows it.

The way the lot and concession numbers ascend through each township displays in a subtle manner how administrators and surveyors perceived the rolling back of the provincial frontier (Figure 4.4). For each township, Concession 1 would be at the front and the higher numbers towards the rear. Townships faced the St Lawrence River, the Bay of Quinte, and Lake Ontario, whereas most of those adjacent to Lake Erie faced northward to inland settlement routes such as the Talbot Road. The scarcity of major port towns along the Erie shore reinforces the feeling that settlers had turned their backs on Lake Erie. Highways 8 west of Stratford and 86 through Listowel are `front'; the parallel county road between them, through Blyth, is `rear.' Sydenham Road northwest of Shelburne, Yonge Street north to Lake Simcoe, and Highway 43 through Kemptville are other penetration routes from which townships opened up on either side. This numbering system offers a unique way of identifying heartland and hinterland and is less haphazard than it appears at first sight.

By providing public road allowances in advance of settlement, Britain's Colonial Office showed its concern for access throughout an inland area. But just how much access was adequate was beyond anyone's experience to determine. Among Ontario's first townships are thirteen in the Niagara peninsula that have road allowances surrounding two 100-acre farms – that is, road allowances on three sides of the lot. Approximately the same number of townships east from Toronto have allowances surrounding two 200-acre farms, still an absurdly high figure.[2] The road allowance changed from forty to sixty-six feet (one chain, approximately twenty metres) in breadth before 1800.

As further versions of land division were instituted, density of roads declined while the size of farm continued to fluctuate. Of the 400 townships laid out

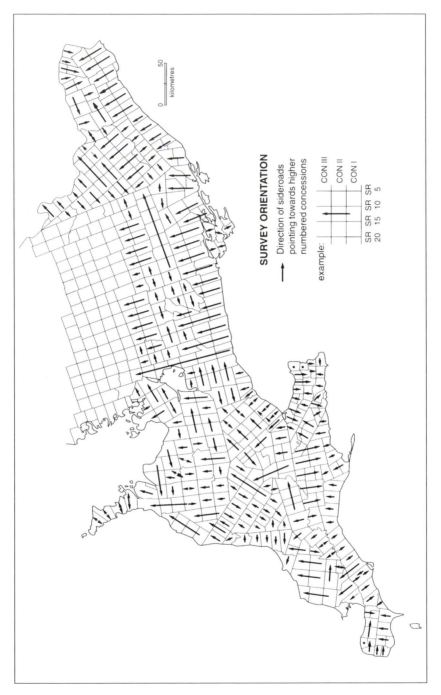

Figure 4·4 TOWNSHIP ORIENTATION. The arrangement of lot and concession numbering in each township gives an impression of the spread of Ontario's development in the nineteenth century.

south of the Precambrian Shield, by far the greatest number have roads surrounding ten 100-acre farms. After 1830, about three dozen townships were
laid out in blocks of six 200-acre lots. The experimenting concluded only when
there was no more land with which to practice, about 1860. The sequence of
trial and error remains forever imprinted on the landscape.

Evaluating the surveyor

Committing a survey system dreamed up on paper to untraversed forest was
a daunting task. The results received mixed reviews: 'How inelegantly Patrick
McNiff has run the line of the third Concession . . . evidently . . . without an
Instrument, without a Compass, without Pickets – without Flag staffs – without
a Head – With Grog – with Confusion – and with a Crookedness that is
characteristic of the work of a bad Surveyor.'[3] McNiff may have been all of
that, or the unfortunate victim of strong magnetic fields distracting his compass, as happened in Belmont Township, east of Peterborough.

An immigrant to Hastings County was, by contrast, highly impressed with
the entire procedure: 'Nearly all the farms in Upper Canada are of either 100
or 200 acres. . . . There are also what are called broken fronts, ie, pieces left
after running the *concession* lines straight; and gores are pieces left after running the *township* lines straight. The fronts are sold to the person holding the
lot adjoining, and the gores are thrown into the last lot of each township, and
there is a county road laid off . . . It is beautifully surveyed, and most advan-
tageously for the farmer.'[4]

Ontarians have rarely given thought to their land surveyors. For decades
scores of individuals, many poorly trained and all underpaid, struggled with
imperfect instruments to position wooden posts properly and drive them into
the ground. Individual townships frequently were under survey for years –
the perimeter first, then concession lines, and still later the lots. Later surveyors
could not easily advance the work of those who went before. One was advised
that 'as [Mr Aitken] has not informed the office where he began, or where he
left off, we cannot with any certainty direct where you are to begin your
operations.'[5] Land lawyers have built careers on the problems of affirming the
survey.

A basic principle of surveying is to work from the whole to the part – that
is, to lay out the broad order of meridians and lines of latitude for such an
area as southern Ontario, and then to subdivide successively into districts (or
counties), townships, concessions, and lots. In the rush to do something before
settlers poured in, and with inadequate resources, the process in Upper Canada
started in the middle, with the townships, and worked towards both extremes.
The result is relatively orderly farm-lot patterns within townships, but a wholly
chaotic scramble of townships across the province.

A further principle of land surveying is to close – that is, to trace out a succession of edges of a parcel of land and end up at the starting point. However, the instructions commonly given to surveyors were to lay out straight lines and not to enclose spaces. This procedure meant that they could not check the accuracy of their own work and take any necessary corrective measures. The outcome is an imperfect version of the precise geometry that would have pleased colonial officials and modern critics. Nevertheless, the survey achieved its goal of dividing the land for settlers to take up farming. Perhaps no one really should be too bothered that irregularities occurred.

Unexpected jogs in country roads are a legacy of the surveying process. Along Highway 12 past Lake Scugog, or Highway 46 south from Woodville, for example, a jog occurs every mile and a quarter (Figure 4.5). As one approaches a cross road village, a distinctive building may fill the view, with the road ahead shifting off to one side at the last moment. Small triangles of unused land mark where sharp corners, antedating fast motoring, have been rounded. The intersecting roads – concession lines – run straight across.

Survey records show that Highway 12 is a side road and that the jogs date back to 1810. In that year the road allowance was laid out according to the single-front survey system (Figure 4.6).[6] In approximately 150 townships

Figure 4.5 THE JOG IN THE ROAD. Irregularities in a rectangular land survey cause sudden, sharp discontinuities. An imperfect intersection, with the side road in the foreground. Manvers Township, Durham County.

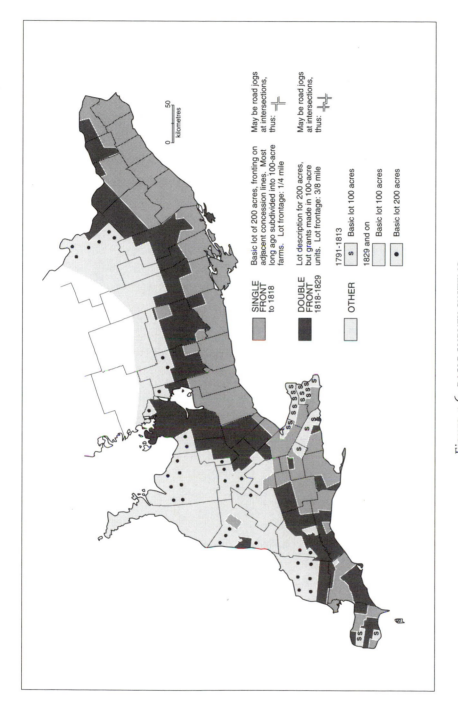

SINGLE FRONT to 1818
Basic lot of 200 acres, fronting on adjacent concession lines. Most long ago subdivided into 100-acre farms. Lot frontage: 1/4 mile

DOUBLE FRONT 1818-1829
Lot description for 200 acres, but grants made in 100-acre units. Lot frontage: 3/8 mile

OTHER

1791-1813
s   Basic lot 100 acres

1829 and on
Basic lot 100 acres

• Basic lot 200 acres

May be road jogs at intersections, thus:

May be road jogs at intersections, thus:

0   50
kilometres

Figure 4.6 BASIC SURVEY SYSTEMS.

across the province, surveyors were instructed first to mark out concession lines parallel to one another at mile-and-a-quarter intervals. They were then to locate the front corners of each lot every quarter mile along one side of each concession line from one end of the township to the other; after every fifth lot, corner posts one chain (sixty-six feet) apart marked the allowance for a side road. Lastly, the surveyor was to lay out each farm-lot and side-road boundary at right angles through to the next concession line.[7] If properly done, each boundary line should have passed one-and-a-quarter miles through the concession land, ending one chain (the width of a concession road allowance) short of the stake marking the front corner of the corresponding lot in the next concession. Crossroads would form a four-corner intersection. Distances incorrectly measured from lot to lot along any concession line became evident at this point. The error produced a jogged crossing, and the irregularity might be repeated from intersection to intersection across the full township.

In the double-front system of the 1820s, applied to more than 100 townships, surveyors were instructed to run lot lines in each direction back from each concession line to the middle of the block. This procedure assured four-square intersections, but, in the event of mismeasurement, created jogs half-way between adjacent lines.[8] Ontario has hundreds of these jogs, each the result of some surveying problem (Figure 4.7). In 1829, the surveyor general required that 'proof lines' (i.e., checking lines for directions) be run between concession roads after every sixth lot. Proof Line Road, in Bosanquet Township, north of Forest in Lambton County, takes its name from this edict. Jogs still might occur on intermediate side roads (every third lot), but the grand, cumulative effect of the double-front jogs across an entire township was eliminated. Ontario's longest stretches of straight road are found in western Ontario, where this improved system was widely applied.

Living with the survey

Early roadways straggled from side to side along the allowances set out for them, following the path of least resistance. In winter, travellers took their sleighs across country with complete disregard for the lot lines. Farm makers cut trees in ever-expanding arcs outward from a chosen spot within what they believed was their lot. They hesitated to work close to the lot boundary, not being absolutely certain of its position,[9] and more than a few pioneers must have sweated mightily in the wrong place.

By the end of the settling era, lotlines and roadsides were becoming sorted out to the onlooker. Each building stood square to the edge of its site, as the site did to the squared fields and the fields to the lot survey.[10] For the pedestrian, 'walking along the concession line, not a tree relieves the eye, except the uniform belt of woods in the rear of the clearings.'[11] Long, straight align-

Figure 4.7 THE WANDERING SIDE ROAD. A supposedly straight side road lurches from side to side across Chinguacousy Township, Peel County.

ments stretch over hill and valley; curves are infrequent, and forks almost non-existent. How orderly it was all becoming.

Ultimately, however, the land division was there to serve the needs of the residents. Hundreds of miles of road allowances provided in Durham and Northumberland counties, for instance, have never been opened. Others were opened briefly, found to be superfluous, and abandoned. Residents simply went ahead and provided themselves with whatever worked best. Overgrown, disused roadways symbolize the residents' disdain for inappropriate rules.

Draping straight lines over rumpled space has had its price. The land shrugged and let the surveyor have his rectangular way in smoothish areas such as Lambton and Kent counties. Elsewhere, as in Markham Township, road allowances encountered watercourses at least once in every kilometre. Culverts have become among the most prevalent of human-made features in the Ontario countryside. In rural Peterborough County, dozens of road cuttings advertise the disharmony with drumlin hills of glacial origin, running in parallel rows diagonally to the imposed road grid. Streams and roads repeatedly bend in deference to each other (Figure 4.8).

Figure 4.8 PHYSIOGRAPHY AND SURVEY IN CONFLICT. A concession road deflects from its straight alignment to cross a stream at right angles. Wilmot Township, Waterloo County.

No amount of brashness could contend with major obstacles. Irregularities caused by lakes, moraines, rivers, or the Niagara Escarpment show how irrelevant the grid frequently was. How very different Ontario's situation is from, say, rural France, where the country roads `follow the lie of the land and speak the very language of the contours.'[12] Fast motorists there squeal their tires on the sharp bends. Their Ontario counterparts fly blindly over sharp crests, bottoming on the other side and soon pulling in for a new set of shock absorbers.

In surveying jargon, longer deviations from the grid are called `given roads.' These rights-of-way, along lot lines or angling irregularly across the survey, have been given by adjacent owners for the public good.[13] Few owners denied their importance, even to themselves, and these alignments have become entrenched. A road allowance near St Catharines `was found in the settlement of the country to present great obstacles to being rendered fit for travel,' and land for a parallel road `was given by the owners of the lots through which [it] runs, and has since been used as a public highway, good at all seasons of the year for travel and sufficient for the public convenience.'[14]

Given roads warp the grid to critical natural points such as lakefront landings or stream fording places. `Dover Given Road,' near Wallaceburg, runs between two lots, like a side road, to a millsite. It is long abandoned, but two small graveyards are reason for keeping the road open across the concession. The lower the density of surveyed allowances, the greater the chance of such places being inaccessible, and the greater the likelihood of given roads. Owners may have been compensated with portions of the road allowance that the given road replaced. One should not presume that an abandoned given road persists as a public footpath.

A good many roads wander across the Ontario landscape for miles, apparently unrelated to the survey. Highway 48 through Goodwood is a prehistoric Indian trail that runs along the Oak Ridges moraine to avoid swampy spots between. The Warsaw Road in Peterborough County is another. Non-survey roads are common in the Bay of Quinte region, skirting the inlets and shorelines. They run across farm lots, even bisecting farmsteads, to give access to peninsulas too small for the grid to serve as intended (Figure 4.9). Stretches of swamp in the United County of Stormont, Dundas and Glengarry so severely obstructed the survey system that lots were rearranged to face given roads laid out on the upland ridges.

Waterloo Township was not provided with road allowances at all, permitting settlers to establish a suitable density of roads without prejudice. Waterloo's local system affirms that having open roads surrounding 1,000 acres (about 400 hectares) at a time has served well. We may conclude that Ontario's local-road system does a satisfactory job, with the help of a good many deviations produced by sensible residents who knew precisely how much road was needed.[15]

Figure 4.9 BISECTED FARM. What looks like a lane leading into a
farmyard is rather a public, given road deflected through a farm lot. Ridge
Road, Bosanquet Township, Lambton County.

Farm-lot size

Colonial officials guessed at the optimal size of land grant when the process
began before 1800. Parcels of 200 acres (eighty hectares) were usual until
1815, and favoured persons received many of them. Subsequently, 100 acres
(forty hectares) was most common. Even that was much too large for the farm
family before Confederation. That generation could manage only about sixteen
hectares, and left the wooded portion as a reserve for fuel and building materials. In due course it became valued space into which machine-equipped
farms could expand.

In 1901, the average Ontario farm property consisted of twenty-eight hectares
(seventy acres) of improved land, and another seventeen hectares (forty-three
acres) in unimproved woodland.[16] One durable Victorian house and barn for
each hundred acres is still very common. Mergers after 1900 have raised the
average farm size and contributed to a continuous range of sizes, up to several
hundred hectares per operation today. `Cattle crossing' signs and slow-moving
farm machinery warn motorists that the concession line is now also a farm
lane for a holding spread over several lots, and even onto other concessions.
Many farmers work several kilometres from the home farm.[17]

The squared-off landscape of hundred-acre units remains strong, however,
in part because of the inheritance system. Farms passed intact to the eldest
son, but with the legal responsibility for fair support of the siblings and
surviving parent.[18] Up to the Confederation period, space was available for the
younger generation to start new farms in the neighbourhood, reinforcing the

family's rootedness, but the next generation had scant prospect of repeating the pattern. Two McCutcheon brothers who took up land in Erin Township in the 1830s each raised a dozen children there, yet five generations later the family name has vanished from the township.[19] Some moved to Manitoba, and others to the cities. To those inheritors of the Ontario farm we may attribute the large Victorian farmhouse, the symbol of farming success.

Place names

Names are the deepest expression of commitment to a place. Each is a signature on the landscape tableau.[20] Names become known far and wide and carry through time; they are not easily changed. Customary names such as Round Lake, Beaver River, or Pine Ridge occur over and over again throughout Ontario, but seldom with more than the most local of associations. They belong more to places dating back to prehistory and ancient tongues.

Native place names at one time must have been in common use everywhere. With few people to defend them, however, and Indian peoples not involved in the map-labelling process that parallelled European settlement, Native place names largely vanished. And if they have not, the place itself has become unrecognizable. The historical plaque in Huronia to the prehistoric site of Cahiague stands in an open field. There has been little movement to reclaim Native names on the modern map. Mississauga, first used as a municipal name in 1968, is exceptional, having won out over Sheridan in a contest to replace the old designation of Toronto Township (itself an Indian name). Rather, we will grow accustomed to Vanier, Clarington, Halton Hills, and Cambridge – all named in the same era as Mississauga. Even archaeological sites bear such names as Draper, Lawson, Hood, Nodwell, and Walker – local names of recent landholders, the originals long lost.[21] They do nothing to strengthen our consciousness of pre-European roots, and indeed they carry no meaning in the mental maps of modern Ontario.

Current Ontario names instead have been parachuted in from outside on the whim of a governor, Colonial Office board, or settler. European surnames are thick across the province. Mallorytown, Talbotville, Martintown, Petersburg, Fowler's Corners, and hundreds more recognize founding families. Streetsville and Churchville, on the Credit River, remember early residents too, despite the generic ring. New Dundee, New Hamburg, New Dublin (but just plain York and London) identify the kind of people one may expect to find in these places.

It is a source of amusement to British visitors that Preston is within Cambridge and that London and Paris are named on the same road sign west of Clappison's Corners. Lincoln County is a fair replication of Lincolnshire (Figure 4.10), but a recitation of the place names en route between Moira (just north of Belleville) and Maynooth, further north, is bound to befuddle an

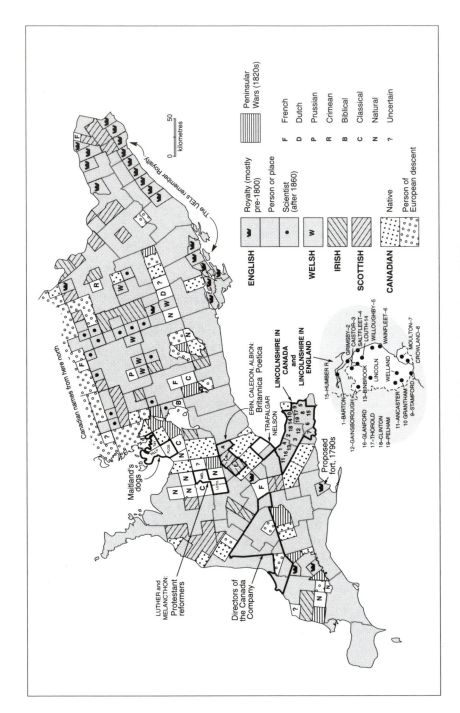

Figure 4.10 SOURCES OF TOWNSHIP NAMES.

Table 4.1
The mixing of place names

Place names encountered en route southward from Maynooth to Moira, Ontario (115 km)		Place names encountered en route northward from Maynooth to Moira, Ireland (135 km)	
Ontario name	Foreign origin	Irish name	Location in Ontario
Maynooth	Co. Kildare, Ireland	**Maynooth**	Hastings County
Bird's Creek	English	Dunboyne	Elgin County
Dungannon	Co. Tyrone, Ireland	Tara	Bruce County
Bancroft	American	Navan	Russell County
L'Amable	French	Boyne River	Dufferin County
Limerick	Co. Limerick, Ireland	Louth	Lincoln County
Steenburg	Dutch	Dundalk	Grey County
Gilmour	Scottish	Newry	Perth County
Tudor	English	Gilford	Simcoe County
Cashel	Co. Tipperary, Ireland	Clare	Grey County
Bannockburn	Scottish	Dromore	Grey County
Eldorado	Spanish	Armagh	Sudbury District
Madoc	Welsh	Lurgan	Bruce County
Ivanhoe	English	**Moira**	Hastings County
Moira	Co. Down, Ireland		

Irishman (Table 4.1). Names on mailboxes or entered on old maps affirm the extensive mixing of origins.

The Ontario map reads like an honour roll to ordinary people and is strong evidence of the durable, personalizing process that occurred in the settlement years. It took a world war for Berlin to be changed to Kitchener in 1916, and few other individuals in the twentieth century have had the stature to have his or her name widely superimposed on ordinary places already named. Sir Isaac Brock was so commemorated in a previous century: Brockville was Snarlington before 1812. Queen Victoria gave her name to countless new places, but seldom as a replacement for established ones. Her great-great-granddaughter Queen Elizabeth II has to be content with a few buildings and parks.

Townships

Between 1783 and the 1860s more than five hundred townships were laid out across southern Ontario, and each one had to be named. The choices constitute a chronology of what successive administrators deemed to be meaningful in their lives (Figure 4.10). It took twenty-five townships, all named before 1800, to do proper honour to the royal family. United Empire Loyalists occupied these, and the names surely helped them to feel at home. Six lakefront townships eastward from Toronto originally had Hanoverian names but were replaced at an early date when no German emigrants showed up to defend them.

Three hundred more townships proclaimed English people and places and were being labelled throughout the settlement period. Tiny, Tay, and Flos – dogs belonging to the wife of Lieutenant-Governor Sir Peregrine Maitland – are the most bizarre recipients of such recognition.

The Scots and Irish communities fared poorly in the exercise. It must have galled a lowlander writing home to relatives in Ayrshire to have had to use a return address such as Oxford or Wolford. The scientist category – Boyle, Cavendish, Kepler, and others – up on the fringes of the Shield in the 1850s was evidence of a broadening of minds. It also reduced the duplication of names already in use for villages, lakes, and so forth. Native populations are remembered in about thirty-five townships. These bear little relationship to the distribution of First Nations peoples today but do offer some evidence as to where these communities were situated in the early years of European contact.

Only after Confederation, when Ontario had achieved enough domestic worthies and a vast northern territory to be labelled, did homegrown names began to appear on townships. Rocky chunks of Precambrian Shield salute a miscellaneous assortment of not-very-famous individuals: names such as Ballantyne, Hendrie, and Pentland. Most of these places are known only to a few prospectors and canoeists.

Township names are subjects of humour as well as dignity, the source of such quaint corporate instructions as `Call your Dummer Plumber´ to deal with septic systems east of Peterborough. And surely Luther and Melancthon are unparalleled examples of surveyor wit: two swampy townships laid out by a Roman Catholic surveyor and purportedly fit only for supporters of the Protestant reformation.

Roads

Numbered survey roads suited the faceless, vacant countryside explored by the surveyor. Naming them indicates a growing sense of place in the landscape, and numbering has frequently fallen out of use. As an example, between the sixth and seventh concessions of Emily Township, north of Omemee, lies `The Orange Line,´ the last east-west linear neighbourhood dominated by Irish Protestants. Beyond, northward, is solid Catholic territory, another world. To call this road the Seventh Line would convey none of the cultural make-up of the township. Again, the survey-numbered side roads in Caledon Township – 5, 10, 15, 20, 25 – became in 1994 the Grange Sideroad, Escarpment Sideroad, Charleston Sideroad, Beech Grove Sideroad, and High Point Sideroad, respectively. These rather pleasant names have local connotations, and retaining the generic `side road´ keeps the survey origins somewhat in view. But history is ever vulnerable, as in Malden Township, at the west end of Lake Erie, where Middle Side Road is also labelled as Middleside Road. Names are that fragile.

The survey labelling has also yielded to urbanization and the province-wide scale of travel that has developed during the twentieth century. Provincial and county road systems carry new numbers freely across township boundaries, and street names run out from cities and towns into the countryside. Well before the First World War Dufferin Street in Toronto ceased to be called the Second Line West, York Township. Highway 2, Kingston Road, and Lakeshore Road are all designations for First Line in a score of townships along the Lake Ontario front. Eglinton Avenue runs west from Scarborough to Flamborough. Numbered roads are becoming scarce in all but truly rural areas, and a voice in the countryside speaking of `the eighth of Elderslie' belongs to a fading age.

Direction and time

Front of Escott and Rear of Escott are two townships in Leeds County – Front on the St Lawrence River and Rear directly north of it. Together the names suggest that Ontario faces a particular direction (Figure 4.4). The architects of Mississauga's city hall had not the slightest doubt and made that post-modern structure, completed in 1987, face south to Lake Ontario as part of its symbolism.[22] With the closing of the fur-trade route westward by way of the Ottawa River in 1821, Lake Ontario became the undisputed artery for commerce and immigration, and from Burlington to Kingston new towns fronted on it. Lots and concessions were numbered northward, and `broken front' survey fragments are strung like footlights across the base of the provincial stage. Court-houses face south with remarkable frequency. Nepean is one of very few townships numbered in reverse, yet Parliament has shunned the river below – symbol of the nation's transcontinental extent – in favour of facing southward. The lonely expanse of the Gatineau Hills forms a laconic backdrop.

The superintendent of Ontario schools in the 1870s expressed Victorian modesty in recommending that a school ought to front on `the street, so that the outbuildings may be thrown into the background.'[23] Furthermore, schools were best situated on the north side of a road, facing south so that the students would sit facing north. That made good use of natural light from the sun during the low season and put the blackboard on the cold, windowless north wall.[24] Besides, `outline maps may be suspended on the north side of the room. Unless a child sees a map for the first time placed in the right position, everything will be turned around for the rest of his life.'[25]

Churches ought then to be at right angles to schools. The narthex door should be to the west, and the chancel at what Anglicans often refer to as the east end. For nearly two centuries parishoners of St John's, York Mills, have wended their way eastward from Yonge Street up a long sloping footpath to the west porch. The churchyard is proper, too, with headstones at the west end of each plot and remains laid out so as to rise to face the dawn on the Day of Judgment.

What looks orderly on paper was far less so on the ground. Yonge Street runs very close to due north, so St John's, York Mills, can be ecclesiastically correct and at the same time face square to the road in proper Enlightenment fashion. But St John's, Nassagaweya, must compromise because what common use calls north in Halton County is actually northwest forty-five degrees (Figure 4.11). 'Ecclesiastical east' is a conveniently varying point on the Ontario compass, appreciably more popular for Ontario churches than is true east. St Mary's Anglican in Metcalfe, Oxford County, achieves proper orientation by standing sideways on its site, but this is exceptional.

In eight townships between Orangeville and Barrie, 55 per cent of the churches were misaligned in 1881; schoolhouses deviated 60 per cent of the time.[26] Clearly, church and school should never stand side by side, if both were properly oriented. But they did (Figure 4.12). Of course, desks could face northward even with a north entrance, and an east-west building would receive more light than a north-south one. Surely an inventive teacher might try hanging the Mercator map of the world on a side wall or, for fun, upside down! The case for southward-facing schools is altogether tenuous.

Weathercocks can confirm our directional suspicions. More and more are

GUELPH LINE

No. 10 SIDE ROAD

Figure 4.11 ORIENTATION. St John's Anglican, Nassagaweya, is square to the survey, but the alignment of its cemetery rows is twisted to hold true to the cardinal direction. Guelph Line, Halton County.

Figure 4.12 MISORIENTATION. Church and school, side by side, with entrances on the south side. The church is ninety degrees out of proper alignment. Notice that the school is finished in metal panels stamped to simulate stone. Ballyduff, Manvers Township, Durham County.

appearing on country non-farm properties, close enough to be checked from the road. We must assume that practical ex–city folks have installed them properly, especially as these people are the first in rural Ontario history to disregard the tradition of building their houses square to the road.

Now, in the 1990s, there is a new, absolute indicator of direction, as reliable as moss growing on the north side of a tree: the satellite receiver dish. Each one points towards Chicago, over which hover North America's television communication satellites. Along the Lake Erie shore, dishes point about fifteen degrees south of due west, gradually increasing eastward to about twenty-five degrees at Pembroke.[27] One need never be lost again!

Evidence of timekeeping is scarce in the Ontario landscape. In the past, life moved to the rhythm of the seasons, the phases of the moon, and the rising and setting of the sun. On the farms, roosters crowed usefully, while house bells, mounted on the summer kitchen roof above the cooking area, rang out over the fields, announcing dinner. Bell-cotes are fragile adornments, and few remain of the thousands once scattered across the landscape. Other bells announced the start of school or worship. Tolling was anticipated, and any bell sounded unexpectedly signalled a fire or other emergency.

On the farms, pocket watches, and then wrist-watches, replaced bells rendered inaudible by noisy tractors. Today the timer on a sound system in the children's bedroom shakes them out in time for the school bus at the end of the lane. Church bells hang idle, and only the occasional clock face on a tower, or a siren atop a fire station, interrupts what has become the complete privatization of time in our landscape.

5

Building materials and arts

Old Ontario was built from wood, soil, and stone, by people familiar with brick, iron, and glass. For them, getting started in a forest was a humbling experience, hard on gentility but good for ingenuity. Everything from treetops to bedrock was hacked, dug, or chipped into useful forms with rudimentary tools. Axe and wedge slew the tree, while the ground yielded to shovel and iron bar. Teams of oxen supplemented human muscle. Gradually, over a few generations, persevering residents achieved a cultural landscape as modern as any in the industrialized world.

As society caught up, local natural resources diminished in importance. By 1900, plate glass, pressed brick, wrought iron, galvanized wire, concrete, and tarmacadam had supplemented, and often replaced, materials previously in use (Figure 5.1). Coal and petroleum were displacing animal feed as fuel. These new consumer items were being manufactured in large quantities at distant locations by unknown hands and shipped by railway and wagon to their destinations. In the twentieth century, aluminum and vinyl wall panels, latex-based stucco, and countless other materials flooded the province. Each innovation disengaged the countryside resident a little more from the basic natural resources of the landscape.

This chapter explores the changing resources and technology of constructing the Ontario landscape.

Wood

Wood is the preferred building material, the world over, wherever it has been an option. It clearly was right for pioneering Ontario – a repeatedly forgiving material, well suited to the relatively unskilled hands into which it fell. White pine is the most versatile of all Ontario trees. It has been used for framing, flooring, and siding and for almost every other building part except those under water. Even the stumps have been employed, for fencing. The export value of white pine is well known,[1] but it also took the lead in domestic matters.

Numerous synthetic materials have been substituted for wood over the years,

Figure 5.1 MATERIALS FOR THE BUILT LANDSCAPE. This barn incorporates a wide range of materials: wood, stone, concrete, aluminum. The gothic window in the hen-house came from a nearby church that received new window sash. Eramosa Township, Wellington County.

but the take-over is far from complete. The very bones of buildings are still wooden. If properly set atop masonry foundations, wooden buildings will allow moderately skilled amateurs to make changes indefinitely into the future, just as they have been doing for all of Ontario's history.

Log walling

Log buildings are the plainest, most utilitarian of all structures in the Ontario landscape. They were easily built and functional and have been remorselessly superseded. It was unnecessary to remove the bark or square the face, and roughly notched logs piled up in criss-cross fashion stood by themselves. House-raising bees brought together untrained settlers, who acquired the simple skills by copying. Even a ham-handed settler could build a house of white pine. A landscape of similar-looking buildings resulted, following a simple, proven design.

Log houses are readily detectable, even if covered over by a veneer. Look for small, gable-end windows, squeezed up under the eaves (Figure 5.2). The top log at eaves level on each end wall holds the top logs of the front and rear walls against the outward forces of the roof. The eaves-level logs are in tension and must not be severed for windows. In a timber-framed house the corresponding beam is at floor level, half a metre or more lower, and windows accordingly can be larger. There is no structural reason preventing small

Figure 5.2 SPOTTING A LOG HOUSE. Small gable-end windows of a log house contrast with the larger ones, preferred, in a non-log house. Compare with Figure 2.6. Note the well in foreground. Near Douro, Peterborough County.

windows high up in a timber-framed house, but it was never done. Bigger windows give better light and ventilation, and we may readily believe that the log-house arrangement was by necessity, not choice.[2] Certainly pseudo-log houses built in the 1990s, with log facing over a framework of lumber, have large gable-end windows. They are popular ski chalets.

With use of the largest logs, forty-five to sixty centimetres across, a building might need as few as six or seven logs from ground level to eaves, but others have up to fourteen. The biggest trees may not have been used in local structures but were instead exported for cash or taken by the crown for ships' masts. Settlers willingly used more manageable, second-rate trees for their houses, some no doubt recycled from temporary lean-tos (`shanties´) built hastily with small trees felled in the first year of settlement.

Logs longer than five to eight metres enclosed more living space than was needed to meet the minimum house size required by law to qualify for title to the land. That dimension, 16 by 20 ft (roughly five by six metres), did not coerce bona fide settlers into any action they would not have taken on their own initiative. But it did establish a benchmark from which houses gradually enlarged, and with remarkable uniformity, through the generations ahead.[3] It took a farm household about thirty years to progress beyond log housing in the pre-Confederation era.[4] There is irony in the durability of log construction for a society that craved more sophisticated housing. Mixed farming provided one use for the embarrassing legacy of settlement. The old house could be converted into a needed outbuilding (and perhaps be moved, piece by piece) and replaced with something grander.

Veneering was another way out, removing the log house from the eye, if not actually in fact (Figure 2.7). Carefully selected, currently fashionable details, together with additions and proper foundation walls, assisted the deception. Veneers have tricked observers ever since into underestimating age, exactly as the self-respecting occupants would have wished.

Barns and houses never veneered stand today along the edge of the Precambrian Shield and in remote recesses of Grey and Bruce counties. Many are abandoned. The powdery lime chinking between the logs, possibly mixed with straw or animal hair, is disintegrating. With no obvious new use for their sites, these derelicts will persist indefinitely in a state of slow, natural self-destruction. Such dwellings signal the honest, but unsuccesful effort after 1860 to extend northward the limits of small family farms in Ontario once the best lands had been taken up. The downturn in farming fortunes prevented a second-generation, framed house from coming into existence.

For all their alleged temporariness, log buildings have proven to be Ontario's most enduring structures. Many have been covered over two or three times, and their existence in the 1990s can be attributed to this wrapper. Now the layers are being peeled off by happy nostalgists, seeking roots.

Plank and stovewood walling

A resident of Medonte Township explained the construction of his old family house, dismantled about 1905 to make way for a railway line. In the 1850 house 'there was a three-inch groove cut in the mud sill right around on the outside. Well then a three-inch plank was stood on end and an oak peg was put in every three feet up the edge of the plank, and then the next plank was bored and that was drove in on to it. . . . There wasn't a nail in it at all. There was a plate on top that sat down on it and it had a three-inch groove and that went right around the house and it was morticed and oak-pinned at the corners.'[5] He never knew all this until the cladding was removed, for the thin walls and full-sized windows were like those of other non-log houses. Had he known, the house might well be standing yet, because it 'was lots strong enough for to move.' Plank buildings are unremarked contemporaries of log ones, being invariably covered with milled boards, brick, or stucco to protect the rough lumber structure.

'Horizontally stacked dimension lumber' is the usual way of describing a style of plank house built of one-by-six or one-by-ten boards[6] (Figure 5.3).

Figure 5.3 PLANK WALL. The double house of a mill worker in stacked plank; previously stuccoed, being refurbished. The intermediate wall in the foreground separates the two dwelling units. Offsetting planks makes a surface to which plaster may adhere. Meadowvale Village, Mississauga.

Layer upon layer of rough planks, each nailed to the ones below, produced a free-standing structure with walls as narrow as fifteen or twenty centimetres – half that of log construction. Windows and doors could be cut without weakening the structure, and such buildings may be extended in small steps. A plank house is a nail and labour extravaganza but could be put up by only two people of no extraordinary talent.

There is no external way to determine how often plank walling was used, but study of ruins suggests that it was uncommon, except in lumber-exporting regions.[7] There commercial sawmills produced large quantities of unmarketable, second-grade lumber, and it became a cheap, unintentional building material locally – around Peterborough in the Confederation era, for example.[8] Far from being a senseless waste of wood, plank walling was opportunistic, `a persistent option within vernacular building, available when needed.'[9]

The stovewood wall is a twentieth-century feature and looks rather like a plastered woodpile. Many can be found in the Lake Simcoe region and the Ottawa valley, made from surplus fence rails cut up during the 1920s and 1930s when small fields were being merged.[10] One man is said to have built a hundred stovewood houses in the Ottawa region between 1910 and 1950; many are found near Manotick.[11] Stovewood walling produces warmer and drier enclosures than does stone, making it attractive for stables. Stovewood might well have become a popular replacement for block or stone had not teams of horses, the chief beneficiaries, been yielding to tractor power.

Timber and balloon framing

Timber framing, also known as bentwork construction, has been by far the most important technology in creating the Ontario landscape. Bents are two-dimensional arrangements of vertical timber posts and horizontal timber beams, lined up parallel to one another, with perhaps five metres between (Figure 5.4). Additional horizontal timbers hold one bent to another – the sill at the ground or foundation level, girts at intermediate levels, and the plate at the eaves. The space between adjacent bents is a bay. A simple timber-framed house has one bay, with the bents supporting the front and rear walls. Framed barns most commonly have three to five bays, formed by four to six bents, lined up. The entire three-dimensional skeleton is stabilized by diagonal braces where the timbers come together, then closed in with boards nailed on.

The fundamental part of the bent is the two-way T joint, formed by a mortice (pocket) cut into the side of one timber and a tenon (projection) carved at the end of another timber. The integrity of the structure depends on the solidness of the tenon. White pine does not rot at the ends, a reason that this species has been indispensable in the fabrication of early Ontario. With an ash or locust dowel inserted through the timbers to secure the joint, framers created a rigid framework without using a single nail. All this detail is open to view inside any barn.

Figure 5.4 TIMBER FRAMING. Mortice-and-tenon technology is displayed in these barn timbers. Bents and beams serve as scaffolding during construction and, here, in dismantling. Adze marks indicate that some of these timbers have been hewn by hand, not milled. Toronto Township, Peel County.

Simplicity and durability are the hallmarks of framing. But this style of construction requires a craftsman able to visualize geometry in three dimensions – the framer – and a cooperative society able to arrange a work crew – the raising bee. Framers and bees were present in the lakefront townships from the start of settlement in the 1780s, carried over from New England and New York. Timber framing is a vernacular art, and skilled craftsmen and their apprentices travelled the province and disseminated an understanding of, and a high degree of standardization in, the procedure. It is still being practised by Mennonites in Waterloo County.

Bents from five to eight metres long are normal, but on some very large barns put up late in the nineteenth century they reached fourteen metres. Timber framing permits far larger openings than is possible with logs because the load is carried by the bents, not the wall covering. It also allows for expansion bay by bay as required, in time with the development of the farm-house and overall property. The timber frame explains the long history of wings, tails, and lean-tos, added on by increments, that distinguish so many of Ontario's houses and barns. In 1833, more than three hundred residents of Caledon Township petitioned for a sawmill `for want of lumber with which to build comfortable habitations.'[12] As fast as local sawmills started up and blacksmiths could cut nails for siding, timber framing became the norm in Ontario, and it continued to be well through the nineteenth century.

If sawmills could make siding, thoughtful people argued that they could also prepare framework, and a much lighter and more manageable one than timber. Thus came about the balloon frame, apparently stimulated by the rapid rise of Chicago in the 1830s.[13] This system uses two-by-four lumber studs (uprights) nailed at 40-cm (16-in) intervals. The wall does not bear a load but does strengthen the lightweight structure – requiring some forty per cent less material than timber framing – because it is nailed to the studs. Circular saws, introduced after 1850, efficiently cut the slender pieces used in ballooning. The machine planer trued them to standard dimensions, and machine-cut nails held everything together.[14]

Not everyone approved of ballooning. One commentator found frame houses either too hot or too cold and preferred to continue with log if he could not jump directly to brick.[15] Others chided the framers as archaic – `old fogy mechanics who ... rob a stick of timber of all its strength and durability by cutting it full of mortices, tenons, and auger holes.'[16]

Balloon framing thrived on capitalization and mass production and was seldom tried in rural Ontario before 1870.[17] New and reconstructed housing sometimes used a studded timber frame – a kind of joiner's (rather than carpenter's) ballooning. It made a heavy building.[18] Much depended on the skills available. As the art of joinery was overtaken by the trade of carpentry, and as apprenticing with a master craftsman began to be replaced by a certificate from a trades school, ballooning made inroads. Timber-framed farmhouses were enlarged with balloon-framed wings. Urbanization gave impetus to balloon framing, and a variant – platform framing – proved well suited to the full two-storey houses coming into fashion.

Timber-framed structures continued to be built and rebuilt well into the twentieth century. The wider spans suited the broad, open spaces needed for churches, schools, and barns. Timber framing produced a cathedral ceiling that improved air circulation.[19] Sidewall bents could enclose a single bay thirteen metres or more wide, held in place by transverse beams or iron tie-rods. Brick buttresses were sometimes added to the outside, largely for decoration. When timbers became scarce, the technology was maintained with laminated planks – five two-by-tens spiked together to form one ten-by-ten beam.

Some new barns erected since about 1920 have prefabricated trusswork structures, combining wall posts and roof rafters as a single unit (Figure 5.5).

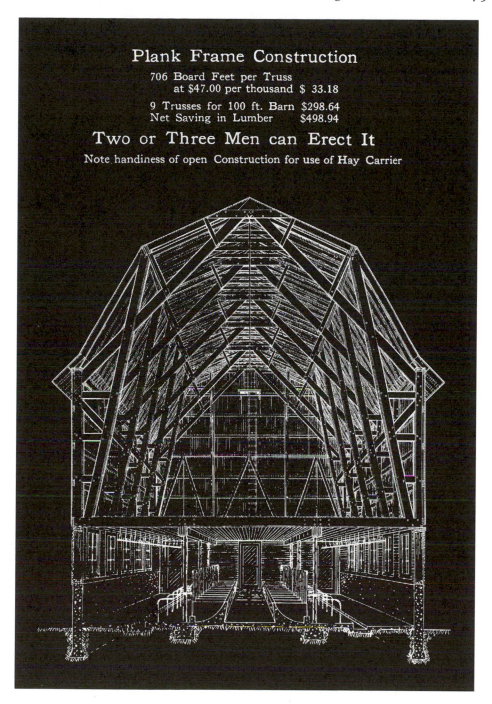

Figure 5.5 TRUSSWORK combines wall and roof support in a single unit.
Beatty Barn Book (1930), 27.

Trusses are, like balloon framing, made of milled lumber, and they too can enclose post-free spaces quite beyond that possibile with timber framing. But old traditions die hard, and a timber-framed barn, replacing one destroyed by fire, was erected near Brampton as recently as 1952, using new timbers from a woodlot in Dufferin County.[20]

Barns as we know them are obsolete in the 1990s, and once a board blows off a vacant building or a foundation starts to crumble, visible decay proceeds rapidly. Hundreds of neglected barns stand in southern Ontario, their erect skeletons testimony to the wisdom and durability of their design. As one decadent barn makes its final collapse from view, another enters its death throes. Somewhere there is always a timber frame available for contemplation.

Siding and roofing

Siding finishes off a building, and rarely is it installed in such a way as to continue to reveal the basic structure. Open nogging – non-structural use of filling between studs, braces, and timbers – is the exception (Figure 5.6). It may be widespread, but we do not know, for normally it is concealed by board or brick siding. Other types of siding, especially in wood, may be replaced from time to time over the life of a building, and they are therefore useful gauges of changing technology and taste.

Split (or `riven´) shingles are the most rudimentary walling, but they can protect logs and make rechinking unnecessary (Figure 5.7). Furthermore, shingles can be prepared at the building site, without a sawmill, from small blocks. Rough boards from a sawmill are another possibility, themselves in need of covering. Planed weatherboard and tapered clapboard (spoken of, and sometimes spelled, as `clabberd´) are very common and not easily distinguishable.[21] Bevelled shiplap – grooved boards nailed to the studs – make a tight and elegant wall (Figure 5.8). Taken together, these types define a sequence of increasing refinement and decorativeness. Each became an option with the introduction successively of pit saws, circular saws, planing mills, and moulding machines through the middle of the nineteenth century.

On houses wooden siding is normally horizontal, overlapped to shed water and keep heat inside. An exception is the board-and-batten technique, which has vertical boards supplemented by narrow strips of wood – battens – covering the cracks. It is expensive, and for show. Barns, in contrast, are usually sided with vertical boards, commonly pine. A gap between them equalizes air pressure and allows the circulation needed to prevent green hay from fermenting. Had the boards been placed horizontally, snow and rainwater would stand on the edges, obstructing circulation and causing rot.

Lath is an invisible use of wood, used to hold plaster to the inside of a wall or stucco to the outside. Strips of rough, unplaned wood, three or four centimetres wide and a quarter the thickness, are nailed to studs, or to vertical

Figure 5.6 NOGGING. Non-structural rubblestone walling fills in a timber frame. Parker's Mill, Rawdon Township, Hastings County, 1925.

Figure 5.7 SHINGLE SIDING over log, as suggested by the small window in the front gable. Near Kenilworth, Wellington County.

Figure 5.8 SHIPLAP achieves tightness with grooved boards nailed flush to the studs. Planed boards are necessary for this sophisticated finish. A simple, Romanesque, `Quebec´-style church. Eau Claire Station, east of North Bay, Nipissing District.

straps nailed on logs, with a half-centimetre space between. The soft plaster oozes through the cracks and hardens around the individual strips. Accordion lath is achieved by taking a thin board, randomly peppering it with hatchet splits, and pulling it apart just enough to create the gaps into which the plaster may set. Sawn lath began to appear after 1830 and rapidly superseded accordion lath in everyday use. Accordion lath is a very good sign that a structure dates back to the first third of the nineteenth century.[22] Since 1950, drywall panelling has made the lath-and-plaster technique obsolete.

Cedar shingle roofing also is largely concealed, but at one time it was universal. Splitting shakes from cedar or pine blocks was a familiar practice to settlers but gave way to milled shingles before Confederation. Roof repair was a task without respite: windstorms lifted shingles and chimney sparks threatened them, and they had to be replaced every ten to fifteen years. Iron sheeting became available in the 1870s, galvanized (zinc-coated) sheet after 1910, and asphalt shingles a few years later. Few innovations were adopted more rapidly, with shingles often being nailed directly on top of the old roofing. There are not enough exposed cedar shingle roofs today to do more than alert us to their onetime prevalence.

Stone

Keppel Township, northwest of Owen Sound, is a stone landscape: exposed bedrock strewn with boulders, stone fencing, and dour stone buildings. Highway 401 between Milton and Cambridge traverses another such area. Stony fields have been the bane of thousands of farmers from Kincardine to Woodville to Picton. With maddening predictability each year's frost lifted a new crop to the surface.

Cursed by amateurs as unworkable and unforgiving, in proper hands stone has yielded some of Ontario's grandest buildings and townscapes. Sydenham Ward, Kingston, is a showcase of the stonemason's craft. Even in utilitarian structures stone has been handled with notable sophistication (Figure 5.9). But stone-cutting has been, by and large, an expensive indulgence, and fewer than 3 per cent of Ontario houses in 1851 were stone. This figure rose only slightly over the next forty years.[23] Stone structures have always been rare, massive and sometimes gloomy, hard to repair, and virtually unassailable.

The ways of working stone remained largely unchanged throughout the nineteenth century. Plain blocks cannot indicate when they were first, or subsequently, used, and the stone itself is not a sensitive sign of the age of a structure. Weathered limestone, found lying on the ground, perhaps has been in use longer than clean, quarried stone; a piece could have been in a field wall or a stone pile for decades before being incorporated into a fine house. When the original Niagara River suspension bridge of 1847 was dismantled in 1900, the limestone abutments were taken down and the blocks reused in new bridge piers. The stone was described as being `practically as good as freshly quarried material.'[24] Construction with previously unused stones occurred only in exceptional cases after the 1880s. Stone buildings that have outlived their usefulness subsequently have been regarded as stonepiles, available for recycling.

Stone construction has had its detractors. In 1808, plans for the proposed brick court-house in Brockville allowed that stone could be substituted in order to reduce costs.[25] The tone is grudging, and brick was indeed used, despite the expense. Stone was less fashionable around Brockville than in Regency England, quite possibly because of a shortage of experienced masons.[26] A stone house, if it stood up at all, was destined to last indefinitely and might become an embarrassment to owners with developing taste. It seems inconceivable today that Confederation-era occupants might have contemplated hid-

Figure 5.9 CRAFTSMANSHIP. Fleet Street Pumping Station (1888). Ottawa.

ing these gems behind veneers, as neighbours were treating log ones. Yet if the buildings were roughly faced and not easily dismantled, disguise must have been a serious option.

Few people scorned stone, however, and well before the eruption of population in the 1830s prideful owners created façades too fine to hide behind a veneer. Cadres of stonemasons recruited to build the Erie, Rideau, second Welland, and St Lawrence canals between 1817 and 1848 subsequently found their way into the general workforce. Stone mills and houses appeared in the Rideau Lakes area in the 1830s and in Kingston, briefly the provincial capital. Hamilton, Guelph, and, to a lesser degree, London followed suit.

In the Paris region stand a number of distinctive houses, dating from the 1840s, finished with rows of fist-sized cobbles. At first glance these look like stone structures, but they are really stucco, with a high proportion of cement in the finish. Similar housing around Rochester, New York, suggests that former Erie Canal masons may have been involved. The examples are admired today and did not go unnoticed in the past; a scatter of later houses use this technique (Figure 5.10). Some built in the early twentieth century have concrete blocks in a cobbled design.[27]

England's gothic revival of the 1840s, focused on medieval pointed churches, thrust stone back into the limelight.[28] A new generation of British architects brought the gothic to Ontario, well timed for Christians and administrators

Figure 5.10 COBBLES. Water-rounded, hand-sized stones laid into lime mortar in neat courses give a delicately textured finish. The degree of labour involved indicates that cobbling was expensive, a high-class activity. House built in the 1860s. Yarmouth Township, Elgin County.

in immediate need of showy buildings. The use of stonework expanded to include slate roofing, sent to Canada from Wales cheaply as ships´ ballast and often arranged into colourful patterns (Figure 5.11). Interest spread to ordinary builders, among them the Saul brothers of Napanee. Between 1860 and 1881 these two stonemasons built twenty-one churches, `all gothick,´ some thirty houses, several factories, mills, and stores, and three bridges – all within an area of three townships.[29]

Along the Niagara Escarpment a number of stone houses date from the period 1850–75. Several dozen stone barns through Nassagaweya and Puslinch townships, southeast of Guelph, stand as examples of the strongly vernacular aspect of stonework in this period. This district was heavily settled by Scots, and there has been the impression that Scots and stone were inseparable.[30] People of Scottish descent also produced non-stone landscapes, however, and stone houses were outnumbered by other types all along the Niagara Escarpment.[31] The alleged connection is not fully convincing.

Figure 5.11 SLATE gives colourful distinction to public buildings. Presbyterian church (1878). Brockville.

Figure 5.12 RECYCLED MILL. Many stood derelict for years until restoration interests began finding them, while still capable of recovery, in the 1960s. Long Island Mill (1860) on the Rideau River, Manotick, Carleton County.

Many country grain mills were made of stone, as were a number of pre-1900 factories. Massive limestone blocks could sustain a tall building, four storeys or more, able to withstand great weight and vibration. Fire has been the main threat to these structures. Those that stand today have passed the endurance test, and obsolete ones often are not worth the expense of dismantling. A few (Figure 5.12) have been recycled: the Mill of Kintail, near Ottawa, is a residence, and the old Ancaster Mill near Hamilton, a restaurant. Many more remain, gaunt and windowless, or utter ruins, bypassed by technological rather than structural obsolescence. Abandoned stone mills are landmarks of the small-scale wheat or textile eras, and many conservation authorities have used them as evocative centrepieces for their recreational parks.

Foundations are the most utilitarian places for stone. Wooden houses flex in frost, and may safely be erected on cornerstones or even bare ground, but brick (solid or veneer) and stone buildings crack and must have foundation walls footed below the frost line. Half a century of land clearing caused erosion along thousands of rivulets, exposing bedrock shales – just what was needed to support the growing stock of masonry houses after Confederation (see Figure 3.4). Shale blocks were also valuable for constructing stables on mixed farms.

There could be no such thing as a temporary stone building, even for the most ordinary use. Public buildings, such as churches and court-houses, were deliberately planned in stone as lasting symbols. But stonework is labour-intensive, each piece having to be shaped and fitted into its unique position in the wall. As soon as factory-made concrete blocks came on the market, around 1900, stone ceased to be used in all but decorative situations. Concrete took over for foundations almost instantly.

Artificial stone facing – a true veneer only a few centimetres thick, set over balloon framing – has brought the look of stone within reach of ordinary consumers late in the twentieth century. It shows that the high regard for stone continues unabated. A lucky few owners have the chance to enjoy the real thing, running their fingers over tooled stone windowsills and around handsome doorways. The rest of us may gaze at modest rubblestone farm-houses in such uncelebrated places as the back of North Crosby Township. The inner yearning of artisans for immortality has given Ontario some of its finest treasures.[32]

Brick

The widespread use of brick is Ontario's most distinctive landscape charac-teristic. Actually, only one-quarter to one-third of Ontario's old buildings have been brick or brick veneer. But even this limited proportion has been enough to catch the eye, particularly of those from outside the province, where brick construction has been almost unknown. Ontario was 27 per cent brick in 1931, compared with 6 per cent for Quebec, and 1 or 2 per cent elsewhere in Canada; figures for the Great Lakes states appear to be correspondingly small, though unrecorded.[33]

Residents have been proud, even smug, about the warm, solid feeling that brick brings to the land. As a civil servant mused on brick in 1904: `the substantial appearance of such cities as Toronto and Hamilton is in decided contrast to the flimsiness of many frame-built American towns.'[34] The clay-and-shale industry has helped shape the province's cultural landscape through most of its history.

Brick is the ultimate unit of prefabrication, the true building block. John Ruskin described it as a `delicious morsel,' and any child who grew up on (chewable) Minibrix in the 1940s or Lego a generation later would agree.[35] The ability to build to any dimension or shape became appreciated more and more as showy, asymmetrical buildings became fashionable in Ontario in the Victorian age. Bricks could also be laid up so as to be decorative in themselves, in designs ranging from the simple strecher bond (all bricks lengthwise) to such elegant versions as Flemish bond (bricks alternately lengthwise and end-on).

Sun-dried brick, or adobe, has been occasionally tried, principally in York County, where there is an abundance of heavy clay (Figure 5.13). It is an odd

Figure 5.13 MUD WALLING. Gable-end windows are elevated, as for log buildings. A horizontal plank beneath them is in tension from front to rear. Yonge Street at Glengrove Avenue, Toronto, 1937.

material for Ontario's moist climate and requires the protection from rain provided by wide eaves, board siding or stucco, and a high stone foundation. A mud house reportedly disintegrated during a sudden freshet in the Don River valley in 1878.[36] Nevertheless, a structure of sun-dried clay blocks was a handy alternative to building with logs or timber framing, and it could stand indefinitely.[37] St Thomas Anglican Church, Shanty Bay, dates from 1840. A good many adobe houses were built between Toronto and Lake Simcoe, and I know of a smithy in Elgin County.[38] More undoubtedly exist, unknown perhaps even to their owners. Mud brick gave way to fired brick well before Confederation.

Quality and colour

Ontario clay is predominantly red and grey, and these clays, along with black, produce red brick. Grey and black produce other colours as well, while yellow clay yields only buff brick, and white only white.[39] Ontario's oldest fired brick is red, made from clay deposits at or close to the surface. These sites are subject to leaching by rainwater, which dissolves and carries downward the lime that gives brick its creamy colour.[40] Erosion, and excavating made possible with machinery after the 1850s, turned up these deeper, lime-rich clays at the very time that mixed red-and-buff designs were gaining poularity. Buff brick predominates west of the Niagara Escarpment, and red to the east, but railways facilitated delivery everywhere of both after 1870.

Fired brick was imperfectly produced in hundreds of little farm pits throughout the province before Confederation. The architects of Stratford's first town hall (1857) had to redesign the building for red brick when local brickmakers could not make white brick of consistent colour.[41] Brick from a single firing came in varying sizes and textures and often was burnt to an uacceptably dark colour. It was very difficult to achieve uniform heat for burning the small numbers needed for a single building, often using poor-quality clay. Perhaps half the bricks in any early firing were defective.[42] I am familiar with a house near Ernestown, built about 1900, in which the entire front wall had to be replaced in the 1960s because the original brick was disintegrating. Impurities were a further problem. Limestone fragments in Dundas County clay, for instance, caused bricks produced in that region to crack.[43]

As long as brick quality was unreliable, discerning consumers specified 'face bricks' in their orders. These are specimens of perfect colour and texture, and owners would be proud to have them showing. Brickmakers had to overproduce to be sure of getting enough face bricks to meet those wishes.[44] Brick veneer consists entirely of face bricks. It may be argued that the large numbers of unsightly 'inferiors' and 'backers' that inevitably were made stimulated solid-brick construction, just to use them up. Bad brick could also be used to nog (fill in) the hollow space between the outer and inner wall coverings of timber-framed buildings. We read that anti-Tory rioters who attacked a store in Brockville in 1838 'broke in all the windows and doors and tore away the clapboarding and all the filling in from one end and part of one side.'[45] With experience the proportion of misburned bricks dropped and the production capacity for veneering rose.

Brickmaking took on added importance after 1860, as more and more towns passed by-laws prohibiting wooden building following disastrous fires.[46] The idea spread into the countryside. Industrialization and standardization came to brickmaking. The soft-mud, mould-filling machine was introduced in 1857 and rapidly replaced hand moulds. Chambers's stiff-mud auger machine of 1862 created an extruded ribbon that was cut off automatically into brick lengths for firing.[47] The older bricks, soft and crumbly and irregular, were superseded by hard, grainy bricks with sharp edges and standard dimensions.

Between 1861 and 1891, the proportion of all dwellings built with brick shot up from 4 to 21 per cent.[48] Bricks offer fine insulation, and a veneer wall had become a recognized aspect of good, functional construction by the 1890s.[49] A double wall controls dampness, and as early as the 1860s brick schools were being designed with an air space between the outer and inner walls for this purpose.[50]

Some farmers meshed brickmaking with the seasonal round of farming duties. Along Brick Street near London, for example, fully twenty farms had kilns in the 1890s.[51] Elsewhere, farmers paid for factory-made bricks with firewood sleighed in for the next season's burn.[52] Railways built after 1870 added substantially to the regional mobility of brick. The bricking of Ontario diluted the impact of the economic downturn after 1873, and brick has been a central element of the landscape ever since.

Solid brick or veneer?

It is practically impossible to determine the extent of brickwork in Ontario. Buildings that we would describe as brick are, in thousands of cases, made of wood – timber frame usually, or occasionally plank-on-plank – and veneered (Figure 5.14). Single-thickness brickwork is evident by the lengthwise orientation of all the bricks, laid up in what is called a stretcher bond. This technique produces a wall that is too weak to support a full building, and to speak of such a building as brick is somewhat misleading.

Thousands more Ontario buildings really are brick – solid brick, consisting

Figure 5.14 VARYING STRUCTURE. The first floor of this house is solid brick, the second a lighter, veneer wall. Rarely is the veneer made so obvious as in this instance of bricks laid on edge (`rat-trap´ or `row-lock´ bond). Wroxeter, Huron County.

of two thicknesses (or even three) of bricks interlinked so as to produce a self-supporting wall. A firm masonry foundation is essential for such structures. Solid brick walls often are discernible by the headers, or half-length bricks, arranged in among the lengthwise stretchers. Headers are the ends of full-length bricks turned at right angles and bind the outer and inner thicknesses together to form the double wall.

It sounds as though one could distinguish solid brick from veneer simply by looking for headers. However, visible headers were considered by fashionable people to be commonplace – 'common bond' is the name for the style – and in need of concealment. A third brick wall – an outside veneer of stretchers – served the purpose, and any hint as to the structure of the building vanished. Brick veneer over brick is more common in towns than in the countryside, perhaps because genteel folks tended to be urban or because town houses had to bear closer scrutiny than did farm-houses. A glance at side or rear walls may reveal headers, however, where critics were not supposed to look.

The uncertainty does not stop there. Headers could be concealed even in double-thickness walls by linking the two parts together by metal clips laid in the mortar and bridging from outside to inside. The same effect could be achieved by hollowing out the back of a front-wall brick and hiding a header behind it.[53] Some chose the other extreme, celebrating headers in a decorative design. The Flemish bond consists of alternate headers and stretchers in every course (layer) of brick. Instructions for brick school buildings in 1870 specified 'best quality dark stretchers' as facing for a nine-inch (i.e., double) wall, 'to be bonded together with alternate headers every fifth course' to give a subtle decoration.[54]

Many brick houses in Ontario are built with a triple wall front and back on the main floor only. These walls carry the upper-storey floor joists. This style of construction encouraged larger buildings to be rectangular, rather than square. The shorter dimension is limited to about five metres, which is the longest practical length for a joist. The end walls on the main floor and all of the upper storey is double thickness, and a light, single wall fills in the gables. In such a building, headers may be evident only in the double-wall portions.

Why is Ontario brick?

Brick construction and veneers are widespread in Ontario not only because the raw material was easily available but also because of the interplay of regional economics and national identity. Following the American Revolution, the new republic undertook to emulate its ancient predecessor, and little Greek temples rose as houses, churches, and public buildings throughout upstate New York, Ohio, and beyond. Fluted columns and large blocks were best replicated in grey stone or whitewashed wood. These set the colour and texture for the northern United States.

One way of resisting the spread of the U.S. Greek revival – and, by inference, American republicanism – into Ontario was to change colour, to brick. This technique also echoed English construction. The new gothicism rising in Ontario after 1840 gave further impetus to brick, but still more important was the accelerating market for lumber in the American midwest. It made sense to cover timber-framed buildings in Ontario with unexportable brick and thus release raw or milled lumber, a cash crop, for export. Free trade between Canada and the United States in primary materials between 1854 and 1866 gave further impetus to the bricking of Ontario.

Ontario lumber exports soared in the 1850s and after.[55] All that cutting created a tremendous residue in unmerchantable inferior pieces in places such as Peterborough and Lindsay, and these items were suitable for plank-on-plank construction. That in turn induced further bricking and kept masons busy. Americans embraced 'carpenter gothic' to perpetuate the woodworking skills of the earlier age.[56] From the Hudson River to beyond the Mississippi they continued to devour still more lumber, leading to yet more brick buildings in Ontario. Trains carrying lumber out of the Kawartha Lakes region and Haliburton returned with bricks from places such as Milton.

Accessible wood became scarcer during the 1870s, giving further reason to reface Ontario in brick. Brick was easily adapted to an age of rebuilding, and its decorative and insulating attributes did not go unnoticed by Victorian society. By 1900, when the age of rebuilding was largely complete, soft bricks, in various tones of red and buff, had made southern Ontario a mellow place. The landscape would have been rather more severe had hard, pressed brick, just coming into production about 1900, been available a decade or two earlier.

That brick image has been perpetuated. Tin sheeting stamped with a bricklike pattern was popular in the First World War era, and asphalt rolls scribed in stretcher bond came into use soon thereafter (see Figure 2.6). The tin is rarely seen today, having rusted away, but the asphalt is still very common.

In the 1990s, old bricks, recycled from demolitions, are in demand, even being sawn in half to go twice as far on a plywood backing (Figure 5.15). Brick is making a comeback, showing up in postmodern architecture and on the streets of immigrant Toronto.[57] From a high-rise hotel near Highway 401 in Scarborough through to the numerous, domestic-looking office blocks and neat brick corner plazas with coppery-green metal roofs, Ontario's brick inheritance is livelier than ever.

Mortar and concrete

Limestone occurs in many places in southern Ontario; when baked and further treated it produces lime mortar (Figure 5.16). The manufacture of lime com-

Figure 5.15 RECYCLED OLD BRICK is being stacked for removal and reuse. The front of this 1840s house is laid up in Flemish bond. Streetsville, Peel County.

plemented quarrying limestone blocks by using the broken fragments. In addition, dozens of small kilns on family farms produced lime, providing welcome income during winters late in the nineteenth century. Lime mortar is a soft, pliable material that bends under strain – a useful property in rural Ontario, where foundations for brick walls were not always well set. Natural cement, which is half clay and half limestone, was an alternative, also widely available. It is identified by hard, gritty joints and was seen by some builders as inferior to lime mortar; they are reported to have used it 'mainly in the foundations and lower stories of farm barns, silos, etc. . . . [and] for many minor uses.'[58] Natural cement cannot be distinguished from other forms of cement, however, and intensive chemical analysis would be needed to establish whether it really was second-rate.

The oldest brick walls in southern Ontario were laid up with lime mortar, while natural cement mortar came into use about 1880. It is not unusual to find both materials in the same wall where patching has occurred. As woodlot fuel supplies dwindled, countryside lime kilns gave way to bigger cement

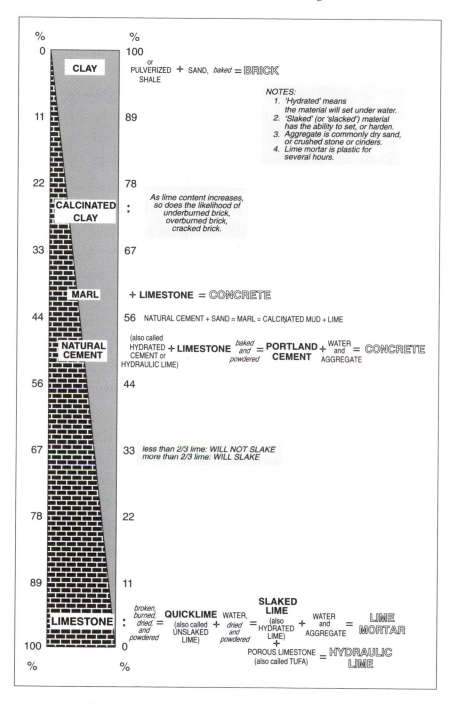

Figure 5.16 COOKING ROCKS.

Figure 5.17 LIME KILN. Careful perusal of topographic maps published before 1960 may lead one to hardy survivors. Coboconk, Victoria County.

plants burning coal, many built about 1900 in response to the growth of cities. All but a few of the old kilns were out of use by the 1920s, though stoic survivors still lurk in obscure corners of the landscape (Figure 5.17).[59] The transition from lime mortar to cement mortar was rapid, and the type of mortar is a useful sign of the age of a masonry wall.

Lime as a plaster wash – stucco – often was applied over logs or rough wall boards when milled lumber or brick was not available. It has also been applied to brick or stone where the mortar has fallen out. One recipe called for 'an equal proportion of pure clay, sand, ashes and lime, thoroughly incorporated together, and mixed with a portion of fresh bullocks blood.'[60] Stucco is a timeless substance, covering up rather than revealing the age of structures (Figure 2.9). Immigrants from Britain after the Napoleonic Wars knew of stucco as a cheap alternative for stone.[61] It suited their desire for show but was not widely used because it cracks in frost. Portland cement became the common stucco base in the 1870s. It is more durable and granular than lime, and the unevenness gives the impression of a darker grey colour.

Concrete

As early as the 1850s, builders began experimenting with gravel concrete walling, a mixture of gravel till (uncovered during railway excavation) and

Figure 5.18 POURED CONCRETE. A dramatic expression of durability and showing off on the front. Elderslie Township, Bruce County.

quicklime.[62] Roughcast is a very similar material, also used as a stucco, but raising poured concrete walls with wooden forms was a fundamentally different process from using individual blocks or bricks. Such walls are easy to maintain, resist vermin and fire, and have good insulating qualities. But they are almost impossible to alter, and manufacturing on site was contrary to the trend towards factory-made products shipped in for installation (Figure 5.18). Furthermore, poured concrete is ugly, and the technique gained little domestic support.[63]

Its great load-bearing capacity, coupled with the property of hardening under water, has made concrete a popular component of the industrial landscape, however. Hundreds of new stables built in the mixed-farming era have floors of poured concrete. Bridges and utility poles, reinforced with steel rods, are very common. A powerhouse at Niagara, locks on the Trent Canal, and a Peterborough factory all were being built in concrete in 1904. They continue to stand up well, as do the oldest Lake Ontario piers, dating from 1912.[64] So do hundreds of concrete silos, some of them the sole remnant of a vanished farmsite.

Portland cement is the principal ingredient of concrete. Marl, a calcareous alternative to lime in the manufacture of Portland cement, is found in wetlands; marl plus limestone makes concrete. The bulkiness of these products is a principal reason that small-scale cement works persisted into the twentieth century, and aggregate (as distinct from block) construction became widely diffused. Marl and natural cement were commercial products for only a few

Figure 5.19 CONCRETE CASTING. Identical blocks cast in pink and grey tones create a decorative effect; rusticated finish simulates stone. Mallorytown, Leeds County.

years before 1905, until the facilities to bake and crush limestone for hydraulic lime, the artificial substitute, became established. Portland cement made poured concrete universally accessible, because water and sand could be added at the construction site.[65] Similarly, slaked lime may be carried dry to the site and mixed there with sand and water to produce lime mortar. By the 1920s the marl beds were once again overgrown wetlands.

Precast blocks were an alternative means of promoting the spread of concrete and were first seen about 1900. Old-time quarrymen warned that block might be less durable than natural stone,[66] but cheapness and convenience of handling gave it a clear advantage. Buildings of concrete block could be put up with considerably less labour than those of brick. Blocks were popular in industrial towns such as Peterborough and Kitchener. Harry and William Boyd of Osgoode, near Ottawa, started producing blocks in 1907, and by 1920 more than one hundred Boyd Block houses were standing in the district.[67] Cylindrical column segments of concrete were in fashion for verandahs early in the twentieth century.

Blocks cast with ripples to look like stone – `rusticated´ – were tried, but they fooled no one (Figure 5.19). They quietly went out of production after a few years, coincident with the end of rural construction in the 1910s. An outer layer of brick has proven a more satisfying means of concealment, and since

1920 concrete has rarely been seen, except for basements. Thousands of city houses of the interwar period have brick facing over block.

Cinder blocks entered the market for a generation, as a creative use of coal residue from city heating and coke from steel mills. Since the 1950s, concrete blocks have once again prevailed as the standard fundaments of small-scale construction in Ontario. In the 1990s, a few huge concrete plants – at Clarkson and Bowmanville, for example – signify the degree of centralization that had become possible.

An abiding regard

From the very first days of settlement, Ontarians were exploiting a wide range of special resources. In skilled hands, promoted by entrepreneurs with investment capital, these would lift society out of the pre-industrial age and make life clearly more comfortable. Sheet-metal roofing, aluminum window sash, steel doors, gypsum wallboard, and plastic trim have brought new life to old buildings. All these materials are substitutes for wood, and wood has always been susceptible to replacement. Fences evolved from stump to wire, utility poles from wood to steel or concrete, heating from brush to manufactured gas, and roads from plank to asphalt. Technological changes such as these carried Ontario towards the age of urban dominance.

Nail production is of particular interest in landscape study because of the rapid succession of technical changes. Country smiths wrought, and subsequently cut, nails manually; factories started producing wire nails after 1870. Each change helps to chronicle when a piece of wood was used.[68]

Decade by decade, common settlers became increasingly estranged from Ontario's resources and from their own ingenuity. The clay pit in the farmyard was no competition for the mechanized, and highly capitalized, brick works set up in the Don River valley in Toronto. Hand-hewn wooden beams may have had the strength of smelted iron ones but were technically crude. If a settler noticed a knot or irregularity, he braced it up to avoid a collapse. But his grandson building a carbide factory in Ottawa, for example, had to rely on the quality-control procedures of a distant foundry to ensure that a metal beam would not crack under load.

Prefabrication grew rapidly during the nineteenth century. Bricks and blocks are only part of a far larger range of ready-made building components. Fence wire panelling, all prepared for stapling to posts, was marketed by the 1880s. Panelled doors and wooden window-sash date from the same era, and iron sash was reported for a church about 1870.[69] The St Lawrence Hotel in Port Hope received cast-iron window casings in 1853, probably by boat from Rochester. The entire front wall of the Canada Life Assurance Company building in Hamilton, built in 1856, was an iron casting.[70] Such buildings may reveal themselves through tell-tale rust stains. Quonset barns, Butler buildings, and mobile homes have lifted the building trades completely away from the farmer's workbench to the factory assembly line.

The opportunity to recycle diminished. Old wood rotted away or, in one last useful gasp, might be burned and the ashes strewn on the vegetable garden. Bad or broken bricks were apt to be thrown in a hole where they would rot and be forgotten. But not aluminum or plastic. More and more, manufacturing processes advanced beyond the capabilities of the local community. When items broke or wore out, they were discarded as unusable. Garbage dumps proliferated.[71]

The low demand for rural building between 1915 and 1950 discouraged Ontario residents from making an all-out commitment to synthetic materials. Though they embraced industrialism, they have always shown high regard for traditional materials. Manufacturers have catered to that loyalty by imitation. The Pedlar Metal Roofing Company of Oshawa, for example, installed pressed-tin ceilings that looked like moulded plaster, put up cast gargoyles and rosettes that aped carved stone, and marketed tin eaves bracketing that looked like wood.[72] Others manufactured asphalt sheeting or galvanized iron panels that were supposed to resemble brick or stone (Figures 2.6 and 4.12).

For a century these deceptions stole across the Ontario landscape unchallenged, at least if contemplated only from a distance. But since the 1950s such well-intentioned but unconvincing frauds have lost favour. Simulated wood trim made from plastic had to be very good if it was to pass the inspection of the new, urbane generation buying up country properties, and reusing authentic, old materials is better still. In an unforgettable, puckish moment, Anthony Adamson once deftly flipped a coin towards the ceiling of a Victorian parlour restoration, gently striking the cornice moulding. To his satisfaction it gave no metallic ring; the work was not tin, but genuine plaster![73]

PART II
READING INDIVIDUAL FEATURES

6

Houses

Ontario has some 300,000 dwellings in the countryside and small towns.[1] Virtually all of them are visible to the passer-by, and each one contributes to the broad picture of economic, social, and technological change. And while most of us have little to say about mills or county registry offices, we all can contribute to a discussion of houses.

The aspect of a house that catches attention varies widely among people. Some may be struck first by Greek columns, others by patterned brick, and still others by double-garage doors or landscaping. Folklorists and anthropologists see ordinary human expression in nondescript abodes, `a means to other ends, a stage for social play, a machine to prolong existence.´[2] Architectural historians look for signs of the hands of great masters. The warmth of soft brick, the patina of weathered boards, and the sparkle of granite boulders add to the list of characteristics to woo the senses. A very few buildings carry detailed historical plaques, but the messages rarely make the connection between the structure and its occupants. The intention here is to establish human intentions by pondering some basic characteristics of houses too frequently taken for granted and then examine evolving types.

Basic characteristics

Massing

As the nineteenth century progressed, southern Ontario´s houses became taller, less symmetrical, and more ostentatious. Compare the Davy house (Figure 2.2) with the cobbled house (Figure 5.10). The American who wrote in 1806 that `buildings standing alone should appear longer than they are high´ could have been speaking of Ontario.[3] Log houses look horizontal, and clapboarding and low side wings reinforce the message. One builder calculated that good aesthetic balance required `the peak of the roof [to] be one third the width of the building higher than the top of the plates.´[4] Early Ontario houses are even lower than that.

The proportions changed with the appearance of modest front gables, which gradually steepened through mid-century. Board-and-batten is another, later development that sends vertical signals. Small upstairs windows and wide doorcases of early buildings contrast with the narrow doorways and tall windows commonly used later in the century. The post-Confederation era was the gothic age – tall, pointed, dark – and set southern Ontario's familiar image.

Symmetry, too, ran deeply through the Ontario mind in the early years, beginning with balanced Loyalist houses. It has been argued that an instinctive response to taking up wilderness land that seems frightening and chaotic was to establish domestic order, and symmetry was a part of that.[5] By the same argument, the nineteenth-century rise in asymmetry may be taken as evidence of a society gaining command and shedding its inhibitions. Among innkeepers the process was apparently well under way by the 1820s: 'to have a ballroom seems to be the height of every publican's ambition in Upper Canada and the convenience, comfort and symmetry of their houses are often sacrificed.'[6]

Most houses up to the 1840s are symmetrical, at least if they are viewed face-on. Additions and alterations regularly contradict both horizontality and balance, but concern for such fine points was decreasing. Any lingering demand for symmetry could be met by placing an accretion behind as a tail, out of sight. A generation later it was concluded that 'symmetry as applied to private architecture ... has had its day ... except in rare cases, where old fogyism holds the sway.'[7] Balanced framed houses evolved freely into other shapes, demonstrating that the forest was no longer forbidding and chaotic.

Build a tower or a mansard (hipped) roof, insert decorative brackets under the eaves, apply contrasting bricks to the corners, and top it off with iron grillwork, crenellated chimney stacks, or lightning rods, and the result is an off-balance, busy Victorian pile (Figure 3.7). Parts stuck out all over. As one promoter admitted, 'a large house is apt to look blank, cheerless [and] unsupported, if built without wings, porticoes, or some projecting feature.'[8] But he cautioned about the proportions: 'we do indeed see many high thin houses, and miserable spectacles they are.' Ontarians' exuberance spent itself rapidly and was fading by 1900.[9] A few further years of boxy houses with low, four-panel roofs and more balanced design quietly closed out this showy era.

A chronology of southern Ontario's housing in high-art, vernacular, and popular groups (Figure 6.1, pp. 106–7) shows how typical examples would have looked as built (or as sensitively restored). The Georgian is horizontal and balanced; details of the Regency anticipate the verticalness to come. The succession from neoclassical to 'common farmhouse' shows the front gable becoming steadily steeper; the Italianate is unbalanced and frivolous. This century has had its own rhythm but has cast repeated backward glances.

Age

The silhouette offers only a first, rough impression of age, and for novice sleuths satisfaction lies in finding a datestone. 'Erbaut von Georg Kreuzer

1875,´ says a block above the front door of a stone farmhouse in Bruce County. The language alone makes this landscape fragment out of the ordinary, but nineteenth-century Ontario houses almost never bear any sort of datestone. Vernacular houses are by nature timeless. Each had many meaningful dates: when the cornerstone was set, when people moved in, or when a long period without alteration or refurbishing began. But the dates of such episodes are almost never displayed. In Prince Edward County, a study during the 1970s showed that only one pre-1900 building in ten can be precisely dated from field evidence, and some of this detail consisted of unverifiable recollections of local residents. Virtually all the datable ones are brick or stone, suggesting that inscribed dating may be associated with permanence. Dates of additions or alterations are almost totally unrecorded.[10]

High-art houses use style to communicate their pedigree, but one probably has to turn to documents to obtain their age. Assessment records, a deed, or a newspaper clipping may exist, but datestones are uncommon. Prestigious houses may well have been constructed all at one time, including the decoration, and that may allow one the chance to date the whole by determining when a particular effect – scrollwork, pediments, or whatever – was in fashion. Knowledgeable travellers well before Confederation were using such evidence to assign an age to at least some buildings.[11] Some builders scratched the date on a foundation stone or door-frame or left a penny of the year beneath the doorstep. This sort of dating was discreet, however, far from the public eye and intended only for private reference.

Houses with showy date blocks are mostly in towns and were built between roughly 1880 and 1930, in the age of rapid urban growth. These labels may be associated with builders who did not want their creations to be mistaken as old-fashioned. Furthermore, town houses are close enough to the street that marks may be read by passing townsfolk. Datestones help today´s inquiring audience, but having such a label undercuts the prideful homeowner´s goal of being eternally modern.

Southern Ontario´s houses are living organisms, responding constantly to cultural forces. That a house would grow was the most natural thing in the world. A log rectangle receives a timber-frame tail, which transforms a temporary shelter into a permanent core for subsequent adaptations. Porches come and go, windows change shape and size, basements are inserted and roofs raised (Figure 6.2).

Much of this activity defies dating, and even dated artefacts can be misleading. In one documented instance, building plans copied in Peterborough from designs published in the *Scientific American* in 1887 and 1888 were not used until 1910.[12] One has to rely instead on such rules as expecting decoration to spread far and wide during prosperity and not to appear in hard times. Thus, for example, Niagara-on-the-Lake has an 1820s look and Perth a look of the 1840s, while most of farmland Ontario features the Victorian age. Each of these places turned from rising to declining fortunes at those times and froze,

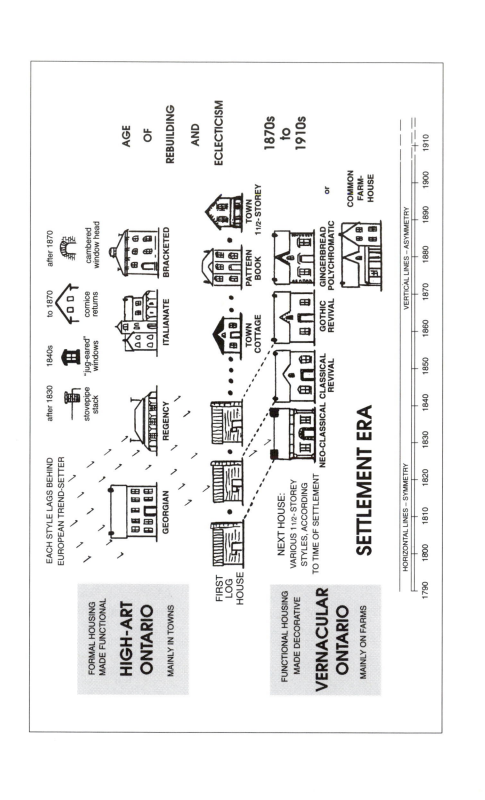

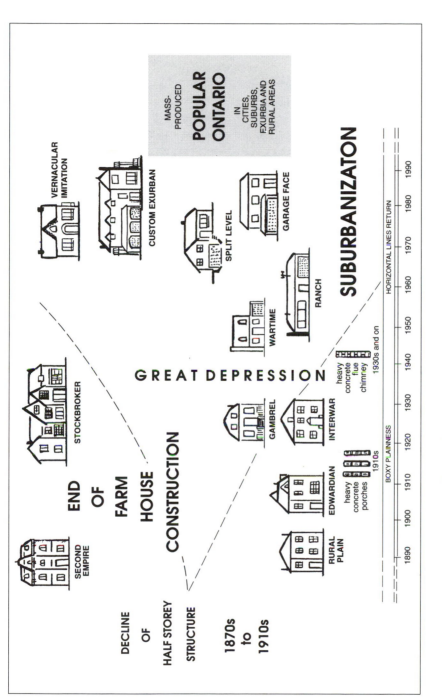

Figure 6.1 A CLASSIFICATION OF DWELLINGS.

Figure 6.2 THE ADDITIVE HOUSE. Add a tail, dig a basement, tack on an umbrage, raise the roof, add another tail: this late Victorian house is alive and always striving to be functionally up-to-date. Huttonville, Peel County.

as replacement gave way to maintenance or abandonment of what was at hand.

Highway 2 from Brighton to Cobourg is a textbook of examples of houses of every age and category. Prosperity and progress, tempered by tradition, assured the simultaneous building of new structures and adaptation of old ones, in all materials. Dating is a skill that blends awareness of technology, materials, economics, and personal whim and the way that they shift by decades and quarter-centuries. That degree of precision should satisfy even the keenest dater.

A few polite houses

A small number of southern Ontario's first generation of houses were two full storeys in height, and five bays (that is, five windows) wide (Figure 6.3). These symmetrical, so-called Georgian houses are associated with United Empire Loyalists and were put up from the 1780s until about 1820, with

Figure 6.3 THE GEORGIAN HOUSE. Two storeys and five bays in sandstone. Quarter-round gable windows and curved doorway transom are neoclassical effects. Augusta Township, Grenville County.

echoes occurring as late as mid-century. Their pretentiousness gives all indications that they were planned and built as complete units by people of means. The style had been familiar in New England and the Atlantic states since the mid-eighteenth century, and under the designation 'federal' or 'Adamesque' it continued in vogue in the United States well into the nineteenth century.

In Upper Canada, the Georgian marks the diffusion of middle-class dwellings throughout the lakefront townships. Despite accounts of initial hardship for some UELs, many quickly picked up their disrupted lives and moved boldly forward. In 1784, no more than a year or two after settlement, one-quarter of the houses at Niagara-on-the-Lake were six metres by nine or larger; this dimension was not regularly surpassed in the province until after Confederation.[13] The Georgian was the first type of large building in old Ontario, and its timber structure was repeated in the earliest inns, churches, and court-houses, not to mention barns. It is a style that shows best standing alone – even aloof – in spacious grounds.

Purest Georgian houses have a distinctively wide space on either side of the central doorway, plus a large central chimney. With as many as three cooking fireplaces (one facing each side, and the third to the rear), the chimney occupied about one-third of the space enclosed by the walls, and the wider central bay was needed to accommodate it. Such houses are rare in Ontario; rather, Georgians here have gable-end chimneys of brick or stone, suited to rather more modest means and needs. The site of the fireplace could become a large central hall. For UELs it was a style filled with nostalgic associations,[14] and the term `Georgian survival' has been applied to examples built as late as Confederation.

The full Georgian design did not fit the needs of Ontario after 1815. Its construction ceased, yet discerning settlers craved the distinctive elements that set the Georgian apart from the rude log cabin. Imagine the Augusta Township house (Figure 6.3), in which the front consists of only the central door and one window on each side: three openings instead of ten. This diminished house, still of horizontal lines and about the dimensions of the wing on the right, is the neoclassical storey-and-a-half house. It is a truly vernacular dwelling and found throughout areas settled before 1830.

Ontario's few Georgian houses have worn well. Most shun additions or conceal them effectively. Often now adapted as professional offices, local museums, apartments, and nursing homes, these Loyalist-era houses stand proudly as some of our most splendid restorations and landmarks. Developers continue to honour the tradition by building duplicates.

The last Georgian survivals were not yet in place when the earliest of the indigenous two-storey houses began to appear. These latter are particularly prevalent in the Germanic regions in Waterloo County and northward to Bruce and Grey. Their roots stretch back into the southern Niagara peninsula and even further into eastern Pennsylvania. The plain ones may be mistaken for Georgian, but the chance of confusion is no greater than that of misreading an altered classical house as late Victorian. Any two-storey house more than about fifty kilometres inland from Lake Erie or Lake Ontario is almost certainly not Georgian. Two-storey town houses of the 1880s and 1890s reintroduce all-at-once, non-additive construction and are discussed at the proper place, later in this chapter.

Greek temples and Regency cottages

The Barnum house is quite possibly Ontario's most celebrated early dwelling (Figure 6.4). Built about 1817, it is very different in style from earlier houses. As one of a mere handful of Greek temple–style houses in the province, it is hardly representative. Rather, its significance is political. Temple houses were – and still are – widespread in the northern United States, and in the British province they became a provocative expression of the persistent effort by Americans to take over Canada.[15] If architecture be considered a weapon, the arsenal had indeed fine craftsmen. `There is no house of similar size and material in the United States that is the superior of the Barnum house in Grafton,' wrote one scholar.[16]

Figure 6.4 THE TEMPLE STYLE shows American influence. A pediment – the low roof triangle – and fluted columns are its hallmark. Barnum house (1817), Grafton, Northumberland County, 1925.

The Davy house of 1819 (Figure 2.2) is a scaled-down Greek temple. It retains the central section and wings, but the boldly projecting pediment has been replaced by a roof of shallow pitch that gives a strong horizontal line to the building. Height has been reduced from two storeys to one plus a loft, and the very subtle false pillars mounted on the wall are mere remnants of vertical lines. The wings look like additions, not integral components. The transition between high art and vernacular is often fuzzy, and the Davy house belongs to both camps.

The Robinson-Adamson house is the counterpoint to the republican temple (Figure 6.5). Known as a Regency house, its dozens of panes of glass suggest that wealth and importance have been judiciously mixed with the practicality of transporting such fragile cargo in small pieces rather than large. The Regency is the one gracious dwelling type clearly associated with Great Britain and has been the architects´ means of entering Ontario´s domestic landscape.[17] It is also a rare type in Ontario, and this is an ambiguous house – horizontal in mass, yet vertical in detail. The cottage roof (that is, four surfaces) squashes any feeling of tallness induced by the long chimneys and French doors that extend from floor to eave.

The Regency cottage is a fancy humble house – the icon of an insecure

Figure 6.5 THE REGENCY. Robinson-Adamson house (1829) following restoration in 1981; Regency style is British. Dundas Street, Mississauga.

colonial elite whose members were as inadequate as the humblest settler in coping with the raw environment – and there is no diminished variant to equate with scaled-down Georgians or Greek temples. Anything plainer and more modest would vanish into the misty beginnings of all housing – the very world that aspiring settlers were striving to leave behind.

The Barnum, Davy, and Robinson-Adamson houses demonstrate the process of simplification in early Ontario. Once stripped to their functional bones, these high-art structures pointed the way for a new generation of domestic building to rise up in sensitive response to the needs of a distinctive society emerging from the Ontario woodland.

The storey-and-a-half in profusion

From 1981 to 1988 the cover page of the Revenue Canada income tax guide for Ontario residents featured three nocturnal skylines. Lights glow late in city high-rise towers, along suburban streets, and out on the farmsteads, as Ontarians pore over their T4 slips in an annual rite of spring. The farmhouse is unmistakably the storey-and-a-half style, described as `the abiding image of the province´ or simply `the typical Ontario house´ (Figure 6.6).[18] This is the basic building-block for the Ontario landscape.

The storey-and-a-half style has been explained by legislative principles, and the case has an appealing simplicity.[19] Upper Canada law in 1807 identified

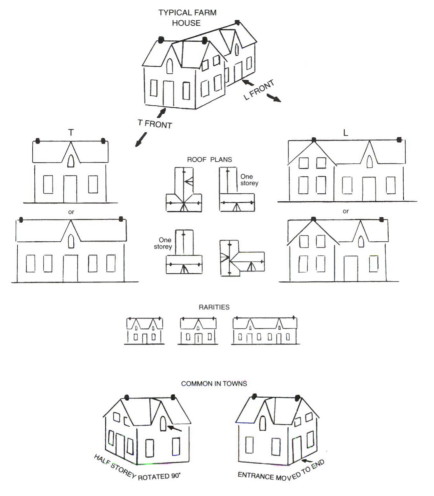

Figure 6.6 VARIATIONS IN THE STOREY-AND-A-HALF HOUSE.

six categories of houses for tax purposes, differentiated by height.[20] Three of these referred to houses of one storey (`round log,´ `square timber,´ and `brick or stone´), two to those of two storeys (`square timber´ and `brick, stone or framed´), and one – `framed´ – to those of less than two storeys. This last type is the storey-and-a-half, which appears to be one storey high when viewed head-on but clearly has two usable floor levels when the end wall is seen. `Two storeys´ meant two floors with full-height walls all around, as distinct from half storeys with sloping ceilings. Of those having two functional floor levels, `square timber, two storey´ was rated at £30 (with no more than two fireplaces or stoves), `brick, stone or framed, two storey´ – the fashionable UEL Georgian house – at £60, and `framed, less than two storey´ at £35.

Storey-and-a-half styles became even more economical as time passed, simply by raising the roof to make the upper level more livable while retaining the definition of being less than two storeys. Legislation in 1820 reduced the £60 rate,[21] evidently responding to the decline and diffusion of UEL wealth or to the rising fashionability of smaller versions. The 1807 system was losing touch with the real situation in housing, and it had long been irrelevant by the time it was finally terminated, in 1853.[22]

The 1807 system helps us to understand how the same house form could occur again and again from one end of the province to the other, over several generations and among a variety of cultural groups. But there were other factors that promoted uniformity. Pine timber was everywhere, for one thing, and neighbourhood building bees using it diffused construction skills widely. Cultural intermixing and similar family structures added to the uniformity of housing. Pioneering Ontarians never hesitated to demonstrate that they knew more about daily life than did remote legislators in York (Toronto, after 1834) or overseas in London. Besides, storey-and-a-half houses were built in places where this legislation did not apply and continued to be put up for half a century after its repeal. The law encouraged selection of the storey-and-a-half, but it surely was not definitive. Ontario's landscape would in all probability have evolved in much the same fashion had no distinctive tax existed.

Half-storey technology

The half-storey configuration suits a society finding its way in a wooden world but not truly at ease using wood and committed to growth by adding to existing structures more than by constructing entirely new ones. For log houses, growth upward is easiest, and two or three logs added upon a one-storey crib make a space beneath the ridge where a person could stand up. The ceiling kept the heat in the main living quarters below and provided a platform for a dormitory loft above, and the loft grew. From the outside, the ends of floor joists showing through the front wall below the eaves indicate the process. As a contrast, the full Georgian involved carpentry and masonry and was not an incremental structure.

Parker's mill (Figures 5.6) is a half-storey, timber-framed building. The nearest corner post supports two horizontal members – the lower one in the end wall (with windows in the upper storey) and the upper one running along the top of the front wall. Each beam forms a two-way T-junction with the post. All junctions in Parker's mill above the foundation level are Ts. This is the conservative, uncomplicated procedure for joining wood by mortice and tenon and is well suited to unsure builders. And because the distance between the two junctions with the post could be as little as the width of a timber or greater than the height of a child, a wide range of upper-storey capacity could be achieved with the same technical details. T-junctions represented a commitment to the half-storey and to the opportunity to enlarge one's dwelling for a marginal extra cost that was 'comparatively small.'[23] Half storeys became the Ontario standard.

How very different the T-joint principle was from the setup of the three-dimensional joint, in which post and beams in the three geometric planes converge at one point. T-junctions avoid the inherent weakness caused by the intricate notching necessary for three-way joints.[24] We can assume that Ontario builders regarded three-way joints as allowing too little margin for error, and such configurations certainly would appear to violate the tendency to over-construction. The technology prevails in New England and southern Pennsylvania, where carpentry was a well-established art. Not surprisingly, these areas are filled with full-storey buildings.

The half-storey discouraged slate or tile roofing, widely used overseas. The prevalence of wood did too, as did high labour costs and the scarcity of slate and tile. The great weight was also a consideration. Slate and tile had to be borne on a heavy roof structure for which the full-storey design was better suited. Some builders went so far as to state that `half stories ought in all cases to be avoided; ... the strain of the roof being thrown upon that part of the wall which is above the beams, causes the front to curve, and is a trait of bad architecture.´[25]

Such was not the case in southern Ontario, however. Pine or cedar roofing shingles have served the storey-and-a-half structure well. Inside the attic, a collar beam ties each opposing pair of rafters together like the letter `A.´ This arrangement redirects the outward thrust of the light-weight roof downward. The rule of thumb allows the collar beam to be as high as two-thirds of the distance from the eaves to the ridge. The low, gloomy loft that once was dormitory space for youngsters who did not need stoves, or `would scorn such,´[26] had room to grow. Adults could stand up without bumping their heads. By inserting a gable window in the front or rear, occupants could see out and have improved ventilation, too.

Timber framing and the half-storey configuration were closely related, and the obsolescence of one foretold the demise of the other. When new or used timbers became scarce in the 1880s and 1890s, sawn boards took over as the universal building material. Balloon framing, built of two-by-four lumber, made inroads. But the half-storey was already going out of fashion because of the increased focus on two-storey houses. It would have faded out of production regardless of the timber supply.

The same sawmills that produced the two-by-fours for ballooning also milled pieces that were assembled into prefabricated roof trusses. These are low triangles resting on the top of the wall, the base of the span establishing the ceiling level of a full storey. Roof trusses are not to be confused with wall trusses (Figure 5.5). Ballooning had prompted that arrangement already, and solid brick construction further favoured the full-storey configuration. The end of timber framing was inevitable.

Cottage-roofed houses were exceptional, and in the timber-bent age only the Regency had it (Figure 6.5). The Regency is a full-storey house – one storey – and the coincidence is significant. A cottage roof cannot spring from a half-storey and is incompatible with it. It requires rafters rising from all four walls and joining in a diagonal arrangement above each corner. The cottage roof is technically more complex than the two-surface gable roof and marks a degree of sophistication beyond the truly vernacular. The evolution of full-storey houses fostered the widespread appearance of cottage roofs, particularly in towns. Cottage roofs produced some rooftop excitement, and many complicated works of geometry adorn the fancy town houses of the high Victorian period. The rise and decline of the half-storey in Ontario illustrate a century of subtle internal and external forces acting on one tangible element, and thereby on the entire cultural landscape.

The storey-and-a-half grows

Almost all storey-and-a-half houses have appendages, either original to the structure or added on (Figure 6.7). In some the tail came first, a starter house to which a big front portion was added later. Many more tails are as large as the front section. Ells and tees in all kinds of arrangements and sizes make the storey-and-a-half an endlessly fascinating structure (Figure 6.6). Town versions built after 1870 are as much as eleven metres by sixteen, equal in size to a small barn (Figure 6.8), while a `cheap double cottage´ or a tiny row-house no more than one-third this size may be found in industrial areas.[27] Ingenious responses to small lots included moving the entrance or rotating the roof a quarter-turn. There are cases of two storey-and-a-halfs being moved together, with an upstairs room serving as a hallway between the two units,

Figure 6.7 THE STOREY-AND-A-HALF GROWS. Front portion dominates tail, 1840s. Wood. Tosorontio Township, Simcoe County.

Figure 6.8 STOREY-AND-A-HALF PLUS. The second-floor rooms of this huge town house are of virtually full height. Note the extra gable-peak window and an unbecoming concrete-block porch. St Williams, Norfolk County.

each with its own staircase. People who were used to improving life by small steps welcomed houses that could do so too.

Decade by decade through the nineteenth century the roof pitch of new houses increased. The shallowest, with base angle as low as thirty degrees, date from the 1820s and 1830s. The angle was up to as much as sixty degrees by the end of the century (Figure 6.2). It seems improbable that many existing buildings had their roofs deliberately replaced with steeper ones, except in cases of fire or wind damage. The old rafters would be too short for reuse, and end walls and chimneys would need rebuilding. Many existing storey-and-a-halfs gained headroom by having their roofs lifted, however. The procedure was to cut through each timber post above the crossbeam, jack up the entire roof structure, insert a timber spacer for each post, and bolt it all back together with a sleeve of reinforcing planks.[28]

The insertion of gables or dormers with windows, on both front and back walls, offered ventilation and light in addition to space. The end-wall windows and the traditional corner staircase with an elbow in it were inadequate if the loft became subdivided into smaller rooms. The answer – reached by a combination of intuition and prodding from the rural press – was to raise a portion of the front or rear wall into a peak and insert a window to illuminate a new stairwell and hallway (Figure 6.9).[29] A straight central stairway could take advantage of headroom created by the gable. Gable-style openings flush with

Figure 6.9 GABLE. The portion of the face of the gable above the front wall of this stone storey-and-a-half is wood. The gable is unquestionably a later addition. Seymour Township, Northumberland County.

the wall are almost universal and suit half-storey construction. Dormers recessed into the roof are the equivalent arrangement in full-storey buildings (Figure 6.10).[30] A front-wall gable window could not be satisfyingly added to a log house because the top log could not be cut (Figure 5.7). Here was one more reason why log construction declined as loft space became more sought after during the nineteenth century.

The shallowest front-wall gables in Ontario are found on the oldest storey-and-a-half houses, in townships fully settled by 1840. They look suspiciously like classical pediments, are sympathetic with other classical features likely to be present, and properly belong with the discussion of polite building of the period before 1840. The term 'classical revival' applies (Figure 6.2). Some of these features are obviously decorative, positioned entirely above the eaves-line, but many more have windows and look useful.

All gable openings on timber-framed buildings interrupt the eaves-line plate, and this timber must therefore be supported by an upright post. The obvious one stands along the side of the doorway, so the broad neoclassical doorcases offered wide footings for a low-pitched gable. The aesthetic appeal of a front peak of the same pitch as the shallow end-wall gable produced front gables that were lower than the roof ridge. It all makes good sense, and few houses in Ontario combine style and structure so clearly.

Front gables were appearing on common houses by 1850.[31] They gave a perfect opportunity for aspiring Ontarians to adopt the gothic (pointed-arch) and vertical themes that were insinuating themselves on the landscape.[32] Narrower doorways took away from lingering classical traits, and front gables steepened and grew to reach the height of the main roof. Transom windows above the front door survived, a last gasp from the broad Georgian front hall and the one element that would enhance up-and-down lines. New storey-and-

Figure 6.10 DORMER windows are recessed in the roof structure of a full-storey house. Northumberland County, 1925.

a-half houses received front peaks as a matter of course. Peaks rejuvenated existing houses, including classical ones in the rebuilding period after Confederation.

The evolved second storey

It is debatable whether the shallow pedimental gable died with classicism or evolved into the steeper, post-Confederation gable, which just happened to be the pointed gothic. Regardless, the movement towards a full second storey continued unabated, all the time making the alleged half-storey deception look more and more insincere (Figure 6.11). A number of variations in the storey-and-a-half might literally be less than two storeys, yet all clearly pointed towards the achievement of full-height upstairs-downstairs buildings.

Kneewall, or bellyflop, windows set close to the floor on the front and rear walls, below the plate, bring light and air to the upper level without structural complications (Figure 6.12). They are fairly common in Leeds County and are occasionally seen elsewhere. With the extension of timber-frame posts towards a full-storey height, kneewall windows evolved into full-size, second-storey windows, and these are found widely throughout the province.

The storey-and-a-half-plus-a-half is the result of steepening the roof to well over sixty degrees in a large building. This produced full head room over most of the upstairs and a triangle of further attic space above that. Some particularly steep examples may be found in towns and are two-storey houses in all but name (Figure 6.8). A little window set high in the peak gives decoration and ventilation.

The mansard roof bestows on a storey-and-a-half house not only the ap-

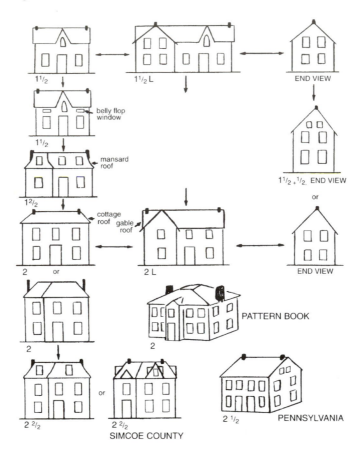

Figure 6.11 EVOLUTION OF THE TWO-STOREY HOUSE.

pearance of a full second storey but the structural detail as well. Think of the peak of the gable roof cut off flat and the rest of it puffed out until virtually vertical (Figure 6.13). The central gable becomes just one of several dormer windows poking through a wall, still shingled to suggest its ancestry as a roof. The Glasgow dormer is a distinctive bay window occupying this position, giving a bright, airy effect to the interior. It is Ontario's oldest dormer, the product of specialized carpentry, and rarely seen except in the Scottish parts of Haldimand, Middlesex, and Elgin counties.[33] The mansard-roofed house is an urban type of the 1870s to 1890s.

Full-storey Victorian housing

In 1865, *Canada Farmer* published a drawing and description of a full two-storey house that its editor considered suitable for the successful agriculturalist (Figure 6.11, `Pattern Book').[34] It was one of the few designs to receive widespread circulation in Ontario, and there are a good many houses that show its influence (Figure 6.14). The front-wall windows are entirely below

Figure 6.12 KNEEWALL WINDOWS. Sometimes known as `bellyflops,´ these shallow openings across the front wall below the eaves illuminate a loft that might otherise have been lit by a central gable. Window spacing and large chimney stack on this 1831 house suggest a fireplace in the end wall. Williamstown, Glengarry County.

the roofline. The gable remains as a windowless, decorative peak and gentle throwback into the neoclassical style. This house, with its distinctive, four-faced cottage roof, affirms the utility already achieved by a generation of swelling storey-and-a-halfs. In 1893, *Canada Farmer's Sun* published an account and illustration of a full-storey house with a `hipped roof prettily broken by gables and dormer windows.´[35] It bears a strong resemblance to a large, folksy type of farmhouse often seen in Simcoe County, along the northern edges of farmland Ontario (Figure 6.11, `Simcoe County´).

Two-storey houses became the backbone of the late-nineteenth-century construction boom, especially in towns. Though it was promoted in rural areas, the *Canada Farmer* model is actually an urban type. The engraving shows it standing in a non-agricultural park atop a plinth that detatches it from the land. Pedestrians are shown approaching the front, as one would when making a call in town. Happy the merchant or doctor who could build such an edifice on a big lot on main street, just beyond the end of the business section; happier still if the site was a corner offering maximum visibility. Here the

Figure 6.13 THE MANSARD. The roof billows out to become virtually a wall while retaining roofing shingles as a finish. Note porte-cochère. Two storeys-and-a-half. Sydenham Ward, Kingston.

Figure 6.14 TWO-STOREY FARMHOUSE. This indigenous, full-storey dwelling is not to be confused with the Georgian of a half-century earlier. Expect Georgians to have gable roofs, while these later ones have cottage roofs. Palermo, Halton County.

successful owner could display his achievement, perhaps in Tuscan (towers and brackets), Italianate (long windows), or Second Empire (mansard roof) modes (Figure 3.7). All stand tall and asymmetrical. By the 1870s town mansions were overtaking court-houses and Anglican churches as the stylish structures. They made wonderful illustrations for the county atlases to which successful citizens were subscribing.

Not all two-storey houses are grand monuments, though many are indeed handsome and size alone gives each one a presence (Figure 6.15). Around Parkhill, where a shortage of good building wood diminished the opportunity for timber framing, full-storey brick houses predominate. Many ‘upright and wing’ (L-shaped) houses in Essex and Kent counties are derived from two-storey styles in adjacent parts of the United States.

Dozens of little one-storey houses, often called ‘Ontario cottages,’ stand in the larger manufacturing towns between Cobourg and London.[36] These diminished storey-and-a-half houses are principally dormitories, with none of the domestic workspace found in big farm-house kitchens. The usual cottage roof left an inconsequential attic. The occupant lived on one floor and worked in a factory near by. Entire streets of them, matched in appearance and mass-produced, and often sold or rented by the neighbouring company, suggest that these are not strictly vernacular buildings. Still, ordinary Ontario shows strongly; the front peak, the gothic louvre, and polychromatic brick all are proper. Some examples, as in Stratford, are stylish little villas (Figure 6.16).

Figure 6.15 VERNACULAR TWO-STOREY, 1903; brick with concrete block trim. East Luther Township, Wellington County.

Figure 6.16 THE TOWN COTTAGE, one storey high, comes in both exuberant and modest versions. Stratford, Perth County.

They have made fine retirement homes for older couples who have moved off the farm, but few small towns had them.

After the First World War, southern Ontario's countryside and small town lost their role as setting the standards of domestic design. The leading styles had urban connotations – names such as stock-broker Tudor, for example – or were produced by contractors for working-class neighbourhoods. They had central heating and inside plumbing. The half-storey structure ceased to be applied, and the new type of half-storey house that developed from the 1940s was balloon-framed and much less roomy upstairs. Housing came to mean a unit in a high-rise building for many people. Garages became integral parts of houses, at first cowering behind but gradually being brought forward boldly. The urban automobile age has transformed the image of housing.

7

Revealing details

As the engineer and author John Mactaggart travelled through the settled townships along the Lake Ontario shore late in the 1820s, he was struck by 'the orders of architecture [that] baffle all description: every one builds his cottage or house according to his fancy.'[1] Such was perhaps the case among higher-class households, where occupants were able to indulge what Mactaggart calls 'whims' and 'conceits.' But such display was not the common experience, and by mid-century the Ontario landscape was a far plainer place, filling with humble classical houses and balanced cabins of limited variety. These buildings expressed the sameness of immigrants' pioneer experience, each using minimally refined materials in a limited range of possible ways.

Simplification was an inevitable aspect of overseas migration.[2] Cultural traits were portable, but tools, materials, and furniture had to be left behind. We have seen the process in the diminished version of the Georgian house, described in chapter 6, and shall again in the domestic origins of institutions, explored in chapter 8. Life's intricacies and amenities dropped from view in the first decades of settlement, when survival was paramount. Thereafter, as more and more people gained control of their circumstances, complexities began to reappear, and the homogeneous landscape that simplification fostered gradually faded. Despite the development of mass production – and potential sameness – people of varied backgrounds and achievement reacted individually, and by 1900 southern Ontario was once again far from being a uniform place.

Decorative details of buildings are particularly sensitive to this sequence, if only because they are optional; these are the subject of this chapter. Functional structures, without decoration, are sure to look much alike. But by soon after Confederation designs for doors, window sash, scroll-work, chimney caps, metal cresting, and terra cotta (clay) panels were being advertised in dozens of catalogues in English, French, and Italian idioms, and these were producing cheerful, even brash chaos throughout the countryside and towns. Brick gave a curious texture and colour to whatever classicalness remained; the many new churches at mid-century helped disseminate gothicism. Freedom from being symmetrical created new opportunities for adding character to a place. Published pattern books, available in public libraries, introduced countless ways to make plain houses picturesque.[3] While editors recommended erecting new buildings, it was the Ontario way to lift ideas that could dress up sound houses already standing, and thereby to contribute further to the busy mixture of sights.

One observer, writing in the 1850s, hoped that a clearly Ontario look would develop: `Though we can scarcely hope to see ... a distinct style of pure architecture formed on the primitive log hut, something may be done to lead the taste of the Province into a direction which may tend to give a local character to our Canadian edifices.´[4] Local character did indeed emerge, but probably not what our writer was anticipating. It was turning out to be eclectic – the care-free mixing of whatever elements one liked best. The English architect A.W. Pugin would have been shocked by `persons so besotted in their mongrel compositions´ as not to value purity.[5] But eclecticism is every bit as honest as the informed expressions of lettered architects, and William Coverdale´s work in Portsmouth, near Kingston, is only one example of professional endorsement of mixing styles.[6] Architects could be anachronistic and avant-garde at the same time, and builders might copy and give advice without fear of being branded naïve. Under such circumstances, no single commercially produced pattern book was likely to dominate. The visual order of the Georgian house seemed remote indeed.

Ontarians have gradually developed an affection for eclecticism. Artists – and in particular A.J. Casson – explored the colours, textures, and moods that had become a way of life. We might think that even the most extravagant elements had, by the 1930s, ceased to be more than faded punctuation marks in the placid Ontario scene. Yet Casson saw in them a vitality that has made eclecticism a popular art form.[7] Late in the twentieth century more and more preservationists are at ease with altered, impure structures. These buildings have come to look acceptable when viewed as social, and not simply architectural, subjects.

Chimneys, lightning rods, verandahs, shutters, carved scrollwork, and attached garages are familiar embellishments that have been appended and removed in unpredictable, even whimsical ways. They add to the eclectic tradition. Because of the ease with which they may be stuck on, such ephemera should not be used to date a structure. Rather, they draw attention to occasions when it was modified. Such details may often be dated with more precision than the buildings bearing them, and they contribute substantially to our ability to read the life story of a structure.

Ephemera tell a good deal about the quality of life of the inhabitants. Chimneys, shutters, and exterior fuel tanks give the history of keeping warm; verandahs and (much more recently) window air-conditioning units tell of keeping cool. Lightning rods are for security, and turned porch spindles are for fashion; belfries and satellite dishes are for communication. All are susceptible to changing whims, and irrelevance of any one quickly shows. Farmer Snug, the upstanding personification of order and good deeds, knew this and maintained a consistently modern farm. Farmer Slack was the opposite.[8] But his sagging porch and broken shutters were perhaps less signs of moral turpitude than they were of the tendency for obsolete bits and pieces to linger indefinitely, unnoticed in their decline.

Verandahs and windows

Catharine Parr Traill tells us that a verandah helped decorate a plain building (Figure 7.1).[9] The gently swagged roof carried by turned spindles and decorated bracing, and the upstairs door opening onto a tiny platform, add interest to a façade otherwise focused only on the front door. Classic aloofness – or simply economy – had produced severe, whitewashed façades, but the gothic was romantic, picturesque, and tied to nature.

To mixed-farming families, the verandah was a sheltered place where members could sit on hot summer evenings, away from kitchen and farmyard

Figure 7.1 VERANDAHS came into fashion after the pressure of farm making eased. The swagged roof echoes a canvas awning.

smells. It shaded the house against searing heat, while in winter it allowed the low sunlight to slant in beneath and give warmth deep within. In town, verandahs were reviewing stands for all the activity passing along the street in front and showed off the best carpentry of the Victorian age. Pattern-book illustrations left little doubt that verandahs or umbrages were intended to denote success.

Verandahs were frequently added to existing houses. The rafters for the roof were nailed to the wooden siding or secured with spikes hammered into wooden dummies or 'bond timber' laid into a brick wall when erected.[10] Too often these verandahs had inadequate footing, however, and as the footstones heaved the wooden structure warped and broke the tarred seal with the wall. Water seeped in, rot followed, and rebuilding or removal became necessary.

Through the 1910s and 1920s, massive porches with concrete or brick columns and poured-concrete decks were fashionable (Figure 6.8). This was a defiant response to nature's disdain for their delicate predecessors but was unable to delay the declining utility of porches. Rural depopulation left fewer people rocking on the porch, and dust stirred up by speeding motorists took the fun out of it. By the time interest in rural housing revived in the 1950s, verandahs had clearly given way to the television room or the back seat of the family automobile. Tar stains and suicide doors are all that remain to show where once clung many a pretty Victorian verandah (Figure 7.2).

The enclosed, or sometimes open, front-door porchlet is a diminished verandah common in towns (Figure 2.6). It faces the street and took hold in the 1920s as family horses and stables yielded to the automobile. At one time visitors drove their carriages in behind, tethered and watered the horse, gave it a dust-free refuge where it was not likely to be startled, and entered the house by the rear. Motorists, contrarily, preferred to park in front and use the front door. Streets were wider, ditches enclosed, and the curbside was a perfect place for showing off the shiny new McLaughlin. Stables were replaced with small garages, and the backs of town lots became appreciably less interesting.

Timber framing and the availability of boxed window glass in various sizes allowed Ontario houses to open up after 1830.[11] Window-panes had been a luxury, for not only was glass expensive and fragile, but a tax on windows that had been in place in England since the 1780s made it daring even to think of having them. 'They get light gratis here,' exclaimed one envious English visitor.[12] By the end of the century the great factories of industrial Ontario were consuming hundreds of panes of glass to let light onto the shop floors.

The extensive use of windows in the Regency style set a standard for showiness (Figure 6.5), and front gable windows in storey-and-a-half houses were the vernacular response. The revival of gothic design gave impetus to decorative glass, while improved technology permitted use of bigger panes. The visual intricacy of façades diminished at the same time as other details of

Figure 7.2 THE SUICIDE DOOR. 'A door upstairs opening on nothing but air? Many houses have this door, and I have never yet been able to find out why. I ask my father and he says they are for walking in your sleep.' Alice Munro, 'Walker Brothers Cowboy,' in *Dance of the Happy Shades* (Toronto: Ryerson Press, 1968), 7–8. The door presumed an upstairs porch, as illustrated in Figure 7.1. Medonte Township, Simcoe County.

houses were becoming more eye-catching; houses pictured throughout this book have the four-pane, double-hung window sash that has become universal during the twentieth century. Here was a contradiction, and it jars the eye of the traditionalist to see a single large pane filling the window opening of a fine old house. In recent years, sash and door mills have stocked trellis-like sets of glazing bars that help restore the impression of many small window panes while retaining the insulating and low-maintenance aspect of modern fenestration (Figures 5.10).

Window shutters have not fared well. They flap and have to be painted. Hinges and wall-anchors rust away, and rotting panels fall out. Inside shutters that fold like an accordion are much more satisfactory. They are not exposed to the weather and may be hidden from sight in pockets in thick walls.[13] Stamped aluminum panels, bolted to front and end walls as decorative hangings, are the order of the day in the 1990s.

Chimneys

Chimneys indicate the cooking and heating characteristics of a house. Cooking hearths, parlour stoves, oil space-heaters, hot-air furnaces, and recreational fireplaces each have distinctive, datable flues or stacks. All-electric houses may have none at all. Iron stoves were known, but not available, to Loyalist-era settlers, and some 50,000 dwellings in use before 1820 must have had open cooking hearths. These fireplaces were invariably built within the building, to retain as much of the heat as possible during cold weather.

UELs knew the big central stone hearths facing into two or three rooms, surmounted by a massive stone stack poking through the middle of the roof. Some Georgian houses have chimney stacks at intermediate points along the roof ridge, for separate, smaller fireplaces backing onto a broad central hall. But simplified living generally led to small, single fireplaces on outside walls and gable-end stacks. The wide spacing of end-wall windows is a good clue that a hearth is there and a persuasive sign of a house built before 1835 (Figure 6.12). Many survivors retain their hearths and chimneys blocked up but intact, and restoration architects have reopened them as cheerful recreational fireplaces.

Improved inland transport, a burgeoning consumer market, and demand for subdivided interior spaces allowed American cast-iron stoves to make inroads in the 1830s.[14] Portable stoves and sectional, sheet-metal stove piping were well suited to owners who altered houses, and stove-pipe stacks at the extremities of the roof ridge have been the universal adornment of the storey-and-a-half (Figure 7.1). Smoke and gases from iron stoves are piped through the house to the chimney stack, a short brick (or occasionally stone) structure mounted on a wooden platform beneath the ridge, and pass safely out through the roof. Gable-end windows were no longer constrained by broad chimney walls and became larger. The compactness of Georgian and classical designs, induced by the fixed focus on the hearth, diminished.

Soot built up in stove-pipes and chimney stacks, raising the threat of chimney fires. This was particularly a problem in regions of softwood forests along the edge of the Precambrian Shield and through the upper Ottawa River valley.[15] Fire ladders, permanently mounted on the roof, are common there (Figure 7.3).[16] Elsewhere, adoption of fire-proof roofing in place of cedar shingles, plus the prevalence of clean-burning hardwood, has made fire ladders practically extinct.

Full-storey houses, with cottage roofs, carry tall chimney stacks. The top had to be above the highest part of the roof in order to draw properly. Together with finials, lightning rods, and ironwork, fancy chimneys were the perfect vertical topping for a flamboyant dwelling. Tall stacks were hazardous, however, easily cracked or toppled by wind. Edwardian houses were rearranged so that the flue – by this time a furnace flue[17] – ran up through the middle

Figure 7.3 ROOF LADDER gives access to the chimney stack in a fire emergency.
Calvin Township, District of Nipissing, east of North Bay.

of the building and issued from the highest part of the roof as a stubby stack
(Figure 7.4). Short stacks had little opportunity for showing off, and they again
became plain, just like their predecessors a century before.

The separation of heating and cooking fires may be discerned on the rooftops.
As wood cookstoves gave way to gas or electric ranges, cooking ceased to be
part of the flue-and-stack system. Wherever kerosene space heaters continue
in use, the flattened oval fuel tank at the side of the house is a sure signal.
Over the past thirty years, most have been replaced by electric baseboard
heating or a central furnace.

Central heating requires a new, straight flue from the basement. Countless
old Ontario houses have undergone this practical conversion, indicated by an
artless concrete-block stack slapped on the outside of the tallest wall (Figures
5.14 and 6.3). Few adornments are so completely functional and lacking in
visual appeal. Many renovators have added a modern recreational fireplace to

Figure 7.4 FURNACE FLUE. A decorated brick stack stands atop a concrete furnace flue, evidence of a house equipped with central heating when built, about 1900. Near Atherley, Ontario County.

an old house. A chimney mounted against, rather than in, the outside wall tells the tale, and more economical renditions have shiny aluminum stovepipes jutting out and up.

Gingerbread

`Cheap and showy´ is the way the *Oxford English Dictionary* defines gingerbread. That description fits well with our thinking about ephemeral bits and pieces. Herbert Walker of Medonte once related that `all you have to do for to warp shingle or anything like that is drop it into a boiler of hot water and then you can put it into any shape you want it.´[18] Beyond the decorative frivolity lies an account of individual accomplishment. Those wooden carvings dripping from gables, eaves, and verandahs relate the history of carpentry and mass production and are among the very best marks of nineteenth-century trades. Gingerbread furthered mass production, the arts, and consumerism.

The gables of vernacular houses are the standard focal points for gingerbread showiness (Figure 7.1). At first, simple curving designs were nailed up, but as gables were added to older houses and more architectural styles became fashionable, the outburst of exuberant trimming adhered less and less to convention. Gingerbread trim popularized eclecticism, and the introduction of scroll saws and lathes in the 1850s induced endless flights of fancy.[19] Each craftsman sought to create a triumph greater than the one just presented by his neighbour. The editors of pattern books egged them on.[20] As the designs became more elaborate, the chance of associating any one of them with a particular individual and region increased. These trademarks provide a rare opportunity to work out the range of operation of a carpenter in Victorian Canada (Figure 7.5).

Later gingerbread gradually filled in the peaks of narrower gables, and then the broader ones. These bargeboards, as they are known, are associated with steeper roofs and altogether bigger storey-and-a-half houses and filled in a wedge of bare wall most grandly (Figure 7.2). Full-storey construction permitted the filling-in process to proceed unchecked. The outcome is window-less, non-functional gables filled with fish-scale, sunburst, and other designs, sometimes in shingle or in pebbles set in stucco. They are common in the industrializing cities and the younger, rural housing of Grey and Simcoe counties built just before 1914. In the plainness of Edwardian Canada showy decoration lost its detailing altogether and became just ordinary wall. As attic rooms were added, windows once again poked through, completing the cycle that began more than half a century earlier (Figure 7.6).

Multi-coloured brickwork is gingerbread in masonry. There is no more ex-uberant expression than a 'hound's-tooth' storey-and-a-half house in Grenville County (Figure 7.7). The neoclassical transom over the door, the classical revival lintels over the windows, and the gothic window in the front gable all antedate patterned brick. The recessed windows and doorcase suggest a veneer, yet the Flemish bonding (alternate headers and stretchers) does not. Nor do the raised stone corner quoins, casting little shadows that add further depth to the façade. As for the hound's-tooth pattern in buff and red, it is simply outrageous, unequalled anywhere in the province. Flemish bonding is a high-art style, with matched bricks skilfully laid up, and the pattern hardly needs to be emphasized by varying the colour. It is as if the builder felt compelled to inflict sophistication upon deprived neighbours. Announcing the date – 1858 – is yet another oddity. Altogether, this house is a showpiece of what that year was *au fait* in domestic design.

The thousands of examples of coloured-brick houses may be placed into two categories. Red with buff trim is the more common, found mainly east of the

Figure 7.5 TORONTO TOWNSHIP GINGERBREAD. This carved confection of hands, crossbars, and spangled circles is one of the most distinctive in Ontario. Fifteen examples have been identified, surely all by a single carpenter and used as a signature on houses he built. All are spread over less than thirty kilometres, between Oakville and Brampton, on houses dated to the early years of Confederation. Near Meadowvale village, Peel County.

Figure 7.6 DECORATION SUBDUED. By the start of the twentieth century, the flamboyance of gingerbread had spent itself, and plain windows poked through simple gables. Fish-scale shingling on this painted brick house dated 1906. New Dundee, Waterloo County.

Niagara Escarpment; the reverse – buff with red trim – occurs to the west. The basic colour is usually local to the region, and the decorative trim was imported. Because neither type was produced everywhere, polychromatic brick treatment often entailed additional costs over a one-colour finish, for material, design, and labour. Owners who really wished to show off reversed the colours from what was usual in their region.

Polychromy may be traced from its Italian roots, through an English church about 1850, to Yorkville's town hall in 1856, to Grenville County, and onward as the principal decorative aspect of the bricking of Ontario.[21] Colourful displays exist in stone, too, by the opportune mixture of granite and limestone (Figure 3.3) and also in slate (Figure 5.11), concrete (Figure 5.19), cobbles (Figure 5.10), and wood (Figure 6.7). Dufferin, Simcoe, Grey, and Bruce counties are the best places in the Ontario countryside to see polychromatic houses.

Figure 7.7 POLYCHROMATIC BRICKWORK. High-art demonstration of
brick bonding (Flemish), colour selection, and architectural eclecticism.
Wolford Township, Grenville County.

Colour and texture

Immigrants writing overseas to relatives repeatedly described the colours of
Ontario. On finds descriptions of glorious autumn foliage, of the stark beauty
of a February full moon casting shadows across the drifted fencelines, and of
the delicate shades of green in early spring. Such scenes, carried from season
to season in the mind's eye, too often contrasted with what these immigrants
built. Everywhere stood unpainted barns, log houses, and fences weathered
to a silvery patina.

What stirred pioneers to boil up vegetable dyes to tint their wooden houses?
The tones – beige, rust, mustard – were muted, perhaps painted on for protection as much as for cheer. We are rather more certain that buildings could
not be white – that would have been too American, too republican. The exuberant mixtures of red and buff brick made the perfect Ontario statement:
gentle frivolity combined with sensible function. We should be grateful that
concrete, the drabbest of all material, came into use in an era when new
construction was rare. Imagine if every cheery brick schoolhouse or riotous
fieldstone farmhouse was, instead, grey slab.

Articulation is the recessing and thrusting forward of parts of a wall, creating
visual interest through the play of light and shadow on surfaces. It is a form
of polychromatic treatment, demonstrated in brick (Figure 7.8) or in board

Figure 7.8 ARTICULATION. Relief-like chimney caps, window-heads, and dentillation beneath the eaves give interest to the buff-brick façade of the Diefenbaker house. Neustadt, Bruce County.

and batten (Figure 7.9). The proposed house for the successful farmer of 1865 was designed so that 'the monotony of the front is relieved by projecting the hall two feet forward.'[22] In addition, it had 'bold wooden brackets' and 'corners ... relieved by having long and short quoins projecting.' Articulation may be structural or, as in the case of verandahs, added on. Drip-courses – projecting bricks above a window to deflect rainwater running down the wall – and terracotta panels – clay castings with relief-like designs – are other instances of non-structural articulation. Rarely does it extend beyond the façade.

External decoration had become big business by the 1880s, when J. Heard and Company of Strathroy advertised that it was in the artificial stone business, manufacturing 'all kinds of trimmings of the most approved designs for the external dressing of ... buildings, both public and private.'[23] It went on to list water-table beltings, sills, label mouldings, buttress caps, copings, window and door caps, keystones, corbels, bosses, pilaster bases, facings and capitals, corner blocks, ashlers, chimney-tops, and more, all of which would be shipped

Figure 7.9 BOARD AND BATTEN. Milled lumber dresses up a simple country school, 1870s, on the corner of a farm lot, far from the nearest farm buildings. Note well with pump in foreground. Markham Township, York County.

by rail in sawdust. Other firms offered tooled stonework, coloured roof slates, ballustrades, weather vanes, roof lanterns, cupolas, belvederes, and anteixia. The very terminology is snobbish, yet the uninitiated customer could still point to whatever gewgaw caught his or her fancy, stick it on, and enjoy it as a decoration with a curious, forgettable name. High art was not completely ethereal.

The craze for gingerbread had burned itself out by 1900, and the new century opened with a plea for simplicity.[24] How well the evidence has withstood the ravages of a century has varied enormously. Many iron bits rusted away with little consequence, while useless eaves brackets have lasted better, tucked under a protective overhang. Early in the twentieth century owners began to paint polychromatic brick white or boxcar red. This was especially true in the older districts of Hamilton and Toronto, intent on distancing themselves from anything that looked small-town. Articulation disappeared under flat veneer, and scrollwork in gables was torn off as soon as bits worked loose.

Older farming people today express surprise when outsiders comment on the faded decoration, no longer a part of their lives. For urbane folks in the 1990s gingerbread is an important part of a happy country retreat and has been restored in plastic and vinyl as well as wood. Young urban professionals are attacking painted brick walls of former working-class housing in such districts as Cabbagetown in Toronto or the North End of Hamilton, taking off the layers to reveal once more the fanciful, polychromatic treatment of a century ago. As a result, such inner-city neighbourhoods seem ever so slightly closer to the countryside than they were a decade or two ago.

8

Community buildings

Ontario's need for spacious, enclosed areas for community gatherings has been almost as strong as the need for personal shelter. Migration to southern Ontario in the nineteenth century upset traditional group activities such as worship and teaching, disruption that was exacerbated by cultural mixing in every local neighbourhood. The absence of sanctuaries and academies was an aspect of the simplification process described in chapter 7, but the activities associated with such buildings survived, albeit at first hardly visible. Long before permanent church buildings appeared on the landscape, for instance, congregations were flourishing and services were being provided (Figure 1.3). Such was the case too with schooling, municipal administration, and the provision of justice. The circuit-court judge and the itinerant preacher fulfilled their duties in private houses or barns and moved on, leaving only the faintest trace.

Terms such as 'meeting house,' 'house of worship,' 'station house,' 'court-house,' and 'public house' are signs of the domestic origins of the institutional landscape. 'Public architecture would be domestic buildings writ large.'[1] Many community buildings even look like houses (Figures 8.1 and 8.2). The Walk-erton pump-house was built about 1890 in the architectural firm's habit 'of basing pump houses on popular domestic patterns' – in this case, the storey-and-a-half.[2] A century later, similar buildings were put up at Meadowvale village and Alton, on the Credit River. Here was high art emulating vernacular, in the time-honoured Ontario manner.

Other public buildings are known as 'halls': parish halls or town halls, for instance. The word 'hall' itself has domestic roots and is suited to the group of buildings considered in this chapter. There are many variations of the simple rectangle, with bellcotes on top, apses at one end and towers recessed or freestanding at the other, and assembly rooms below. Transverse wings add still more variety, as do cornerstones and other labels, and it all adds up to the institutional mate to the irregular Victorian house (Figures 3.7 and 6.1, above). I address the public structures of the Ontario countryside as a generic group of similar-looking, hall-type buildings.[3]

Figure 8.1 BANKING HOUSE. Exchange Bank of Canada, Second Empire style, c. 1890; note coloured roof slates. Parkhill, Middlesex County.

Figure 8.2 JAIL HOUSE, with Georgian elements. Cobourg, Northumberland County.

Halls are ideal entry points into the landscape. They stand next to the road within easy view, and their grounds are sufficiently public as not to inhibit those who wish to walk up for a closer look. Large windows along each side permit one to see right through the single room, adding to the impression of a public place, and visitors may well be permitted to step inside. Notice boards and date stones make unsolicited announcements, and steeples and flagpoles send further signals. Halls are like large-print books, lying open at the roadside for perusal.

Yet there are pitfalls. The country church on the corner may not be a church at all. Window curtains, a vegetable garden, or a tethered dog are warnings that what looks like a house of God may be a house of mere mortals (Figure 8.3). Conversely, a dwelling could be made a house of worship simply by decree (Figure 8.4), and some church buildings have attached residences (Figure 8.5). Providing and maintaining the right amount of public and private space for a changing community that takes pride in being efficient are exacting tasks. The distinction between workplace and dwelling place in Ontario has not always been clear, and adaptability has been a proven asset.

The majority of halls bear a close resemblance to the storey-and-a-half building turned sideways (Figure 7.3). The upright front wall and its entrance provide a focus in the tradition of the Greek temple (Figure 8.6; see also Figure 6.4). The steep roof and a tower standing against the gable-end wall have further impact (Figure 8.7). Inside, exposed crossbeams in a cathedral ceiling display the half-storey bent structure. Institutions have taken the lead in the trend towards taller buildings as the nineteenth century progressed. None the less, the basic hall functions as a one-storey building. Galleries or choir lofts at the rear of many church sanctuaries create partial upper storeys, but few halls use the half-storey other than for air circulation. Windows reaching to the eaves reinforce the impression that these are one-storey buildings.

The architecture of institutional buildings has proceeded through the same sequence as identified above for dwellings (Figure 6.2). From rare Georgian beginnings followed classical, gothic, and the diverse Victorian styles. Welling up through this high-art sequence is the domestic expression, and trickling down from it are ideas diluted and simplified to become the vernacular. From these extremes has come Ontario's particular, eclectic blend.

The origins of Ontario's high-art public buildings are British. Many of the grander ones were designed by reputable architects, some of whom, like William Storm, made their careers here.[4] A few dozen pace-setting buildings occupied prominent places in the lakefront townships, and from these vantage points they were unashamedly copied by a progressive society eager to propel itself into the forefront of taste. The Guelph town hall of 1857 initiated a sequence of copying in which the same architect did houses there and a more modest town hall for Orangeville in 1864 (Figure 8.8). Caledon township hall, ten kilometres further into the countryside, echoes the design in the 1880s

Figure 8.3 CHURCH DOMESTICATED. Inborn impressions of houses and churches may be deceptive. `Parish Apartments,´ with former gothic openings showing through ageing stucco. Campbellford, Northumberland County.

Figure 8.4 HOUSE INSTITUTIONALIZED. `Some places of worship are specimens rather of domestic than ecclesiastical architecture, and more suitable for dwelling houses or barns than temples of the living God.´ *Christian Guardian*, 18 June 1845, 138. True also in the late twentieth century. Meaford, Grey County.

Figure 8.5 RESIDENTIAL INSTITUTION. Clay-tile residence is appended to a brick church. Notice decaying bricks in front wall. Rosedale United, formerly Methodist. Enniskillen Township, Lambton County.

and may be a sequel (Figure 8.9). Romanesque detail shows in a Mono school house of 1875 and housing in Amaranth by 1890. At some point the roots of any one building's design become lost in the pervasiveness of diffusion. High art was diluted by rude copiers, who, by adopting features and mixing in details as much as their resources and understanding allowed, contributed to eclecticism.

Churches

When the Province of Upper Canada was constituted in 1791, the Anglican church – the Church of England – took immediate steps to become visible. A parish could be declared, a building raised on public land, and the clergy engaged – all with public funds. Until 1831, only Church of England (and Presbyterian, Church of Scotland) clergy could perform marriages.[5] The church was the state made manifest and authoritative in a pre-eminent way in a landscape of struggle, where the rudest shelter was the norm.

Early Anglican churches were dignified, high-art imports, built with such forthright materials as stone or stucco over timber-frame (Figure 8.10). Clas-

Figure 8.6 HIGH-ART HALL. Registry Office; Romanesque, with recessed wall panels and a classical pediment. Napanee, Lennox and Addington County.

Figure 8.7 VERNACULAR HALL. Headford United Church, with separate tower, and meeting rooms below. Markham Township, York County.

Figure 8.8 TRICKLING DOWN. Carved animal-head keystones in the Orangeville town hall (1864) may be traced to the Guelph town hall, several years older. Dufferin County.

Figure 8.9 RURAL COPYING. Stylistic details from Orangeville's town hall (Figure 8.8) are repeated in the community hall (1880). Caledon village, Peel County.

Figure 8.10 THE ESTABLISHMENT. Anglican Church, in the Georgian style. St John's UEL Anglican, founded 1787. Roughcast. Cataraqui, Frontenac County.

sical or Georgian style has prevailed, and a bell tower was commonly attached to the narthex. Most of these structures were in the bigger towns, much too far away to be of use to most settlers early in the nineteenth century. It was

Christianity for the privileged. A great many of the buildings remain, and their histories have been extensively researched.[6]

For other Christians – 74 per cent of the population in the 1840s[7] – getting started was a struggle. As late as the 1870s, Dundalk (south of Owen Sound) had three Christian congregations but no church buildings.[8] At a country crossroads nearby in Melancthon Township, about 1850, several Methodist groups vied for their turn in a schoolhouse: 'The "Noo Connexion," a body which had only recently sought representation in this part of the country, and having, as yet, only a limited influence, had been obliged to content itself with the privilege of the school house on Sunday, and other evenings, after the Wesleyans, the Primitives, and the Episcopaleans were done with it.'[9]

For Roman Catholics worship in a formal sanctuary was vital, and they built early, if modestly (Figure 5.8) but other denominations accepted log construction as a first step, on donated land. Apses, transepts, towers, and spires came later, and sometimes not at all. At the dedication of St Andrews Presbyterian, Camden East, in 1881, the trustees proudly announced that there would be no spire, 'the building committee not being ambitious enough to ornament the church with both a spire and a mortgage, so it will have neither.'[10] One is reminded of the generations taken to build the great mediaeval cathedrals.

Nearly half of land-breaking Ontarians were Methodist, and they followed a different course. Itinerant preachers ('circuit riders') and lay volunteers functioned without church buildings, and adherents freely offered their houses and barns as places of worship. Even one repentant Anglican in Peterborough during the 1830s invited the local Methodists to meet in his house (but not his church!).[11] The Anglicans of St Peter's, at Erindale, Toronto Township, shared their cemetery. But the Methodists were not of the same standing of course, and had to rest in peace (one hopes) in what the Anglicans patronizingly called 'the Methodist corner.'[12]

For the most part, however, the Methodist population made do by its own ingenuity. Huge communal camp meetings held outdoors in summer gave Methodism far-reaching influence throughout pioneering Ontario, yet for years little showed on the landscape. It was truly a grass-roots, vernacular beginning, but far better suited to the pioneering spirit than was the imperious approach of the Anglicans.

If one were to accept the view set forth by the Earl of Durham in his 1840 report, Methodism – or indeed any other religion – might never have contributed to the visible landscape. Durham held the very American idea that political stability was based on economic growth, not on any established church. 'Progress,' one scholar has declared, 'was to replace religion as the new opiate of the masses.'[13] Yet at this very moment residents of Upper Canada embarked on a spree of building churches. As population density increased, the circuit that one man could ride shrank until it became feasible for him to stay in place. At this point, having a dedicated sanctuary made sense.

Methodist buildings began to appear about 1840, and Baptists and Lutherans, and disestablished Presbyterians, also began building.

For Methodists, there was no contradiction in being progressive; those involved in making worship visible would be recognized for their Good Works.[14] It was a strongly vernacular, self-help undertaking – the equivalent of domestic log cabins – and even the Anglicans started to participate.[15] Between 1851 and 1881, the number of Anglicans, Presbyterians, and Baptists in Ontario doubled, while the number of their church buildings tripled, to nearly two thousand. Methodists' numbers were up threefold, and their buildings up nearly fivefold, to more than twenty-three hundred.[16] Congregations that should have been growing divided into smaller units instead, and the expectation that worshippers would fill all the pews in due course became impossible to achieve.

Some of the impulse for church construction resulted from immigrants bringing with them various old-county organizational disputes. Presbyterians disagreed on how to select ministers, for example, and other denominations argued about the relationship between church and state.[17] Some splintered three or more ways (Figure 8.11), and towns that might have had two or three prominent churches instead had five or six undistinguished ones. Damascus, a hamlet near Arthur with a population of fifty in 1881, had five churches.[18] Ontario had become a landscape of little country churches, setting a vernacular tone that remains deeply ingrained to this day.

The degree of showiness of vernacular church buildings is a rough indication of denomination. The most modest are the Mennonite meeting-houses found in Waterloo, Wellington, and Bruce counties (Figure 8.12). Baptist churches are more decorative, and Methodist and Presbyterian places of worship still more so. The Roman Catholics' and Anglicans' are the most self-conscious, filled with icons and symbolism. Knox or Chalmers churches were probably Free Presbyterian, which chose reformers' names; the established Church of Scotland preferred saints, such as Andrew, John, and Columba.

Anglican and Roman Catholic buildings have split choirs, altars at the chancel wall, and a communion rail; Methodist ones have a chancel-wall choir, central table, and no communion rail. Anglicans and Catholic buildings are likely to have an apse, those of the other denominations not (Figure 8.13). Anglicans and Catholics focus on a high pulpit and chancel window, and others on a central table. Vestiges of these preferences that survive changes in ownership hint at the complex denominational interaction in Ontario's landscape at the time its institutions put down tangible roots.

Ontario gothic

The pointed gothic window is a universal architectural signal of the Christian church. The revival of gothicism in the Western world in the 1830s was just one more upswing in the cyclical way styles rise and fall in favour. By chance, it coincided with Upper Canada's first widespread demand for church build-

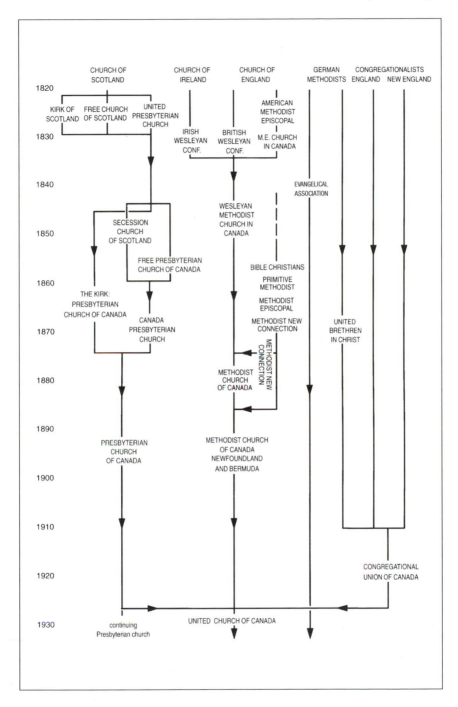

Figure 8.11 DENOMINATIONAL SPLINTERING. Disputes split Protestant denominations, and each faction built churches as one way to consolidate its position. Adapted from panel in Emmanuel College, Victoria University, Toronto.

Figure 8.12 MEETING-HOUSE. Mennonite meeting-houses follow a standard design, with five doors and a plain exterior. Elmira, Waterloo County.

Figure 8.13 APSE. The curved apse is associated with Anglican and Roman Catholic congregations, in which the service focuses on the high altar. Burnbrae, Hastings County.

ings, and the result is a landscape of gothic churches. The gothic style gained widespread recognition with Pugin's treatise, published in 1843, which asserted that classical design was pagan and that the true Christian idiom was medieval, or pointed.[19] Fortunately, he went on, because `styles are now adopted instead of generated,' this oversight could be quickly rectified.[20] Ontarians, always seeking to be current, have demonstrated this dictum.

Architects and builders in Ontario had in fact been putting up picturesque gothic buildings for some time. St John's Anglican at York Mills and Christ Church at Holland Landing, both in brick, and Christ Church at Tyendinaga in stone, antedated Pugin by several years.[21] A small building in gothic revival was the Methodists' choice, and hundreds were built. Others were altered to conform, as both Anglicans and Methodists sought a common image following the decline of privilege and revivalism.[22] Gothic style became very visible on the landscape and a strong contributor to the mixture of styles (Figure 2.3).

Ontario gothic has also a domestic aspect. Stoves cast with gothic motifs warmed home parlours as well as church sanctuaries, and hardly a country road or small town street lacks a storey-and-a-half house bearing a little gothic window in its front gable (Figure 7.7). Prince Edward County is particularly rich in this respect. Flamboyant examples have curved panes and glazing bars, whereas on the plainest the curved arch is flattened to a triangle.

A gothic window neatly tops off the central bay of a farm-house and helps the storey-and-a-half style to stand tall. It was a shape that suited brick, for it depended on the wedge-shaped key-brick rather than the long stone slab that spans the flat-topped classical opening. The pointed arch has been described as `the best and most dignified' way to top off a window opening and `should be used, where practical, in all Gothic buildings.'[23]

Domestic gothic expresses the spiritual dimension of ground-breaking and farming – life-long, devotional acts – and the pointed window takes its place, with grace at the dinner table and reading from the family Bible, as part of the mingling of Christianity and the daily agricultural routine. The gothic design reflects the conservative maturity of farmland Ontario in the Victorian age. It never caught on except in the front gable and is less prominent in manufacturing centres than in the service towns and countryside.[24] As full-storey construction became dominant, front gables disappeared and gothic windows went out of fashion.

Merger, decline, and revival

By the 1870s, dissension among the Protestant denominations was waning and consolidation was under way. Merged congregations agreed to share one building and dispose of another. Some sold their sanctuaries to other denominations in the growing towns. Anglicans in Brampton, for example, bought an Episcopal Methodist building in 1884 and added a chancel; Roman Cath-

Figure 8.14 MEDIEVAL REVIVAL. St Albans Anglican church, in a style espoused only
by Anglicans; built 1887. Glen Williams, Halton County.

olics bought another surplus Methodist church, in Toronto Junction, in 1876.[25]
Proceeds from such sales allowed Methodists and Presbyterians to erect showy
churches to match the larger Catholic and Anglican ones appearing in new
idioms such as Romanesque and medieval (Figure 8.14). New St Paul's (Woodstock), Holy Trinity (Chatham), Trinity (St Thomas), and St John's (Morpeth)
are four bold Anglican churches of the 1870s of a Detroit firm's design.[26]

Other denominations preferred celebrating their vernacular pedigree: for instance 'Toronto Methodist: a style occupied by our Primitive Methodist friends for some years.'[27]

Many central churches added offices and classrooms to meet the widening needs of the urban age. Additions generally were handled with more dignity in churches than was the case in housing. Anglicans preferred separate parish halls, built on the adjacent glebelands of the parish; the space could be squarer than was possible if placed beneath the sanctuary.[28] Presbyterians, in contrast, were among those who usually inserted basement halls beneath existing sanctuaries. This procedure retained visual balance while giving the building more height and thus more prominence (Figure 8.7). It also allowed for efficient central heating[29] and avoided disturbing existing burials (perhaps unknown) in the adjacent churchyard. The basement hall was a vernacular solution, easier for small buildings and reminiscent of lifting barns atop new stables.

Closing a church was painful and too often postponed. Many structures lingered on for decades after their members should have been folded in with others.[30] As a result, multiple charges reappeared. The revived circuit rider of the Depression era drove a well-worn Model-T over dusty country roads to conduct three Sunday services to small residual congregations, mostly elderly. Creation of the United Church of Canada in 1925 induced further rationalization, but still church buildings remained, carefully boarded up and ready for rededication should ever the call come again. Hay Bay Methodist opened in 1792, was enlarged in 1834, and was abandoned in 1860; it was repurchased in 1911, reopened in 1912, and abandoned once more in 1925.[31]

Surplus church buildings have provided a steady supply of roadside space for other uses. This is the only reason that many are still present today. Selby United and Alton Baptist became township halls; sanctuaries in Melancthon and Forest Mills became Orange halls. Others went into more mundane uses. The Amaranth Township Roads Department parks machinery in a former church at Campania, west of Shelburne. In Orangeville, a Roman Catholic church became a dry-cleaning shop – cleanliness next to godliness! – and another an apartment building. Hundreds more have become residences (Figure 8.15).

Since the Second World War, immigration and mobility have created new religious use for abandoned church buildings. In Odessa, a few kilometres west of Kingston, the Methodist Episcoplal church of 1870 has been taken over as a Roman Catholic sanctuary. About 1980, a Ukrainian Orthodox congregation placed an onion dome on a plain country church building on Dundas Street north of Oakville. Italian, Polish, Portuguese, West Indian, and Chinese congregations have all seized similar opportunities. Fundamentalist sects and pentecostal groups have reactivated other sanctuaries. By starting out unobtrusively, they are repeating the pattern of institutional beginnings in Upper Canada nearly two centuries ago.

Figure 8.15 REDUNDANCY. Church consolidation has provided a steady supply of small buildings for other uses. A brick-veneer church of the 1870s is converted to domestic use. Oil Springs, Lambton County.

Lodges

The Orange Order

The old Sydenham Road (Highway 10) passes through `the Orange Valley´ north of Flesherton. `The Orange Line´ crosses Haldimand County. `O´ Hill is well known to skiers on the Blue Mountain near Collingwood; it takes its name from the large letter once painted on the limestone crest of the escarpment, flanked by an `L´ on each adjacent promontory. Together the three letters LOL announced the Loyal Orange Lodge far out into Georgian Bay. These local expressions do not appear on ordinary maps but are deeply etched in the memories of members of their communities. They identify the men´s society of Protestant Irish origin that came with Irish immigrants to Canada in the 1830s. It flourished as both a patriotic and benevolent organization into the middle of the present century, and despite the odds continues today not entirely out of sight.[32]

Some six hundred Orange Lodge branches were scattered throughout old Ontario when the organization was at its peak in the 1870s.[33] Most occupied hall-type buildings that are today fraught with mystery: terse label stones, shuttered windows, bare flagpoles, overgrown sites, and dereliction (Figure 8.16). They are likely to be wooden, starkly plain, very small, and on tiny plots with virtually no grounds. Orange halls enclose some of Ontario´s most im-

Figure 8.16 THE ORANGE ORDER. Lodge No. 2320 has a closed-up look, though it is still actually in use and was one of Ontario's last lodges to be chartered. Oddly unsymmetrical building, concrete block (1914). Corbyville, Hastings County.

penetrable inner spaces, yet do so in a type of building that is normally outward-looking.

By electing to conduct its affairs in private, the Orange Order has achieved appreciable visibility. Farmhouse kitchens or bar-rooms in country inns were not sufficiently private places to conduct business; sharing school-houses had other complications. Construction of individual halls provided the answer. Orangeism was a beneficiary of surplus churches late in the nineteenth century, and the substantialness of its buildings increased again as school-houses were being abandoned a half-century later. These have actually helped the lodge to maintain its privacy, perhaps, as they may be easily mistaken for something else more familiar.

The one time the Orange express themselves outside the hall is on the Glorious Twelfth of July. Each year on that day roads throughout the province became parade grounds for celebration of the victory of Protestantism over Catholicism in Ireland at the River Boyne in 1690. Clearly such festivities were not for all neighbourhoods, and we can understand why the Orange Line was an identifiable boundary in a countryside of divergent religious backgrounds.

Throughout the year lodge members were quietly going about the neighbourhoods, performing a self-initiated welfare function. To victims of fire they offered housing, to injured fellows they gave help on the farm, and for widows and orphans they underwrote debts. The Orange Lodge was part of urbanization too and became a potent force in Toronto politics from the 1890s until after the Second World War. Several mayors have been Orange, and the hall on College Street West is a fine brick building of high-art spirit. A ladies' wing established a few halls in towns early in the twentieth century and undertook social work.[34]

Since the 1930s, the political strength and social welfare role of Orangeism have been eroded by bureaucracy and multiculturalism, and the fraternity began a slow decline. On the site of the hall in the Orange Valley, run to seed by 1975 and now gone, only a burying ground from its pre-Orange days remains. As the old rural social fabric unravels, it takes a sixth sense to descry Orange remnants in the custody of tired old men clutching tattered warrants. The relict graveyard in the Orange valley is a strangely fitting companion.

Others

The upper storeys of town retail blocks have been common locations for the Masons, Oddfellows, and other fraternities. The illustrated county atlases of the 1870s and 1880s are filled with instances: Park Hill, in Middlesex, is just one example.[35] These groups were based on trades and labour, and their roots were not on the farm. By sharing town retail buildings with lawyers, small workshops, and apartments, they made their meeting rooms even less visible than those used by the Orange Order. Orillia's Masonic temple, for instance,

Figure 8.17 RECYCLED HALLS. Painted clocks in the cupola stand in for real ones, awaited since this former township hall was built in 1875; each face registers a different time. Royal Canadian Legion Hall, Branch No. 607. Keene, Peterborough County.

has been only faintly identified by the impression of calipers etched in the pavement outside the store above which it is located.

Surplus halls in the countryside have become attractive sites, in part because of their convenience to ageing members. Senior citizens may park the car by the door and do not have stairs to climb. Masons meet in a disused country church near Acton, and the Royal Canadian Legion uses the former township hall at Keene (Figure 8.17). Two other rural organizations – the Women's

Institute and the Tweedsmuir Society – took up still more of the little, relict halls. Economical, conservative instincts quickly identify space made redundant amid social change and snap it up.

Schools and libraries

If one person can be said to have shaped the landscape of public education in Ontario, it was J. George Hodgins. As deputy superintendent of education from the 1850s until 1876, deputy minister until 1890, and an inexhaustible promoter of literacy, he presided over the period when compulsory, free public education took its place as one of the taken-for-granted aspects of provincial life.[36] Attractive, durable, functional schoolhouses were the centrepieces of Hodgins's policy. Hundreds are scattered across the province, readily identified by their hall-like lines, roadside site, shade trees, and dated marker, frequently with the township name (Figure 8.18).

The Public School Act of 1846 bound the province to providing free education for all children up to age sixteen. Buildings were to be designed for the purpose and spread across the countryside for easy access.[37] Qualified teachers, spinster or bachelor, were to board inconspicuously in the neighbourhood; they would leave no trace. By 1863 there were nearly four thousand public schools in Ontario, seven or eight buildings in every township south of the Precambrian Shield.[38] More than four out of five were wooden.

Figure 8.18 ROMANESQUE COUNTRY SCHOOL. Polychromatic brick, 1889. Rob Roy, Osprey Township, Grey County.

Hodgins's great hope was that each building would be 'the most attractive spot in the neighbourhood.'[39] His treatise, *The School House*, opens with more than thirty pages picturing showy school buildings for the aspiring town or township. But in reality early school buildings were indistinguishable from dwellings.[40] The majority were log and, we may suspect, superannuated houses donated with every best intention but far below Hodgins's rather high standards.

Sharing space with church congregations was common in the earliest days. It was not practical, however, as a regular arrangement. Current educational theory required that desks be ranged around the walls and facing outward, for example. There was the matter of pride, too, and by the 1870s country schools and country churches everywhere stood adjacent to one another, but aloof (Figure 4.12).

Changes rapidly followed passage of the Free Schools Act and abolition of fees for primary schooling in 1871.[41] Three windows on each side became standard, and some schools had separate entrances for boys and girls. Ventilation flues and raised ceilings improved air circulation, and interior arrangements and equipment were upgraded.[42] In Halton County we read of 'a very marked improvement in school houses, grounds and furniture' by 1877.[43] Brick or stone country schoolhouses continue to be a highly visible aspect of the general rebuilding in that era. Some were entirely new; the best of the older ones were modernized and veneered, and still others were redesigned surplus churches.

Despite this variety of origins, Hodgins worried about 'such an uninteresting sameness' among schoolhouses.[44] He urged that full attention be given to architectural detail. Cambered, Romanesque, and flat-headed windows all were widely used; end walls received gothic treatment. Vernacular forces and personal pride were sufficiently strong that variation on the standard theme occurred naturally.

School grounds also came under Hodgins's scrutiny. The 1876 manual prescribed that the lot be one acre (0.4 ha), and certainly not less than half an acre, with the building centred from side to side.[45] The site ought to be planted in species of trees that the children could study.[46] This practice would help re-establish respect after generations of forest destruction. Sugar maple was popular, and the centrepiece of many an Arbor Day ceremony in May. Huge, mature specimens continue to shade school sites all over the province. Paling fences were required, faced on the boys' side of the play yard (boys pushed harder than girls). A two-seat outhouse was similarly divided down the middle. A well and pump were mandatory (Figure 7.9).[47]

Hierarchy and consolidation

Despite standard textbooks and wall maps, education was an isolated activity during most of the nineteenth century, carried out by hundreds of dedicated,

Figure 8.19 BIGGER SCHOOLS. Streetsville grammar (`high´) school, 1877–1950. It has since provided various municipal functions. Peel County.

but lonely teachers. Progress much beyond the three Rs was unachievable. Two-room schools began to appear in the countryside after 1880, and grade schools with several rooms in the towns. A straggling few rural school buildings were replaced as late as the 1920s, and one in Palermo in 1941 (later converted to a theatre studio). A four-room country school was built in Adolphustown Township in 1962 and adapted for residential use barely ten years later.

Secondary schooling was developing in the cities and larger towns before 1900.[48] It was accessible to country youngsters only if they could afford a train ride or could board in town (Figure 8.19). Continuation schools brought limited secondary education to those students immobilized in the declining countryside between 1907 and the 1950s. Fewer than two hundred existed, and they have left only a fragmentary imprint on the landscape.[49] Another approach was short courses, offered in the 1940s `even in vacant houses on the back concessions.´[50]

So much of what Hodgins had put in place was wearing away, and by the 1930s the province could no longer disregard what one critic described as its rural `educational slums.´[51] Attempts at consolidation into fewer buildings, combined with busing, began in the 1920s. We read of Mallorytown (Leeds County) in 1923, where `horsedrawn vans are used on all the routes, and in winter are made very comfortable by tightly curtained tops,´ and of motorized vans being tried in the same decade in Tweed, Dundas, and Gooderham (near

Haliburton).[52] Hundreds of underused little schools were closed between 1938 and 1945.[53]

The first substantial use of school buses occurred late in the 1940s, and as hundreds upon hundreds more hit the roads in the ensuing decades, more and more country school buildings became redundant.[54] One eight-room school could replace eight single-room ones. Children could be redistributed into grades, and teachers could become specialists at particular levels. Additions, not always well matched, were made to existing schools in villages and towns. Since about 1970, introduction of portable classrooms has made adaptation to changing enrolment patterns even more rapid.

Few consolidated schools occupied rural settings before the 1970s. But expensive town sites once again made open farmland attractive, just as it had been 150 years earlier, and schools moved out. In 1985 the Peel Board of Education set up its headquarters in a field on Hurontario Street in Mississauga, adjacent to the restored Britannia country school of 1852, using an architecturally sympathetic style. An operating farm adds to the rural spirit, and city children studying pioneer life must tramp along the roadside to get to class.

Surplus rural schoolhouses came to the attention of city folks out on Sunday drives in the 1950s, and many have been bought up for conversion to residences. Having a well gave them an advantage over many churches, and they generally were in better condition. Some townships placed resident custodians in their buildings at the time of closing, to secure them for possible future educational needs. Sale for housing may not have been contemplated at the time, but no doubt councillors have applauded such wise decisions of their predecessors.

Owners of country schoolhouses tend to keep them looking like schools. Twin outhouses rarely now stand at the back of the lot, but a swing may dangle from a century-old maple in front. These buildings have taken on a new, informal educational role simply by existing. Sightings trigger nostalgic childhood recollections, even among people who never attended a country school.[55] It is surely part of the high value that Ontarians have given education that the little red schoolhouse has been so thoroughly romanticized.[56]

Private schooling

Several religious denominations had set up schools long before the Public School Act of 1846. Bishop John Strachan's school in Cornwall (1804), Booth Academy in Norfolk (1819), King's College (1827) and Upper Canada College (1829) in Toronto, and Victoria College in Cobourg (1840) all had church affiliation. A plaque in front of the West Lake Boarding School, of late Georgian domestic design and situated west of Picton, relates that it was operated by the Society of Friends (Quakers) from the time of its construction in 1839 until 1859.

From these institutions sprang Ontario's first generation of home-grown elite, some trained up to the age of twenty, well beyond the common school-leaving age. Tuition was paid, and some fine semi-public buildings came to grace selected townscapes. It was the familiar pattern of catering first to privilege, with a more broadly based component gradually taking hold in the 1830s.[57]

Church-sponsored education for common settlers was rare before 1846, but the act that year provided support for parochial schools. Legislation in 1859 specified that, at the request of five householders in a local area, a Roman Catholic school would be provided. By 1863 there were 109 separate schools throughout the province.[58] This was about 3 per cent of the total, and since its buildings look the same as others, parochial schooling does not stand out of the general educational landscape. An inscription such as `Sep[arate] School Sec[tion] No. 10, Carrick' (Township, in Bruce County), almost unintelligible, is typical of the extent of visibility.

The great growth of Roman Catholicism in Ontario has been in the cities, beginning with Italian immigration in the 1920s and sustained with southern and eastern Europeans arriving since 1950. Full public funding through the high-school years was instituted in the 1980s. It demonstrates the spreading influence of the Roman church but has not made unusual marks upon the visible landscape.

Libraries and Mechanics' Institutes

Many of those who migrated to Canada from the United States or overseas before the 1860s took a step backward on the path towards literacy. Public education was sufficiently well established in those homelands to ensure that the concept would be carried to the new areas, but once again the means of implementing appeared only slowly. Schools made sure that native-born youths would grow up literate, but there had to be some means of maintaining that achievement and fostering use of books and magazines more widely through society. The subject became all the more crucial when agricultural mechanization took hold after 1850, introducing complicated machinery and instruction manuals on how to use it. `Book farming' was part of the mixed-farming development, and more and more specialized crops and crop combinations had to be understood. Literacy was becoming an essential tool itself.

The first public libraries were established in the 1850s in the cities.[59] In addition to literature, they housed growing collections of pattern books and farming periodicals.[60] Called Mechanics' Institutes, 268 of them were scattered throughout the towns and countryside in 1892,[61] or one for every twenty to thirty schools. Programs of public lectures and exhibits gave the institutes further reason for being; the Hamilton Mechanics' Institute became the home of the Hamilton Association, founded in 1857 to promote natural history and

Figure 8.20 CARNEGIE LIBRARY. More than one hundred of these cottage-roofed, full-storey buildings of the early twentieth century grace townscapes throughout the province. Lindsay, Victoria County.

philosophy.[62] Such bodies tap the deeper intellectual undercurrents of a maturing society. They leave faint archival spoors in themselves but contribute to an atmosphere in which new, tangible expressions might erupt at any time.

Public library buildings were slow to materialize in Ontario, apparently because money was directed instead into school-library collections, housed within school buildings.[63] Then, in the 1890s, Ontario's library resources received a big boost when the Scottish-American entrepreneur and philanthropist Andrew Carnegie initiated a program to construct and furnish public libraries throughout North America. Drawing on his immense wealth, accumulated through the Carnegie Steel Company of Pittsburgh, he underwrote 111 library buildings throughout Ontario between 1895 and 1915 (Figure 8.20).[64] The standard Carnegie library plan was squarer than the usual Ontario hall. It was symmetrical and had a wide, low front. Carnegie libraries are examples of mass-produced high-art construction, consciously laid out for the specialized public purpose of having people congregating without necessarily interacting – an unusual specification. Most Carnegie library buildings remain standing today and continue in their intended use.

Government buildings

The Municipal Act of 1849[65] was a landmark in the process of decentralizing local government following the decline of Old Tory power after the 1837 rebellion. Before 1849, authority had rested with the provincial legislature, district courts (originally four, then eight, and later twenty), circuit courts of quarter session, a few incorporated town councils, and, after 1834, the council of the City of Toronto. At the other extreme, business was conducted in the field by supervisors of roadwork and inspectors of land clearing, fences, and mills. These part-time public servants rode around to meet the country people at the farmhouse door. They kept ledger books at home in the sideboard and met, when necessary, around the kitchen table or in the crossroads tavern. The trace of their activity is the built landscape conforming to government expectations.

As a result of the 1849 act, some five hundred townships, fifty counties, and increasing numbers of incorporated towns needed offices, council chambers, and other public works promptly. Grand town buildings here and there set the tone and were the envy of all (Figure 5.9). Most administration, however, was conducted in vernacular halls, looking very much like the churches and schoolhouses everywhere at that time under construction (Figure 8.9). A half upper storey may have been tolerable in a back township that was given a redundant church but was an affront to a village on the make.

The town hall in Meaford is typical, a two-storey building with a cottage roof, built during the 1870s (Figure 8.21). The upper floor is a full-height council chamber and meeting room with a stage, and offices occupy the ground floor. The tradition of large, open upstairs spaces casts back to the dormitory in early inns and houses and makes structural sense. This space could be readily appropriated for political rallies, public lectures, railway promotions, or temperance meetings. Clinton's town hall is of similar vintage, with a Second Empire (or mansard) motif. It has been praised for 'the excellent stage which Ontarians had come to expect in their assembly halls by 1880.'[66]

Town halls helped popularize the Italianate and Second Empire styles of architecture. A far greater variety of styles has been used for public buildings than for dwellings, but some have rubbed off on business blocks and more expensive housing. Southern Ontario's late Victorian townscapes are, as a result, rather more heterogeneous than the adjacent countryside.

The high point for decentralized administration was reached late in the nineteenth century. Since that time growth of the public service has been almost entirely an urban phenomenon, centred at Queen's Park in Toronto. Town and township halls rarely have additions, maybe for design reasons but more probably a silent signal of their declining importance. Out on the dusty back roads repose ageing country halls experiencing the same neglect as have rural churches and schools. Regional government has given a new cast to the political map since 1960, merging towns with their surrounding countryside and producing large municipal buildings among the farms where land is cheap and parking lots are large. The offices of Halton Region, on Bronte Road at the Queen Elizabeth Way, fit this modern pattern.

Ontario has had a number of parliament houses in Toronto, Kingston, and

Figure 8.21 FULL-STOREY HALLS. The upper storey of Meaford town hall (1878) has one large room with stage. The building is grandly billed as an opera house. The contemporary fire-house, next along, strives to be as tall, with its high, parapet-like wall above the second floor, and then reaches further still with the four-storey, hose-drying tower. Grey County.

Ottawa, and each one has been unique. The currently existing assemblies at Queen´s Park – a red sandstone, Romanesque building of the 1890s – and the Centre Block, Parliament Hill, Ottawa – collegiate gothic revival in grey granite, dating from the 1920s – are among Ontario´s best-known landmarks. But the buildings themselves have no more bearing on the look of the province´s landscape than does a particular Romanesque mansion or gothic cathedral. Queen´s Park is echoed in urban structures such as Toronto´s York Club and 1899 City Hall, but the Centre Block in Ottawa came at a time when its style was passing from fashion. A degree of uncertainty in national identity is shown by the variety of architectural styles on Parliament Hill.[67]

Court-houses and registries

Evidence of the legal system in Ontario almost antedates settlement. The earliest court-house, planned for Cornwall in 1793, was designed to double as a military blockhouse.[68] It draws attention to the close ties between civil obedience and territorial sovereignty, and, again, the very names of these places are evidence of domestic origins. Like the Church of England, the judiciary had the benefit of British capital for investing in appropriate quarters to administer both criminal and civil matters. Court-houses should have been tasteful buildings, reflecting current British fashion, but not even the treasury in Whitehall could avoid the starkness of the earliest days in a raw colony. The first court-house in Charlotteville was of hewn timber and the jail 'merely of rough logs.'[69] Circuit courts were the judicial equivalent of circuit-riding preachers, meeting in inns and being similarly invisible.

Just as soon as feasible, however, court-houses began appearing in solid, durable-looking styles befitting an intentionally visible hand of authority. They were quite without ordinary domestic overtones. Classical façades and baronial castles were widely fashionable (Figure 8.22). They remain imposing structures in a landscape of small houses. Inside, the royal arms tell that Ontario is by and large a peaceable kingdom, home to a droll menagerie of gold-leaf lions variously ferocious or tusked, but also pessimistic and underfed, sharing the field with unicorns triumphant, supercilious, and occasionally irritable.[70]

Despite their high-art pretensions, judicial buildings frequently grew by the small steps asociated with the vernacular. Osgoode Hall, seat of the provincial supreme court, was built in stages beginning in the 1820s. Only in 1856 did it take on its current appearance and become, in the eyes of subsequent generations, unalterable. Kingston Penitentiary grew between the 1840s and 1890s. Both it and Osgoode are rare examples of high-art eclecticism and helped in making this familiar process respectable. The Middlesex County court-house in London (1827) displays classical, gothic, and Romanesque styles in succession.[71] Others were conscious architectural mixtures as, for example, Doric Greek elements combined with a Roman cupola on the Whitby court-house of 1852.[72] But the majority of court-houses sprang from a single tradition, and their broad façades easily concealed any little afterthoughts tacked on behind.

Registries are tied to the expanding land-transfer business after 1830, and one may be found in every county seat in the province. As private transactions succeeded the initial distribution of crown land, a local office to handle and secure records became essential. Registries are solidly built little masonry vaults, hall-like in mass and very often Romanesque in detail (Figure 8.6). They stand apart from other buildings to minimize the consequences of fire. Court-houses and registries usually occupy adjacent lots, but rarely match. Both are monumental buildings and illustrate the development of Ontario's architecture.

A government presence

The Canadian postal service became prominent in the decades between Confederation and the First World War with the erection of fine stone, and oc-

Figure 8.22 COURT-HOUSE, Renfrew County (1867), built in primeval wilderness, to assert majesty of law. Pembroke, Renfrew County.

casionally brick, buildings on bold sites centrally in the cities and larger towns (Figure 8.23). Thomas Fuller, Canada´s chief architect between 1881 and 1896, used Romanesque detailing on a basic plan, with a corner tower, in dozens of instances across Canada.[73]

Further down the hierarchy, in villages and crossroad hamlets, the postal system was outwardly invisible. It was carried on in rented space in private

Figure 8.23 TOWN POST OFFICE. A building designed by Dominion Architect Thomas Fuller was a small-town status symbol. Dozens were built across the country, dwarfing adjacent buildings on main street. Sandstone, c. 1890. Deseronto, Hastings County.

premises such as a general store. Rural delivery produced tens of thousands of mailboxes strung out along country roads – minuscule service centres that have had an unremarkable technological and architectural history. Late in the twentieth century they are disappearing, and so too is the opportunity to read names and get a feeling for the ethnic mix as one drives by. As more and more customers choose the security of a locked pigeon-hole box in town, or shift to the fax-modem or electronic-mail technologies, countryside postal activity is being pushed towards extinction.

The post office has touched the very pulse of rural society. Generations of postmasters have moderated neighbourhood social interaction, cutting across religious and educational lines. The postal wicket has been a secure, secular rendezvous, for some no doubt a confessional. From 1920 onward, the income from postal franchises was increasingly coveted in withering villages. As retail buildings vanished, services wound up in such unlikely places as the grain elevator at Indian River, east of Peterborough, or in modern, nondescript little buildings shared with no one (Figure 3.10). Hundreds of branch post offices have been closed over recent decades. The process has gone practically unnoticed to the country at large, but each instance has been perceived as the death knell for neighbourly interaction and has been sadly and vehemently lamented.[74]

The Ontario landscape is virtually undefended, and few regions betray less evidence of a military presence. Yet Lieutenant-Governor John Graves Simcoe's original road plan was executed in the 1790s as a military operation. There ought to be a plaque at the corner of Queen and Yonge streets in Toronto to mark the pivotal point from which military roads fan out over the province. These benign streets identify the principal east-west and northward axes of the province, along which troops could be moved.

For Simcoe, 'no hillock [caught] his eye without exciting in his mind the idea of a fort.'[75] Several materialized. High-art engineering skills created fortifications at Penetanguishene, Malden, Niagara, York, Kingston, and Prescott. After the end of the War of 1812, such talents were directed to constructing the Rideau Canal and Grand Trunk Railway. Both were perceived, at least partly, as defensive works against lingering threats of American invasion. Only military circles had the discipline and the knowledge to carry through such elaborate projects. Today, the military installations of early Upper Canada are grassy parks dotted with handsome Georgian buildings converted to little museums. Stanley Barracks, in Toronto's Exhibition Place, is an example, truly a case of beating swords into lawnmowers.

A good many towns have armouries, almost invariably in red brick. The demolition of the University Avenue Armoury in Toronto in the 1960s, and its replacement with a new court-house, signifies the authority of the pen in modern Ontario. In London, the armoury has become a hotel. Military bases at Trenton, Hagersville, and Petawawa are only slightly oppressive, and Borden's evergreen plantings and regimental museum are quite inviting. Martello towers were erected on the Kingston waterfront in the 1840s to defend what was currently the provincial capital from American expansionism, but they function as decorations in today's cultural landscape. Along with blockhouses put up in the 1830s along the Rideau Canal, these are signs more of Canadian paranoia than truly useful defensive installations. Military emplacements are oddities and have had attention lavished on them in the way that folklorists have revered octagonal barns and covered bridges.

In Ontario's lakefront towns – Port Hope, for example – the customs house (and there is that domestic connotation again) has occupied a prominent position at the landing.[76] Immigrants and importers passed through these obtrusive structures even before they had actually gained the shore. The physical positioning of the customs house speaks of the province's defence of its economic interests, in the seats of commerce. Since those early, waterborne days, they have receded into the more and more complex trade and business landscape (Figure 8.24). 'Customs' today means a mundane stone building at the Niagara or St Clair border crossing, or a supermarket-style checkout counter in the depths of Pearson International Airport.

Ontario's public structures aspire to be expressions of high art but largely fall short. The overwhelming majority spring from the vernacular domestic fabric.

Figure 8.24 CUSTOM HOUSE. Pink sandstone, 1884. Custom house and post office, Brockville.

The functions performed by pastor, teacher, reeve, and magistrate were pervasive. These have been conducted for the benefit of countryside society in the same way that the country storekeeper has provided for the economy. The structure that has served all these people, out of satisfaction as well as necessity, has been the humble hall.

9
Barns

The Ontario barn is a practical, general-purpose building. It is the place to store crops and tools, shelter livestock, and provide working space for such mechanical operations as threshing. British immigrants would have been familiar with such terms as `stable,´ `granary,´ and `byre´ and would have known each as a separate building. Individual farm buildings in Ontario rarely bore these names, however, though parts of barns did. Rather, Ontario farm makers were content at having protective roofs and walls and cared little for what they were called.

A chronology of Ontario barn types is easily traced by changes in the farming economy and in building technology. Grain storage gave way to haylofts as the wheat export economy was followed by mixed farming after Confederation. Stables and silos augmented the initial, all-purpose, rectangular building. Gabled roofs were supplemented by gambrel (`hipped´) roofs before 1900, and the overall size more than doubled. Timber framing gave way to lumber framing in the First World War era; galvanized (zinc-coated) steel panels replaced roofing shingles, and cement block, stone. Each successive move was made with an eye for efficiency and reuse.

Rarely have farmers deviated from this logical path, even though many took frivolous liberties with their houses. A few owners have been persuaded that placing windows in the roof of the barn, or adding cupolas, for instance, made sense. Most farmers, however, agreed with the more sober commentator who advised that, for barns, `there ought to be no mock windows, mock doors, or arches; no false gables. Let every thing be real, and expressive of its use.´[1]

Beatty Brothers Limited of Fergus, the premier name in barn publications early in the twentieth century in Ontario, urged that `the appearance of the barn can be made to have a big cash value.´[2] The response of some owners was to sell advertising space on the sides. Recall the castor-oil promotion `Children cry for Castoria,´ dating from the 1940s. Others believed that paying thousands of dollars for painting the barn red or white was a worthwhile investment. But these efforts are exceptional today, and beyond most normal budgets. They probably always have been.

Figure 9.1 THE BROODING BARN. Barns are the largest buildings on the Ontario landscape and easily catch the eye. Howe Island, Leeds County.

Figure 9.2 DATED BARN. June 1903. June was a popular month for barn construction, between planting and harvesting the first hay crop. Cramahe Township, Northumberland County.

Figure 9.3 THE DIAMOND CROSS (see detail, bottom right) is an opening found high up in the gable end of barns in many parts of Ontario. Its origin and meaning are obscure. 1892. Douro Township, Peterborough County.

The barns of old Ontario speak for themselves as ageless artistic works of great power, built for the millennium (Figure 9.1). Gaps between barn boards are not the result of carelessness but were deliberately included, to provide for air circulation. They also admit filtered light, and an empty barn in June, just before the first hay is garnered, can inspire thoughts of medieval cathedrals. The silver-grey boards and lustreless steel roofs signal a timeless commitment to the land.

Dating barns seems contrary to their spirit, and only occasionally is it done (Figure 9.2). I have seen barns in Ontario labelled as early as 1858, which gives an idea of how long siding lasts – if it is original. Are the few barns that bear dates the last of many, once with visible dates, to have had their boards replaced, or are these barns a fairly complete set of the small portion that ever bore carved dates? My instincts favour the latter interpretation because of the scarcity of reboarded barns seen over the past thirty years and because of the known durability of pine boards. They had to be renailed, but not replaced.

The diamond cross is a much more intriguing mark on Ontario barns (Figure 9.3).[3] Many Ontario gable-roofed barns from Bruce County through to the Rideau Lakes carry this device high up in the gable end, sawn into the siding.

Singles predominate, but groups of two or three are found in Bruce and Hastings counties; dated examples range from 1858 to 1904. Farming people call them pigeon holes, and some believe the shape to be heraldic. Could it be the symbol of a farm organization or religious group? The diamond cross is not functional, other than to let air pass. It is too widespread to be a local builder's trademark. It is found, among other places, in British Columbia, on sixteenth-century barns in Andalusia, and on Chinese ceramics several thousand years old. Though not as generic as a square or circle, it is more universal than one might initially suppose. The diamond cross remains one of Ontario's mysteries.

The simple wheat barn

The most rudimentary barn is a single log cribwork, five or six metres on a side, standing on four cornerstones or on the bare ground, flexing with the frost.[4] It has a simple gable roof, and the gable ends are filled with vertical boards; there is one entryway. A great many buildings of this type continue standing one hundred and fifty years or more after construction, testimony to the solid materials as much as to careful maintenance. A few log barns will hang on indefinitely on moribund farms along the fringe of the Precambrian Shield, where land improvement ceased after a few hard years and rebuilding never occurred.

Some log cribs may be the remains of a building that was once three times the size. The full barn consisted of a pair of cribs set apart by a passage hung with doors at each end and spanned by a gable roof (Figure 9.4). A central drive floor five metres in breadth between the cribs is wide enough for a yoke of oxen and wagon to pass through. This is a consistent dimension for Ontario barns of all ages, and the barn door may be used as a scale for rough measurements in the field. A log barn five metres by fifteen is a common shape and size. It contrasts with later, squarer barns.

Construction of the first barn on a lot was probably related to an individual's entry into the export wheat trade. Log building was cheap – £5, as compared to £50 for a framed barn, by one estimate[5] – and the stout walls, properly chinked, could easily withstand the force of a heavy stack of grain. Log cribs could not be expanded by small steps as production grew, however, and framed structures were destined to take over. Framed barns were appearing among log houses along the Lake Ontario front as early as the 1830s.[6]

The timber-framed, three-bay (or English) barn, gable-roofed and sheathed in vertical pine boards, and entered along the long side, is one of Ontario's most common buildings (Figure 9.5). Four bents, each eleven to thirteen metres in length and set five to six metres apart, define three chambers, or

Figure 9.4 EXPEDIENT BARN. In 1903, after a new house was built, a log barn was moved from an adjacent farm to join with the old log house to make a new barn. The face of the original house shows in the bottom six logs of the right-hand crib. Douro Township, Peterborough County.

bays. The middle one is the drive floor, onto which wagons can be drawn through large doors. On either side are two levels for storage. Such three-bay barns, thirteen metres by fifteen, are six times the size of a basic log crib and are unencumbered by internal walls. Bays from four to six metres wide could be added simply by erecting more bents, securing each with new beams and an extension to the plate (the eaves-line beam), and moving the cladding outward to enclose the space created. The drive floor was sufficiently wide for a span of oxen or horses and has set the dimensions for tractors.[7] Lean-tos gave further opportunity for crosswise extension.

Five bays – two on each side of a central drive floor – is as wide as Ontario barns normally have grown, and the ratio of breadth to depth has been no more than two to one. This layout allowed a through draft for winnowing – a manual process of separating grain from the chaff that survived until field threshers (combines) and fanning mills (small blowers used inside the barn) became available in the last third of the nineteenth century.[8] Thereafter, a squarer building, or one with irregular extensions, was not a drawback. Practical matters induced symmetrical barns when symmetry was in fashion and did not inhibit irregularity at the time of the picturesque and gothic movements. We will never know whether barn design reinforced current fashion by chance, or if sensible farming procedures validated the current acceptance of oddly shaped buildings.

Barns provided temporary storage for cash crops headed to large, central

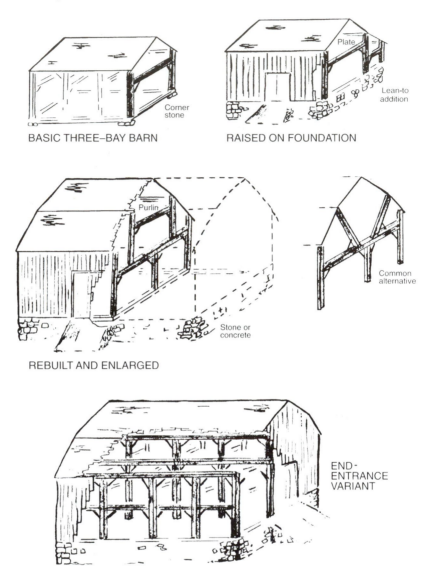

BASIC THREE–BAY BARN   RAISED ON FOUNDATION

REBUILT AND ENLARGED

Figure 9.5 EVOLUTION OF THE FRAME BARN.

warehouses and commercial mills in the pre-Confederation era. They filled up with wheat late each summer and were emptied out each fall and winter at a rate depending on market conditions. Barns on farms existed more or less by default, for grain prices were so volatile that the big traders did not wish to claim ownership for a moment longer than necessary. The system caused the goods to be kept back in the hands of each farmer until the optimum moment for sale.[9] Fortunately, wheat is relatively hardy and, as long as vermin could be controlled, did not require specialized storage space. Barns might not even have come into being at all if marketing conditions had been different.

Expansion

The fundamental change of the mixed-farm era was the insertion of stables beneath timber-frame English barns (Figure 9.5). Pry up the barn, build the wall beneath it, pour a cement floor, and set the building down. Contrary to the modesty shown in dating superstructures, foundations frequently are etched with a date. I know of one instance – 1874 – beside a stable doorway in Toronto Township. That date is consistent with what we know of the timing and circumstances of raising barns.

Most existing farms in the 1870s would have had small stables, probably log, for oxen or horses, and other little structures such as smoke-houses or root-cellars. All had earth floors. But nothing resembled the open stalls needed to house a herd of cattle during the four or five months each year when pasturing was not possible. In a raised barn, feed was stored in the overhead mows at harvest time and then forked down to the livestock in the stable below in winter. Thousands of raised barns were built. Thousands more obsolete wheat barns were jacked up in place and had stone basements built beneath.

The decision to lift a barn sent woodsmen back into the bush to cut the biggest trunks still available, for use as joists bearing the new floor above the stable. Sawmills cut two-by-tens, or trued up logs salvaged from the crude log pens that the stables superseded. Elm and tamarack were used in addition to pine, and smaller pieces made flooring. Cement pillars were inserted in the bigger stables to help take the load, and the joists were notched into the timber sills resting on top of the foundation wall.

Raised barns have entrances at two levels – to the stable at ground level and to the drive floor one storey above. The most expedient way of achieving access is by digging the stable into a slope, which acts as a ramp to the upper level. We speak of banked barns, and the rolling Ontario terrain has provided numerous sites for them. In flat places, farmers built earth ramps, frequently with a root cellar beneath.[10] A free-standing ramp, with a tiny bridge to the drive floor, prevents the foundation wall from being pushed over. Long after a barn and foundation have been removed, these ramps may survive as faint signals of the enterprise once centred on that spot.

A good many raised and/or banked barns in the Grand River region have a forebay, or overhang, along one of the eaves sides (Figure 9.6). The forebay was popular in colonial Pennsylvania and was transferred into the Waterloo

Figure 9.6 FOREBAY BARN. Lighweight construction beneath the overhanging portion indicates that the floor-joists are cantilevered out, supporting the superstructure. A ramp to the drive floor rises on the far side. Logan Township, Huron County. See also Figure 12.7.

region and beyond after 1830. From the overhang feed is dropped into a sheltered feedlot outside, instead of into mangers inside. It is an efficient arrangement for mixed farming, but farmers specializing in field crops late in the twentieth century have found the forebay unnecessary. Some forebays have been enclosed for storing machinery, reasserting the more familiar, full-foundation configuration.

The builders of barn foundations once again reveal Ontario resourcefulness in the post-pioneering age. 'Them stones there in that corner they came out of the fireplace of the other [1850] house up yonder.'[11] So reported a long-time resident of Medonte on his barn's foundation wall and, incidentally, on the replacement of open fires with wood stoves. Stone was also culled directly from fields being cleared, and a great many more Ontario barn foundations are made from flat riverstones (Figure 3.4). Walls are one-third to a half-metre thick, totalling more than one hundred linear metres in the larger barns. The introduction of poured cement, and then concrete blocks after 1900, rendered stone once again an unwanted byproduct of farm making.

Between the 1860s and 1890s, a few dozen full stone barns were built in Ontario. Stone construction inhibits expansion and is often combined with wood. Load-bearing walls act as bent-posts. The concentration of these ponderous buildings astride the Niagara Escarpment gives them considerable visibility in local areas – Nassagaweya Township, for instance. Limestone predominates, with granites worked in. Instead of having bents, the walls carry the timber plates and rafters to support the wooden roof. Narrow slits, seven to ten centimetres wide on the outside and flaring to about forty-five centimetres on the inside, allow air circulation without being draughty. Stone barns are handsome but not overly practical. They could be made to any dimension but are not adaptable. Too few were built to effect any appreciable saving in timber.

Some of Ontario's grandest barns are crowned with handsomely louvred cupolas. These are the outward expressions of a system for removing foul air from stables by 'natural forces.'[12] Other components are hinged windows in the basement stable and a boxed tube, about a metre on a side, extending vertically down from each ventilator to the stable ceiling. Temperature differences between the warm air of the stable filled with animals and the cooler air outside cause convection currents that draw fresh air in through the basement windows and force the warm air up the shafts and out the roof.[13] A valve in the ventilator prevents reverse draughts.

Rooftop ventilators are yet another expression of mixed farming and date from the beginning of stabling in the 1860s. Trade catalogues were very keen about layouts promoting air circulation and are helpful in identifying and dating vent types with precision.[14] With the introduction of electricity to rural areas between 1920 and 1950, fans came into use. Interior shafts and rooftop cupolas disappeared, except in Waterloo County, where they are instant indicators of unelectrified Amish farms.

Consolidation and enlargement

In the Ontario style of growth by small steps, farms sprouted gaggles of little buildings (Figure 9.7). These may have made sense individually, but the cumulations became more and more incoherent as modernization proceeded. One editor observed, in 1881, that 'in constructing farm buildings, the error is usually on the side of too small structures, as the thousands of leanto sheds, ``annex'' stables, and hay stacks, etc, through the country testify to.'[15] For a good many years before that, the farm press in Ontario had been urging farmers to consolidate their small buildings into orderly clusters.[16]

The Ontario Agricultural College, founded in Guelph in 1874, took the lead in disseminating ideas and literature on barn design. Researchers encouraged farmers to erect entirely new, large barns, laid out for the efficient flow of livestock, feed, and air (Figure 9.5). Basement stables were evidence that thoughtful rebuilding was a sounder activity than clustering. By 1880 there began to appear raised barns of more than twenty-five metres length and thirteen in breadth. This was the maximum width of a self-supporting roof and set a practical upper limit for the size of barns.[17]

Figure 9.7 INCREMENTAL GROWTH. In this quadrangle of small barns, feed filled one, straw another, animals a third, and machines yet another. Trafalgar Township, Halton County.

The biggest of this new generation of consolidated barns have more than ten times the volume capacity of those English barns they replaced. They were well suited to storing large quantities of loose feed and livestock bedding then in demand. Many, as in the Flesherton area, have double-width drive floors, permitting a team and wagon to turn around inside. With roof pitch at least as steep as their smaller predecessors, these big barns soar to heights of ten metres or more. They reasserted the vertical dimension slowly being eroded by decades of low, shed-like additions spreading outward from the many little barns. So much had changed by the era of the First World War that one could properly speak of 'old-fashioned barns of 25 years ago' and agree with the adviser who wrote that 'the building or remodelling of your barn is one of the most important events of your lifetime.'[18]

Rebuilt barns reused the materials of the barns they replaced. The barn in Figure 2.4 was built – 'assembled' is perhaps a better word – with parts salvaged from three small, gable barns.[19] Recycling was the obvious procedure. There were no bulldozers, and burning was wasteful and dangerous. The site could be used again, with parts ready for reuse. The safe and sensible way to remove a framed building was to strip off the siding and dismantle the roof and frame, peg by peg and piece by piece.

Recycling shows. The timbers in Figure 2.4 have open notches and slots in them, and others have rows of rusty nail stains. In some barns the rafters are too short and are overlapped and braced. Bents may not match. Those on the end walls are particularly likely to be a mixture of small pieces left over, placed there, where large openings would not be needed. But the finished product was what counted. Lean-tos and the old log house–turned-piggery vanished into a single building that heralded its owner's achievements. The symmetry of the big barn rebuffed the chaotic clutter that had accumulated and swept aside evidence of the halting progress of earlier decades (Figure 9.7).[20] The new barn, somber and business-like, became a solid counterpoint to the asymmetrical frivolity showing up on houses at the same time. At no moment in Ontario's history did the farm landscape look as neat as it must have about 1900.

Barn enlargement could be made to sound easy. 'In 1914 ... we split the barn to make it wider and bigger. You just split it, build it up and tie it in.'[21] The reality was trickier and called for the skills of an itinerant framer who could rearrange all the pieces into new bents. The idea was to use as many existing joints as possible. The bent, a braced H, may be pulled apart into a sideways T plus a spare post. Two sideways T pieces, overlapped at a central post, could support on top a third, unchanged bent. The result was like having a small barn perched on top of two-thirds of two other barns. Three bents became one, and three small rectangular buildings became a single, larger, squarer one.

Builders watched out for hefty pieces suitable for crossbeams more than twelve metres in length. Former plates, corner posts, and sills worked, if supported by one or more central posts rising from masonry pillars in the stable below. Sometimes a single massive timber – a 'summer beam' – was available, spanning the full breadth of the bent without support. We can only guess that summer beams came from large log buildings or were cut new from the few prehistoric trees still standing.

The gambrel effect

The new, large barns of the 1880s had roof profiles that varied from gable through slightly hipped to substantially hipped. Efficient reuse of materials suggests that the old roof should span the topmost H portion of the bent, and the side sections of the roof, adjacent to the walls, use rafters left over from the other barns. No used rafters would be long enough to reach the full length from the new eaves line to the new ridge. For this reason a widened building needs braced timbers in the roof, running from bent to bent. Purlins, as they are called (Figure 9.5), offer a new use for timbers from dismantled small barns and are further evidence of recycling.[22]

The clerestory roof (also known as the 'monitor' or 'Rhode Island' roof) involves the same structure, but the lower roof panels have a shallower slope (Figure 9.8). The clerestory is a raised section of a gabled roof that lets in more light and air than permitted by the gaps between the boards. Purlins are mandatory, and the bents may well be of the vertical-post style.

There is a popular impression that hipped roofs enclose significantly more space than do gabled ones. For instance, one author wrote that, 'in order to be able to store larger quantities of hay, the traditional pitched roof gave way to the gambrel.'[23] Certainly, if gable-roofed and gambrel-roofed barns occupy the same ground area, the gambrel must have more interior volume beneath the roof. But steepening a gable roof from thirty degrees to forty-five degrees offers similar opportunity, and even an exaggerated bulge adds only marginally to capacity (Figure 9.9). The fact that small barns practically never carry gambrel roofs suggests that farmers have long known that the way to increase volume was to merge barns, not puff out the roof. The gambrel roof on the rebuilt timber-frame barn is nothing more than the unintentional mark of a technical procedure put into effect thousands of times between 1880 and 1910.

Trusswork construction, using lumber, also produces a gambrel roof (Figure 5.5). One could save from forty to sixty per cent in material by using the truss – 'a not small item . . . when timber for building purposes has become a scarce

Figure 9.8 CLERESTORY barns. Bell's Corners, Carleton County.

Figure 9.9 GAMBREL CAPACITY. The gambrel-roofed barn has greater loft capacity because of larger floor area and higher roof ridge, not because of the gambrel shape. Flos Township, Simcoe County.

article' by 1904.[24] Trusses were slow to make inroads on Ontario's farm landscape, however, so long as the supply of reusable timbers held up. Trusswork barns were reported in Ontario before 1900,[25] and, as Beatty indicates, they promoted do-it-yourself construction. They offered other compensations, too, in an increasingly busy world: 'In cases where farmers' wives are expected to board and lodge the builders, [there is] a saving in labour and vexation of two or three weeks' unnecessary time for framing old style barns.'[26] The building bee, that great means of disseminating sameness through the vernacular landscape, was giving way to the printed manual, read quietly at home, alone. Trusswork was the accepted procedure by the 1920s, but this was well after the age of new barns in Ontario. Big truss barns are not common.

The mows

Loose hay – winter feed – is voluminous and heavy, and lifting it for storage was a new challenge for the mixed-farming era. Farmers initially forked it up to the mows from the drive floor, a back-breaking task that began to be replaced in the 1880s by pulleys. The rack-lifter is a winch mounted from adjacent bents and spanning the central drive floor of a gable-roofed barn (Figure 9.10). It slings a wagon-box, or rack, of hay up high enough for the contents to be forked across into storage. It is a simple but awkward invention, not able to

Figure 9.10 RACK-LIFTERS are common on small, gabled barns. This one, exposed during dismantling, is identified as a McConnell lifter, patented 1885 and manufactured by C.O. Armstrong, Brampton. Toronto Township, Peel County.

transfer a load horizontally. Nor could the rack-lifter raise a load more than about three metres, the height of the supporting bent. Gable roofs were not built to take such a weight. Still, for small, labour-intensive operations the rack-lifter must have been a great boon. It was widely marketed and is often seen, disused, in barns today.

A track mounted in the roof ridge proved a better solution for moving hay. Along it travelled tongs or a sling on a pulley, suspending loose or baled hay or sheaves of grain. The roof could support this lighter load, and trusses were still better, described as the 'strongest possible support' for hay forks.[27] Furthermore, the wide passage below the roof ridge of the gambrel gave ample space for the load to move. A large, hinged hay door, cut high up in the gable end of the barn, allowed farm-hands to swing clutches of hay up from the outside. It made for a cooler and less dusty job than working inside.

The end-drive barn is a logical consequence of installing the hay track (Figure 9.5). Here the drive floor has been turned to be parallel to the roof ridge. It gives the option of unloading outside or inside. End-drives are like very long, three-bay barns, and long multiple bents may be linked end to end. Transverse beams tie the two side sections together, and the roof maintains ample drainage slope. This arrangement gives shallow mows into which loose hay may be steered easily. The end-drive barn is found throughout Halton County and adjacent parts west of Toronto, on the more progressive farms of the early twentieth century.

A projecting peak, protecting the end of the track, used to be a common feature on big barns throughout Ontario, especially southwest from the Grand River. Peaks are rarely seen now, sawn off, with the unused tracks rusty. Bales of hay ride gasoline-powered, portable conveyors. Elsewhere, the hay door is nailed shut and the barn empty, and a forklift truck raises great coils of hay from the field onto a trailer for shipment to a corner of the farmyard.

Specialized spaces

Green fodder, or silage, became a part of Ontario agriculture about 1880, when farmers began to think of breeding and of diets for the new dairy herds. Silage reduces the incidence of sour hay and bad-tasting milk. Ontario's earliest silage containers were rectangular, lined bins inside barns, but a position outside reduced the chance of absorbing barn smells, and a cylinder better withstands weight and pressure. The first tower silos were built with vertical wooden tongue-and-groove staves wrapped in iron hoops or wooden cribs (Figure 9.11).[28] A silo of no more than six metres in diameter could store the product of about ten acres (four hectares) of cropland without its becoming mouldy – enough to support four or five dairy cows through the winter.[29]

Early in the twentieth century silos were built with clay tiles. Far more common are silos of poured concrete with steel reinforcing rods (Figure 5.1). These were built from before 1900 until the 1950s and are as much as twelve metres high. They are almost indestructible, and many persist in the company of steel Harvestore-brand silos or with clusters of smaller steel bins filled through inclined chutes (Figure 9.12). Haylage, or grass embalmed in white plastic bundles that look like giant marshmallows, is the latest development in farm-feed science. It is designed for the efficient release of nutrients for livestock. Together with concrete pit silos lying below grade, haylage is contributing to the declining profile of livestock farming on the landscape.

Feed corn sheds water when still in the ear and may be stored outside before being chopped and blown into the silo. Some farmers leave it in the field, hoping to take it off on a firm, dry day in February. Lattice-work corn cribs, perhaps three metres wide and endlessly long, are preferable and have demarcated the edges of barnyards throughout southwestern Ontario since the introduction of feed corn in the 1920s. Despite their rudimentary looks they are neither temporary nor inefficient, just another example of resourceful Ontarians dealing with varying seasonal demands on storage space. Alternatively, trucks carry the product away to feed mills for chopping and mixing with nutrients, then return it, bagged and labelled, to the feedlot.

Figure 9.11 WOODEN SILO. Vertical boards, bound with lapped planks. Dundela, Leeds County.

Figure 9.12 AGRIBUSINESS. Modern farm elevator and grain bins conceal a traditional barn. These are commonly seen in the vast, flat farmlands from Woodstock westward and increasingly, in the 1990s, on farms further east. Near Hickson, Oxford County.

The mark of grain storage on the Ontario landscape is now subdued. Wheat seed has a weight of more than two hundred kilograms per cubic metre – four times that of baled hay and twelve times that of loose hay.[30] It exerts a substantial outward pressure, as do oats and barley, feed for work horses. Horizontal siding is the field mark of a granary. It sheds water and repels the circulation of air and mice, impossible with vertical planks. A lining of horizontal lumber stands behind, with both walls nailed to studs to create a solid, compact bin. This is house construction, and it served horses, which are very susceptible to damp, as well as grain storage. Board and batten achieved the same purpose, as did brick, and small, free-standing barns for horses and their feed were common in Ontario prior to 1950.

Continued adaptation and decline

Thirty years of consolidation still left a great many farms in which the barns displayed the successive stages of growth. A catalogue of farms for sale across the province in 1909 lists many with several barns each.[31] Beatty Brothers remarked on the geography of barn rebuilding in the course of illustrating their 1918 book: their `expert commercial photographers from the principal cities ... prefer[red] to work in some of the big barns near their homes than to go far out into the country to take pictures of small barns.'[32] Automatic expectation of an expanding future was fading, especially on marginal land.

By the 1920s aesthetic reasons for consolidating buildings – for instance, that barns more than eleven metres long ought to be widened, to `correspond´ – made little sense.[33] Modest adaptation was preferable. Existing barns, big and small, went on sprouting lean-tos and ells, as had been the case for a century.[34] Dismantled buildings, brought over from farms perhaps a kilometre or more distant and reassembled, added to the disarray. Losses from fire or storm created misfits: barn superstructures awkwardly fitted to foundation stables with lean-tos. Cladding only partially obscures ingenious adaptations, and barns will for ever bear the scars of change.

The traditional, rectangular, all-purpose barn has been outmoded for decades, victim of changing marketing and industrial procedures.[35] Tower silos are the earliest outbuildings of distinctive shape, their scientific design chosen for a particular purpose. They are evidence that the beginning of the end for ordinary barns occurred before 1900. The prefabricated steel garage and the farm elevator are more recent expressions of labour-saving farm technology that shunned the old barn. They make running a farm less risky than was the case with the wooden barn, always susceptible to fire.

Timber-framed barns continue in use, despite the odds. In Waterloo County it is not uncommon for resourceful Mennonite farmers to dismantle a barn piecemeal, in the path of suburban development, and then, after perhaps years of storage, to re-erect it elsewhere. As farming economics and technology evolve, adaptable space will continue to be in demand. Amid the scatter of Quonset huts and steel bins, pole barns and former houses, and undatable lean-tos, timber-framed barns may well outlast their modern counterparts. One barn in York Region has found reprieve as a retirement home for pleasure horses, but such opportunities for new life for the old form are rare.

Hundreds of Ontario barns stand gaunt and empty. Crops once stored in them now are loaded directly into trucks and hauled off to cannery or mill. Vacant stone stables deteriorate from freezing and thawing, no longer controlled by the body heat of livestock housed there. Each incipient ruin offers unmatched opportunity for roadside contemplation of a barn´s technology and meaning. Concrete silos are so difficult to remove that they take on unplanned roles as memorials to vanished farms. Municipalities could do well to recognize the value of memories evoked by these, and also by ramps and foundation walls, and consider incorporating such features into open-space planning. Imaginative landscaping, incuding lilac bushes, will permit such parts to stand for generations to come as firm reminders of the agricultural base on which the province has been built.

10

Fences

Fences and gates are to farm fields what walls and doors are to a barn or mill. They contain the workspace and give access to it. Fields are deliberately open to the elements, but in other ways equivalent to the drive floor or milling room, where production occurs. Brush, tree trunks, and stumps made primitive fencing, still occasionally seen, and split rails and peeled posts were hardly more sophisticated. By the 1870s, however, baling wire was being used to bind the wooden parts together, and a generation later box wire was supplanting all wood but the posts. Slender steel bars, introduced as fenceposts after the Second World War, complete the transition from natural to synthetic material.

The principle of private landownership, and the possessiveness it fostered, ensured that fencing would flourish in southern Ontario. Fence viewers were among the first local public officials, and even before 1800 they were making their rounds, empowered to discourage trespassing.[1] In the rangelands of the Canadian West the livestock was branded; in Ontario it was the land that got marked for identification. Open space became a significant artefact.

For Catharine Parr Traill, fences signified the completion of farm making. `The field,´ she wrote, `is fenced with split timbers and the great work of clearing is finished.´[2] Not only should fences look as if they would last, they were supposed to be attractive as well. A traveller from overseas wrote that `logs laid zigzag with end resting on each other ... offend Englishmen who are used to walls and hedges.´[3] The fencing requirement for receiving land title might possibly have led to replication of an English landscape. But neither of these commentators realized that, for ordinary settlers (which they were not), the fence was largely irrelevant to the farm-making age in Ontario. The pig or cow ran loose in the summer and was slaughtered at the end of the scavenging season in November; it needed no fence.

Try as one might to argue that long piles of brush or boulders were fences, they were really no more than the residue of land clearing. Still, the very act of piling stones created a resource where none had previously existed. Many a field heap and stone wall has been fed into a lime kiln for making lime mortar. Others contributed to basement walls. Stone-crushing machines, coming into use late in the nineteenth century, demonstrated that field piles were a repository of road-building material.[4] They have often served this purpose, particularly since the 1920s.

Tree limbs and rocks strung out in a line were good neither at preventing trespass nor at giving crisp definition to a boundary (Figure 10.1). They wasted precious cleared land and were a base from which weeds might recolonize adjacent fields. They were virtually immovable, and it was too bad if they ended up in the wrong place as clearing spread. Such straggly heaps gave pioneer Ontario much of its appearance of being a construction site, and prideful residents looked on such inadvertent fencing, like shanties, as only temporary.

Respectable-looking fences, deliberately built, began to become evident about the middle of the nineteenth century. As neighbouring occupants cleared off the full breadth of their lots, the countryside opened up and property boundaries took on importance. Samuel Strickland was sensitive to this process of coalescence and, writing in 1853, asserted that the greatest danger from fire was its potential destruction of these boundary fences.[5]

Fencing proliferated with mixed farming, both along boundaries and within farms (Figure 10.2). Every field had to be enclosed so that livestock could be moved from one to another from season to season. A farm lot of eight to ten

Figire 10.1 INADVERTENT FENCE. Poles stacked and stones strewn at the edge of a clearing are doubtful deterrents to aggressive livestock. Seymour Township, Northumberland County.

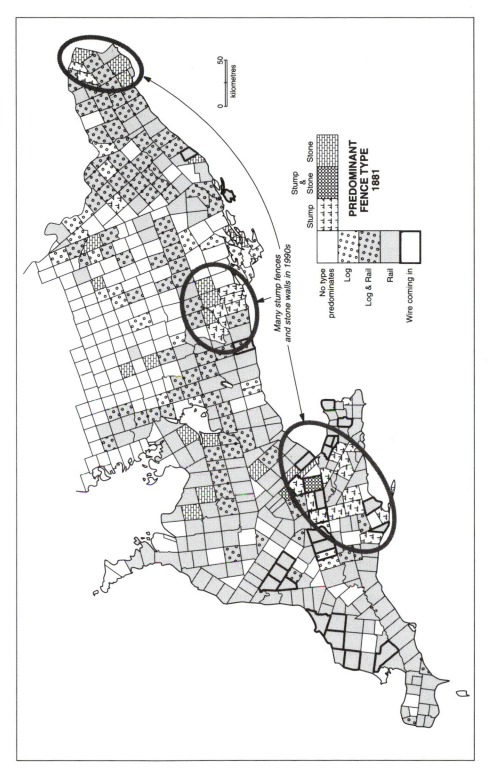

Figure 10.2 FENCE GEOGRAPHY, 1881. Compiled from *Report on Agriculture* (Toronto: Ontario Agricultural Commission, 1881), questions 16 and 17.

Many stump fences and stone walls in 1990s

PREDOMINANT FENCE TYPE 1881

Stump
Stump & Stone
Stone

No type predominates
Log
Log & Rail
Rail
Wire coming in

0   50
kilometres

fields would require two to three kilometres of fencing to enclose them. Add that much again for boundary fencing, shared with a neighbour, and the Ontario mixed farm may truly be said to have grown fences.

It is paradoxical that property boundaries are the most durable features on Ontario's landscape, yet the devices used to mark them are among the most susceptible to replacement. The sequence followed in this chapter is based on the progress in making a phenomenon fixed in one's land title into an artefact with corresponding permanence on the ground.[6]

Fence types

Planned fencing, resting on the ground

Fence types mirror the relative availability of land, labour, capital, and entrepreneurship in Ontario over the past two centuries. The earliest consciously conceived fences followed the inadvertent ones in being profligate with land but negligible consumers of the other components. The labour necessary for digging post-holes was unavailable. Instead, fences rested on the ground, with outward bracing occupying a wide swath. Here was a use for those tree limbs and rocks that were otherwise nuisances.

Split cedar rails and formal stone walls identify the beginning of a new era in the look of the Ontario landscape. One good tree trunk could yield up to eighty 12-ft (4-m) rails twenty to thirty centimetres across, capable of creating a stretch of zigzag fence longer than the height of the tree from which its parts came (Figure 10.3).[7] 'There is a good deal of ground lost in this way,' wrote one Irish emigrant, 'but land is not so valuable here as at home.'[8] Bracing with other rails or boulders took up still more space, while the angles gave niches in which elm and other trees could grow untrampled. These shaded cattle and broke up the open landscape visually.

Snake fences may be moved, a capability that ensured their popularity well into the mixed-farming era. The farmer who noted in his diary that he had 'been moving fence' thought this not at all unusual.[9] Portable fences demonstrate the mutability of a developing land adjusting to new technological and economic conditions and helped prevent farms from becoming obsolete.

As pressure grew to cultivate every fragment of farmable land, more and more farmers saw the potential of the unused area along their snake-rail fences. Building straight rail fences in their place added two or three furrows to the field, and one-quarter of the rails were left over (Figure 10.4). Some that had been embedded on the ground may have been unusable, and others were needed for bracing the replacement fence, but many more surely found their way into entirely new fences bordering the small fields characteristic of the mixed farm. Construction and reconstruction of fencing were labour-intensive

Figure 10.3 SNAKE-RAIL FENCE cuts a wide swath. The transparency of wire promotes openness, contrasting with the opaque panels of split-cedar rails. Near Singhampton, Grey County.

tasks and constituted one of the reasons for the era of hired farm-hands in late Victorian Ontario.

Straight rail fences 'occupy less ground, are much stronger, more durable, and less ugly' than the snake.[10] They are the style of the progressive farmer, anxious to slough off the old, makeshift ways for something more becoming. Snake-rail fences were for those who could not keep up. They survive along the Shield fringe, where modern farming never firmly took hold and pressure on the land has remained low. Today, such areas are appealing to city folks looking for country retreats, and the snake fence has regained favour as a picturesque selling point.

Stump fences look like the oldest of all types (Figure 10.5). There is something primordial about uprooted trees, but in truth stump fences are not as old as split-rail ones. The rot-free characteristic of white pine applies to the root, too. A resurvey of Esquesing Township lands in 1883, sixty-four years after the original lines were run, speaks of 'stumps that still remain, as many of the trees marked were pine and of a lasting nature.'[11] By comparison, hardwood roots rotted within ten years.

Pioneering farmers could postpone the difficult task of pulling out stumps as long as hand-cultivation techniques were in use. But once machines began

Figure 10.4 POST-AND-RAIL FENCE marks a transition from wide and portable to narrow and fixed. The straggly stones once supported a snake fence, leaving the actual boundary line unclear. Puslinch Township, Wellington County.

Figure 10.5 STUMP FENCE. The grotesque shapes of dried roots, writhing in the air, are darkly gothic, but stump fences are not the oldest in Ontario. This one was probably combined with shrubbery and debris recently removed. Blandford Township, Oxford County.

taking over, after 1850, old pine stumps were liabilities. Fifteen or more of them could clutter a hectare of cleared land. Extracted stumps decay even more slowly than those in the ground, and pine well over a century old continues as fencing today. Stump fences are the non-portable byproducts of farm mechanization in the second half of the nineteenth century. Fences that were needed while clearing was under way had to be constructed from more accessible and portable materials.

The drystone wall is a rather different type of planned wide fencing. It is clearly immovable and calls on the talents of relatively skilled craftsmen (Figure 10.6). It was reported in 1856 that 'a few farmers in Caledon have built a considerable quantity of stone wall, which answers admirably, forming the most durable of all fences, and at the same time ridding the land of a troublesome incumbrance.'[12] Such walls may consist of fieldstone, river stone, quarry stone or mixtures. The intensity of workmanship varies from heaping to sorting to fitting, with corresponding durability. A stone wall should be set in a trench below the frost line, or it will gradually be thrown out of alignment. In the absence of mortar, water drains away freely and very little maintenance is needed. Field consolidation and road widening made fences of all types vulnerable following the First World War, and many stone walls were dismantled and crushed into road metal.[13] Southern Ontario's most attractive stone walls stand today on poor land, evidence that their creators were perhaps more accomplished at masonry than at farming.

The tripod fence consists of horizontal split rails supported by three poles wired at the crossing point and standing on the ground (Figure 10.7). The

Figure 10.6 DRYSTONE WALL. Glacial debris, mostly limestone, laid up in regular courses, forms a mortar-free wall. Caledon Township, Peel County.

Figure 10.7 THE TRIPOD FENCE is particularly prevalent in the Kawartha Lakes region and towards Smiths Falls. Mariposa Township, Victoria County.

lower log is suspended from another loop of wire. This style, sometimes known as the Workman fence, is a sensible response to fencing needs within the farm in the mixed-farming age. It could be picked up and repositioned again and again until a suitable arrangement of fields had been achieved. It occupies less space than earlier fence types, and its introduction coincided with rising land prices. The tripod fence uses only slightly more than half the wood of a snake-rail fence, and much of this was plundered from older fences. Baling wire was a new material on farms, readily available new or reused.

Tripod fences have been popular in areas of thin or stony soil, where digging post-holes is difficult. Today they are most commonly found in a belt running east from the Lake Huron shore through to Lake Simcoe and on to the Rideau Lakes and St Lawrence valley. They are a legacy of the mixed-farming era of small fields in a region that, for the most part, has suffered from shallow soils and has not adopted the large-scale agribusiness arrangements of the late twentieth century.

Planned fencing, set into the ground

Livestock and railways do not mix. This incompatibility induced permanent fences, mounted on posts dug more than a metre into the ground. The deaths of a good many crazed horses and cows in the 1850s, not to mention crew members and passengers in derailed trains, convinced citizens that the tracks would have to be fenced off. Railway companies were slow to take the matter seriously, however. Contractors for one line were instructed to build a snake fence 'with a worm of four feet.'[14] Such a shallow angle – more than one hundred and twenty degrees, compared with the ideal of ninety degrees – was hardly adequate, considering that the posts and braces were barely planted, if at all. It was to all intents and purposes a cheap, straight fence, destined for a short life. The Bruce County wind storm of Good Friday, 1912, flattened straight rail fences but left proper zigzag ones standing.[15]

Board fences were popular for a few years, particularly along railway lines.[16] They were a sign of the surplus sawmilling capacity created by the decline of American markets after Confederation. Boards were cheap to purchase, but expensive to maintain. Even though they were mounted on the side of the posts away from the track, animals still pushed them off the posts; nails rusted. By 1900, board fences had vanished, the seasoned planks given new life as barn siding or other products. Some turned up as silo lining, as well, 'made from fencing ripped in two.'[17]

Wire was replacing wooden rails and boards before 1860. Snake fences were cheaply secured with telegraph wire,[18] and single, barbed strands held back cattle and horses. Rows of barbed strands have been useful for crossing streams because they could be rolled back during the spring flood before the livestock were put to pasture. A cedar-rail fence might stand as an orderly structure for only six years, but its life could be extended with baling wire at little cost.[19]

It took woven wire (or box wire) mounted on posts and well anchored at the corners, however, to restrain hogs and sheep (Figure 10.8). This came into use during the 1880s and was swiftly adopted by railways.[20] From West Toronto to Norwood, `the line is fenced throughout with wire,´ according to an inspection of the Ontario and Quebec Railway in 1884.[21] By 1898, `all of the leading railroads, and most of the best farmers of this country, now use Page Coiled Spring Woven Wire Fencing.´[22] Wherever the layout of fields stabilized and property boundaries became defined to the satisfaction of the adjoining parties, permanent wire fencing became common.

Wire required less maintenance than wooden rails and took up only a quarter of the swath cut by a snake fence or rock wall. The labour invested in digging post-holes was substantial, however, and the initial and continuing cost of the material was high. Galvanized (zinc-coated) wire and staples last about thirty years; oak fence posts are good for only six to eight years, ordinary cedar posts fifteen to twenty, and treated ones up to forty.[23] Large, sap-free fence posts last longer than small sap-filled ones, but posts with sap in them can be barked more easily and the tanbark sold for cash.[24] As long as new or recycled rails were available for panels, posts, and braces, purchase of wire and seasoned posts could be delayed. Despite steady modernization, fence maintenance has continued to be as routine a matter as ploughing and harvesting.

Hawthorn bushes are found widely throughout the province in conjunction with other fences. But hedges alone have not been important for Ontario fencing. They have none of the advantages of other types. They are not portable, they take up a wide swath of land, and they are easily penetrated until well established. Hawthorns have proven to be little better than living brush heaps in a land provided with much more satisfactory fencing materials.

The landscape of fencing

Ontario by the 1920s was acquiring a new openness. Views once cut up by lines of rails became expansive, as a result of installing wire fences or of removing fences altogether. Wire fences are about as utilitarian a feature as one could imagine, and it is a source of satisfaction that, with almost any field crop as backdrop, a wire fence all but disappears from view (Figure 10.7); raindrops or an ice storm causes it to be visible again, but not for long. Fence wire casts no shade, and wire fences allow cultivation much closer to the fencing than do more opaque types. As farmers installed them, they cleaned out years of underbrush and stones, adding to the open effect. Two out of every three posts are now steel stakes. These are hammered in even more easily than drilling for wooden ones with an auger and are so slim as to be almost invisible.

Surplus rails have been recycled as stovewood foundations or used for fire-

Figure 10.8 FENCE POST. Roadside erosion exposes an eight-foot fence post, bearing remnants of boxwire fencing. The hole, taking half the post, is measured by the standard length of the shovel handle. Given Road, west of Newcastle, Durham County.

wood. In recent years, thousands more rails have been sold for suburban landscaping. It is not uncommon to come upon a stack of several hundred rails in the back of Northumberland County, say, ready for shipping to a regional garden centre. Country owners are scavenging derelict fences on the backs of their farms and setting them up as picturesque attractions along the roadsides.

Rural travellers pass along the edges of properties rather than through them, and entrances rarely are marked by more than a letterbox or a line of trees. Functioning field gates today are galvanized steel panels no more than a few years old and always fresh-looking. The overhead suspension farm gate used in the shallow soils of the Precambrian Shield is a rare instance of ordinary entrances making bold statements. Seldom, however, does one encounter truly grand gates that draw ceremonious attention to the threshold of private space. The public and private spaces in Ontario have always run together, and our visual participation in rural life beyond the roadside has been little restricted.

Parts of Ontario southwest of Woodstock today are almost without fencing, and crops are planted to the very edge of the roadway in many places. That is nothing new, for a century ago farmers in Scarborough Township showed `a disposition to do with as few fences as possible,´ and in Saltfleet Township `the fruit district fences are being removed almost entirely.´[25] Wire rusts, posts rot, fields merge, and feedlots restrain the livestock.

Having few is today´s response to the question of fences. But the issue is not likely ever to disappear. Boundary trees indicate the reluctance of owners to allow demarcation of the land to recede entirely into the land-title books. In a litigious world, handsome trees stand for domain and authority and are more than pretty decorations on the skyline. The more elemental the marker, the more enduring the fence, and the happier the neighbour.

11
Power and mills

Ontario took hold in an age of bulky, unrefined exports, most notably wheat and wood. Harvest, transport, and storage of these products created a landscape of fields, roads, and barns. Sawmills and grist mills were the landmarks, but such small parts of the broad setting as to be relatively unseen. Other specialists were no more visible. The workshop of the itinerant artisan – shoemaker, barn framer, or gravestone carver – was the set of tools carried about the countryside in his saddlebag. His skill, acquired through apprenticeship, was carried safely in his head.[1] These country specialists boarded with their customers and then moved on, leaving their products as the only evidence of their passage.

Identifiable workplaces began to appear in substantial numbers as the mixed-farming era unfolded. Many were adapted dwellings (Figure 11.1), perhaps moved, and they became larger over time. Still more looked like halls (Figure 11.2). The sensitive citizen who wrote, 'I do not like to have a traveller ask, when passing the place where I worship, is that a mill, or a barn, or a factory, or what is it?', was living in the early years, when spaces frequently lacked identity.[2] The word 'factory' crept into the terminology, supplementing 'workshop,' 'mill,' and 'manufactory' and introduced corporate enterprise into a land of family operations and simple partnerships.

Each business was facilitated by a widening range of transport, warehouse, wholesale, and retail functions. Increasingly sophisticated forms of power were being harnessed to supplement and replace human and animal effort. Mill-wheels were superseded by boilers with chimneys and then overwhelmed by poles carrying electric wires. Pipelines carry oil and natural gas. Work has left a rich trace over the landscape, and that is the subject of this chapter.

Animate power

The original Ontario landscape is handmade. The reason that wood has been of such pre-eminence is that the axe was such a simple (albeit sometimes deadly) instrument. The axe chopped trees, it squared logs, and it split shingles.

Figure 11.1 WORKSHOP HOUSE. The laboratory and office of the Ontario Portland
Cement Company, with domestic lines; c. 1905. Blue Lake, Brant County.

The axe was suited to little jobs, in the hands of little people, often quite
unskilled but filled with vision. And when it had to tackle the big jobs – cutting
through roots, or whatever – it did so by thousands of tiny bites. The human
exertion was enormous, over decades, by tens of thousands of people, all
working one by one.

The humble axe should be the most highly prized exhibit in any museum
of pioneering, but it is not. Broad-axes and adzes draw attention more readily,
perhaps because they are so obviously old-fashioned. With a succession of
new handles and new heads, great-grandfather's axe is old in spirit but not
in fact. The landscape that celebrates a storey-and-a-half house has found no
corresponding place for the tool that created it, and we easily forget. There
should be memorials for old axes, just as we erect gravestones to celebrate
the hands that used them.

So it went, through the building age. A mallet drove a peg through a timber

Figure 11.2 HALL-LIKE WORKSHOP. Carriage shops resemble halls with an active upper floor. A temporary ramp run up from the road in front gives access when needed. The upper level of this clapboard building is lined with tongue-and-groove boards that keep sawdust from billowing up from below while still admitting heat for painting and drying. Pinkerton, Bruce County.

joint; a pair of tongs turned an ox shoe in the forge; an iron bar pried a stump. Grandmother's foot pumped the treadle on a spinning-wheel; a small boy's arms ached from hours of squeezing the bellows in the blacksmith's shop. Everywhere human energy made things happen, and the artefacts of that output – human bodies – wore out and were gone. What they have left behind is not the mill, if we can speak of ourselves as mills (or pumps), but the products.

Animal power, properly supervised, supplemented human power. With a length of chain, oxen lugged heavy logs into place and hauled rocks to the edge of the field. At first they too left no greater landscape mark than their passing hoof-prints in the woods and clearings. But settlers built, by their energy, stables where these bovine sources of power could be stored and serviced. The origins of the tractor shed are obvious, in retrospect. Other buildings were put up to store the seed drills, ploughs, rakes, and harvesters that teams of oxen or horses drew about the fields. Houses housed energy, but we remember them for other reasons. Animal shelters and machine sheds are the rudimentary features of the landscape that we might comfortably associate with power.

From the start of the nineteenth century Ontario was headed for industrial capitalism. In every district individuals knew about productive processes and labour-saving machinery, even if conditions at first precluded their use. The water turbine and steam piston were proven inventions by the 1820s, for example, yet few entrepreneurs could afford boilers or large castings until domestic machine shops were set up in the 1860s and railways made shipment practical. The wind was free, but windpumps depended on the ability to drill wells before they began to become the common means of raising water (Figure 3.8). In a windswept place such as Lambton County, it was the 1890s before windpumps were used for cutting and grinding corn.[3]

Animate power would have to suffice for the time being in the pioneering community. But the constraints that it created among progressive people spurred interest in developing more substantial forms of power.

Water power

Inland Ontario is well-watered. Thousands of kilometres of small watercourses and still smaller tributaries tumble off the highlands of Dundalk, Haliburton, and Madawaska. Glacial deposits and bedrock ledges have discouraged their use for transport but have provided superb conditions for the widespread, almost limitless generation of water-power.[4]

From the beginning of settlement, land surveyors were instructed to record in their journals potential water-power mill sites.[5] Legislation encouraged skilled artisans and mechanics to occupy these places and to develop their sawing, grinding, and other talents for a waiting community.[6] The result has been a landscape sprinkled with dams in industrial ravines traversed by low-level bridges. Where necessary, given (that is, non-survey) roads connected mills with the survey grid.

As soon as any one site was harnessed, it diminished the utility of adjacent ones. Millponds stretched back hundreds of metres, drowning other sites further upstream. A river such as the Ganaraska could have been developed in more than twenty places in its eighty-kilometre course to Lake Ontario at Port Hope, but only about eight sites were brought into use. The South Saugeen, between Mount Forest and Southampton, has had eleven mill sites in 320 m of drop (Figure 11.3).

A good vertical drop gave no assurance of success. As one land surveyor reported in 1863, 'the stream is very small, there only being power enough with a twenty feet overshot wheel to drive a single shingle machine for about six hours out of twenty-four for three or four months in the year in Spring and Fall seasons. I should not consider the mill privilege of any value.'[7]

The earliest mill-wheels were called 'undershots' and consisted of simple vanes against which a freely flowing stream slapped as it passed beneath. The power of the rotating axle passed through rudimentary gearing to the saw or millstones. Artificial channels were unnecessary for the steady flows of a forested watershed.

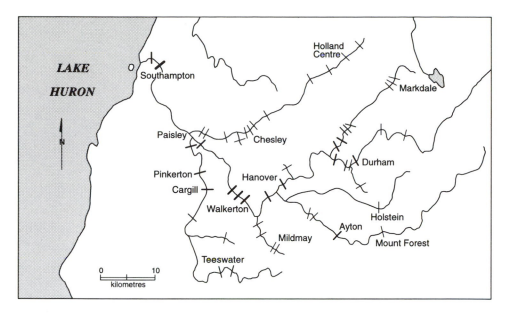

Figure 11.3 MILL SITES, Saugeen River basin, Bruce County, 1925. The heavier the line, the bigger the installation. Compiled from *Water Powers in Ontario* (Toronto: Ontario Department of Lands and Forests, 1925).

Clearing off trees changed all that, however, for it reduced the water-storage capacity of the soil, which led to wide fluctuations in run-off throughout the year. If a drought did not leave the wheel high and dry, a flood might carry it off, and perhaps the mill with it. Others just faded away as a result of changed conditions, often within a few years of first settlement. Nature rapidly reclaimed such rudimentary sites, and they are impossible to recognize today.

Settlers responded with artificial structures, and the utility of river mill sites steadily improved during the nineteenth century. A dam was the central element. It was built like a railway embankment by putting up a scaffold `to serve as a track on which to wheel the dirt out'[8] and filling it with logs and brush packed with clay. Southern Ontario's dams are generally low and wide, backing up one or more hectares of water in the typically shallow valleys. The reservoir pond behind the dam evened out the irregularity of flow in the natural stream.

Water `on the dam' transferred control of the power supply from nature to the miller. Directing the water through an elevated flume to the mill-wheel could turn as much as three-quarters of the river's flowing energy into mechanical energy, compared with less than one-quarter where no millpond was involved.[9] Overshot, breast, and poncelet wheels had horizontal axles and could be more than five metres in diameter. All worked on the principle of water being poured onto the wheel, where it collected in little buckets, thus rotating the wheel by weight and gravity. The water spilled out into an exit channel at the bottom, and the empty buckets returned on the upward portion of the circuit until positioned again for refilling.

As little as three metres of falling water was adequate for a commercial installation. Wide wheels were more powerful than narrow ones, and the shorter the radius the greater the torque.[10] The turbine, introduced after 1850, was more efficient still (Figure 11.4). It has a vertical shaft, with inclined vanes that are pushed sideways by the weight of water falling through. Turbines may use even smaller heads of water than open wheels and are more efficient still, making previously unused sites developable.

Water-wheels and turbines fed through a flume could be started or stopped at will, simply by opening or closing water gates. Turbines were enclosed and warmed by heat from the mill, eliminating ice problems associated with outside wheels. Water stored behind the dam could be drawn off beneath the ice, stretching the work season into the sleighing period – the best time for hauling grain or logs overland.

The flume could be routed anywhere in the valley, permitting the entrepreneur to separate the workplace from the power site. Mills took up sure-footed positions above the floodplain, freed from the damps and alleged noxious airs of the bottoms and from the threat of flooding. Scots liked long mill-races leading to mills well off the stream, whereas millers from the United States preferred mills on top of the dam, fed by short races; Ontario, so often a

Figure 11.4 TURBINE, with shaft and gearing, displayed at a former mill site in the Saugeen valley. Lockerby, Bruce County.

compromise, has had both.[11] Bigger mills frequently replaced the open channel with an iron pipe and sometimes, as at Walter's Falls in Bruce County, erected a standpipe to assure a strong head of water when starting up.

The discharge channel, on the downstream side of the mill, returns used water to the main stream. If the gradient permits, the outflow may be directed immediately to another mill at a lower elevation. Spencer Creek, cascading through Crook's Hollow in the Niagara Escarpment above Dundas, offered a succession of opportunities using the same water. All hydraulic systems also included an overflow channel from the millpond, controlled by stoplogs that could be hastily removed in the event of a freshet. Flood energy cumulates downstream, and any chance to send excess water off from the main channel until the crest had passed could spare mills further down from possible damage. Every Ontario mill seat has been tested by floodwaters, and repair and recovery were part of most millers' lives well into the twentieth century.

Small, water-powered sites are irrelevant today, and each spring run-off carries away a bit more of Ontario's industrial history. After 1945, conservation authorities accelerated the decline by pulling down disused dams and foundations and installing flood-control structures. The best-preserved sites occur near the heads of watersheds along lanes long overgrown and are known only to anglers. There flooding has been less destructive than further downstream. Long ago the limited waterflow in such places committed millers to family-scale business. A few mills still look much as they did more than a century ago, and a tiny handful in Grey and Bruce counties continue to run on water.

Country industry

Country sawmills are rare today, their role in establishing the wooden landscape being long gone. They have commonly been artless wooden sheds overhanging a stream and displaying a degree of impermanence consistent with their function. The long, low silhouette defined the carriage on which the logs rode through the saws. The simplest of mechanisms was used to transfer the torque of a water-wheel to a vertical saw and later to one or more circular saw blades. Large openings let logs in and planks out. Sawdust fell through and washed away, becoming someone else's problem downstream.[12]

Sawmilling made the massive timber-framing technique obsolete. The rough boards fed huge pioneer markets for joists, flooring, siding, lath, rafters, and shingles, but maturing communities demanded finished wood products. Planing mills and sash-and-door works began to appear in the 1850s, using specialized machinery to produce window-frames, tongue-and-groove flooring, staircases, turned balustrades or porch posts, and all the gingerbread trim for which high Victorian Ontario is known. Cabinetry followed, undertaken in a factory.

Portable sawmills have always been poorly acknowledged fragments of the built environment. Driven by up to eight horses or by steam, these could follow the timber supply far away from the watercourses. Wherever the wave of pioneer construction passed, surplus sawmills were dismantled and the machinery was used to start the process over again further out, on the edge of settlement. They were part of the decline of river-bottom industry and hastened the era when balloon framing would prevail over timber.[13] Gasoline-powered mills may still be found doing this kind of itinerant job.

The custom grist mill was the other main industrial building of the settlement era. It was the successor to the household mortar-and-pestle for meeting domestic needs and still highly labour-intensive. A pair of granite grindstones crushed the seeds, producing a flour embedded with shell fragments and difficult to separate into grades.[14] It was all the country miller could do to lug bags of grain up the stairs into the attic of a storey-and-a half building, pour it down through the stones, bag the grindings in the cellar, and heave the eighty-kilogram sacks back to the main floor (Figure 5.6). Custom grist mills often have a decidedly domestic look, and some millers even lived there. Datable details are scarce and most likely to be found in doorways and eaves, mimicking the architecture of vernacular housing.

Commercial manufactories

Blacksmiths, gristmillers, sawyers, and other country craftsmen all dreamed of the day they would be prosperous factory owners. Sawyers wanted lathes and moulding machines. Millers eyed sifters, driers, and the new porcelain roller machines that began replacing granite grindstones in the 1870s.[15] Blacksmiths coveted trip-hammers and rolling mills. Weavers wanted looms and carding and fulling machines. Each would have products moving among many workstations.

Lineshafting, a system of transmitting power by belts and pulleys, was the technology that made such dreams possible (Figure 11.5).[16] After conversion of water-power into mechanical motion, the energy could be carried about one hundred metres horizontally and five or six storeys vertically.[17] Lineshafting broke the drudgery of such manual routines as cranking and chopping. Conveyors replaced the tedium of lifting and pulling. In conjunction with more efficient water-wheels, lineshafting increased the number of machines at any one mill site from two or three saws or pairs of grindstones to as many as twenty distinct operations. Not all the machines might run at once, but the efficiency with which they could be cut in or out marked a breakthrough in industrial organization.

Flour millers put up buildings as tall as four-and-one-half storeys, the maximum without steel framing. Height was essential, for the repeated sifting and sorting necessary to produce a variety of grades of flour were performed by gravity flow, from the top of the mill to the basement (Figure 11.6). Little

Shafting and Iron Work

Our facilities for manufacturing Pulleys, Shafting, Couplings, Hangers, and other iron work are unsurpassed in this country, and our patterns are numerous and varied. All Shafting made by us is turned and finished perfectly straight and to a standard size.

We use only the best and finest qualities of iron and steel.

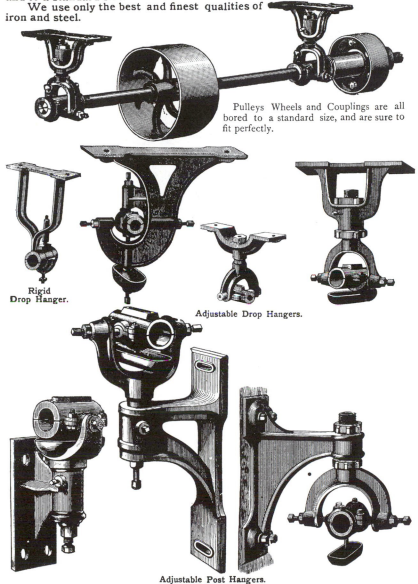

Pulleys Wheels and Couplings are all bored to a standard size, and are sure to fit perfectly.

Rigid
Drop Hanger.

Adjustable Drop Hangers.

Adjustable Post Hangers.

Figure 11.5 LINESHAFTING. In the years before electricity, power was transmitted mechanically through gears, shafts, pulleys, and belts. Display of fittings in W. and J.G. Greey, *Toronto Mill Furnishing Works: Illustrated General Catalogue of Mill Machinery and Supplies* (Toronto, 1888), 182.

Figure 11.6 VERTICAL TECHNOLOGY. Mills are tall in order to move flour first raised by elevator through the various operations by gravity. The granary, on the right, worked on the same principle. Elevator bins are lined on the insides of the posts, to prevent boards being sprung off. Stark's Mill, Paisley, Bruce County.

tin cups hooked to a continuous cloth belt revolving in a vertical wooden tube mechanically lifted seed or milled flour, which was sorted into tall bins by a swivelled spout. Moving also cooled it and prevented the bolting (sifting) cloths from clogging.[18] Heavy framing was needed for these buildings to withstand the relentless vibrations. It also permitted large window openings for light and for dissipating the heat generated in milling.

Local milling pushed the capabilities of water-power to the limit. Along the Mississippi River and its powerful tributaries an exceptional number of textile mill towns rose late in the nineteenth century: Lanark, Innisville, Carleton Place, Appleton, Almonte, Pakenham, and Galetta. They constituted one of Canada's principal industrial districts, and only gradually were they super-seded by huge mills in, particularly, Cornwall. Milling complexes also developed around the biggest water-power sites along the Grand River, anchored by labour and capital pools available in places such as Berlin (Kitchener), Hespeler, Preston, and Brantford.

When Ontario's wheat production declined after Confederation, dozens of small commercial mills throughout the province gradually switched to grinding prairie grain. Through the early years of the twentieth century, family

Figure 11.7 MILL RUIN. Straight-furrowed grindstones serve as doorstep to an abandoned country mill. Percy Creek, near Warkworth, Northumberland County.

operations such as Stark Brothers of Paisley and the McClures of Chesley, in Bruce County, received grain shipped through Fort William by water to Owen Sound and thence by rail to their mills.[19] After grinding, the flour went by rail to Montreal or Saint John for shipping overseas. From the Lake Huron shore through to east of Lake Simcoe, dozens of mills engaged in this 'foreign' business. A few of the sturdy timber bins still stand, but in the undulating Ontario countryside they lack the visual impact of their prairie counterparts (Figure 11.6).

All but a few very large commercial mill buildings have become obsolete. Some were doomed by water-flow problems, many more by failing to innovate. Here and there mills have reverted to regional needs for livestock feed. Others have been reused as warehouses and space for other industries. Odd ones, standing alone in country ravines, are now dwellings, restaurants, antique shops, and fashionable country inns (Figure 5.12). In the past sixty years it has not been unusual for a miller simply to close down and walk away from a dying business, leaving the machinery intact. Such was the case with the Starks of Paisley, for instance. Mills fade away only with reluctance, and their ruins add charm to the landscape (Figure 11.7).

Steam power

Industrial might was outstripping the capabilities of Ontario's streams by the Confederation era. The land of little watercourses had served well a small-scale, pioneering society strapped for capital. Wheat could always be exported unmilled, as it so often had been, for want of refining capacity. But basic to national industrialization was the ability to break away from the export of unrefined staples and do the refining at home. Water alone could not handle the desired expansion.

Steam power was a logical supplement. As far back as 1824, before there was a mile of steam railway anywhere in North America, the machinery from a Lake Ontario steamboat was being removed in the winter and used to run a sawmill.[20] The technology was simple: steam fed into a piston connected by a crank to a fly-wheel. That fly-wheel provided the torque in the same way a water-wheel did and could be connected directly to existing lineshafting or pieces of machinery.

It is not unusual, then, that the brick chimney, landmark of steam, may often be found at water-power sites (Figure 11.8). The mill at Upper Canada Village, for example, combines the two forms of power. For the risk-taking entrepreneur, steam allowed for expansion beyond the capability of the stream. The conservative miller installed steam to maintain output when the water supply in the pond became too low, as it frequently did. Scrap wood fuel for the boiler was cheap, and, as much as possible, the water-wheel performed at still less cost when the river flow permitted. Steam breathed continuing life into many existing water-power sites.

Steam allowed industrialists to break free from water-power sites altogether. Some were enterprising farmers, living on the high ground far from the river valleys, who took up manufacturing to complement the yearly round of activities (Figure 11.9). The lakeport grain elevator is another example, first commercially applied in Buffalo late in the 1840s.[21] Steam power was essential, because of both the volume of cargo and the absence of water-power sites at river mouths, and could be added on almost without limit. Witness the regiments of poured concrete silos in Goderich, Depot Harbour, or Toronto. They endure in such unlikely uses as artists' boutiques at St Jacobs and are as indestructible as their solitary mates down on the farm.

Steam power could also be mobilized, as the railway locomotive so obviously demonstrates. The first farm steam-engines of the 1860s were intended only as portable industrial power, not replacements for draught animals. They were towed to the field by teams that also hauled wagonloads of cut or threshed grain back to the barn and drew the firewood to stoke the firebox. By 1890, however, self-propelled models had been introduced, and over the next half-century they were followed by kerosene, gasoline, and diesel tractors.[22] These retired the horse and that building now rarely seen in southern Ontario – the brick horse-barn. The tractor has given the farm movable inan-

Figure 11.8 INERTIA. Water-power sites persisted as industrial focal points into the ages of steam and electrical power. Elora, on the Grand River, Wellington County.

imate power, essential to maintaining the dispersed rural landscape.

By the 1880s, major industries – foundries and machine shops, agricultural implements, textiles, paper making, and flour milling – were gravitating to the lower reaches of rivers. There the discharge was greatest, and firms shared dams and welcomed municipal bonuses for basic works.[23] But the inadequacy of water-power was obvious, and steam, generated from wood, and increasingly after the 1870s from coal, supplemented and gradually displaced water. Steam power was attractive first in the flatter, more westerly parts of the province

Figure 11.9 `FOGORIG,´ a farm-wagon works, powered by steam, 1867. Seymour Township, Northumberland County.

and accelerated the depletion of forest there. The Hamilton Pumping Station is exemplary of Ontario´s steam era (Figure 11.10).[24]

Steam stimulated industrial growth in Hamilton, Toronto, the lakeshore towns east towards Kingston, along the Welland Canal, and in the Ottawa and Grand river valleys.[25] Big factories frequently bore Italianate and other vertically oriented, high-art embellishments of urbanization (Figure 11.11). Tall brick chimneys challenged church spires for symbolic attention.[26] `Berlin [Kitchener] is a town of smokestacks . . . [and] . . . smoke which no matter where the wind is, floats over the houses.´[27] Heat was a useful byproduct, both in production – for warping parts of furniture, for example – and for the comfort of workers on the shop floor or in the office. Heat was the main product for dozens of greenhouses in the Kingsville area, each cluster with its little brick boiler house and squat chimney (Figure 11.12). Slabs of wood from sawmills fuelled many fireboxes and brought to an end plank-on-plank house construction.

Some steam mills modernized by converting to gasoline or diesel generators, as did water mills. Every such move after the 1890s carried one away from the mainstream of technological change, however. Water, steam, gasoline, and diesel each retained the commitment to lineshafting. Electricity was making that form of transmission obsolete, and even the most efficiently powered lineshafting system could not compete. Those who undertook partial mod-

Figure 11.10 HAMILTON PUMPING STATION. Pump-house, engine-house, wood-house, and chimney comprise an indusrial site remote from water. From 1859 to 1928 the steam-engine pumped Lake Ontario water through an eight-kilometre iron pipe to a reservoir atop 'The Mountain.' The engine survived scrap-metal purges of the Second World War and runs again as a technological display.

Figure 11.11 FACTORY AS LANDMARK. Vertical building lines suited the use of Italianate and Second Empire motifs. Textile mill, steam powered (1873). Port Dalhousie, Lincoln County.

Figure 11.12 HOTHOUSE farming. Seacliffe, Essex County.

ernization set themselves on a downward course, slowly and gently, towards oblivion. The principal beneficiaries of this process are landscape observers such as we. Failure to modernize offers rare opportunities to witness a technology several generations out of date.

Electricity

In 1828, the English traveller F.H. Baddeley found his way to the industrial heartland of Upper Canada: Marmora.[28] There, deep in the Hastings County forest, he found two large furnaces for smelting local iron ore. Two hammer-forges and a casting house could refine the output, relying on wood cut in the surrounding forest for fuel or charcoal. A potashery consumed the brush, and a tannery used the excess heat. A grist mill and sawmill could draw power from two flumes; there were twelve water-wheels in all. Storehouses, stables, a blacksmith's shop, a provision store, a counting house, and much more added to this self-sufficient industrial site. Marmora was a ghost town, however, even at that early date. Only three houses stood where barely a few years before two hundred people had lived.

Marmora fell victim to the limitations of transmission. Neither water-power nor steam power could be carried more than a few hundred metres from where it was generated. Without railways, the raw and refined materials faced arduous overland journeys between mine and market. From its earliest years, Ontario's industry was abreast of the world's technology but had trouble competing. Vestiges of Marmora still visible in the undergrowth are reminders of the transformation of the landscape made possible by more than a century of the changing technology of power and its transmission.

Transmission

During the 1880s, inventors discovered that the familiar water turbine, if properly wound with copper wire and rotated (by water or steam) within a casing, could produce electricity.[29] The energy from this generator could be sent through steel or copper wires and a motor connected at the other end to reverse the procedure and produce mechanical motion in a machine. The pedigree of the watermill is obvious.

Electricity freed users from locating their industries at water-power or steam-powered sites. One could of course electrify an existing lineshafting mill with a few metres of wire and a motor for each machine, and many industrialists did. But that approach failed to exploit a distinctive feature of electricity: its transmissibility. The range of electric power was measured in kilometres, not metres.

Electrical power could also be assigned to the tiniest jobs. This capability set the stage for Edison's patented electric light bulb to provide cheap, safe lighting in every household and business in the province. For most of its history, Ontario had been a daytime society, with scant need for illumination. Farming and farm making coincided with the long-light season; those making winter deliveries of wheat to the lakefront relied on the reflected light of stars and moon, if need be. Lighting took on importance, however, with mixed farming. Cows had to be milked and fed at night, and more and more farm activities had to be performed in the dark seasons.

Poles and overhead wires were spreading out along the country roads by 1900. Power from the Credit River at Cataract lit up Erin township by 1909, for example, well before many Toronto households had the same opportunity. Niagara power began to be used in Toronto in 1906, and office workers on fixed, long hours – 8 a.m. to 6 p.m. was common for years – were among the first to benefit. Commuters had been riding electric streetcars since the 1890s and were well aware of the benefits of electricity.

Every installation invited other users to share the wires and poles. Street lamps lit the way for office workers and factory hands on night shifts. Lines ran out into residential neighbourhoods. Use of motors in manufacturing and in street railways led directly to development of every conceivable domestic electric appliance and wiring of houses to receive them.

By 1940, electricity poles lined country roads and farm lanes throughout the province, each carrying a pair of wires on a short cross-arm (Figure 11.13;

Figure 11.13 ELECTRICAL POWER. Steel towers of 1920s' vintage and wooden poles of indeterminate age follow a concession road. Trees in the way are removed or severely amputated. North Easthope Township, Perth County.

see also Figure 4.5). Feeder lines with many wires carried power at higher voltage to big metal transformer boxes hung on the poles. Steel towers brought still higher-voltage trunk lines from generators at Niagara or Muskoka Falls or Grenville to transformer stations occupying several hectares each. The power grid – the hierarchy of major and minor links – ties us all in everywhere, and it was all standardized at an AC frequency of sixty cycles per second by 1960.

Buried cables have supplanted the maze of overhead wires in some places. Microwave technology has too, while producing its own, distinctive hilltop tower. Steel or concrete poles have been introduced in specialized situations. But wooden poles continue to be universal, just as they have been since the first railway telegraph lines were strung in the 1840s and telephone wires in the 1880s. Wooden pole lines are likely always to be with us.

In the wake of electricity

Electricity has become as universal as air, water, space, and mobility. It stimulated the concentration of industrial activity in cities and at the same time ensured the continued viability of a diffuse countryside of towns and farms. Cheese making, canning, brewing, weaving, and tanning all had an agricultural base, and all have benefited from electricity. As transmission problems were overcome, production of electricity became concentrated in fewer generating stations. Some of that power returned to run modernized machinery in the old factories located on water-power sites in such places as Carleton Place and Preston. Elsewhere, mills lived out their days in the old style. The Starks' mill at Paisley did not even have electric lights when, as a chop mill, it closed in the 1970s. It looked very much as it had ninety years earlier.

Electricity made the tall mill and factory buildings of the mechanical era obsolete. High ceilings for shafts and pulleys were no longer needed. Gravity feed was replaced with horizontal conveyor belts, run on electricity. The assembly line (not 'assembly column') and the fork-lift truck prevailed. Electric lighting made it unnecessary to have so many windows, and many older factories blocked them up to cut heating costs (Figure 11.11).

The village of Leaside, founded in the 1920s high above the Don River valley bottoms, is the prototype of the twentieth-century industrial landscape. Wide, single-storey factories, the early ones with saw-tooth roof skylighting, were built. Among the founding firms of this residential and industrial community were Sangamo Electric, builders of electric motors; Canada Wire and Cable; and Square D, the fuse-box people. Since that time factories have been superseded by unobtrusive, compact industrial estates in buildings not easily distinguished from town housing. The wheel has turned back to the domestic model.

Few provincial institutions have excited more passion than Ontario Hydro.

Enthusiasm for universal, clean energy is tempered by disdain for the artefacts and, in the 1990s, anxiety over a huge debt and the disposal of nuclear wastes.[30] Massive granite hydro-generating stations brood in the Precambrian Shield, and strobe lights on the chimneys at Lakeview, Ashbridge's Bay, and Bath are beacons of thermal industrial might. The nuclear stations at Douglas Point, Pickering, and Darlington are almost too big for comprehension. Policy requires that they be fenced against intrusion, but to hide them is impossible.

High-voltage transmission lines likewise are uncompromisingly obtrusive. Echelons of tall steel towers stride boldly across the Niagara Escarpment along Highway 401, empty cross-arms reaching out for more wires to join those already draped in place. A new rank of towers appeared through the Port Hope area in 1994. The location of, and increasingly the need for, high-voltage towers has come under some of the closest scrutiny ever provided for within the environmental-review process in Ontario. Serious doubts are being voiced about the need for more central power sources, and these strobe-lit stations noted above are, for the most part, inactive in 1996. Co-generation, or electricity manufactured at home, offers an alternative. Yet despite these indications, poles and wires are unlikely to fade out of the landscape any time soon.

Back in Niagara where it all began, the power-house of the Electrical Development Company built adjacent to the Falls between 1903 and 1913 has been superseded, and the generator hall stands inactive (Figure 11.14).[31] But what grand obsolescence this classical façade is! Such majestic decoration of nearly a century ago is pure prescience; a simple slab wall would have stood as long. Niagara Power is a link between the century past, back to the Kingston town hall and earlier (Figure 2.2), and the full flowering of twentieth-century Ontario life. It is a worthy companion to the Falls thundering close by.

Figure 11.14 POWER AND ART. The classical-style generating hall for 'Toronto Power' at Niagara Falls (1903–13).

12

Graves and monuments

Life´s celebration

The family home was almost the only place for dealing with personal well-being during the nineteenth century. People were born there, sheltered there, and died there, with the family. The doctor ministered to people where they lived, making his rounds by horse and buggy, toting the familiar black bag.[1] A gentleman in Bruce County described his boyhood tonsillectomy in 1912, performed by the village doctor on the welltop behind his house, with a spot of iodine, a pair of scissors, and the promise of a penknife when it was over.[2] The criminally insane were taken away to the Asylum in Toronto (built 1846), but others who were mentally or physically handicapped were cared for, perhaps incarcerated, at home.

Lives passed through the land unobtrusively. In the doddy house, a self-contained wing of the family home, ageing parents lived out their years quietly, close to the children but not under foot (Figure 12.1). When the end came, the local cabinet-maker or sawmill hand switched to his undertaker´s role, embalming at home and delivering the casket. A church funeral and burial beside parents in the churchyard completed the family cycle, all in an ageless, familiar setting. Only in death did there appear a lasting, visible link to the land and to the place where one lived – a burial marker.

Death is as old as life and touched all ages. In Springcreek Cemetery, Clarkson, founded in the 1820s, in a special section, set apart, markers no more than thirty years old all record the deaths of children. The names suggest that the parents are recent immigrants, still young and not yet rooted or sufficiently concerned with their own mortality, let alone their children´s, to have arranged a family burying place. So it was also in the years leading up to the consecration of Springcreek. One errant swing of the axe clearing the forest could inflict a fatal wound in the healthiest young immigrant.

Untold numbers of burials were made on the backs of farm sites during the early nineteenth century. From time to time, diaries record these, but otherwise they are lost. The occasional family burial plot, on the edge of the farm, is

Figure 12.1 THE FAMILY FOCUS. The doddy-house extension (1848) to this four-bay house, built in 1837 by emigrants from Pennsylvania, is a senior citizens' dwelling that permitted ageing parents to live out their years within the family unit. Vineland, Lincoln County.

the closest today's landscape comes to acknowledging this old practice. Stephen Leacock once stumbled on an ancient grave and was struck by the fact 'that the old grave that stood among the brambles at the foot of our farm was *history.*'[3] Indeed it was, for burial markers are the credit lines of the countryside, supplemented by names on mailboxes, storefronts, cornerstones, and road signs.

The transitory nature of life yields a good deal of maudlin prose and tearful farewells for those 'gone home': 'Young people all as you pass by, / O think of me for you must die. / Repent in time, make no delay. / I in my prime was called away.'[4] Cemeteries are active places where we all may celebrate lives once played out on the Ontario stage. Even the traveller moved so deeply as to aver that 'a glance at this beautiful cemetery almost excites a wish to die' had his heart, if not his words, in the right place.[5]

Cemeteries

Colour, texture, and shape give to all but the smallest burying grounds discernible geographies. Polished pink or grey granite blocks dominate one section and look like they would endure until the Judgment Day, and beyond.

Thin, creamy-white marble slabs, some carrying olive- or orange-coloured lichens, stand out in another part. These communicate fragility, and many lie flat on the ground; others reel at awkward angles. Between these well-defined precincts one finds a transition area, highlighted by tall obelisks in both materials.

Ontario's oldest gravestones, still widely found, are the slim white panels, row on row, often intricately decorated and inscribed. Few bear dates later than about 1880, and some are more than half a century older than that.[6] These markers of soft marble have proven easy to carve with hand tools, and they take us back to the shadowy beginnings of non-native settlement. The obelisks span the period from Confederation until the First World War. The granites date from before 1900 and continue in use as the dominant material to this day.

In Niagara, a few black slate markers even older than the marble ones record New England roots. Most graveyards also contain one or two cast cement markers from the late Victorian era, often in the form of a felled or gnarled tree. In the 1980s cemetery boards started erecting granite plaques with a running list of those whose cremated remains were placed there – a new burial style for a crowded, footloose, and less family-oriented society.[6]

Years of wind and rain have carried wooden markers away entirely. Lichens and acid rain have effaced soft marble into illegibility, and, cracked, pitted, and fallen, these markers, too, are disappearing for ever. Frost action first throws over stones and then gradually causes them to settle lower and lower into the sod, finally being grown over altogether. Hardly a cemetery exists in which the oldest section does not peter out into vacant ground. Decay, plus loss of written records, presents a problem for cemetery boards anxious to use the land wisely while not desecrating human remains. It would never do to dig up old remains while preparing for a burial today. This concern has given rise to a slightly bizarre profession: divining for burials with metal rods.[7] The procedure appears to involve electromagnetic interaction between buried and living bodies, and there are similarities to dowsing for water with a forked stick.

Not all burying grounds tail off into such shadowy beginnings. A granite stone in the Huxley Cemetery in Erin Township reports an interment in 1884 as the 'first burial in the cemetery.' In Phelpston (northwest of Barrie), the oldest stones in the Roman Catholic graveyard date from the 1860s, yet substantial houses in the neighbourhood are older. Exploration along a disused road allowance to an old river fording point leads to another burying ground with the missing older stones that help to fill out the local settlement history.

Superseded graveyards are easily forgotten. A cemetery board manual of 1875 records that 'the dead have hitherto been interred in denominational or local burial grounds of small size. ... Nearly all [are] ... almost filled, and [have] begun to assume the neglected appearance that seems to be their lot.'[8] But they are hard to close. The sense of place in Ontario is strong, and the spinster granddaughter goes home to the family plot perhaps decades after regular burying ceased.

Renewed interest in ancestry since the 1960s, supported by 1979 legislation, has stimulated the restoration of many neglected graveyards (Figure 12.2).[9] In St Cyprian's in Mono Township, stones had been untended for such a long time that some had to be pried from trees growing around them.[10] Reconstruction reasserts faith in the collective performance of the ancestral community and provides a grip on the past amid profound cultural changes late in the twentieth century. For immigrant groups, their own cemeteries offer communal peace in their adopted land. Toronto's Ukrainians, for instance, have opened a site near Oakville Creek at Dundas Street.

Markers

Along the Port Franks Road in a corner of Lambton County, the Ward cemetery demonstrates one manner of grave-marker restoration: pull up the stones, intact or broken, and build a concrete wall into which they may be set and secured from further decay. One tall, slender marble marker mounted here remembers

JOEL.
SON OF
Allen & Clarissa
KENNEDY.
WHO DIED
4th May 1866

These words are followed by age, verse, half a metre of blank stone, and, then, offset to the right:

Wiliam Nieghor
Hamilton

and below that, carved on the stem that was intended always to be below ground level,

Waognbdepqsvc
bfgaoultivibyher
ABCDEGVWOPMNL

We think of gravemarkers first and foremost as sources of genealogical information, but they also speak to us indirectly as works of art, as geological

Figure 12.2 CEMETERY 'RESTORATION.' Gravestones line up in rows on a cement platform, like a school class picture but no longer associated with individual burial plots. Highway 6, north of Shelburne, Dufferin County.

Figure 12.3 BOUNSALL BROTHERS MARBLE AND GRANITE WORKS of Bowmanville, Durham County. *Illustrated Historical Atlas of the County of Northumberland and Durham* (1878), 25.

specimens, and as commercial products. Joel Kennedy's is all of these and seems also to have been a scribbler: these last three lines of characters in various sizes and fonts suggests an apprentice carver honing his talents. Many early gravestones are poorly executed – characters badly shaped, unevenly spaced and improperly centred, and with names misspelled – and only gradually did itinerant stone carvers achieve quality. No one was ever supposed to know how William Nieghor sought perfection, nor would they have, had not our yearning for immortality induced some local enthusiasts to revive this derelict site.

Gravestones are often marked with the carver's name and the place of manufacture: Nieghor of Hamilton, in Kennedy's case. They are in select company with iron stoves, bricks, pickle crocks, and farm implements – all durable consumer products. Within any one cemetery, manufacturers' labels give a rare idea of market areas over which individual towns had influence, perhaps even how that role changed from decade to decade. Of 700 gravemarkers in cemeteries in Euphrasia Township, Grey County, in 1974, 111 indicate place of origin. Meaford and Owen Sound were the most common sources, but twenty came from Hamilton, well over one hundred kilometres distant.[11] A stone dated 1861 in Formosa, Bruce County, bears the label of a Guelph firm, almost as far. One can imagine a farmer taking a sleighload of grain to a warehouse on the Grand Trunk Railway in February and returning with a

Figure 12.4   WHITE BRONZE COMPANY of St Thomas. Cast-metal grave marker, with inscriptions bolted on. Fairfield Plains, Burford Township, Brant County.

carved gravestone ready for erecting in May when the ground dried out. Stones were shipped across Lake Ontario from Rochester to Port Hope and on to Peterborough, earning backhaul income for schooners carrying grain or wood to the United States.

The cemetery is a free showroom, and the signature at the base of the stone has been a discreet means of reminding relatives whom to call in future times of need. For example, Bounsall, a common signature in graveyards back from Lake Ontario towards Lindsay, can be traced to the Bounsall Brothers Marble and Granite Works of Bowmanville.[12] The Bounsalls must have been a progressive firm to be promoting granite markers in 1870, an early date for that material. They were clearly anything but modest, judging from the relative scale of stones and people in an engraving from 1878 (Figure 12.3).

The White Bronze Monument Company of St Thomas flourished between about 1883 and 1900, producing distinctive, rust-resistant, weatherproof zinc grave markers (Figure 12.4).[13] The markers were sanded in such a way as to look like granite, especially when wet. Most are obelisks and bear exquisitely detailed cast reliefs. Customized inscription panels were bolted on to a limited number of standard models. New ones could be added later as required, ensuring repeat business. White Bronze products were sold through locally franchised agents, a remarkably innovative idea for the 1880s. J. Heard and Company of Strathroy, for example, advertised in 1883 that it was the exclusive agent for `the Celebrated White Bronze Monuments, Headstones [and] Statuary for the County of Middlesex west of London.'[14]

White Bronze markers are light and were easily shipped. Examples are scattered throughout Ontario, two or three in any one graveyard, and may be found at least as far away as the Annapolis valley in Nova Scotia. The greatest concentration is in Parry Sound, Muskoka, and Nipissing districts, looking as fresh as on the day of manufacture. Zinc monuments made no significant impression on the more traditional granite ones, however, and one would have to conclude that consumers were not yet ready for catalogue shopping in the cemetery.[15]

Inscriptions

It may sound insensitive to describe gravestones as field sources for demographic analysis. But they are. Names and birthplaces await the ethnic historian, life spans the actuary, and decorative motifs the artist. Numerical treatment has been hard to resist, though in no Ontario cemetery is the sample of gravestones sufficiently complete today to provide data that would withstand statistical tests. Stones are illegible, adherents are buried elsewhere, and paupers have no stones at all. Existing grave markers identify a biased sample of Ontarians, perhaps no more than half of them, and the evidence will continue to diminish.

Gravestones are nevertheless tremendously important cue-cards.[16] Local roots were strong before the First World War, and markers from that period are expressions of the make-up of the neighbourhood. Every old cemetery bears names matching those of local villages, streets, shops, and telephone book entries. `James McDonald, 13-4 Lancaster,' appears on a 1903 stone at Glen Nevis, one kilometre from the McDonald farm on Lot 13, Concession 4, Lancaster Township. Descendants have made certain that his link with the land would not not soon be lost, nor that he be mistaken for a neighbour of the same name.

Names indicate ethnic background. The Scottish `Mac´ or Mc´ and the Irish `O´ are well known, and catalogues of names by nationality identify others.[17]

Anglicization of surnames – for instance Schmidt to Smith, Müaller to Miller, or O´Brian to Brian – is powerful evidence that the English cultural group set the standard. Birthplaces take on significance in these cases, and a good many gravestones of those who died in the era of soft marble stones identify the parish or county of birth. Thus, we read of Nelly Campbell, `spouse of Donald Campbell of the House of Duntroun, natives of Kilmanna Parish, Argyleshire, Scotland, who emigrated to Canada in June, 1819, and departed this life on the 28th day of Dec, 1851, aged 81 years.´[18] Identifying birthplace is less frequent among the English for whom, like anonymous coins and postage stamps, their ancestry was too obvious for words.

Those of American birth generally found it imprudent to be expansive, but not so Scots and Irish. It has been estimated that Irish immigrants to Ontario outnumbered all others from the British Isles almost every year between 1820 and 1845, and throughout the province grave markers record the diversity of their birthplaces.[19] The Presbyterian graveyard in Dunvegan, Glengarry County, is quite the reverse. It records a remarkably narrow range of home parishes and is occupied by fellow emigrants, plus kinfolk later joining relatives or friends. Similar examples are found in the Scottish parts of Elgin and Bruce counties, where highland games and quite possibly even the Gaelic tongue persist. Reference to the place of birth disappeared as the emigrant generation died off.

French stones invariably stand aside from the Ontario mainstream and occupy their own cemeteries. Near the shore of Lake St Clair at St Joachim, in Essex County, `repose le Rev Joseph Gabriel Edmond Courtois, né à Gentilly PQ le 21 août 1862, ordoné [sic] prêtre le 25 août 1889, vicaire à Windsor 1889–1890, curé de French Settlement 1890–1901, Paincourt 1901–1911, St Joachim 1911–1912, décédé le 7 avril 1912.´ Franco-Ontarian graveyards are not obtrusive, however, taking on the North American lawn look rather than the European appearance of raised vaults and stonework.

German immigrants began assimilating from the time of their arrival in the 1850s, and many of their markers are bilingual. At Formosa, Bruce County, is a gravestone inscribed as follows: `Zum andenken von Anna Victoria, geliebte Ehefrau von F.X. Mesner, gestorben den 29 Aug 1861, alt 25 Jahre . . . In memory of Anne Victoria, beloved wife of F.X. Mesner, died Aug 29 1861, aged 25 years.´ English verse follows. All this was committed to stone after barely a decade of settlement. Anti-German sentiments caused script and language to vanish almost overnight during the First World War. For example, Karl Teuber, buried in 1915 in Alsfeldt, Bruce County, is recorded in German; his wife, Matilda Damm, buried in 1926, is named on the same stone in English. German grave markers have never made a comeback, and the language has just about died out in the rural regions.

Some gravestones record the cause of death, especially if it was at all unusual. We are told that in 1861 nineteen-year-old Robert Hayes `was accidentally

killed while in the discharge of his duties as brakesman.´ The marker was
`erected by the employees of the PHL&B Railroad.´[20] Robert Burleigh died in
1865 `by a fall from the topmast of the Schooner ``Star of Hope.´´´ His
gravestone, on Amherst Island, Lennox and Addington County, carries a sail-
ing ship on it. A barely legible stone nearby in Bath identifies a victim of one
of Ontario´s major tragedies during the nineteenth century: `In memory . .
George M. ., son of Joseph and Jane Den. ., a passenger who was killed on
the great Railway ca. . of the 12th March 1857, . . Desjardins Canal bridge . .
of the great . . Ae 18y 9m . . .´ More than sixty people died when a Great
Western Railway train plunged through a bridge near Hamilton.[21]

Death from illness or domestic affliction rarely is stated. Perhaps it was too
futile to engender more than pity at the youthful age of the victim or the
destruction of a family. In a small cemetery on the edge of Pearson International Airport (Malton) lies Sarah Holmes, who died 7 November 1858,
apparently in childbirth, and with her `also infant Matilda.´ An adjacent plot
marks the Lundy family, four of whom were in all likelihood victims of the
outbreak of cholera in 1849 (Figure 12.5).[22]

Gravestones speak indirectly too, as works of art. Children´s markers are
tiny, and the catafalques of famous people are massive. Lambs and doves are
used for children, while draped urns-of-life and hands pointing heavenward
are common for adults. Celtic crosses identify Anglicans and Roman Catholics.
A Scottish thistle intertwined with an English rose tells of cultural mixing;
calipers identify a Mason, and ladders are for Orangemen (Figure 12.6).

Weeping willows are standard expression of sorrow, and were probably the
most popular of all the motifs used on marble gravestones. As a purely practical
matter, living willows are very common in cemeteries because they soak up
water in prodigious quantities. Willows keep the ground dry and lengthen the
burying season. The adoption of granite signalled the decline of the hand-
crafted, vernacular era for Ontario gravestones, but highly personalized designs
began to appear once again late in the twentieth century (Figure 12.7).

Ontario´s gravestones are business-like on vital statistics but rarely expansive
on the character of the deceased. Here and there a sentence appears: about
George Elliott of Norfolk County, for instance, `one of the most active and
useful inhabitants of this district.´ Gravestone text becomes still more terse
after about 1880, about the same time that improved stone-cutting saws were
making granite blocks more popular than the old marble ones. Who can tell
whether the interest in one´s forebears was waning or the cost of inscribing
it was rising? Either way, the late Victorians were increasingly reticent about
the accomplishments of those who preceded them.

Reporting the age of the deceased yielded to giving the date of birth. The
new procedure was economical, but empathy for an infant carried off before
its first birthday, or for a young man felled by a kick from a horse, or for a
work-weary patriarch who died after a full life is diminished if one has to

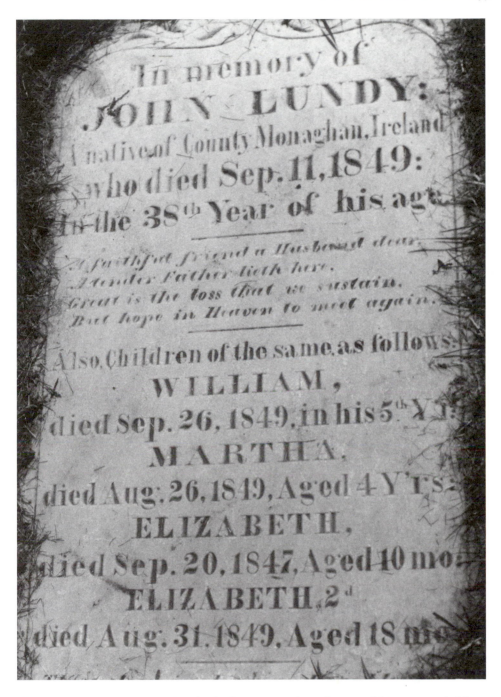

Figure 12.5 DISEASE. John Lundy died 11 September 1849, and his young children Martha 26 August, Elizabeth 31 August, and William 26 September. Cholera was rampant that summer. Another child, also named Elizabeth, had died two years earlier. Malton, Peel County.

Figure 12.6 SYMBOLISM. Orange symbols surround a family burial plot. McCabe Cemetery, North Fredericksburg Township, Lennox and Addington County.

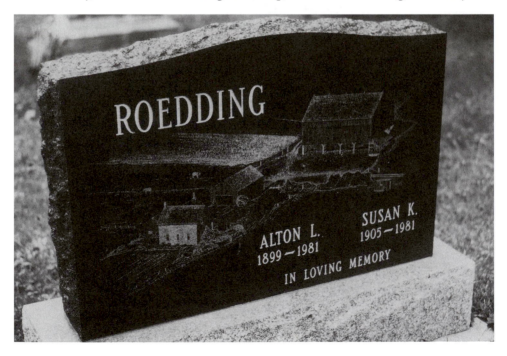

Figure 12.7 FAMILY FARM. A forebay barn and storey-and-a-half house were at the centre of the Roedding family's life. Alsfeldt, Normanby Township, Bruce County.

pause and calculate how long each lived. Birth and death dates are for actuarial measurement, whereas age recognizes the span of life. Some of the personality of Ontario's graveyards fell away with the adoption of granite.

Gravestone text sheds light on the structure of the family in Ontario history. We read of a patriarchal society, seen in the frequency of inscriptions through the nineteenth century specifying 'wife of . . .' in contrast to the relatively few that say 'husband of . . .,' regardless of which spouse died first. Many couples share a stone prepared for them when the second partner died. Separate stones for maiden aunts, children, and connections through marriage add to the scene. It is not unusual for the same name to appear more than once, on different stones.

For the successful family, a new marker – a granite column, probably – appeared in the years around 1900, collecting all the names together as a recognizable family tree. It stands in the midst of a tract bounded by tiny footstones for 'Mother,' 'Father,' 'James,' 'Elizabeth,' and so on. The more elegant plots are set off by iron railings, and a private vault serves the very well-to-do (Figure 12.8).

This streamlining of family affairs bears a resemblance to the consolidation of farm outbuildings in the same period. One gets the impression that late Victorians in Ontario were great tidiers but also intent on remembering, and one wonders what was done with the older stones that became redundant. I know of one in a basement in eastern Ontario, where it has leaned, out of the weather, for a century; there must be more in barns and sheds across the province.

Extended family plots record the fullest flowering of rural Ontario, just before 1900. Several families of the same name or with obvious intermarriages rest together, members of a kinship network that gave entire townships a coherence unequalled since. However, the seeds of change are evident in inscriptions such as 'Mary, 1861–.' Members were lost to other families or moved to the cities, and the number of new family monuments declined after 1900. Once again stones recording the passage of couples and perhaps an unmarried child became characteristic as the countryside unravelled into the broader provincial and national dimension. Many more gravestones with entries since the 1950s speak of husbands than was the case a century earlier, evidence of the demise of paternalistic attitudes.

Memorials

A marker for Alexander Kidd and Christiana White lies in a graveyard in Dummer Township, looking like the fallen headstone for their burial plot. We learn a lot about them: 'Sacred to the memory of Alexander Kidd, who died on the 30th of December, 1868, aged 88 yrs & 2 1/2 mos. He was born at

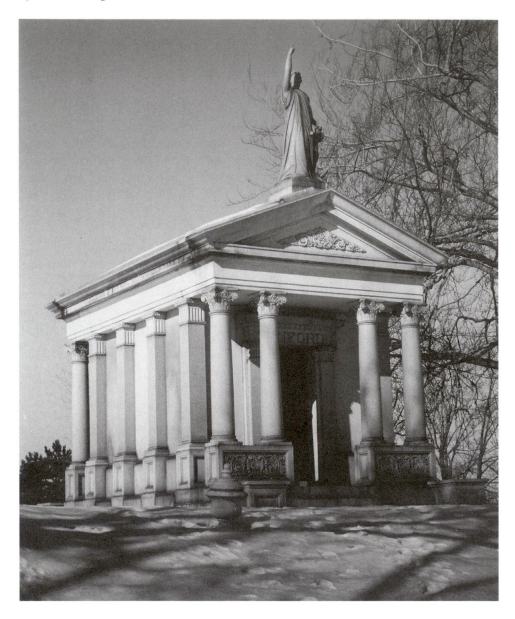

Figure 12.8 MAUSOLEUM. The Sanford family has erected a little Greek temple as its memorial, in the best high-art tradition. York Blvd, Hamilton.

Boness, Scotland. Also of his wife, Christiana White, who died on the 13th of August, 1866, aged 85 years & 1 1/2 mo. She was born at Linlithgow, Scotland. They came to Canada in 1815, settled at Perth, Co. Lanark, in 1816. In 1831, they removed to Dummer, where they died full of years and in hope of glorious immortality . . .´ It further records that `this monument is erected by their grandchildren in token of their affection and respect to their memories.´ The marker is a memorial as much as a burial marker. The ornate drapery style of the stone dates to the 1880s, twenty years after the deaths. The grandchildren were responsible for this monument and its extensive biographical detail, and quite possibly it replaced ordinary gravestones.

Other graveyard stones are more obviously momuments. In St Peter´s churchyard, Erindale, one marker recalls a man who died in England in 1799, nearly thirty years before the graveyard was even established. The name on the stone affirms family continuity across the Atlantic Ocean, as worthy a matter of recognition in the absence of the body as with it. Monuments record burials at sea, too. `Thomas G . . . was drowned rounding Cape Horn, June 24, 1853,´ is typical of this type of inscription.[23] Then there was `John Youart, who died of diptheria [sic] while on a visit to his native land, 10th Dec 1860, aged 40 years, and whose body now lies in Leicester Cemetery, Leicestershire, England.´[24]

Monuments

Brock´s Monument on Queenston Heights is a an exceptional example of the adulation of heroes. Since its erection in the 1840s, and destruction and replacement shortly thereafter,[25] Ontario has added few monuments of that dimension. It has been enough occasionally to review an illustrious career on a gravestone. James McQueen, buried at Fingal in Elgin County in 1877, `served under Gen Sir Isaac Brock at Queenston Heights. He was at the taking of Detroit. Was wounded at the battle of Lake Erie. Appointed lieutenant by Gen Riel Feb 1812, and promoted to Col of the Talbot Regiment at the close of the war.´

Following the First World War, cenotaphs were erected in almost every town in the province (Figure 8.21). They provided an opportunity to think back to the victims of the Boer War and the Northwest Rebellion as well. Military cemeteries, with their identical markers set out in precise ranks, are also monumental (Figure 12.9). Churches mounted plaques on their walls alongside those to clergy and distinguished parishoners or benefactors, and universities did the same. By the end of the Second World War circumstances had changed, and the widespread inadequacy of public facilities led to dedication of usable spaces, such as memorial arenas.

Cenotaphs fit most easily into urban settings, in the presence of other monumental forms. On Remembrance Day each November, the town´s war memorial provides a place for collective remembering of those buried on distant battlefields. The Ontario countryside – except for a few battles in the War of

Figure 12.9 MILITARY CEMETERY. The impact of these personal markers collectively creates a monument. Woodlawn Cemetery, Aldershot, Wentworth County.

1812 – never has been a theatre of war, and death here, rather, has been a normal part of life. The great, vernacular celebration takes place on a daily basis, family by family, inconspicuously in hundreds of cemeteries across the province. Life's cycle is a cherished feature of the Ontario landscape.

PART III
EXAMINING CLUSTERS OF FEATURES

13

Farms

Ontario's farms are the creations of immigrants of varied backgrounds who often showed disdain, if not outright hostility, for their neighbours (Figure 13.1). The landscape mirrors this outlook: no residential farmer villages, a system of public roads that bypass farm buildings, and private lanes leading to them. Building sites varied with local conditions but tended to be set well back on the lots. Here was privacy, freedom from the `disagreeable necessity´ of gazing at one's neighbour, and security from passers-by helping themselves to the orchard or kitchen garden.[1] We are told that the spread of idle gossip and rumour would be suppressed.[2]

Such moderate paranoia may be the effect of strangers thrown together in an unfamiliar setting. Still, location in the middle of the farm gave best access to the fields, was within earshot of the dinner bell, and made driving the cows home for milking easy regardless of which field was in pasture.[3] In homogeneous areas barns stand one to two hundred metres from the concession road, midway from the side boundaries, in the middle of the standard wheat-era farm of twelve or sixteen hectares (thirty or forty acres). A good setback has proven a useful buffer against road dust, too.

Expeditions off the farm were relatively infrequent in the first generation of settlement, and the need to open a roadway lane was not a decisive factor in choosing the building site. In due course, mechanization permitted more of the lot to be cultivated, and the centre of gravity receded. Southern Ontario's longest farm lanes are in Grey and Bruce counties, where machinery was being introduced early in the settlement era; some lanes are five hundred metres in length. Merger of farms across the concessions, beginning early in the twentieth century, exacerbated the problem of buildings being set far back, for the middle of an extended farming operation could now truly be at the roadside. New buildings after the First World War would probably have been raised close to the roads, but by then the building era had passed and inertia kept the landscape the way it was. An exception is the winter roadside shelter for the car. It surely beats having to plough out a long lane before going to work on a snowy morning.[4]

Figure 13.1 SCATTERED FARM BUILDINGS. A landscape of free-standing farm units is an Ontario hallmark. Credit River valley in Caledon Township, Peel County.

Water has been crucial in the location of farm buildings. The earliest settlers relied on surface streams – `living water´ – but land clearance and regraded fields caused muddy and irregular flow. Groundwater was preferable, and increasing numbers of wells were dug from the 1860s onward. Houses and barns are known to have been moved as part of the process,[5] but once a well was in place it was an anchor around which further expansion took place. After 1920 inside plumbing, a hot-water tank, a furnace, and an excavated basement – visible by the outside, hinged lid – further tied the old house to its site. Next came a septic tank and weeping tile bed, both unmovable. The kitchen-door pump handle gave way to an electric pump, served by a pole line of wires from the roadside – one more factor discouraging relocation of the modern farm buildings.

It was well known in British experience that `the old farmsteads . . . ride high on the hills´ (Figure 1.2).[6] More prosaically, we are told that the barn site `should be well-drained and high.´[7] These raised areas are generally composed of glacial gravels and tills, are well drained, and are suited for excavating wells and basements. The flank sloping away from the house was ideal for a septic-system tile bed. Elevated sites also escaped the early frost, and a sloping orchard benefited from air drainage. The barn, nestled in the slope, could be entered on two levels.

The elevation also embodied the intangible matter of view. Landownership has been a heady experience for Ontario´s residents, and to gaze on one´s domain from the house has been immensely satisfying.[8] One writer rated view as important as water supply and more so than drainage or wind protection.[9] Altogether, Ontario´s farm building sites express a remarkable fusion of practicality and emotion.

Buildings

The house and barn compete for attention on many Ontario farms, and there is no clear-cut winner.[10] A traveller describing a farm he visited in 1832 makes the case for the house: 'The original shanty ... still remains, ... degraded into a piggery; the more substantial loghouse ... has ... become a chapel of ease to the stable or cowhouse; and the glaring and staring bright-red brick house is brought forward close upon the road, that the frame dwelling, which at one time the proprietor looked upon as the very acmé of his ambition, may at once serve as a kitchen to, and be concealed by, its more aspiring and aristocratic successor.'[11]

This is the essence of a farm layout in southern Ontario: a showy house at the front, and all else more utilitarian concealed behind. Silos, smoke-houses, wells, corn cribs, sheds, driveways, utility lines, windmills, and tree-line wind-breaks are among the other elements that have made up the nerve centre of an operating farm (Figure 13.2). The farm kitchen – in the house, usually at the back – is part of the workings of the farm enterprise, too; preserving kettles, drying herbs, and maybe a spinning-wheel are signs of the activity centred there. Some structures are obsolete relics – the spring-house super-seded by an electric refrigerator, say – and others, such as a dish for receiving satellite television signals, are brand new. A root cellar beneath the house is both an outbuilding, reaching by an outside entrance, and a basement of the dwelling, accessible through a trap door in the kitchen. Lines blur.

Outward-looking house fronts notwithstanding, farm families for generations have come and gone through the back door, in the kitchen wing. A plank walkway leading to the front of a log house was uncommon enough to catch

Figure 13.2 THE FARMYARD. Scattered buildings, rising ground, electricity, fuel tank, wind-pump, shed, corn crib, steel bins, and a fine house with bellyflop windows: this farm-building cluster conceals little about itself. The barn is out of sight to the right. Seymour Township, Hastings County.

the attention of one backwoods scribe.[12] At one time inviting, most façades now mock and are defensive (Figure 1.2).[13] Typically the doorstep is sunken and overgrown. Suicide doors and tar-stained walls mark vanished porches that once were both useful and ornamental (Figure 7.2), and the family wash flaps from a line strung out in full view from the road. Plastic sheeting seals the doorcase from wintry draughts, and some front doors have been closed up altogether.

Back-door farmhouses may stand unlocked day and night, but the necessity of passing through the yard to gain entry serves as a screen. In secure societies the kitchen is not a truly private space, but an open spot where neighbours and visitors may gather. Ontarians had to learn to be neighbourly, and the landscape suggests a persistent guardedness. Outward-facing, defensive houses have the accessible kitchen in an inconspicuous place. One writer went so far as to call Ontario's farm buildings introverted fortresses.[14]

Ontario's farms today rarely have more than one obviously nineteenth-century house. Between Confederation and the First World War, however, many of these dwellings contained two or more households. Families stretched out to three-generation units, as ageing settlers entered grandparenthood, and mixed farming created opportunities for hired labour. It was common for the hired hand and his family to occupy the upper floor of the kitchen wing; in other instances they lived poorly in outdated log houses.[15] These extra dwelling places hardly showed on the landscape, and a ground-level wing for grandparents was only slightly more evident (Figure 12.1).

Early in the twentieth century the provincial government was advocating separate dwellings for hired workers.[16] It was not an onerous requirement, for conditions were moving in that direction anyhow. Farm consolidation permitted some tenants to take over vacated houses away from the base farm. Many went off to war and came back to a rather less labour-oriented agriculture. Retired farmers chose to live nearby in town, and one household per farm again became the rule. A surplus of houses developed, and these became outbuildings or were demolished.

Outbuildings and plantings

The buildings on Ontario's farms are spread out. Everyone understood that 'the barn, being very liable to destruction by fire, is too dangerous to be a very near neighbour of the dwelling,'[17] and so it stands at a distance. Space was needed for turning a horse and wagon.[18] Tower silos had to be placed so as not to impede light entering the stable area and had to be well away from the manure pile. So did creameries, the sprawling bunker silos, and, of course, the house. The privy – 'that diminutive house to which a name is applied that expresses the absolute importance of such a retreat'[19] – took up its discreet niche on the perimeter under the most favourable light, drainage, and prevailing wind conditions. Lilac bushes may still hide the site.

The farm yard outside the kitchen door has been, in many respects, an extension of the house, especially of the summer kitchen. It adds to the spacious effect. It was the site for much of the family cottage industry: washing wool, slaughtering pigs, cleaning vegetables, growing herbs, and more. Clean water entered into all these processes, and here the well was located.

In remote parts of Renfrew County one can find examples of the connected farm buildings known in central Europe. These sombre clusters, of log or shingle siding, are associated with farmers who emigrated from Poland to the Opeongo Road region – Barry's Bay – following the Crimean War in the 1850s. Those who prospered joined the Ontario mainstream and its cultural landscape of separate houses and barns. But in this harsh land, many struggled to survive. Their descendants maintain the arrangement even today.

The sun is an inconclusive factor in the arrangement of farm buildings. Southeast slopes are favourable, and contemporary observers urged that barn extensions enclose a winter feeding area on those sides, while windbreaks occupy north and west.[20] Approximately half of the townships in Ontario are laid out so that the fronts of the farmhouses may face south to southeast. But every house that basks in the wan winter sun also exposes itself to the fury of easterly winter storms. The number of townships aligned roughly east-west equals those running north-south, creating every possible lighting situation throughout the year.

Not much more can be said regarding the wind. `Square to the road, hogs to the east,'[21] is an old expression showing concern for livestock smells, yet a sampling from King Township shows that more than half the farmhouses are downwind from the barn. Livestock herds were latecomers to Ontario agriculture, and stable smells are strongest in winter when the farmhouse windows are closed, so odours have perhaps been overrated.

Arguments for straight lines of planted trees are considerably stronger. Along the driveway or across the front, they announce the farm to the passing world. Trees planted upwind of the buildings give shelter and behave like snow-fencing for a distance of up to thirty times their height.[22] They also act as lightning rods: `I believe that if farmers would plant a cordon of common poplar trees around their barns, at a distance of from fifty to one hundred feet, . . . it would prove an almost effectual protection. These trees grow very fast and are easily grown, and very soon would be taller than the barn; and though ugly to look at, are not quite so ugly as the remains of a burned barn.'[23] Lombardy poplar are short-lived as well as ugly and have been only limited competition for itinerant lightning-rod salesmen. These pedlars criss-crossed the province selling their wares. They had considerable success, judging from the profusion of lightning rods seen on roof crests today (Figure 9.7).[24]

Lawns are high-art stages on which prosperous people have shown off to the neighbourhood. They must have been particularly conspicuous along the main roads, and huge, if they filled the space forward of a well-recessed house. Patrician activities – parading horses or oneself and playing croquet – are clearly visible in many of the county atlas engravings published about 1880.[25] Flower beds, ornamental shrubs, and bird-baths decorate the foreground, and the margins demonstrate renewed interest in trees. Deciduous species have been planted to complement asymmetrical buildings, while conifers dignify classic designs. Oddly, the decline of classicism coincides with the clearing of the pineries. Shrubbery cushions the sudden change where tall Victorian houses meet the ground.[26]

The house, with its decorative carvings or brickwork, was a respectable backdrop for the lawn, and the verandah an observation gallery for less-spry family members. This vision contrasts strongly with the abandoned front face of so many farmhouses today. Modern non-farm residents install lawns as a matter of course, as a means of maintaining connection with the outside world. Chances are they are not conscious of the high-class connotation lawns long have held.

Orchards have been part of the building group. Fruit trees serve also as shelter and landscaping and provide a site where chickens could scratch and calves graze under supervision. Beehives were sometimes nearby, and collecting both honey and fruit has been part of the domestic round of duties performed by women and children. Severe winter cold in 1917–18 and again in 1933–34 killed large numbers of trees, including dozens of apple grafts.[27] Inland, small-scale orcharding has declined since 1934, overtaken by commercial fruit farms. Gnarled old apple trees continue to be scattered across southern Ontario's countryside and are another of the guideposts, along with silos and lilacs, to a building site long after the buildings have gone.

Field and woods

It takes an orchard, or a stand of mature corn tall enough to hide the fencing, to focus our attention on the land itself. At any season particular farm prospects may well catch the eye: a tractor ploughing in April, trailing a swirl of gulls; hectares of butter-yellow sunflower blossoms gently dipping in July heat; coiled hay scattered across a snow-swept meadow. At most times, however, the countryside is merely fields, filling up every space that is not obviously in some other use. It is indeed odd that rural life would not exist without arable land, yet we can find so little to say about it.

Farmers who found the soil too thin after clearing quarried the glacial tills immediately below. Railways and township road commissions were steady customers through the later nineteenth century. Commercial extraction became big business after 1890, but for decades thereafter 'the small quarry, worked by the farmer and his boys in a desultory way ... still survives.'[28] Entire farms, or groups of farms, have been obliterated since the 1950s to meet the demands of highways and suburban construction. The huge pits have been the targets of environmental legislation since the 1960s and are supposed to be neatly concealed behind berms made from the topsoil stripped off.[29] This same material is used for restoration, often with ponds and undulating topography (Figure 13.3).

Southern Ontario's woodlots are residual places, left after apparently loftier purposes have been met. Unlike the clear-cutting by settlers for fields, woodlots have been drawn on selectively. They have been thinned for logs, firewood, and fence-rails. Specialty trees have been harvested: walnut and hickory for their nuts and maple for its sap (Figure 13.4). Woodlots are more truly reserves than workplaces and have been exploited but never entirely removed.

Woodlots occur anywhere on the farm property, but for smooth sites 'residual' has meant remote, even sinister. As Alice Munro has written, 'Bush lots at the back of the farms hold shade, black pine-shade like pools nobody can ever get to.'[30] Through much of the province the pressure to clear the land abated before these strips of trees across the rear of farms shrank and disappeared along a fence line between open fields. Even the skimpiest of woods puts some reassuring limits on the vastness of the land. Where the woodland has disappeared, the great expanse of Foodland Ontario lies exposed, stretching from Dufferin to Oxford and on to Kent and Essex counties.

Ontario's woodland has regenerated substantially during the twentieth century. Some counties had as little as twenty per cent in woods in 1890, when the American Association for the Advancement of Science made a plea for forest conservation. Ontario's first tree-farm planting occurred early in the twentieth century, and trees were being planted to stabilize soils in sandy areas north of Bowmanville soon after the First World War. Norway spruce, and then other evergreens, have been popular. Acreage that should never have

Figure 13.3 FARM POND, for watering cattle, fire protection, or simple aesthetics. St Vincent Township, Grey County.

Figure 13.4 THE SUGAR CAMP is well concealed, but maple sugaring is one of those rare farm activities in which the public is invited to participate. Centreview, Bangor Township, Hastings County.

been cleared is once more greening up under provisions of the Woodland Improvement Act, 1966.[31] Old fences straggle through the regrowth. Harvesting programs give the feeling that these are not like the old woodlots. Rather, tree plantations are more like field crops, maturing somewhat more slowly than most.

Replanting rural Ontario has increased its attractiveness for country living. Since the 1950s, many farmers have found sudden wealth by selling off house lots along the roadside. Sloping sites with thin soil are hard to farm but may well be picturesque attractions for countryside commuters. In the Oak Ridges, out through the Rideau Lakes, and on the back slope of the Niagara Escarpment, many a poor field is prospering by growing houses on lots from one-tenth to four hectares. Such sprawl clashes with the old rural scene, and some effort was made during the 1970s to control severances. But interest in that seems to have abated, and subdividing resumed a decade later. As a new generation of shade trees matures in front of these lots, a leafy roadside veneer is destined to fill out over the farmlands.

14

Roadsides

One day in 1978, five university geography students set up little wooden stools along a country road and prepared to draw the Ontario landscape. A late-summer haze gave a mellowing cast to rural Charlottenburg Township, south of Simcoe, and the group was gradually absorbed into the tranquil scene. Grasshoppers rasped, starlings wheeled, somewhere beyond sight cattle lowed, and, on four of the clipboards, vistas of farmsteads or close-ups of barn siding were taking shape. On the fifth sheet a different scene unfolded: a straggly mass of lines between a recognizable fence post on one edge and the blacktop road on the other. Behind the pencil sat an Asian student, focused on the roadside ditch. In his experience, crops grew right to the edge of the traffic surface, and the sight of a swath of untended vegetation was a source first of puzzlement but gradually of anger. He saw more than two thousand square metres of inactive land lying in front of every farm lot, and that was, to him, an entire farm.

Some 5 per cent of all land in southern Ontario is vacant, roadside land, and that does not include unopened or abandoned allowances. There is little solace in knowing that ditches have long been condemned as habitats for such pernicious plants as the Canada thistle[1] or that today they are recognized as refuge habitats for threatened native plants and animals.[2] Ditches still look so terribly wasteful.

Roadsides acquired definition and value as the mixed-farming era took hold late in the nineteenth century. Gravelling made a solid, crowned roadbed from what used to be a muddy way that became hollowed out as wagons passed. Flanking drainage ditches would take the run-off without becoming clogged with mud sprayed aside by passing traffic. Culverts directed water beneath farm lanes and intersecting roads. Roadside ditches carried off water from adjacent fields, thus marrying land management with transport.[3] Ditching (and fencing) caused the end of the old winter practice of driving sleighs on short-cuts across fields.

Before the end of the nineteenth century, special drainage projects for such sodden places as the Luther marsh (Wellington County) were being worked

Figure 14.1 ROADSIDE DITCHING is the rearrangement of Ontario's tiny streams to conform to the rectangular survey of fields and roads. A particularly deep ditch. Near Blytheswood, Essex County.

into this developing pattern of water control.[4] Essex County is another place where deep drainage ditches have been necessary to keep the roads usable, and at times one seems to be driving on a dike (Figure 14.1). In the tobacco lands of Elgin County and vegetable areas of Kent, drainage channels are covered, and fields and roadways run together without ditch, fence, or wasted land.[5] The traveller has the sensation of driving through farms rather than past them. In towns the open ditch has disappeared beneath a curbed street as a storm sewer fed through curbside drains. Occasionally a date stamped on the drain lid states that this step was taken between the 1870s and the 1920s, but subsequent rebuilding has obscured just about all evidence of the process.

The margin

Roadside trees are as much a human-made element of rural Ontario as the ditch in front, the fence beneath, or the farmstead behind (Figure 4.8). They give articulation to a landscape where the next-highest field feature may be the fence post. Roadside trees are not remnants of clearing but were consciously reintroduced after that era amid the widespread belief that trees 'for shade and ornament' contributed to the virtue of country life.[6] Poets were aroused by the frightening prospect of a treeless landscape, and Arbor Day plantings became regular spring events at country schools late in the nineteenth century.

Farmers pointed out that shade and beauty did not increase their income, and we read in *Canada Farmer's Sun* of the resident who cut down his line of 'non-productive forest trees.'[7] The journalist urged others, as a compromise, to plant nut trees at the roadside. Shade benefited church-goers, weary travellers, and sweaty kine on sultry August afternoons. It did not matter that such trees did not grow ramrod straight for the satisfaction of lumber merchants. As for the romantics, the play of light and shadow through basswood or hemlock added immeasurably to the maturing landscape. Wrote one, trees 'relieve the parched and dusty appearance of the country in summer, and break the dreary monotony of the winter landscape.'[8]

As the forest cover diminished, ground-level winds increased and blowing snow became a menace to winter travel. Wind swept the raised roadways clean in some places. Newly erected rail fences disrupted the flow of air and caused deep drifts to accumulate elsewhere.[9] Neither sleighs nor wagons could be used properly.

Experiments during the 1870s suggested that wire fences might be a satisfactory compromise.[10] Legislation soon followed, intended to ensure that sleighing could take place.[11] Local councils could require farmers to move a fence, change its material, or install wire.[12] They made such alterations more appealing by permitting owners to encroach up to six feet onto the road allowance, or by buying the wire, or by paying the farmers to install it.[13] Roadways that appear to be of one chain's width between fences may actually be considerably narrower, and wire fencing took over as the standard roadside material.

Roadside planting also helped. Limbs broke the scouring effect of the wind, and trees properly placed upwind caused driven snow to fall deeply on the roadway.[14] Starting in 1883 municipalities could pay farmers up to twenty-five cents for each roadside hardwood tree planted, on either side of the fence (Figure 10.4).[15] Careful positioning helped control erosion, just as day-lilies (or 'gully-lilies') have done, and keep the ditches clear for carrying the spring run-off. Grants were offered for internal lot-line planting too, and trees recommended for all field boundaries. The principle was to break up the wind, and the small fields of mixed farms provided tens of thousands of kilometres of new edge where trees could grow up.

By the 1920s, motorists began demanding that roads be ploughed in winter.[16] In Sunnidale Township, Simcoe County, provincial highways were ploughed during the 1930s, but county and township ones were not.[17] During the transition, the Ford Motor Company marketed a tracked truck.[18] Ageing, taller trees unintentionally helped by channelling the wind below their boughs, thus scouring the roadway.[19] But some firm initiative had to be taken to keep the snow off.

Portable snow fencing was the answer. This simple device was made of vertical wooden slats wired together and held up with metal stakes hammered into the ground. Set about thirty metres back from the road, snow fences (Figure 14.2) caused snow to drop harmlessly on the fields, where it melted

Figure 14.2 SNOW FENCING causes drifts to accumulate downwind. Municipal by-laws authorized the erection of snowfences on private lands. They had to be removable to permit cultivation, normally by 1 April; this picture was taken 12 April. Near Belfountain, Peel County.

into the ground in spring. The motorists' victory over sleighing was swift, achieved with only slight impact on roadside trees.

A century after planting, the big roadside maples are disappearing. Along main routes they are victims of widening projects.[20] Many others are dying off, and much of the prettiness of the countryside will be lost where replanting has not been initiated. The current case for trees is largely aesthetic, but roadside trees are known to reduce monotony and make motorists more conscious of their speed.[21] Road widening has actually fostered much roadside renewal, for planting is a cheap and politically sensitive way of responding to those agitated by cutting. The cycle of decay and rejuvenation continues.

Life along the roads

In the distant beginnings of Ontario community life, itinerant preachers and magistrates spoke forth from a barn, tinkers mended pots in a summer kitchen, and journeying school-teachers gave lessons in the parlour. Pioneer patriarchs and matriarchs were laid to rest at the back of the clearing. Social life, as well as business, was focused on the farm buildings. But always the understanding was that this was only a temporary condition and that community-wide services would in time become established at convenient, central sites (Figure 1.1).

The permanent structures of local services took shape along the roadsides, at points that were the greatest distance from the centres of the farm lots where the farm buildings stood: 'In a rising settlement it is an object to have one of the corner lots, for the owner has the advantage of a road on two sides; and if the place should happen to grow to any importance it will be here it will begin and in the usual way, with a tavern, a blacksmith shop, and so on.'[22]

Corners of lots are generally awkward places for individual farms but conveniently accessible for neighbours travelling the rural roads, going to church or school (Figure 7.9). We must believe that the farmers who donated church and school sites during the nineteenth century were not so altruistic as to give up their best parcels, and many sites were leased.[23] It is a happy coincidence that donors could look like good citizens without unduly impeding their livelihoods. Under uniform land conditions, farm building sites and neighbourhood service sites have established a complementary relationship, giving stability to the landscape.

Rising ground answers the needs of roadside services just as it does farmhouses. A rural school 'stands back from the highway, on an elevated site – as school-house sites ought to be.'[24] Furthermore, it should be on the south side of a gentle slope, sheltered from severe weather from the northeast and set back from the 'noise, and dust, and danger' of the road. In 1856 Chatham relocated its cemetery, prematurely chosen in a bottomland and found to be 'altogether unfit ... by reason of the wetness of the soil and the great difficulties ... in draining the same.'[25] Rural cemeteries usually stand on elevated sites, in light soil where possible, competing with the better farmland and far from the water-powered mill down in the valley.

In the 1860s and 1870s many townships had ten or more Protestant denominations, and the crest of a hill along a rural road gave each a platform from which to announce itself. The open countryside must have aroused competition among denominations, and one struggles to believe that a sense of Christian mission prevailed and suspects a strong promotional undercurrent. Roman Catholic churches have been particularly well positioned for establishing authority visually (Figure 14.3). Raising a tower or spire could be postponed in cases where such prominence was given to the building itself.

The land survey, as we saw above, induced neighbourliness along concession lines. Lines that are also main routes – Yonge Street and Talbot Road, for instance – further strengthened this neighbourliness by prompting landowners to divide their lots lengthwise. These long, narrow 'string hundreds' gave more properties direct access to the main stem than did the usual square-hundred arrangement. A density of farm buildings twice the normal contrasts

Figure 14.3 ROMAN CATHOLIC CHURCH. Maryhill, Wellington County.

with the scarcity of buildings along the next concession road back. Quite possibly this rear road passes the deep woods that, in square hundreds, would have been half-way between concession lines. String hundreds used roads efficiently, thus enhancing the arterial role and attracting still more users.

The layout of farm lots discouraged neighbouring integration across the concessions, but institutions counteracted this tendency. As an example, legislation in 1874 set the maximum catchment area per school as four square miles (nine square kilometres),[26] or a maximum journey of two miles (three kilometres). For many children, the nearest school was in the next concession, and each school section evolved to as round a shape as the rectangular lot survey would allow (Figure 14.4). Roads rarely were the boundaries of school sections, and even township boundaries could pass through the centre of a section by the creation of a Union School Section (`U.S.S.´), shared by two townships. Compliance with the distance regulation was not easy, and many schools were moved to new sites at one time or another, in addition to others built new. Churches, post offices, and municipal halls offered the same opportunity to tie the concessions together. Mills, railway depots, and retailing likewise had the same effect.

The concession line once again became a stronger focus with rural depopulation. In the 1940s, schoolhouses situated on sideroads in Hay and Stanley townships (south of Goderich) were moved out to the concession lines.[27] Minor roads low on the priority list for winter ploughing suited pupils on foot, but not school buses. Wellington County closed sideroads to save maintenance on bridges, and postal routes have been changed.[28] Rural electrification gave further impetus to this change, for transmission wires generally ran along the concession roads.

Farmers, too, became part of the roadside world. Buck wrote that `in the field along the road the farmer made bricks; in the others he grew his crops.´[29] `The road´ is Brick Street (Commissioners Road), west of London, and about 1900 fifteen or twenty farmers had diversified; some of them could make enough bricks in a day `to veneer a fair-sized house.´[30] Farm sawmills flourished, too,[31] and there were small breweries, shingle mills, cheese factories, and carriage shops, to name but a few, that were attracted to countryside locations.

Workers lived in tiny houses, without summer kitchens or outbuildings and with room enough only for a small vegetable garden (Figure 14.5). These were not farmhouses; rather, they were part of the roadside community. Many housed millworkers, happy to be up on the higher lands, well away from the dampness and supposed foul air of the valleys where the mills were situated (Figure 14.6). Farmside industries were the first to succumb to urban industrialism, amid the general process of rural decline after 1880, and these specialized dwellings have largely vanished.

Today´s farm operator continues the tradition of participating in off-farm

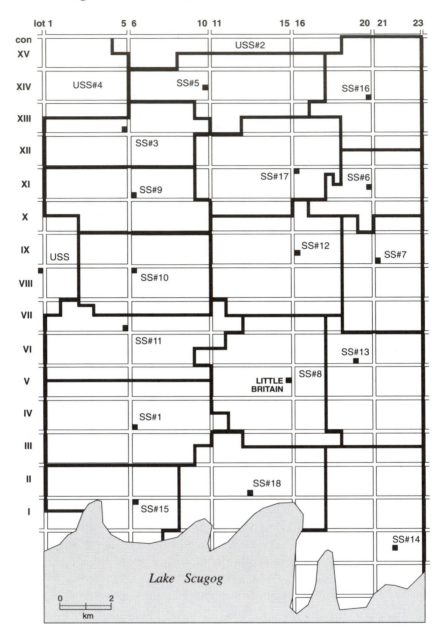

Figure 14.4 SCHOOL SECTION ('S.S.') boundaries demonstrate efforts to create circular hinterlands in a rectilinear landscape. Mariposa Township, Victoria County, 1877. From Paterson map of Victoria County, Archives of Ontario.

life by selling residential lots in the field along the road. These are easy to spot, taken up by houses of similar design to those in suburban tracts. Many fail to stand square to the lot boundaries, violating one of southern Ontario's most revered traditions, and the usual farm outbuildings are absent. Com-

Figure 14.5 ROADSIDE INDUSTRY. A tiny storey-and-a-half dwelling next to the road is a faint reminder of rural industrial hamlets once scattered throughout southern Ontario. Oldfield, Chatham Township, Kent County.

Figure 14.6 RURAL WORKFORCE. Millhands' housing, two units per building. Credit River at Barberton, Streetsville, Peel County.

muting has become an accepted, if tedious, part of country road life, and motorists dressed for the office and driving late-model cars or vans mix with tractors and farm trucks. The Ontario countryside, at one time a residential farming quarter, has witnessed generations of multifunctional diversity and is returning once more to a primarily domestic role, with farmers interspersed.

Intersections

The need for a central site where neighbourhood services could gather is deeply rooted. It was enunciated, for instance, in a draft of grammar-school legislation in 1832 calling for `a commodious school house´ and teacher´s residence to be built where sessions of the circuit court of quarter session met.[32] General stores and country taverns filled this need. Inns offered rest and refreshment for the traveller and residence for the keeper and family.[33] They provided space for conviviality, public meetings, trials, church services, and theatrical performances (Figure 14.7).

The blacksmith´s shop, harness shop, and carriage works were among the first non-agricultural activities to move off the farm and join the roadside store. They took the prime sites, at the very corner. Churches, schools, and halls in turn took positions next along from the corner as they outgrew the domestic settings in which they were nurtured. Non-farm houses filled in. All establishments had direct access to roads in any direction. This is the southern Ontario hamlet, with well-defined edges.

A country church is a familiar focus and includes a cemetery, a rectory or manse, and perhaps a shed where parishoners could place their wagons and horses under cover (Figure 14.8). Chances are that the burial ground is older than the church building, while the congregation is the oldest of all (Figure 1.2). Douro, east of Peterborough, is a hamlet where institutions, not businesses, take over the intersection. The church and manse stand on one corner, and the cemetery is diagonally across. The parish hall occupies a third corner. The entire crossroads becomes a kind of churchyard.

The link between church and cemetery has been weakening over the generations. Non-denominational lawn cemeteries first appeared in cities in the 1830s to serve increasing numbers of people not connected with a church. Many of rural Ontario´s little churches of the nineteenth century were raised on sites too small for burials. Adherents were laid to rest elsewhere, without a church building. New burying grounds today occupy open fields and bear no visible association with a church building or the countryside. Flat markers make these places largely invisible, and they will come to look like parks as the trees mature. The old country graveyards have stayed in place, even if their church buildings and most of the markers have gone. The intersection of Highways 427 and 401 in Etobicoke was designed around a cemetery, and

Figure 14.7 COUNTRY INN. The corner bar-room entrance is a sure sign, as is the location at a crossroads or close to a railway station stop. Station hotel, Bowmanville, Durham County.

Figure 14.8 CHRISTIAN CLUSTER. A cemetery is the only element not visible in this crossroads grouping along the 12th Concession of Dover Township. Grace United Church, Baldoon, Kent County.

the runways nearby at Pearson International Airport were laid out to avoid the old cemetery at Elmbank. No other artefacts are more tenacious.

Schools have not induced such lasting clusters. The teacher was a poorly paid tenant, hired as a single person and expected to remain so. He or she roomed in a nearby farmhouse. Swings, flagpoles, and outhouses barely out-lasted the functioning school, and even the shade trees have reached maturity and are dying off. The schoolhouse itself, surviving as a country dwelling today, is, and has always been, the principal artefact of rural education.

Rise or decline

Before completion of the Grand Trunk Railway through Lambton County in 1859, the town of Thedford did not exist. But immediately a station was established there `for the accommodation of the little Village of Widder, one and a half miles to the south-west [southeast, actually] . . . The hamlet which sprang up . . . was thereafter for many years known only as Widder Station. It was intended as a ``branch'' of the older village, but soon outgrew the parent stem, and subsequently absorbed the major part of its life and vitality; and gathering speed with every stride, it soon reached a place among the acknowl-edged villages of the west.'[34] Widder declined into an assortment of odd-sized vacant lots and mysterious entries long forgotten in title deeds. Likewise, Iona Station, on the Michigan Central Railroad in Elgin County, prospered, and Iona faded.[35] There were many more.

Some towns withstood the stigma of being bypassed. The Canadian Pacific missed Craighurst village by a kilometre. The road crossing is marked by a hotel and cement-block house contemporaneous with the line's opening through Simcoe County in 1906, while the town, founded nearly seventy years earlier, continues on. Names such as Mono Road and Vineland Station direct one to nearby, pre-existing centres. Towns such as Haliburton, founded during the railway-building era, grew up surrounding their railways. They replaced nothing, and each has a clear, central focus on the railway.

Villages, towns, and cities emerged as an interconnected system and took up positions scattered along a network of improved minor, intermediate, and major highways and railways. The process was symbiotic: big towns com-manded, and fostered, big roads that spilled over adjacent farmlands. In 1936, the hamlet of Sheridan, at the intersection of two country roads east of Oakville, had nearly one hundred people, living in a dozen buildings; it also had a church and a store. Today the site is buried completely beneath the interchange of the Queen Elizabeth Way and Winston Churchill Blvd., with the curving ramps cutting through the nearest farmyards, supposedly well back from the old crossroads. A historical map on a monument at the site dramatizes the effect.

On the back roads languish the remnants of urban places that failed to advance. Slow dereliction set in with rural depopulation and continues visible because the road has never encroached beyond its surveyed right-of-way. After most of a century of decline, many hamlets now consist of little more than a reduced speed–zone sign and a clutter of fences and treelines that define old parcels of land. Corner stores and workshops not easily recycled into other uses have vanished, leaving vacant spaces where the roads crossed. Motorists appreciate the improved visibility. Adaptable structures and maybe some new suburban houses stand beyond this hollow centre. They function as part of somewhere else.

15

Transport systems

Workplace and home were the same for most people in old Ontario, well into the twentieth century. The shopkeeper lived above the store, the railway agent was quartered in the station, the farm family worked in the kitchen, and the doctor had an office in the house with a separate entrance labelled `Surgery.´ Factory hands and managers in towns such as Alton or Almonte walked between the house on the hill and the mill in the valley, but it was hardly commuting in the modern sense of that term. The roads reflected this living style, being useful for getting around in the neighbourhood but not intended to carry large numbers of travellers over long distances.

Conditions changed early in the twentieth century, with urbanization, industrialization, and a new degree of mobility made possible by motor vehicles and the accumulated wealth to buy them. Some towns grew and others withered, and gradually a system of major and minor roads and railways emerged in response; some arteries disappeared altogether. Rebuilding the Ontario transport system to meet regional and province-wide needs was done with bold strokes, and these have had a profound impact on the cultural landscape during the twentieth century. This undertaking contrasts with the modest and inconspicuous renewal occurring on farms and in service towns, already well established.

A Bruce County resident in 1972 recalled a minor episode in his neighbourhood nearly forty years earlier: `The road was black-topped between Paisley and Walkerton in 1936. They tore up the logs; it was corduroy in the swampy places, with gravel on top of it. They built the new roadway all up with stone and gravel and then put black top on it. The grader came along and turned it over and they put so much tar in and then they would turn it over the other way. They would just do a mile and a quarter at a time.´[1] The references to corduroy, and to stretches of a mile and a quarter, carry us back to the very start of settlement. Tearing out that century-old road structure wiped away an archaeological stratum, but this is the normal way to make a modern road. The resident might also have mentioned the temporary road camp where young men from the surrounding area boarded that summer and were paid a cash wage. All signs of that have vanished, too.[2]

Wooden roads should never have existed, as wood lying on moist ground and exposed to air decays rapidly. Yet corduroy, planking, and wooden culverts were as natural as wooden houses or wooden fences. They made transport feasible in a countryside of tiny streams and poor drainage before machinery was available for building gravel roads. From time to time remnants, embalmed for decades, have reappeared during grading or rebuilding.

The process of making modern roads shows across the landscape surprisingly well. This is the case even though no one campaigns to recreate an old-style roadway in the way enthusiasts advocate restoring a century-old house. `Heritage Highways,´ such as No. 2 along the Lake Ontario shore or No. 3 near Lake Erie, pass through historic areas along rights-of-way dating from the beginning of settlement, but no motorist would tolerate the stumps or river fords that prevailed when the landscape was young. The road as an artefact does not count, regardless of how sensitive the community may be to heritage conservation in general.[3] Transport, rather, offers lessons in cultural change from the residual fragments, frequently visible, of a phenomenon that seeks to be eternally modern.

Corridors

Within a few years of British rule being established in southern Ontario, the basic transportation corridors had been identified. Lieutenant-Governor John Graves Simcoe laid out, and to some extent executed, a military road system radiating from Toronto to Niagara, the Thames River, Georgian Bay, and the St Lawrence valley. Details of the alignment, engineering, and means of conveyance have constantly changed, but the routes remain as always. Yonge Street (1794), the Welland Canal (1830), the Grand Trunk Railway (1856), Lakeshore Road paved (1914), the Queen Elizabeth Way, or QEW (1939), and the 400-series super-highways starting in the 1950s have, era by era, repeated Simcoe´s plan. Barrie, London, Guelph, Brighton, Lancaster, and dozens of other urban places stand on little stems off the 401 spine, just as Port Credit has off the QEW since 1939. But all continue part of the basic corridors.

The QEW through Mississauga is the latest upgrading of the first Concession Line south of Dundas Street (`CON I, S.D.S.´), opened in the first quarter of the nineteenth century. No other segment of road in Ontario has gone through all the stages from stumpy track to gravel, to concrete, to multiple lanes with level crossings, to fully controlled access ramps with signal lights and television cameras monitoring traffic flow.[4] It shows up on every map since the 1790s.

Artefacts from various periods recall the route´s ancient lineage. The Credit River bridge is an outstanding example of concrete-arch design dating from the 1930s, though few motorists are aware of the architectural gem, with its ten graceful, monogrammed (ER) lampposts, that bears them. Near Cawthra and Dixie roads stand storey-and-a-half farmhouses of the 1870s. Once their laneways issued directly on to CON I, S.D.S. Now, however, these houses hide behind noise-deflecting walls erected in the 1980s and are reoriented into residential neighbourhoods that have filled in around. Even the visual link to the road they were built to face on has vanished.

New alignments devised to reduce grades, ease curves, and avoid congestion always leave evidence of what went before. The Canadian National Railways line east of Oshawa is on a right-of-way several hundred metres south of the original 1856 roadbed, still visible after abandonment more than a century ago. The Bronte Creek crossing of Dundas Street has outgrown previous alignments on four occasions, and abutments and bridge piers still remain to identify the stages (Figure 15.1). The Welland Canal is in its fifth manifestation, each change having involved substantial relocation and a chapter of engineering history.[5] At Merritton a lock, built for the first Welland Canal in 1824 and superseded twenty years later, lay buried 140 years before being exhumed for archaeological study and then reburied.[6]

Parts of the corridors remain in use unaltered. The English built the Grand Trunk Railway as a prestigious social instrument and a landscape *objet d´art*, and no structure on it could be too strong or too big. The stone piers of the

Figure 15.1 PERSISTENCE OF A ROUTE. Superseded structures mark the progressive modernization of the Dundas Street crossing of Bronte Creek. Tansley, Nelson Township, Halton County.

Figure 15.2 BUILT TO LAST. The Grand Trunk Railway is an overbuilt monument to English expectations of massive volumes of traffic. Passenger station and ticket office (1856). Ernestown, Lennox and Addington County.

Credit River bridge at Georgetown stand securely after 140 years, bearing loads unimagined when erected. Romanesque stone stations at Belleville and other places continue in use, setting the style then and of undiminished presence today (Figure 15.2).[7]

Even so, the Grand Trunk was scaled down from what it might have been had work started a few years earlier. The distinguished engineer Frederick Cumberland described the Humber River bridge as a `simple and satisfactory´ combination of brick piers and wrought-iron girders but pined for `those not very distant times ... when the crossing ... would have been effected by a structure involving much more intricacy of design, vastly more material, and far heavier expense.´[8] He particularly regretted the `hard horizontal lines´ that he anticipated would `mar every landscape and parallyze [sic] the hand of the most soulless artist.´ But graceful arches made little sense in Canada, and most other lines, including Cumberland´s own Northern Railway between Toronto and Georgian Bay, are functional, and certainly not monumental.

Hierarchy

Earliest transport was, like most else in Ontario, vernacular. It was based on simple responses to common needs. In 1871, on average, one blacksmith served every twenty-eight farms; one could usually be found within a radius of two kilometres. One grist mill served sixty farms, one brewery 150, and one cheese factory 200.[9] For most people, most of the time, trips were short, and they remained so well into the twentieth century. They and everything they carried moved at one speed – very slowly – over roadways that were invariably bad. The similar appearance of so many of the buildings in old Ontario occurred despite – or perhaps because of – inadequate communication.

From this sameness has emerged, generation by generation, a sophisticated transport system tuned to carrying large shipments and small, at high speeds and low, over long distances and short. With this a landscape of specialized buildings has developed. Once there was a brewery on practically every stream, yet by 1980 nine million Ontarians were supplied by just three corporations. The Boyd firm's catalogue of concrete blocks in Osgoode, a country store in Newington, a business premises in Tweed, the freight shed in West Lorne, the Sawyer's farm-machinery warehouse in Hamilton, and the Canada Air Line Railway repair shops in St Thomas all are late Victorian expressions of a regional, even provincial scale of marketing the products of the urban-industrial era.

The layout of roads to this day remains rectangular, but it has come to function radially. Far out in the countryside, road signs and mailboxes carry city street numbers and addresses, which, followed down to their origin, put one in a town. Different types of vehicles have sorted themselves onto major and minor alignments for safety and efficiency. Entirely new roadways have been built where expansion of the grid proved impractical. Public and private corporations maintain waterways, railways, and highways and open, expand, contract, and close them according to the wishes of the users.

Lanes and minor roads

The lowest in rank is the farm lane, a private road that ties farm buildings to the public road system. Often the lane is defined by an avenue of trees – basswood or maple, for instance – and these give definition and focus to the cluster of buildings off towards the centre of the lot. Even the remnant stumps at the Smith-Armstrong farm draw the eye towards the house and barns (Figure 1.4). As much as one-quarter of the road mileage in a typical southern Ontario township consists of lanes. This was the price paid by farmers wishing to build in the middle of lots served by road allowances running along the edges. Lanes have continued in use as field access routes under farm consolidation during the twentieth century.

Next in the sequence are the surveyed concession roads and crossroads. Customary use determined that some allowances were important and others should not even have been opened. Statute labour – roadwork performed by residents in lieu of taxes – was allocated unevenly across the concessions,

according to the local pathmaster's perception of this distinction. His neighbours endorsed this impression with hard work in critical spots and careless
uninterest elsewhere.[10]

The surveyed road allowance of one chain-width – sixty-six feet (about twenty
metres) – is a Renaissance measure.[11] It was suitable for settled land with
plenty of traffic but seems overly generous in Ontario. A number of private
companies incorporated to build toll roads on the surveyed allowances designed driving surfaces narrower than three metres.[12] Vast flows at some time
in the future were an obvious expectation, and in the meanwhile the wide
right-of-way permitted roadways to weave among stumps and boulders without
encroaching on private lands (Figure 15.3). Unused portions were free pas-
tureland.[13]

Figure 15.3 UNDERUSED ROAD ALLOWANCES. Road allowances have been more
than adequate for roadways and drainage ditches throughout most of
southern Ontario's history. Westover Road, north of Dundas, Wentworth
County, 1880s.

In the late nineteenth century one chain continued to serve adequately for roadway and ditching. Twelve-foot (four-metre) driving surfaces allowed slow-moving vehicles to scrape past and remained characteristic up until 1939. The generous allowances have permitted the survival of early examples of rail and stump fencing. Had roads been only as wide as needed, fences and borderline trees would have been destroyed as each successive widening took place. There must be satisfaction in knowing that Highway 401 and its kin, on entirely new rights-of-way, have further reduced the roadside destruction dealt by expanding roads.

Major roads

Municipal and provincial funds supplemented, and then replaced, statute labour between 1880 and 1940, allowing important roads to be given extra attention. They were cambered (arched), ditched, and gravelled, which made them suitable for horses, not just oxen, and in all seasons.[14] Gravel was the key element, for an earth road could not hold its camber or keep its ditches clean. Names such as 'Minto Gravel Road' and 'Thorold Stone Road' tell of all-weather transport not much inferior to a 'rail' road, and far cheaper. The Northern Gravel Road between Collingwood and Owen Sound was in fact an extension of the Northern Railroad from Toronto. In 1896, Ontario appointed an instructor in roadmaking in the Department of Agriculture, a sign of the vital role that roadside ditches played in field drainage. In 1901 the provincial government made its first direct budget allocation for rural roads.[15]

As rural depopulation proceeded after 1900, the mobility of the remaining residents increased. They sought more distant destinations, and travel became concentrated on still fewer roads. When farms merged, the home farm was likely to be on one of these main roads. Thousands of kilometres more settled into the status of 'back roads.' A half-century later many of these were losing their mail routes and school-bus runs, and municipalities chose not to keep them open in winter. Many have since disappeared from the map altogether.

The province-wide system of King's Highways began branching out from Queen's Park after the First World War.[16] Those portions of township and county roads appropriated and gradually upgraded were linked by common numbering and destination signs to establish such routes as Highway 7, zig-zagging between Sarnia and Ottawa. The long-distance motorist passed through every town along the way, becoming familiar with the storefront restaurant with oilcloth on the tables, the curbside filling station, and the Central Hotel that shared main street in each. By the early 1930s, one mile of road in seven was asphalt, concrete, or macadam. Lane-marking stripes were soon painted on these surfaces – surely one of the most pervasive expressions of authority ever wrought on the landscape of the province.[17]

Most roads continued to fit within their allowances through the interwar years. Six metres (twenty feet) was adequate for two vehicles to pass easily at modest speeds. But with the construction of raised surfaces, broader shoulders, smoothed jogs, and deeper ditches, road structures suited for steady motor traffic were filling allowances to their full width and then spilling beyond.

Cuttings and embankments nibbled at adjacent fields. Highway 10 south of Caledon village sways from side to side, its widened right-of-way of the 1960s encroaching on whichever side provided less resistance. At the Delaware Township hall west of London in 1949 'motor vehicles failing to make the turn on Number 2 highway have repeatedly smashed into the structure';[18] council retreated to a remodelled, less vulnerable, Presbyterian church. The 1977 cornerstone on Munn's Church tells of similar discretion (Figure 1.3). Expropriations for multiple-lane highways have made a mockery of the one-chain width.

Since 1945, the emphasis has been on separating incompatible types of traffic and making roads safe for higher speeds. Tractors turning left into a farm lane do not belong on the Queen Elizabeth Way, nor should trans-provincial transport trucks be creeping through Port Hope, Simcoe, or Forest on a Saturday morning. Hundreds of overpass bridges have appeared, and a place such as Chesterville no longer entertains the Highway 43 traffic between Smiths Falls and the Quebec boundary. Both the Gravenhurst bypass and the entire length of Highway 401 each have contributed to the survival of small towns.

Canals and railways

Canals and railways were built to occupy a higher niche in the order of mobility. Even the feeblest tramroad or narrow-gauge light railway was destined to assume main-road status, and Grand Trunk Railway contractors were in-structed in the 1850s to build 'a first-class single-track railway, with the foun-dations of all the large structures sufficient for a double line, equal in per-manence and stability to any railway in England' (Figure 15.4).[19]

Such cautious reading of the needs of a raw colony was not always re-spected. Cobourg entrepreneurs boldly laid the railway to Peterborough straight across Rice Lake on a causeway that lasted only from 1857 to 1859 before being crushed by ice.[20] Remnants of this folly still obstruct pleasure boaters. Kingston promoters struck out directly for the U.S. railway network with a water route slicing through Wolfe Island. Within twenty years the canal was a weed-grown lagoon that today does not even look artificial.[21] The Brockville tunnel (1860) provided railway access inland from the downtown riverfront without disturbing the townscape. It was an aesthetic success and

Figure 15.4 EXPANSION ANTICIPATED. Grand Trunk Railway bridge abutment and piers designed for two tracks (1856). Only one such structure was ever built. Speed River, Guelph.

a prestigious monument, but it hardly reflected sound business practice. The south portal today houses a small museum and is wonderfully cool in summer (Figure 15.5).

By the early twentieth century, the possibilities for canals and railways were just about exhausted. Proposals died in the legislature, and a few projects that got started were never completed. North of Newmarket, locks for the Holland River canal have stood unfinished since 1912. Others were obsolete practically before they were open; electric suburban railways built in the 1910s died early deaths at the hands of the motorist coming on strongly in the 1920s.[22] The Trent-Severn and Rideau waterways have managed to adapt to recreational use and survive relatively unchanged from the days of lumbering and small steamboats.[23] They were installed as alternative transport to secondary railways that surely would have been abandoned by the 1990s. The Trent and Rideau are fine living museums of engineering progress between 1840 and 1920. Hog's Back dam south of Ottawa, the Severn River marine railway, swing bridges, and hydraulic locks are among the jewels strung along these fascinating systems, awaiting the touring motorist or boater.

Figure 15.5 FOLLY. The Brockville railway tunnel (1850s) as it appeared in 1969, a few years after abandonment. A museum display was set up in the south portal in the 1980s. A stretch of railway track laid to the broad (provincial) gauge (5 ft, 6 in.), in use between the 1850s and the 1870s, adds an authentic touch.

Pipelines

Pipelines are at the high-art end of the transport hierarchy, but almost invisible. Those low, wooden signs with large numbers painted on them, aimed skyward, that one sometimes encounters along a country road mark the path of a buried oil- or natural gas-transmission pipe. An inconspicuous pressure station may present itself. Oil jerkers around Petrolia and the natural gas-pumping station at Port Alma are just about all there is, fixed on the ground, of oil and gas transmission. Both look ancient but would not be functioning unless, like all else under transport regulation, they were fully modern.

Crossings

For several decades before 1975, Ort Road, near Fort Erie, was one of several earth roads making level crossings with the Queen Elizabeth Way.[24] Such a meeting of highest- and lowest-level roadways aroused little thought in the 1940s, when grade crossings were common all along the QEW. By the 1960s, however, it was becoming a dangerous oddity, hardly used but always there. About 1975 the crossing was closed, and this interesting feature no longer tells its story.

Among the forty thousand spots where country roads meet in Ontario it is highly improbable that any two cross on separate grades. Grade, or level crossings allow maximum access at minimum cost – just what was wanted. But these places are not strictly on one level. Each displays the careful engineering of intersecting culverts and drainage ditches that keeps surface waterflow separated from public movement. Since most Ontario streams are not navigable and the terrain is rarely rougher than a gentle roll, this is a landscape of low bridges and culverts, not high viaducts. Bronte Creek and a few others in deep glacial ravines along the Lake Ontario front are exceptional (Figure 15.1).

Bridges

Ontario was constructing bridging well before bridges, as we would call them, were being built. It opened many corduroy roads – with poles laid crosswise to traverse low, wet land. After years of filling and refilling, these have become solid ground (Figure 15.6). Such embankments are like landforms, almost free from maintenance. In the last quarter of the nineteenth century, farm-machinery firms adapted their talents to the production of the graders and ditchers required for such work.

The simplest bridge has a deck of logs lying across log or timber cribs set on bare ground. It was like a log barn with a flat roof, and southern Ontario had thousands and thousands of them. Rot is a slow killer of these heavy structures, and, with individual pieces freely replaceable, some still exist in

Figure 15.6 DRAINAGE. A country road in the poorly drained backslope of the Niagara Escarpment looks like a causeway in springtime. Nassagaweya Township, Halton County.

Figure 15.7 TRESTLE AND TRUSS. Trestles (background) carried railways across ravines, with truss spans (foreground) used where footing could not be secured. Canada Air Line Railway, 1870s. Near St Thomas, Elgin County.

the marginal townships where neither need nor resources have induced modernization. Most, however, have given way to corrugated steel piping and are hidden from sight by layers of gravel and asphalt. Installation of culverts on Ontario roads was a major activity during the 1920s and had the effect of diminishing our awareness of the presence of water flowing through the countryside.

Trestles – columns of timber bents bolted together – provided somewhat more sophisticated bridging than did landfilling (Figure 15.7). They blended the skills of a vernacular barn framer and a high-art civil engineer but were expected to last no more than ten years.[25] Trestles spanned ravines and allowed railways to start earning money well before lines were fully ready to receive heavy traffic at high speeds. In due course carloads of spoil were dumped through the latticework, burying it and building up an elongated cone that, once compacted and sprouting vegetation on its flanks, was as solid as natural ground. Filling in transparent trestles with these opaque embankments has made the railway even more visible.

Where a railway line cut through a farm lot, the corporation was obliged to install a private farm crossing joining the two pieces. If the topography called for a bridge, it put up a beam bridge or simple trusswork of braced, diagonal timbers. Almost all such structures have been wooden, and their numbers have gradually diminished as severed parcels have been attached to other farms on the same side. More have disappeared as the tracks that they spanned have been abandoned, and we may expect to see earth filled back into cuttings across disused roadbeds.

The common Ontario bridge consists of boxlike superstructures, either girders (that is, beams) or latticework trusses (Figure 15.7). Wooden ones were hardly more permanent than trestles. But since the 1890s wide steel beams, spanning between concrete (or occasionally stone) piers, have been used for hundreds of bridges, especially on railways. Most girder bridges are low-level and fixed in place, but more costly versions that could be swung, lifted, or tipped were needed for crossing Ontario's few navigable waterways. The Scherzer rolling lift bridge at Smiths Falls is an example of this genre.[26]

Railways introduced truss bridges to Ontario after 1850, and they became essential elements of the highway and railway net that developed to serve mixed farming and industrialization over the next half-century (Figure 15.8).

Figure 15.8 IMPORTED STEEL. Swing-truss railway bridge built by Carengie Steel in Pittsburgh, Pennsylvania. Numbered pieces allowed for easy assembly. Trent Canal at Nassau Mills, Peterborough County.

Compared with beam construction, trusses were light and portable, and by the 1880s U.S. steel mills were exporting knocked-down models that a literate foreman and squad of unskilled hands could assemble on site. Pins were sometimes used because they were simpler than riveting. American bridges were popular first in southwestern Ontario, where timber supplies dwindled before Canadian manufacturers of steel products had come into production.[27] After 1900, firms in Hamilton and Walkerville picked up the business, and hundreds of their products may be identified by cast builder-plates boldly displayed.

Individual truss components are replaceable, perpetuating the basic design from wooden origins through cast iron (1850s), wrought iron (1860s), and then steel after 1880. Mixed materials allowed each to do what it could do best. Cedar decking was replaced with concrete by the first decade of the twentieth century. This required stronger structures.[28] Wooden trusses could be enclosed to retard decay from accumulated snow, but this was done probably fewer than ten times in Ontario. For all its notoriety, the covered bridge at West Montrose in Wellington County is nevertheless an oddity. Iron and steel made enclosed bridges irrelevant, and had creosote been available before the 1930s, covered bridges might not have existed at all.

The market for steel truss bridges continued well into the automobile era. By the 1920s it was normal to mount them high above a stream's flood level, with substantial earthwork ramps and stone or cement abutments at each end. They replaced river fords or wooden bridges. Some were dismantled and re-erected in secondary locations as they became inadequate for main roads. The pony truss, a light open-topped bridge, has been popular for small crossings for a century but is gradually being replaced by concrete girders or culverts. Truss bridges demonstrate the benefits of timely adaptation and give a glimpse far back into the history of structural metal design.

The bow-string bridge is a truss that looks like a concrete arch (Figure 15.9). Construction with reinforced concrete reduced the steel content substantially and made it possible for contractors to use material excavated locally.[29] Steel or iron reinforcing rods allow the concrete to be in tension. The load bears down, not outward, on light piers. One designer built some five hundred bow-strings on country roads throughout the province in the 1910s and 1920s.[30] The first massive structures were followed by lighter and cheaper ones. During the 1930s it became apparent that the concrete was being corroded by salt, newly applied to keep routes passable for cars in winter. The exposed rods began rusting away. Salt preserved wood, as did creosote, and the result was a modest revival of wooden truss construction.[31]

Since the 1950s girder bridges, in steel or pre-stressed concrete, obtrude unharmoniously into the landscape. Their size is unlimited, as elevated road-ways such as the Queensway in Ottawa show. Many have replaced older (but not old), more graceful spans emblazoned with castings of Ontario's coat of

Figure 15.9 THE BOW-STRING. A concrete truss bridge with steel reinforcing rods in the deck in tension, holding the ends of the arched superstructure. Load bears down, not outward, on light piers. Grand River at Bridgeport, Waterloo County.

arms. Against its graceful steel-arched mate, the second Burlington Beach Skyway bridge at Hamilton shows the shift towards utilitarian bridge design in recent decades.

Bridges in the landscape

Had the British tradition of grade separations for railways and public roads carried over into southern Ontario, there would have been perhaps five thousand more bridges on the landscape. But the costs were simply too great and the density of traffic and population was too slight to justify this massive outlay. Grade crossings prevailed, and whatever difference in elevation there may have been was invariably absorbed by the road (Figure 15.10). With their long curves and gentle slopes, railways have been set into the landscape, slicing through hills and riding above ravines. Roads, in contrast, have always rested on top of the undulating land surface. As railroad lines are abandoned, these uneven grade crossings are smoothed, leaving tell-tale embankments or cuttings on either side. The enduring road resumes its appointed way.

Highway 400 was built in the 1950s as a controlled-access road yet made a level crossing with a railway south of Barrie. It may be considered arrogant that Department of Highways officials presumed that this line would rapidly succumb to the motor traffic generated by the new highway. The decline of the railway was slower than anticipated, however, and motor traffic built up so rapidly that an overpass had to be installed, about 1960. Still, automobiles and trucks have killed thousands of miles of railways, and after not very many years Highway 400 was swooping up and down over a trackless roadbed. One

Figure 15.10 THE UNLEVEL GRADE CROSSING. Railway engineering invariably determined the configuration of road crossings and may not well serve the motorist. East of Hornby, Halton County.

Figure 15.11 ROAD CONQUERS RAILWAY. Highway 6 grade separation, built c. 1960, crossing the Canadian Pacific Railway; rails lifted 1988. The previous grade crossing is in the foreground. Near Mount Forest, Wellington County.

finds similar overpasses along Highway 401 and elsewhere (Figure 15.11). We may expect these spans to be demolished when their useful lives are over.

The Great Lakes shoreline

Ontario has a water transport tradition that goes back to its very inception. Settlers sailed the Great Lakes and arrived at little landings at the mouths of dozens of rivers and creeks. Land transport took priority immediately, but the landscape continues to mirror the early elements and the changeover. Along the length of the Lake Ontario and Lake Erie shores, ferry slips have fallen into disuse; in their place bridges carry the lakeshore road or railway across the river mouths. On the waterfronts of Oshawa and Port Burwell, or Trenton and Dunnville, the change has been uncelebrated.

At the broader scale of the Great Lakes region, spectacular bridges span the Ottawa, St Lawrence, Niagara, Detroit, St Clair, and St Mary's rivers, asserting the supremacy of land communication. Railway tunnels at Windsor and Sarnia belong in this group of major links with the rest of the continent. The harbours persist at such places as Bayfield, Port Burwell, Bronte, and Brighton, but they have been relegated to the edge of Ontario. Some of these small ports host a few commercial fishing boats, and others are home to large flotillas of recreational craft moored at shiny new marinas.

The transport role of lakefront towns has vanished, save possibly for a lighthouse guiding commercial ships offshore (Figure 3.12). Navigation was a principal outdoor night-time activity before the twentieth century, and tall lighthouses are original components of dozens of Great Lakes harbours. But use of rivers for power and introduction of railways reduced waterborne commerce to a handful of international enterprises using no more than a dozen lakeports with regularity. Changed shipping lanes and electronic navigational gear introduced since the Second World War have accelerated the decline of the old lighthouse. Lighthouses are quaint relics and constitute a minute component of the Ontario landscape.

Space and time

Railway stations

Transportation requires buildings as well as arteries. Taverns, passenger depots, and freight sheds conveyed customers and their goods through time in the same way that roadways, tracks, and bridges carried them across space. Station lunch rooms and station hotels offered sustenance and shelter until a scheduled connecting stage or train arrived. Warehouses give secure space for repackaging, sorting, inspecting, and taxing goods. Other structures have provided for the transport service itself: lockkeepers' houses, locomotive sheds, and the railway YMCA where crews away from home could rest between assignments, for example.

Buildings can be as homey as the enterprises they support. The works de-

partments of Elderslie and Amaranth townships, to name but two, park machinery in former halls – a school in one case and a church in the other. The
Schomberg terminus of the Schomberg and Aurora Railway, opened in 1904,
looked like a farmyard. The S&A was a shoestring operation, and taking over
extant buildings was part of its strategy for survival. Service ended just twenty-
three years later, and the station melted back into the rural scene.[32] It continues
as a house in the village today.

Erecting distinctive passenger stations was a favourite means used by successful railways to promote themselves. The Grand Trunk Railway's pretentious Romanesque stations, in stone or brick, boldly announced the company's
presence throughout the Ontario countryside in the 1850s (Figure 15.2). They
took a lead in architectural design and added impetus to the diffusion of the
Romanesque style through public buildings over ensuing decades. Stations
are among Ontario's first mass-produced buildings, and more matched sets
appeared during the first period of railway consolidation, in the 1880s. Canadian Pacific, the Midland Railway, and other companies had one or a few
standard designs and distributed bigger and smaller versions along their lines,
according to traffic needs.

High-art pretension had to face vernacular reality, however. The Grand Trunk
planned that at every stopping place signalmen, track crews, freight-handlers,
and dispatchers each would have their own buildings.[33] All would be separate
from the one for passengers and ticket agent. That was the British way, tried
at Ernestown and elsewhere, but was out of touch with the less-specialized
style of North American business practice. In Ontario, the residency station
prevailed. The Ottawa, Arnprior and Parry Sound Railway (later Canadian
National), for instance, put up identical station buildings at many stopping
points in the 1890s. Each had passenger, freight, and train-operation facilities
on the ground floor and residential space upstairs for the operator and family.
In Whitney, Wilno, Carp, Kinburn, Canoe Lake, Edgington, and elsewhere,
the OA&PS presented a consistent corporate image in a single, all-purpose
building.

Recognizing a railway station used to offer no challenge. The tracks and
loading platform in front and a name-board on each end left no doubt. Decades
of decline have resulted in the demolition of hundreds of these buildings, yet
many others have been taken over for new uses, often far from the routes
they served. But they continue to have the look of stations. The Italianate style
has been especially popular, with its broad, bracketed eaves that sheltered
waiting passengers in all types of weather. The operator's bay window and
the large baggage-room door are other diagnostic features. The inside walls
are surely panelled in wood because plaster cracks from the pounding of
passing trains. Streetsville's first railway station, built in 1879, becomes readily
discernible in its setting on a residential street where it has stood for nearly
eighty years.

Parking spots

Cars and trucks have shrunk waiting time and have made transport a highly private matter. Travellers no longer chat or doze in the Sharbot Lake station waiting room while making connections for Pembroke or Kingston, or Smiths Falls or Peterborough. They drive on through. In place of the livery stables and main-street hotels that served a slower-paced clientelle stand the big motels, of international renown, out at the interchange with Highway 401.

The opportunity to get home for the night, and not to rest en route, has never been greater, and the urban landscape mirrors it. Virtually every new dwelling built in the last half-century comes with its own garage. Most of these project obtrusively from the front and, when signalled by a remote control to open their doors, swallow up arriving household members and then slam shut. Broad asphalt driveways provide overflow parking. The curbsides of residential streets perform the same function in densely built city neighbourhoods. Thousands of self-service gas bars (not `service stations´) line highways, and parking lots stretch endlessly around suburban shopping malls, industries, container terminals, and airports. All these features keep people and goods moving rapidly and headed for a final destination.

The artefacts of personal mobility are all around us, but not altogether pretty. One term – `parking spot´ – sums up the gradual impoverishment of the old Ontario landscape. A few old country inns that have hung on have been beneficiaries of the recent renewal of interest in touring rural areas. Country-living magazines have stimulated revival of such hostelries as The Little Inn in Bayfield, one of many with a gourmet menu popular with the summer-theatre and antique-shop set. Cars are put in their place behind hedges or board fences, and for a moment one may be able to look back on a period when moving about was a congregating rather than an isolating experience.

16
Townscapes

The town is the apogee of Ontario achievement, if literature be our guide. Sara Jeannette Duncan, Stephen Leacock, Hugh Garner, and Robertson Davies have done as much in words to promote Ontario as the Group of Seven painters have done on canvas. Out there in Jubilee, a couple of generations ago, Alice Munro found a pleasing scene, of `Sidewalks, street lights, lined-up shade trees, milkmen's and icemen's carts, birdbaths, flower borders, verandas with wicker chairs, from which ladies watched the street – all these civilized, desirable things.'[1] Not roads with ditches, but streets with sidewalks that are stages for the steady interplay of personalities and situations. Towns invite interaction, and the landscape recedes into a more submissive posture than it possesses on the farm.

Sightlines

The edges of prosperous towns are among southern Ontario's least attractive places today. Fringed with fast-food restaurants, propane-fuel depots, `garden centres,' lumber stores, and the local Ontario Provincial Police detachment, they are ragged places, approached without their offering clear evidence of when one is actually entering. Their skylines add little more cause for celebration, if only because they offer no unobstructed view. Notable exceptions are the Franco-Ontarian communities of extreme eastern Ontario, dominated by the glistening roof and spire of the local Roman Catholic church.

Hundreds of crossroads towns have a translucent quality distinctive to southern Ontario. Grand Valley is a town one just looks straight through (Figure 16.1). The concession road pierces the heart and runs out the other side, and the side road perpendicular to it does the same. Where they cross, there is just a stop sign. No village green, no widened market street, and nothing like the anomalous central roundabout in Goderich obstructs the clear view.

A thick, low plinth of deciduous trees greets the motorist approaching a typical southern Ontario town. It screens all but the chimney-tops of prosperous houses and the business buildings lying at the centre. As one proceeds

Figure 16.1 CENTRE OF TOWN, looking outward from the retail to the residential section, 1977. Background extensively damaged by tornado in 1985. Grand Valley, Dufferin County.

into town, rural concessions give way to blocks, farms to house-lots, and gravel surfacing to blacktop. Lots shrink and houses draw closer to the curbside, displacing front-lawn trees. The roof ridgelines on buildings reorient to line up at right angles to the street.

A house with a storefront added on marks the beginning of the business section. A windowless end wall of a retail building indicates that the builder expected a continuous terrace to develop. A *porte-cochère* opens through a wall of storefronts, offering a brief glimpse of the alley behind (Figure 6.13). Buildings reach three floors in height, and mansard roofs and fluted pilasters give still greater display. Such a showpiece as the Grand Central Hotel in Orangeville is the tallest in its block, but the entire top floor is a fake. False fronts may be necessary for draining rainwater to the rear, but the reasons for such designs frequently go well beyond simple necessity (Figure 16.2).

The central intersection is not necessarily a focus. One just stares directly on through the centre of places such as Harriston or Seaforth, the eye finally being arrested by a church spire and the resumption of trees. Beyond the last brick store block the side scene once more opens out, back to a church and its grounds, possibly, or to a Carnegie library. Fleeting views of carriage houses, vegetable patches, and the backs of side-street housing show between spreading maples and the ornate façades of the mansions of wealthy townsfolk. The

Figure 16.2 A FALSE FRONT makes a modest building pretentious. The storefront storey-and-a-half house next door is a transitional link to the residential part of the street beyond. Frankford, Northumberland County.

town shrinks to one house-lot deep. Quite suddenly the view opens wide to the farmland horizon, and the town is over.

Main street

Business blocks were the largest countryside building investments outside of mills or factories before 1914. They represent the full flowering of a commercial society that, in southern Ontario, is as old as settlement. Perth, a stone town, preserves the early commercial style of shops that look like houses (Figure 16.3). Many towns at Confederation had main streets much in the style and scale of Perth, but built in wood. At one time or another, most burned (Figure 16.4).

Fire destroyed fifty businesses and several houses in Drumbo in 1862, and 125 in Bradford in 1871.[2] Drumbo was hit again two years later, and Sykes Street, Meaford, had major fires on eight occasions between 1881 and 1921, each eroding the old streetscape more.[3] Commercial streets had grown piece-meal, with individual buildings filling in gaps. Frame showrooms jutted out to the street from houses set further back, and wooden sheds stood everywhere. Flames jumped from roof to roof, and church spires created draughts that

Figure 16.3 DOMESTIC-LOOKING BUSINESS STREET. Perth was one of the first inland towns in Ontario, rising to prominence with the opening of a branch of the Rideau Canal in the 1830s. It declined, but did not disappear, when missed by railways a generation later. Perth´s stone construction has borne up well, unremodelled, in an essentially pre-retail style.

made them blaze like torches. Great town conflagrations passed into history only with the disappearance of wooden roofing shingles in the 1920s.[4]

Following a fire among buildings described as ʿmostly roughcast [i.e., stucco] and lumberʾ in Orangeville in 1860, several merchants chose to rebuild in brick.[5] In Barrie a decade later, town council proposed that no wooden houses be allowed on two main streets.[6] Belleville ruled that a party wall be required for terrace-type housing, of brick at least 30 cm thick or stone 40 cm. Further,

Figure 16.4 FIRE destroyed at least twenty buildings in Barrie in June 1875. The chimneys standing in the foreground suggest that these buildings were free-standing, house-like shops, of wood. A newer, more fire-resistant streetscape stands opposite, largely spared.

a bylaw dictated that 'no wooden clapboarded, or frame dwelling-house' could be built in the inner part of the town.[7]

Everywhere precautions were being taken, and even without fire the urban fabric was being transformed. Brick and concrete came to the fore, able to withstand fire better than either stone or sheet metal.[8] As we have seen, solid brick was a recipe for full-storey construction, and across the province full-storey brick buildings took over main street after Confederation. Firewalls and watermains with hydrants have added immeasurable assurance. Only Toronto, Kingston, and Hamilton had water systems prior to 1863, but by 1900 more than two hundred Canadian towns (mostly in southern Ontario) had this utility.[9]

Fire stations took up commanding central positions. The hose-drying tower is their unmistakable hallmark (Figure 8.21). Italianate or Romanesque detail enhances their vertical lines, and many survive. Trade catalogues promoted fire-resistant materials such as lead-based paint,[10] asphalt shingles, asphalt ('insulbrick' or 'insulstone') siding, cast iron, and pressed tin. Use of metal seems to have been regarded as untruthful, and manufacturers attempted to disguise it as wood, stone, or brick, with indifferent results. Rust stains streaked down walls are tell-tales of iron window casings above, for instance. Metal gave some protection to wooden structures cheaply, as did brick veneer.

New brick blocks rose up amid unbridled optimism, offering shops below and rental apartments above. Each is testimony to success in business, proudly announced by a name and datestone mounted prominently on the façade. The *Peterborough Examiner* effusively described the Morrow Building of 1878: 'in the French Classic style with an arcaded ground storey from which spring pilasters supporting a panelled frieze and medallioned cornice with ballustrade and pediment windows, being roofed with a mansard roof.'[11]

Buildings of all descriptions carried frivolous iron castings of urns, acanthus leaves, fluted columns, and other devices representing various architectural revivals sweeping the high-art world. Stone and brick, in many shades and textures, and sometimes used together, created endless variations. Congregations attempted to place their big new churches on corner sites along the main street and designed them with corner towers so as to show off their architecture fully in all directions (Figure 5.11).[12] Post office buildings did the same (Figure 8.23).

Main-street hotels look much like retail buildings, except for the fire escape and maybe an encircling verandah, if street widening has not taken it. Livery stables may still stand behind. Hotels survive in towns of 1,000 to 3,000 people, too small or remote to draw modern motels and restaurants, but big enough for a loyal cadre of customers at the bar. Room guests who are satisfied with worn furnishings, squeaky staircases, a bathroom at the end of the hall, and an escape rope coiled by the window may thank the customers of the lively bar below – once the commercial traveller's showroom – for subsidizing southern Ontario's least expensive accommodation. Town hotels are fascinating vantage points from which to discover the region's streetscapes and to feel a bit closer to the local scene.

Straight streets and four-square intersections offer few head-on views of buildings. Sites opposite the head of a T-junction are among the few that give special opportunity for showing off. The old town hall in Milton and parish church in Romford occupy such prominent spots. The showy location of Stratford city hall is accidental: five streets, representing five orientations of the survey grid, come together there.

Too rarely has a truly spectacular site been properly used, but St Mary's Roman Catholic Church in Guelph measures up. Not only does this massive church building command a broad, busy retail street from its lofty elevation, but the spire may be seen well beyond the city limits. Far to the southeast, around Arkell, one may see the church seemingly float over the region, much as Chartres Cathedral does over the Beauce region of France.

Domestic architecture paralleled business and public designs. Stretches of Lakeshore Road through Burlington, Grafton, Trenton, Napanee, Gananoque, and Brockville display the finest of stately Victorian town housing (Figure 3.7). An address on main street trumpeted personal success. The verandah was a reviewing stand for ladies strolling, young men driving fast buggies, and parades and funeral cortèges.[13] Victorian townsfolk made the street a place, not merely the way out of town. Indeed, only muted echoes reached the farms – 'the mansard roof and vaguely Italianate details, which become vaguer as one moves away from the sophisticated urban centres.'[14] Architecturally, Victorian towns outgrew their countryside origins, and few farmscapes embraced main-street elements.

Back streets

Plenty of Ontario town life is missing from main street and must be tracked down in the separate quarters defined by the major intersection. The railway stop might be in one of these quadrants, a mill dam and industrial grouping in another, a church or school or court-house in the third, and the farmers' marketplace and the fairground off in the fourth.

Residential sections followed a defined hierarchy (Figure 16.5): `A town lot is to be granted in the front street only on the condition that you shall build a house of not less than forty-seven feet frontage, two stories high, and of a certain order of architecture. In the second street they may be somewhat less in front, but the two stories and the mode of architecture are indispensable; and it is only on the back streets and alleys that the tinkers and taylors [*sic*] will be allowed to consult their taste and circumstances in the structure of their habitation.´[15]

Away from the main street lots are narrower, and storey-and-a-half houses turned sideways make best use of the small lot (Figure 6.6). Here also are one-storey town-houses, and structural alterations that are not vainly concealed.

Figure 16.5 OFF THE MAIN STREET. Wellington Street. Orangeville, Dufferin County.

Styles, materials, setbacks, scale, and upkeep are more varied, and these streets are altogether more vernacular. Parallel streets in one direction may be numbered, and those crossing them carry given names, as was the fashion late in the nineteenth century: William, George, Mary, Charlotte, Victoria, James, Margaret, Peter, John, and others; royalty was high on the list of choices. Beyond lie subdivisions laid out since 1960 with curving streets and cul-de-sacs, contrasting sharply with the old, square quarters they enclose.

Back streets have surprises. The lawn-bowling green, a high school, a Catholic church, or a particularly grand house can break the vernacular run. And buried far in, along the side streets of county towns – St Thomas, Milton, Orangeville, Lindsay, and Napanee among them – sits the judiciary. The court-house, jail, and land registry form a grouping clearly removed from the business focus. The parts do not always match. Orangeville's ornate brick court-house contrasts with the rough stone prison wall of apparently earlier vintage, for instance – or is this just another example of the familiar practice of putting up a showy front wall?

Ontario law is rooted in centralized, oligarchic rule established before 1800, an age when circuit courts met in a village inn or at the residence of a prominent Tory. It took decades for the judicial process to be transformed into localized institutions. By the time the Municipal Act of 1849 authorized creation of county governments and construction of court-house buildings, prominent central sites were taken. Perhaps, too, an out-of-the-way site better suited the tone of invisible authority prevalent in the generation following the demise of the old Family Compact.

In 1841 Upper Canada had only thirteen local jails to serve both welfare and disciplinary cases,[16] but by 1850 Toronto had orphanages and houses of industry, and the central prison stood adjacent to its military garrison and close to the provincial psychiatric hospital. Both prison and hospital were high-art landmarks, built in the classical tradition of the Dublin customs house (Figure 2.2).[17] Such early concentration in one city – though Kingston had the penitentiary – plus the strong family role in matters of moral behaviour left justice almost out of sight in the countryside fabric. John Kenneth Galbraith could not recollect ever having seen a police constable in his home district of Elgin County in the 1920s.[18]

'Railway Street' or 'Station Street' is another name found off in one of the corners of town. It led to that distinctive cluster: station house, freight house, tool shed, cattle pen, elevator, water tank, and paired privies. Trackwork, signal masts, and platforms with baggage carts added interesting furniture; crew members' housing sometimes stood near by. Country hotels were common at junctions with other railway lines. At Georgetown and dozens of other places, passengers took a drink or meal, or put up for the night before continuing onward by connecting train in the morning (Figure 16.6).

Railways skirted around built-up areas, coming as close as topography and land prices allowed and the amount of local financial assistance dictated.

Figure 16.6 JUNCTIONS. The station hotel provided respite for weary travellers. Georgetown, Halton County.

Tracks bullied their way into the middle of town only in exceptional cases. Toronto is one, and filling the bay for tracks during the 1850s is the surest sign that this was to be the great city of the Lake Ontario shoreline.[19] Generally, however, engineers found it necessary to lay out routes 'at a distance from towns and villages in search of a practicable alignment.'[20] In places such as Port Hope, Brantford, and Paisley, this meant bridges carrying tracks high above the valley and a station perched on the edge of the tableland, well removed from the centre of town. Beyond was the wrong side of the tracks, a shabby and insecure-looking place.

Decline and revival

Small-town business districts today present some of the most arresting contrasts found anywhere in Ontario's landscape. Plate-glass show windows display shiny appliances or designer jeans, while overhead broken venetian blinds dangle behind cracked dusty panes, encased in peeling paint, rusting ironwork, or crumbling brick. Merchants have tried to deflect the wandering eye with awnings and gaudy signs. But a glance from the other side of the street reveals the decay wrought by more than half a century of underuse, caused primarily by car-oriented suburban shopping malls. In many towns entire buildings have vanished, breaking up the continuity of the streetscape.

Rarely is the pulse of the province brought so intensely into the public eye.

And there is more, in behind, along the lanes and alleys: workshops, garages, barns, bits of machinery, tethered dogs, clotheslines, vacant lots, sagging walls, and so on. But there may be also a load of new automobiles, a drive-up video store of cinder blocks (and barred windows), and a farm truck creeping past with a load of feed. The back side of a town's business street is disorganized and seemingly in a state of transition, yet with the decay is mixed hope and evidence of people doing more than barely hanging on.

Each corner of the intersection of Queen and Hurontario streets in Brampton is occupied by a branch office of a major chartered bank. Each building is a variant of the one-storey, glass-and-concrete banking-hall style of the 1960s. All the sites were once filled by taller buildings, two still recalled by ghostly stains on adjacent walls. Despite so much apparent inattention to the old fabric, business streets might be even paler shadows without such initiative in reconstruction. Throughout Ontario, people are being induced to look again at the old downtown. What took place at Queen and Hurontario in the 1960s marks the beginning of main-street rejuvenation and has kindled awareness of the built landscape in many citizens who had never thought about the subject before.[21]

By the 1980s, century-old buildings were becoming assets once again. Entrepreneurs competed to use them rather than replace them (Figure 16.7).

Figure 16.7 DOWNTOWN REJUVENATION. An 1858 business block with a harmonious, street-level façade of the 1980s adds to the vitality of a downtown area. Guelph.

Empty market space around town halls, vacated years ago for street-side shopping and later for drive-in convenience on the edge of town, is being reoccupied. Byward in Ottawa, the Kitchener Farmers´ Market, and the city hall marketplace in Kingston have found a clientele that appreciates the old-style ambience (Figure 16.8). Nineteenth-century buildings are contributing to downtown renewal in a score of towns across the province. Fashionable shopping districts in Elora, Kleinburg, and Unionville have set a tone that has been applied to the conduct of routine business in Cobourg, Dundas, Stratford, and other old towns. And now suburban malls and office complexes are copying old Ontario mainstreet designs on the façades of their cinder-block buildings. Polychromatic brick has made a strong comeback. Such imitation bodes well for the continued renaissance of downtown streetscapes.[22]

No element of the landscape has generated as much heritage attention as small-town mansions. Prideful owners care for their treasures, and local committees select for recognition – ´designate´ – singles, or entire streets of them, under the Ontario Heritage Act, 1974. These buildings are as architecturally pure as any, public or private, in the province. The large lots on which they stand have enhanced their prominence. Infilling with more modest houses began at least as far back as the 1920s – in Hamilton´s North End, for example – and is a distraction prompted by changes in fortune and demography.

Many fine mansions have been converted to apartment houses, accountants´ offices, or nursing homes; the Perth County Board of Education occupies one

Figure 16.8 MARKET SQUARES exist in only a few, planned instances – Ottawa, Cobourg, Toronto, and Kitchener among them. Behind city hall, Kingston.

in Stratford. In each instance, fire escapes hooked unharmoniously to exterior walls signal the change in function. Other houses have become funeral homes, their high ceilings and domestic detail harmonizing gently with the laying-out tradition in the old family parlour. As decentralization of business activity continues into the twenty-first century, the grand streets of Ingersoll, Owen Sound, and dozens of other Ontario towns stand ready to absorb new small firms. They should be able to do so while maintaining their distinctive nineteenth-century character.

The boundary between commercial and residential functions has always been fuzzy. In his painting *Grey March Day, 1974*, A.J. Casson captures an L-shaped, storey-and-a-half house with a storefront built onto it before 1900.[23] Workplace and dwelling place were one, and the journey to work was a matter of a few footsteps. Mixing of the two roles is somewhat different today. Consider the example of Dundas Street in Waterdown, which has outgrown its Victorian retail stretch. Houses in the adjacent residential segment have taken on commercial functions, but very discreetly; with a modest lawn sign (of the `for sale´ size) and a simple display in a front window. One gets a feeling of going into someone´s home, which is very fitting for selling handicrafts and specialty clothing.

Conversely, in such villages as Bright (north of Woodstock) and Brussels (in Huron County) commerce has withered. Business blocks are being converted into apartment units occupied by people commuting to distant jobs. Bricked-up display windows, a row of mailboxes, and a line of electricity metres mark the encroachment of residential use on former retailing space.

Such interchange of commercial and domestic roles has taken place quietly, within an existing and serviceable town fabric. Communities´ satisfaction at having such options is evident in increased care shown for the buildings: brick being cleaned and repointed, ironwork scraped and painted, windows and woodwork spruced up. Adaptability and good business sense have contributed to the survival of established settings. The opportunity to make alterations has strengthened the continuity from one generation to the next, and that approach has in turn enhanced a region´s identity. The continued vitality of Ontario´s small towns reinforces those literary images of Davies, Munro, and their circle.

PART IV
FINDING LIMITS

17

Boundaries

It is so easy to assume that Ontario as outlined sharply on the familiar provincial road map will stand for all time. The Great Lakes shoreline looks absolutely definitive. Such apparent stability has deflected our attention from regional cultures welling up within the province and spreading beyond its boundaries, and others that have spilled in from adjacent places. Exact congruence of political and cultural areas might occur in a static, pre-industrial world, but there has been no such match here.

Coffee-table gift books provide one type of view of Ontario. Prize-winning photographs – of Queen's Park, Fort Henry, a fall fair, Tillsonburg's main street, Agawa Canyon, gingerbread trim, the steamboat *Segwun*, the Blue Jays, Mennonites haying, and so on – present Ontario as a recreational playground in a benign setting. The heritage village at Lang – or Doon, or Black Creek, or Morrisburg – has its page, too. It is the predictable reminder that history is found behind a ticket window, through a turnstile. `Foodland Ontario´ is another popular subject: a roadside stall of sweet corn in Leeds County, a `U-pick´ strawberry or apple farm in Halton, the weekly vegetable market in the corner of a shopping mall in Waterdown, or an estate winery's tasting boutique in Grimsby.

Counties and townships are another way of thinking about Ontario and offer a regional or local focus for an area not easily comprehended all at once. They are the traditional units of organization for local historical societies. Heritage advisory groups created under terms of the Ontario Heritage Act, 1974, perpetuate these political divisions, while others are organized by cities and towns.

These familiar limits have not gone unchallenged, however. A Scot who recognized the unity of peninsular Ontario, southward from the Precambrian Shield, could not make the lowland east of Ottawa and Morrisburg fit.[1] A Carleton University student in Ottawa found Ontario west of Kingston a foreign place. In their `sampling of what pleased us in travelling over country roads,´ Blake and Greenhill identified a rural Ontario that excluded everything southwest of London. Historian Arthur Lower once asked whether Ontario even exists.[2]

There are many sorts of boundaries that we rarely ponder, and some of these may offer fresh perspectives. Conservation authorities are established watershed by watershed. Welland Canal studies focus on technology; those of the Ottawa Valley mills concentrate on manufacturing.[3] The domains of ethnic Germans in south Bruce, or of Catholic Scots in Glengarry, make up other similarly orderly units. Linear transects – Dundas Street, the Trent waterway, and dozens of walking tours – are popular field approaches to organizing Ontario.[4] All invite the integrated celebration of natural and cultural features, such as has been done in Brantford with the recent stabilization of factory ruins along the Grand River.[5]

My Ontario is a mélange of nineteenth-century images stirred up in the Credit River valley over more than thirty years.[6] The Smith-Armstrong house is one such element (Figure 1.4). From this starting point on the Credit, Ontario spreads outward for hundreds of kilometres in some directions and much less in others. But sooner or later something extraordinary registers. The slightest feeling of unfamiliarity kindles awareness of the dimensions of Ontario. Home turf yields to edge, and in due course all that is familiar is left behind. This experience is universal to all travellers. The age-old question of where a place is in the larger scheme is the subject of this chapter.

Between city and cottage

After a brilliant analysis of a thousand years of landscape change in the British Isles up to 1914, W.G. Hoskins declared that Britain in the twentieth century was too urban for his taste and so terminated his study.[7] Land sprouting houses instead of crops somehow had ceased to be land at all. In the minds of some observers, `cityscape is not landscape.'[8]

As cities outgrow the nurturing countryside, their evolution becomes part of an international process well removed from parochial events in the townships. Richardsonian Romanesque building style is one such international element (Figures 3.2 and 8.23). The massive classical façade of banks and public buildings of the 1920s is another, and the very term `International Style' for office blocks and high-rise apartment buildings since 1950 – types rarely found in small towns – says the same. Each type of structure has its ultimate, high-art representative, always in a city and rated in a still wider global circle of peers. It has been true even to the grave (Figure 12.8). The Ontario countryside is not known for showy places, but seldom either does it present scenes of abject city-style poverty. Openness dilutes and diminishes the extremes.

No matter how much Hamilton, London, or Ottawa (to say nothing of Toronto) seek to be urbane, however, pre-urban roots persist in their fabrics. The discerning eye can pick out one-time country-crossroad clusters of houses in a 1950s Etobicoke neighbourhood or an Edwardian farmhouse on a side street in Hespeler (Figure 17.1). The storey-and-a-half farmhouse reappears as

Figure 17.1 RURAL REMNANT. A blocky, fieldstone farmhouse (c. 1905) survives in the suburban neighbourhood that was the family farm into the 1970s. Hespeler, Wellington County.

a gabled worker's cottage or swells up into a two-storey terrace unit, and the gable with its gothic window is everywhere.

Block upon block of polychromatic brick town houses were painted over after the First World War, as burgeoning cities tried to shake the small-town look. Then, in the 1970s, individuals and developers started stripping off the layers of red or white paint, restoring some of the feeling of rural Ontario close to the centre of even the biggest cities.[9] The fashion has taken hold, and suburban houses and small business blocks finished in patterned brick provide a further bridge between town and country.

On the other side of rural Ontario lies cottage country. There generations of patricians from Rosedale or Rockcliffe Park have passed their summers. On Lake Simcoe and Lake Muskoka, among the Thousand Islands or Rideau Lakes, and around the Great Lakes shorelines, cottages and summer resorts, and youth camps for children, have been Ontario institutions for as much as a century.

Vacationers travelling to these retreats by train and steamboat were entirely detached from the rural scene they crossed. Beginning about 1920 the automobile brought outsiders as close to the countryside as the roadside fruit stand, but few cottagers did more to involve themselves with the land than count cows as they sped on. Highway 400, built north from Toronto in the 1950s, made bypassing the countryside once again easy. More recently the rebuilding of Highways 35 and 115 towards the Kawartha Lakes and Haliburton has had the same effect.

Rural Ontario has reverted to being an unknown land, lying between the shady city street at home and the marina on the lake. Road names put us in touch with the two solitudes. Along Highway 35 in Sommerville Township south of Coboconk, 3rd Line, 5th Line, and 7th Line strike eastward into farmland,while Lightning Point Road and Juniper Point Road wind westward towards the Balsam Lake shore. The laundromat and pizzeria in Lakefield, or the Rockcliff Hotel in Minden, are reassuring signs that one has not really strayed far.

Rural Ontario besieged

The old Ontario landscape is a remnant and has being attacked from both the city side and the cottage side for years. Suburbanization is rural renewal with no opportunity of going back to an earlier, less crowded era. Beyond, former city folks (`exurbanites´) attempt to maintain a country look, but with no intention of being rural. An overgrown field becomes a recreational place, where city-based owners enjoy rambling over moraines and squidging past bogs. A rototiller is an urbane plough for the vegetable garden, the nearest that most exurbanites come to farming. The front door looks as if it is to be used. On Monday morning this precinct of riding clubs and gentleman farmers is as empty as the suburban high-rise apartment house.

Cottage country has also been expanding, and its diffusion seems even more encompassing. It has been growing into the poorer farmlands of the province, and farmers have been happy to sell some or all such land. One of Matt Cohen´s fictional characters speaks for hundreds of owners of marginal farmland: `The easiest way to make money from the farm would be to sell it . . . for cottage lots and a trailer park, put the proceeds in the bank and live off the interest.´[10]

Around Pigeon Lake, in the Rideau, along Prince Edward County´s outer shore, near Port Stanley, Meaford, or Roche´s Point, and on the Trent Waterway north of Campbellford the story is the same. As more and more cottages are winterized for year-round retreats or principal residences, waterfronts are taking on a nearby urban appearance of fashionable neighbourhoods on estate lots. Skiing is winter cottaging without the lake, and chalet neighbourhoods have much the same visual impact as suburban tracts.

Farmhouses, too, from Artemesia to Eldon to Plantagenet have been sold for recreational residences. For thirty years, buyers personified by the fictional Walt Wingfield have been purchasing farms in decline, thereby expanding the cottage culture into a pervasive countryside one.[11] The number of operating farms in Ontario fell from over 227,000 in 1911 to fewer than seventy thousand seventy years later,[12] and this change represents a vast pool of reclaimable marginal land and buildings. Families on adjacent functioning farms have been hired by the new owners fresh from the city to make renovations and repairs, to mow acres of lawn, and to store boats, plough the lane, and provide security when the place is empty. After Christmas some of these experienced country neighbours go away too, towing a boat to Florida for three months of their own cottaging.

Does rural Ontario any longer really exist? Wingfield was determined that it would, at least in outward appearance, and believed that he could help by setting up Wingfield Farm. The results were uproarious, and one suspects not unlike those of hundreds of kindred spirits, scattered over the countryside, who discovered that thirty years on Bay Street was not the best preparation for a second career on the land.

In truly rural areas a farmer shores up a rail fence because he has to and gives little thought to the piece of gingerbread trim missing under the eaves of his house. No one has moved into the old Methodist church, the store does not stock bayberry candles made in South Carolina, and the brick veneer has never been cleaned. No sign warns of the danger of entering a mill ruin, everybody knows what you mean by 'the Eighth of Elderslie,' and the Presbyterian church at the corner is unlocked. Signs of creeping citification have not yet appeared. Such spots have all but vanished, however, either rotted away or spruced up.

A drive between Shelburne and Collingwood is a showcase of rural Ontario in the 1990s. This is a countryside of marketing boards, crop insurance, RRSPs, and CD players. Farm kitchens have filing cabinets, personal computers, and fax machines. The number of low metal farm buildings is greater than seems proper. The nineteenth-century houses are more and more noteworthy amid so many new dwellings, both at the roadside and back on the farm. It may still be rural, but the feeling is changing. The city has become the standard, and the old, comfortable countryside is rapidly becoming part of folklore.

Subtle variations within Ontario

The tension between homogenizing and personalizing the Ontario landscape has always existed. Many commentators on the process of settlement urged that ideas be shared, and construction bees did just this. Others, including the editors of building-pattern books, suggested that immigrants be sure to bring along their own building plans.[13] Communal barn raisings and quilting bees produced a functional, uniform landscape, and reconstruction of buildings after Confederation deepened the consensus. Yet individuality was not lost. Barn types display regional variation,[14] and a particular style of paired eaves brackets, for example, gives a signature to houses in and around Brighton and Napanee. The exuberant decoration found in Toronto Township gingerbread (Figure 7.5) is only one of dozens of such localized designs.

Physical undercurrents

Sometimes physical conditions establish local character. Distinctive climate and the American boundary explain the concentration of fruit trees and vineyards along the Lake Ontario shoreline through Vineland and Jordan, for example. Elsewhere, draining the Holland and Innisfil marshes in the 1920s produced new land and farming vistas taken up with prefabricated houses sold from catalogues and intended for urban sites. Much of eastern Lambton County was brought into production only when drained, after 1870. An unusually large proportion of two-storey houses and fewer gable-roofed barns there are evidence of the late start; barns and houses stand close to the road, suggesting the importance of off-farm activity and of scattered plots, under one management, from the first days of settlement.

Norfolk County is a case in point. A sandy region, it supported some of Ontario's finest stands of pine timber. Stump fences are widespread, and split rails are seldom seen in this well-drained area. Wheat was lucrative, and post-Confederation rebuilding in Townsend Township, for example, swept away almost all evidence of classical housing. Reliance on a single crop did severe damage to such fragile soil, however, and mixed farming came too late to remedy the situation. Land abandonment followed, and by 1914 shabby, patterned brick houses stood amid untended fields.

Cigarette tobacco, well suited to the light sandy soil, restored optimism to Norfolk in the 1920s. Rejuvenation took the form of squat plain brick farmhouses and rows of tobacco kilns clad in green asphalt sheeting (Figure 17.2).[15] Stump fencing was cut up and burned in the kilns, gradually sweeping out the untidy, confining effect. Prosperity continued, and by the 1950s another round of housing replacement took place, this time with ranch-style bungalows and prominent garages. As tobacco farmers struggle with declining markets in the 1990s, the county may become locked into a faded 1920s or 1960s image, perpetuating its maverick role. Or maybe not; in this non-conforming part of southern Ontario, ginseng and mushrooms are the latest specialty crops to provide wealth and brand-new, 1990s housing.

Cultural undercurrents

Ontario has been known as a cultural mosaic, but its landscape is in large measure a melting pot. Public and separate schools look the same; houses in Irish Protestant areas do not stand out from those in Irish Catholic areas.

Figure 17.2 NORFOLK SAND PLAIN. Flue-curing of tobacco became established about the First World War, as ciagarette smoking took on importance. Squat houses and plain tobacco kilns date from an era when new buildings in rural Ontario were rare. Blenheim Township, Oxford County.

During the 1840s Dawn Township, near Chatham, was the promised land for hundreds of escaped American slaves who took up small lots along roads occupied by Scots and English; established residents showed the way for these destitute immigrants, who followed by example, and as a result the Ontario landscape has no distinct physical markers from that immigration today.

In Rainham and South Cayuga townships, west of Dunnville, the first permanent houses built by Pennsylvania Germans about 1800 were their familiar, six-bay type, with four front windows and two front doors (Figure 2.10). These houses set the standard at the time, but over the century they became less and less conspicuous among the large numbers of simpler storey-and-a-halfs. Most of the old, founding houses were gradually altered to join the mainstream.[16] Had this been a more prosperous area, all might have vanished; as it is, the transition still shows.

Oshweken, on the Six Nations reserve south of Brantford, blends in with some of the mellowest rural and small-town countryside in Ontario. The grid road system and framed houses squared to the lot lines are familiar. Government signs that announce regional service offices occupy storefronts and modified storey-and-a-half houses in a fashion seen all over the province. Gasoline is tax free but service stations look like those anywhere. Satellite dishes, pickup trucks parked at the supermarket, land for lease, and a Chinese restaurant are ordinary parts of reserve life.

The band's Council House, dated 1863, is as typical a fragment of old Ontario as one could imagine. It is a hall-like building that could be taken for a country church at first glance. It was sided in wood when built and then veneered in brick in 1896. At this time it was raised up, and basement space was built beneath. There once was a tower, but that has since been cut down to a trim porch.[17] The Council House has undergone a sequence of changes experienced dozens of times in Ontario. The Mohawk reserve is a landscape of alterable, yet finished, objects, to be held as possessions and to be lamented when they are destroyed. In short, the Six Nations landscape looks Western.

Yet for the Mohawk, and for First Nations communities everywhere, satisfaction lies in demonstrating creative talents rather than in having finished objects. Decay is a natural step in a timeless, circular sequence. Thus, for example, a mask is carved from a living tree with ritual and respect. The tree, culturally modified, lives and grows, and eventually the mask is discarded and fades back into the soil. In Western eyes the tree is damaged; in Native eyes it has shared and is healing. The process of creating and re-creating means that decay is always present, and a First Nations landscape is all too easily misread as impoverished and untidy.

Storey-and-a-half houses and frame country churches add to the Mohawk dilemma. Band members are caught between the inevitability of using building styles and indestructible materials of European origin and their own wish to adhere to the cycle of constant renewal. The Six Nations have had no heritage conservation group to respond as log houses rot. So long as the making of indelible marks on the land occurs, Native reserves will continue to reveal what is non-Native about them, and therefore to blend in with the rest of Ontario.[18]

United Empire Loyalists were very different. They craved immortality. Their descendants, some of them among the most influential of Ontario residents even late in the twentieth century, have promoted it in the landscape. Roadside signs between Gananoque and Cornwall announcing 'Loyalist Country' arouse expectations of a distinctive appearance to the region. That there is none must puzzle and sadden more than a few prideful Loyalist descendants. Had UELs received farmlots side by side, small enough that individual families could manage, today there might be a Loyalist landscape. Instead, the excessively large rewards of land made to them – hundreds of hectares, in many instances – left households widely scattered.

Loyalists built well, but not so distinctively as to mark a difference from other Americans who followed them and overran the old townships. By the second quarter of the nineteenth century, simplified housing of good quality, new or rebuilt, was setting the standard.[19] Dilution proceeded, and Loyalist Upper Canada lives on most visibly at Upper Canada Village near Morrisburg, its influence beyond the museum gates a baffling memory of faded patriotism.

Others' landscapes within Ontario

American influences

For generations commentators have suggested that Ontario looks like an extension of the adjacent United States. Canada in 1888 'is half-annexed already socially – hotels, newspapers, advertizing, etc, all on the American pattern. Yankee blood will have its way and abolish this ridiculous boundary line.'[20] Still, despite all the American house-design books and immigrants crossing into Ontario, the boundary persists, visibly as well as politically.

New England landscape stereotypes – salt-box and Cape Cod clapboarded houses, massive central stone chimneys, houses connected to barns, and covered bridges – are rare in Ontario. In Vermont villages are too compact and too white, graveyards too black, valleys too narrow, roads too winding, and vistas too short, and everywhere the forest creeps over walls and all. Rural New England is claustrophobic, and altogether different from the counties along Lake Ontario or Lake Erie. New York state is very different from Ontario too, despite similar age of settlement and its rectangular survey. Roads sweep through broad vistas, barns hug the roadsides, and little domestic Parthenons are dotted about, announcing republicanism.[21]

Such a contrast with Ontario may seem strange, for New York and New England were major sources of Ontario settlement, and immigrants brought their landscapes with them. Classical styles, with their republican allusions, may have made Canadian administrators jittery, but immigrants from overseas also used them. Some UELs from New York built big, five-over-five 'New England' houses, cunningly labelled 'Georgian' (Figure 6.3). Late Loyalists built in the same style, or smaller. Ontario's few Greek-temple buildings, truly Yankee in spirit, smack of American inclinations to annex Canada in due course (Figure 6.4), but such was the nature of changing architectural whims that the classical tradition in Ontario could be attributed to the English revival as much as to the American.

The countryside marks made in Upper Canada by American immigrants prior to 1815 might still predominate had settlement not been scattered and rapidly filled in by non-Americans. Ontario's best pre-1815 American landscapes are urban, where buildings were clustered. The Greek-revival style of Niagara-on-the-Lake is in keeping with Canandaigua or Geneva, New York, and contrasts with rural Louth Township, immediately to the west. Nowhere else in Ontario are Georgian houses called 'federal' or 'Adamesque.' Niagara actually is a deception, largely rebuilt after being burned during the War of 1812. The Americans destroyed a town built in an image that the United States was consciously fostering for nationalistic purposes; after announcing that further American immigrants would not be welcome, loyal British subjects in Niagara rebuilt it in the American idiom.

Completion of the Erie Canal from the Hudson River to Buffalo in 1825 opened Upper Canada's Lake Erie shore to Americans pressing westward. No laws could stifle this natural movement, and the pillars and pediments of American classicism showed up in Welland, Haldimand, and Norfolk counties. Methodist Episcopal churches may be found there too. All were matched across Lake Erie on the Ohio shore, known as the Connecticut Western Reserve.[22]

Americans competed with thousands of British immigrants north of Lake Erie, and the landscape displays a standoff. King, Queen, William, and Victoria are common street names. But there are some imposters: Washington Street in Union (Elgin County), and Jefferson Street in Port Bruce, for example. For every bit of reputed American classicism there is some English gothic, and mixtures softened the foreigners' influence (Figure 17.3). Pugin would have been only slightly dismayed, Ruskin considerably more so.

The Lake Erie townships of Essex County constitute Canada's little corner of the American midwest. It is a startlingly flat landscape of fine-textured sandy soil, tile silos, half-raised barns, and few fences. Between Kingsville and Leamington, heated greenhouses with bold brick chimney stacks assure fresh tomatoes in March (Figure 11.12). Across on Pelee Island a tobacco barn decays not far from the intersection of Centre Dyke and West Pump roads. Burley tobacco – the dark, air-cured leaves favoured for cigars – was one of a succession of specialized crops suited to Pelee's mild climate; market gardening, soy beans, and viticulture have been others.

The literature lacks stylistic names for buildings in Essex, and illustrated books of barns or churches in Ontario barely acknowledge that the place exists. American writing supplies such terms as 'upright-and-wing' and the 'I house' to describe the dwellings, sprung from roots in Maryland and Pennsylvania, carried west by way of the Ohio River valley.[23] The upright-and-wing is not so very different from the storey-and-a-half stretched upward, and originals and sequels stand together in vernacular Ontario. The difference is easily articulated in Essex, and the cultural watershed may be traced through the Chatham-Tilbury region.

Of all American immigrants, Mennonites from eastern Pennsylvania have put the most enduring imprint on the land (Figure 17.4). The wide roadsides and warning signs for horse-drawn buggies announce Ontario's most easily spotted cultural landscape; 'Rural Carriage Supplies' occupies a metal-sheathed shed west of Elmira. These conservative farming people moved into the Niagara peninsula after 1820 and spread up the Grand River valley to the Waterloo and Elmira region by the 1860s. Today pockets live as far north as Owen Sound.

Penetration inland at such an early date permitted Mennonites to put down secure roots prior to the arrival of English-speaking settlers. Their landscape emerged fully in Waterloo County. The forebay barn (Figure 9.6) is evidence

Figure 17.3 AMERICANNESS NEUTRALIZED. Zion Baptist Church blends classic with brick. St Williams, Norfolk County. See also Figure 2.3.

Figure 17.4 MENNONITE ONTARIO. The two-and-a-half-storey house with tiny attic windows is a link between Waterloo County and roots in southern Pennsylvania. Note the doddy-house on the near end. Near Elmira, Waterloo County. See also Figures 2.10 and 12.1.

of mixed farming, different from the wheat-exporting conditions that produced unraised English barns elsewhere. Houses with two front doors, and the low-roofed meeting-house (Figure 8.12) with five doors, are other landmarks.

The Mennonite landscape is seriously threatened in the 1990s. A meeting-house at the north end of Waterloo closed in 1994 because driving buggies through the suburban sprawl that had built up around it had become too dangerous. Many Mennonites have given up farming and taken places in the towns. But little of their contribution to urban life is strongly visual, and therefore they do not make a mark. Others Mennonites, displaced by urban sprawl, have moved to existing farms further west, in Perth County. Taking over farms that do not have the 'Waterloo County look' has again diminished the Mennonite landscape.

Quebec

The inland line with Quebec, near Dalhousie Mills, is southern Ontario's only non-water boundary. At the time it was established, in 1791, it separated settled, francophone Lower Canada, functioning under seigneurial terms, from the newly settling areas further west, where residents preferred the British freehold land system. By 1841, when this line ceased to be an intercolonial boundary at the time of union, a cultural landscape had taken shape on the westward side that had distinct differences from that to the east. In 1867 the line reappeared on maps as a provincial boundary, just as new forces started to diminish the contrast on the ground.

For some eighty kilometres west into Ontario the landscape offers evidence of Quebec's influence and frequently communicates the feeling that this is not entirely the Ontario one knows further west. To the motorist on the Macdonald-Cartier Freeway (Highway 401), the clue may be no more than the bilingual roadsigns (Figure 17.5). The more experienced eye may catch a good deal more. Take Riceville and Fournier, villages on a secondary road well back from the St Lawrence River, midway between Ottawa and the Quebec line. In Riceville the Orange hall, Presbyterian church, and red-brick houses occupy tree-lined streets; a country crossroads church and former schoolhouse stand close by. Even the name brands Riceville an Ontario town.

Fournier, a kilometre east, is a striking contrast, a white, wooden village of modest houses closely spaced along treeless Rue Fortin. Picture windows stare across to the greystone Roman Catholic church, with its gleaming silver (*fer blanc*) roof and large stone manse. The scene is all very reminiscent of Quebec, right down to the side-by-side positioning of barns on the farm at the edge of town. The seeming power of the church over the dwellers of those simple houses contrasts sharply with the matched scale for public and private buildings in Riceville.

On the road connecting the two villages stands a house with elements of both traditions (Figure 17.6). It gives every indication of being an Ontario structure from the eaves down yet sends strong Quebec signals from above the eaves. Striking similarity to the Smith-Armstrong house (Figure 1.4) puts it into the Ontario camp; the *fer blanc* roof, in the mansard style so popular in Second Empire France, suggests it is the product of a Quebec artisan. Perhaps there was an earlier gabled roof, destroyed in a fire. A Scottish family, such as probably first occupied the site, would have rebuilt with gables; it also might have topped off the blunt tower. But the Scots were in retreat late in the century, and perhaps migrants from an overcrowded part of Quebec were now in charge and employed their own style.

East of Fournier the landscape often evokes Quebec. In some places the long, narrow, 'string-hundred' farmlots look seigneurial, and older buildings must be studied with care to determine that the French have not always been there. The parish church at L'Orignal provides another blend; it was built in the 1830s with English Regency windows and a Quebec *clocher double* spire.[24] L'Orignal's seigneurial origins suggest a reason for this mixture. It became all the more appropriate when the Ontario side of the Ottawa River was drawn into the ecclesiastical province of Quebec in 1847. Quebecers, overcrowded in their traditional lands, spread into what seemed like friendly territory, taking up poorly drained vacant sites in Prescott and Russell counties.[25] Drier parts were taken over after 1880, as Scots resettled further west.

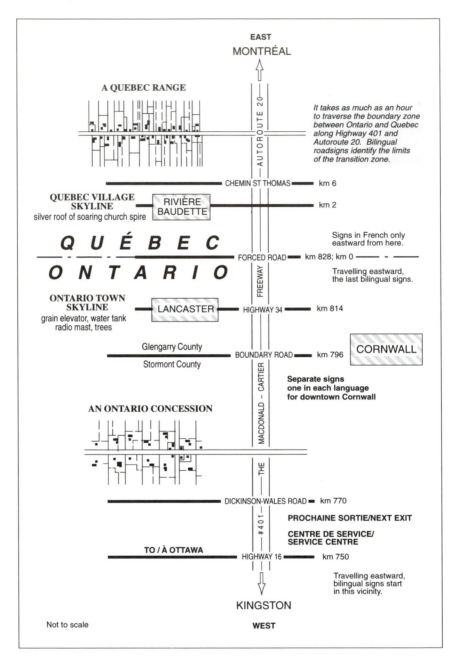

Figure 17.5 THE ONTARIO-QUEBEC TRANSITION.

The Detroit River separates southwestern Ontario from Michigan, yet where the frontier there is not American it may be eighteenth-century French. Long, narrow farms are as suggestive of Quebec as any along Autoroute 20 east of the Ontario boundary. Red and white diamond or arched patterns on barn

Figure 17.6 TRANSITIONAL HOUSE. Ontario walls combine with a Quebec roof. Between Riceville and Fournier, Prescott County.

doors are similar to those in Quebec. The design is alleged to signal ownership and not tenancy or simply to help one find home in a fog.[26] Essex County in 1851 was more than ten times as French as the provincial average, and twice as Catholic.[27] The Lafontaine region, near Midland, is another offshoot from Quebec. Villages strung out along country roads and side-by-side double barns are characteristic of this region. In Lafontaine and through Kent and Essex counties, French names – on streets, mailboxes, churches, and gravemarkers – draw attention to the French presence and the influence of Quebec.

The north

The cultural landscape of the north is shallow. Lonely highways, microwave towers, derelict cars, and summer camps (not cottages) are some of the images of northern Ontario, and each inclines the mind to another place and another time. The remains of mining headframes, lumberers' bunk-houses, and the warping engines that drew the logs through the lakes – these and many more artefacts signal short successes and broken dreams and await canoeists and backpackers wherever they dive into the forest.[28] There is scant incentive to eradicate the skeleton. Ghostly landscapes are arguably the region's most enduring.[29] Even the towns seem not to be indigenous. Company housing for papermill labourers in Kapuskasing looks like the Toronto suburb of Leaside, also built up between the world wars. Gazing across one´s domain – the settler´s dream in the south – was replaced with the twentieth-century aspiration of a paycheque and a Sears-Roebuck catalogue.

Northerners pioneered with prefabricated buildings, sent in by boat or railway to make instant settlements. Some prefabs never left their wheels: railway coaches were adapted as mobile school rooms or church sanctuaries, for instance.[30] Packing crates and metal left over from railway construction or mining camps added to the variety of dwelling places. A rootless vernacular, sprung from high-art components, characterizes the cultural landscape.

Passage into the north is marked by the end of continuous farmland and by one´s first encounter with the northern town. The two phenomena do not coincide. Northward on Highway 11, the southern townscape is strong through Huntsville, well beyond the farmscape, and seems to disappear only after South River. Powassan is different, with its false-fronted, free-standing wooden shops and post-Victorian houses among the rock outcrops (Figure 17.7). Likewise,

Figure 17.7 NORTHERN ONTARIO. A boom-town façade in tin, insulbrick, and wood – no brick. Highway 11, Powassan, Parry Sound District.

Figure 17.8 SHIELD FARM. Highway 11, south of Huntsville, Muskoka District.

Pembroke is southern and Mattawa is not. Lake Joseph, well into the Shield along Highway 69, marks the beginning of the north on that route. Sault Ste Marie and Thunder Bay are tiny southern bridgeheads in a sea of northernness.

Naïve hope and breezy promotion encouraged farming settlers to spread over the Precambrian Shield, taking up pockets of land northward to Lake Nipissing and Algoma in the years after Confederation (Figure 17.8).[31] Much of this land should never have been cleared for farming. Once the prairie west became accessible in the 1880s, any lingering farming appeal to the fringes of southern Ontario dissipated.[32] Such unreceptive land simply could not engender pride. Some occupants moved on, and others pursued non-rural goals in the north, or moved back to the south.

Shield farms tend to have many small buildings, scattered wherever rock and swamp allowed. Some houses are log. Others are the first of the frame era that followed and were never superseded. These buildings are survivors, tarpapered and augmented by a century's accumulation of miscellaneous pieces common in rural settings on the edge of the good earth. Many settlers who tried to work the land gave up, and the decaying ruins of their best efforts have gradually been overtaken by second-growth scrub forest.[33] Those who persisted have a satellite dish and 4 x 4 truck to mark their spot, not barns or fields.

A few pockets of choice farmland in the Sudbury and Algoma regions, around Lake Superior and towards Rainy River, were not even accessible before 1885. There farms graduated directly from log shanties to big gambrel barns and turn-of-the-century houses. Around Earlton, in the Great Clay Belt, the rectangular survey shows through. In haying season one could almost believe it was southern Ontario – but only until the country road is swallowed up again by black spruce forest.

Ontario-like landscapes beyond Ontario

Every cultural region has a core and a periphery, and we ought to look around for the wider areal context of any particular place. Residents of Niagara-on-the-Lake might reasonably propose that their neighbourhood is typical of Ontario, and all else within the province is extraordinary. This is an honest, if also inexcusably egocentric, position to take. And if it is true, then much of western New York state could also be construed as belonging to the Ontario landscape. Residents of Fournier could make the same case with respect to much of the St Lawrence River valley. Yet Niagara and Fournier both also lie at the margins of cultural regions centred well beyond the Ontario boundary. And old Ontario has affected areas beyond its boundaries and also shares common ancestral roots with distant parts of the world.

Pontiac County is an Ontario landscape lying outside Ontario, across the Ottawa River in Quebec. 'The Pontiac' was taken up after 1820 by Americans and Irish lumbermen, some of whom were moving into Renfrew County, on the Ontario side, at the same time. The two counties share a common settlement history, recalled today in the brick streetscapes and big houses of Hull and Campbell's Bay, which are similar to those that can be found in Pembroke and Almonte (Figure 17.9).

Pontiac County began to take on French elements in the 1870s, but the English-speaking landholders and farmers had an Ontario style well in hand. The style persists despite the predominantly francophone status that has prevailed since the 1960s. The English-speaking character is deep-seated, and Pontiac's residents have often dreamed of annexation to Ontario.[34] Much the same may be said for the valley of the Rouge River, a tributary of the Ottawa River flowing southward from Arundel and St Jovite to Grenville. There the transition is notable for the way symmetrical structures are overtaking asymmetrical ones.[35]

Ontario has been exporting itself to other parts of the world since well back in the nineteenth century. As early as the 1830s Ontarians were drifting into Michigan, creating landscapes much like Grey or Simcoe counties. Enclaves reminiscent of old Ontario lie along the Trans-Canada Highway east of Brandon, Manitoba, and in Puget Sound in Washington state. Mossy-green roofs are all that prevent many storey-and-a-half houses in southern British Columbia from fitting into, say, Hastings County. Barns in that region bear diamond crosses, too (Figure 9.3), identical to those in Ontario.

The Canterbury Plain of South Island, New Zealand, in the 1950s looked much like rural Ontario. Both regions have a common ancestry, and it is not altogether strange that they should establish similar features, despite the great distance between them. In Great Britain, rural structures nestle in with gen-

Figure 17.9 PONTIAC COUNTY, Quebec, has a striking resemblance to Ontario. 'Pontiac Motosport Repair' occupies an 1875 church west of Aylmer.

erations of others types, and the Ontario-like components have no opportunity to stand out. But look beyond the British world, to storey-and-a-half houses standing in such places as Brittany and southern Quebec. Ultimately, one may be reminded of old Ontario almost anywhere in the world.

18

Decay and renewal

Oakville, November 1979. A theatre group staged Shakespeare's *Hamlet* against a set consisting of a pair of worn, fluted wooden columns. A note in the playbill stated that these had been taken from the porch of the Petrie house in Bronte, recently demolished. After more than two thousand years of revivals of classical architecture, one more use had been found for a surplus piece of the Ontario fabric. Maybe these columns had already been recycled from a forgotten log house.

Niagara-on-the-Lake, 1967. New granite gravestones were erected at the Butler's Rangers burial site, no doubt as a Canadian Centennial project (Figure 18.1). They took over duty from badly weathered limestone slabs that were more than a century old, keeping the message and the memory alive. By 1990 these replicas were themselves becoming chipped and worn, like their predecessors. Modern recollection of those people once again was under threat.

Erin Township, 1986. I happened upon a Canadian Pacific Railway branch line laid with rails stamped `Cammel Toughened Steel, 1889´ and `Barrow Steel, 1891.´ These British imports antedate domestic steel manufacture and would originally have been laid on the main line.[1] Worn rails could serve on minor lines, and declining use ensured that they remained indefinitely – but not for ever. In 1989 the route was abandoned, the trackwork was lifted, and with it to the scrap heap went a few more artefacts of Canadian economic history.

Niagara again, 1892. A ceremony on Queen Street unveiled a cast metal drinking fountain stamped 1792 to mark the founding of the province of Upper Canada. A century after that centennial, patrons of the Shaw Festival still stroll past the battered memorial. At every turn we are reminded to remember.

Barberton, on the Credit River, early 1970s. The main building of this milling complex was plastered, concealing handsome riverstone walls erected in 1863. Decayed mortar had been washing out with each rainfall, and frost would

Figure 18.1 MEMORIAL GRAVESTONES. Word-for-word replacements in 1967 for badly weathered gravestones are showing signs of decay that will lead to their eventual disappearance or, possibly again, to their resurrection. Niagara-on-the-Lake, Lincoln County.

soon have started dislodging the stones. Dismayed preservationists learned that this apparent desecration was an honest next step in a process that was generations old, in which function was more important than appearance. For Barberton, it was either a plastered finish or no building at all.

Memory in the landscape builds on the interplay of decline and recovery. Pugin roused the Christian style in the 1840s partly from concern that nine-teenth-century England might not otherwise be remembered. He believed that the era had produced nothing of its own.[2] The same argument has been invoked by heritage conservation groups determined to see that suburbs do not totally obliterate the farming landscapes they are built on.

When the Ontario Historical Society tried to set up a provincial museum in 1899, detractors said there was no point. They claimed that too little heritage was left to save because of decades of rapid change.[3] It was the wrong moment in history to argue that the land is a living organism exuding vitality when consumers were craving instead new and shiny products. Those supporters of the museum project, and a few kindred spirits since then, have recognized that derelict barns and scrap-metal yards add to that vitality. Like dead trees sinking into a swamp, and the earthly remains of departed souls, these offer the sustenance for new lives to participate in renewed landscapes.

Boneyards

In the farm-making era Ontarians recycled everything. Every brick, skillet, spoon, pickle crock, millstone, and drive shaft was a treasure coveted and used over and over. People sifted through the ruins of burned houses gathering up the nails; they awaited anxiously the passage of the itinerant potmender. Un-wanted field stones were piled up into useful field walls; unmerchantable tree brush was burned to produce saleable potash. Ontario started without refuse, and with barely the concept of it.

Reuse declined as mass production took hold. Remanufacture of industrial products was beyond the capability or will of most individuals. Railway com-panies rerolled their worn iron, and blacksmiths reworked tire-hoops, but there was not much use for broken window panes, rusted lengths of fence-wire, or empty tin cans. Old crankcase oil was spread on gravel roads to lay the dust for years before the danger of heavy metals was acknowledged. A bent axle became a prying bar and later just leaned the years away against the shed wall; it finally came to rusty rest with other unusable bits in a heap at the back of the farm. Replacement was so much simpler than repair.

Discarded objects began piling up. In the 1930s Charles Buck recalled seeing 'on the edges of three Elgin County sideroads . . . heavy mill-stones lying in the deep grass.'[4] All were near the former sites of flour and grist mills (Figure 11.7). They may have been resting there for seventy years, replaced by porcelain rollers. Or they may have been there just a few years, the least reusable and most durable remnants of entire mills closed since the First World War.

Since the Second World War, the cumulation of discards has come to include items still usable but no longer stylish, and others built cheaply with obsolescence in mind. Consumption came to be of consuming interest, and shopping malls have spelled the demise of the country store, with its stock of rubber boots and castor oil. The childhood duty of saving string has gone, and individual packaging has accelerated the pace of turnover and throwing away.

Every farm has its trash heap, hidden well back in a swale. Old bedsprings and broken teapots languish with the remains of grandfather's '38 Nash. The Madoc area is particularly rich in the debris of mining, forestry, and farming. In a tiny cemetery near Smiths Falls lies `CM1876,´ the datestone from a demolished church building. A dump for old railway bridges flourished in East Toronto during the 1980s, and near Hay Bay, in the Bay of Quinte area, the last resting places for human beings and automobiles may be found side by side.

Refuse heaps are places where people have disowned what once they prized, and where later generations have explored in search of memories. Refuse blends losing with recovering, but the personal family dump is itself becoming lost to corporate enterprise.[5] Drive along a township road on a weekday morning and see the plastic garbage bags and blue boxes lined up at the end of every lane, awaiting the municipal recyclables pickup (a.k.a. `garbage´) truck. Watch the regional waste-management site rise, a garbage mountain crawling with yellow earth-moving machinery, surrounded by a prison fence splattered with blown paper and enwreathed with swirls of gulls.

Factory-made products defy easy reuse and do not decay cleanly or quickly. Still, we escape being overwhelmed by landscapes of disposal and despair because Ontario has always been a vital place. Abandoned farmhouses, collapsing barns, or run-down business buildings in town are temporary features in a world of progressive agriculture and commerce; shabbiness and rot indicate transition, not an epidemic. And on the edges, where expectations of prosperity have gone unfulfilled, nature rapidly heals. Near the Precambrian Shield, overgrown pasture reverting to forest looks less and less wasted as each year passes. Crumbling buildings and rusting machinery catch the fancies of artists and poets, and the abandoned quarry works at Dundas or the badlands of Caledon do not seem to fit the usual definition of despair. In chronically depressed areas, one may hear of `the backlog of dereliction,´[6] but this expression has not suited old Ontario.

Reshaping

Long before front-end loaders made earthmoving easy, Ontarians were pushing the land around. They created structures that were both subtle and long-lasting. Barn ramps and levelled fields are part of the geometry of farming; roadbeds and ditches are the shape of transportation. Breakwaters, jetties, and embankments converted sloping shorelines into sharp edges, where schooners and wagons could stand side by side to transfer cargoes.

Builders of dikes and embankments must have believed that their products would last for ever. Farmers ploughing fields probably never thought of themselves as engineering the countryside, but what they have done is likewise impressive and durable. The earthworks themselves are so rudimentary as to be undateable. At the same time, ploughing, widening, and resurfacing have consistently obliterated even the most recent manifestation. It is an odd paradox of modern antiquities. Earthworks are more functions than artefacts and best dated by association with other features and events of known age.

The Welland and Rideau canals demonstrate alternate approaches to shaping early Ontario. Both are bold enterprises, dating from the 1820s. The Welland was dug, and set within the land (Figure 18.2). Its route was notched back into the face of the Niagara Escarpment, and a tunnelled section was even contemplated. In contrast, the Rideau stands on the landscape, built up with great dams that flooded vast expanses of unsettled townships for unobstructed

Figure 18.2 WELLAND CANAL is a ditch, dug into the landscape. This is a portion of the first rebuilding, during the 1840s, bypassed in the 1930s. Barkley Road, Thorold, Lincoln County.

navigation (Figure 18.3).[7] An engineer writing in 1865 concluded that drowning the land was a cheap way to construct the canal, but that `a heavy expense is exacted to retain proper control of the large bodies of water collected and maintained by artificial works.'[8] The Rideau area is poor farm country, and those reservoir lakes have long since taken on recreational value. What was expediency in the 1820s now looks like enlightened foresight.

Gravel, ground up and sorted by thousands of years of glacial action, is the basis for southern Ontario's earthworks. It is available everywhere. Railway builders discovered Ontario's gravel deposits during the 1850s as they sliced through the landscape in quest of smooth alignments. They cut down and built up, using steam-powered machinery that was soon adopted by municipal roads boards and quarry operators.[9] We read of quarrying from a railway cut in Thurlow Township and of clay `exposed in cutting CP railway, Goderich.'[10] Along the Ontario and Quebec Railway during the 1880s, building stone was drawn from a cutting east of Havelock.[11] Deep cuts were susceptible to being plugged with snow unless they were widened out, however, and that produced still more building material. Railway cuttings and embankments, as well as wayside pits, will endure long after the tracks have been taken up.

Figure 18.3 RIDEAU CANAL sprawls on the landscape as a series of long, shallow lakes that flooded over the land; stumps of drowned trees appear beyond the timber raft. Watercolour of Mud Lake c. 1840 by Thomas Burrowes.

Building up

Embankments could be established temporarily with timber. The pre-Confederation miller built a bentwork trestle for a wooden trough to carry water off the millpond to the top of the mill-wheel. The dam was of wood and stones, packed with clay scraped from the pond site – a minimal excavation – and the pond settled into the natural undulations. This was enough to get business started, and mill dams were later reinforced with more earth scooped from the millpond and banked up on the edges. Pond storage capacity increased, the evaporation surface diminished, and stable banks replaced marshy bits.

Country roads laid with transverse poles (corduroy) through low areas were eventually filled in and built up by road crews with machinery and talent paid for with taxpayers' money. Lakefront piers stood on stone-filled cribwork piles before being filled in solidly. From Komoka to the Forks of the Credit river to the Madawaska valley, railway engineers threw bentwork trestles across ravines. All those structures have been replaced: railway cars of fill were run out onto the trestles and discharged their loads until the originals were buried in new embankments.[12] A culvert at the bottom prevented them from becoming dams. Railway embankments are the boldest evidence today that a now-abandoned line once passed through.

Bigger and bigger earthworks have been undertaken in the twentieth century. In the 1920s, dikes diverted the Holland River at Bradford and exposed its fertile bed for market gardening. The Shand Dam on the Grand River at Belwood, built in 1941, provides flood control through to Lake Erie. In the late 1950s the St Lawrence River was backed up behind a massive dam at Cornwall, flooding thousands of hectares of old Loyalist riverfront for the Seaway and power development. Everywhere on the outer fringes of suburbia in the 1990s, graders casually throw up huge lozenges of topsoil, heralding yet another subdivision. A year or two later they spread it all out again, ready for instant lawns to be rolled out around rows of matching houses. Each project gradually stabilizes, evidence of nature's boundless healing power.

A raised roadbed, properly drained for all-season use, is complemented by a ditch alongside. The relatively low real-estate value of Ontario's countryside has ensured that these universal features remain as open channels. Field underdrainage usually is covered, concealing the colossal commitment of manual labour using in laying stone drains or clay tiling, especially in low-lying areas such as Essex and Lambton counties.[13]

Since Confederation, thousands of acres of wetlands, especially southwest of London, have been made farmable through tile drainage. Plastic piping has superseded clay tiles since 1970. A few excavated channels – Government Drain No. 3, for example, seen from Highway 401 – are the sole visible expression of an elaborate system that has dried out thousands of hectares since the 1870s. Laser technology and mechanical trenching have brought a high degree of sophistication to this invisible engineering in the 1990s.

Digging out

Open pits and quarries punctuate the landscape in such scattered places as Picton, Kirkfield, Bancroft, Beachville, Dundas, Uhthoff, Caledon, Marmora, Don Valley, and most recently Newtonville, supplying material for the Darlington nuclear power station (Figure 18.4). Hundreds more wayside pits, many formerly operated on an incidental basis by farmers, are used by county roads departments. These holes have scarred the countryside for urban-industrial purposes, much as cutting trees did for agriculture in an earlier era, but the land does not heal as readily. Since 1964, legislation to plant berms of trees, and to restore cover and topography, has helped conceal much of the activity.[14] Flooding is an inexpensive way to cover watertight holes and, as with the quarry in Elora, produce a recreational facility. Jackson Park in Peterborough is a botanical garden made from a limestone pit, as are parts of the Royal Botanical Gardens in Burlington.

From the 1830s until after the First World War, the Lake Ontario front between the Credit River and Burlington Bay was busy with men in shabby scows lifting blocks of shale off the lake bottom and delivering them to Toronto for house foundations and street pavers. Stonehooking, in combination with occasional severe storms, has had serious effects on lakefront lands. Wrote one resident in 1856: 'I had a grove of trees near the Lake, which has been taken away in consequence of the removal of Stone from the shore, by these

Figure 18.4 PITS AND QUARRIES. Limestone quarry. Pelee Island, Essex County.

Stone-gatherers, and in some places causing a loss of three rods of land.'[15] The shoreline has receded as much as two hundred and fifty metres in some places west of Oakville. By 1920, the availability of concrete and opposition from lakefront landowners made stonehooking no longer economical. But thirty years of reclamation has barely stabilized, much less reversed, the effects of a century of quarrying.[16]

Smoothing

Roadcuts are good places to note the stoniness of adjacent fields; bracing wires supporting gateposts indicate shallow soils; clay shows as large, shiny clods in a ploughed field. None of these signals of the composition of the land was available to original settlers, for only the surface showed. Settlers had to accept the physical and chemical composition of the land they occupied and live with the irregular contours while figuring it out. Many had never farmed, and only by experience did they discover that non-acidic soils lay atop the Niagara Escarpment, that cedar and elm indicated poor drainage, that slopes washed away, and so forth. Corn was a fine crop for breaking up clay but did not ripen well, whereas corn planted in sand 'has its ears up.'[17]

Farm fields were levelled and cleared of stumps manually. The intention was that such laborious activities as sowing seeds broadcast, tilling with a hoe, and harvesting with a scythe could be replaced by animal-drawn machines parading grandly back and forth in straight, uninterrupted lines. Pastures remained irregular, but wherever the plough passed it smoothed the land in a few seasons. Graders flattened steep hills on roads and filled up depressions.

Dumping of excavated materials, coal cinders, and vegetable wastes smoothed Toronto's streets during the nineteenth century. It also raised them more than a metre above ground levels of the 1830s.[18] Smooth gravel thoroughfares sweep dispassionately through the countryside, and asphalt and cement have further ironed out the land's wrinkles.

Abandonment of even the strongest earthwork leads to smoothing. Barn ramps and stone-heaps stand indefinitely, but hundreds of stable walls collapse and farmhouse basement holes slowly cave into oblivion, with a lilac bush perhaps marking the spot. Septic fields slump. Railway embankments may actually be bulldozed after the tracks are lifted, as farmers reclaim allowances that had long before been deeded across their lots.[19] As streams carve new channels through the silty bottom and plants encroach over the rim, dozens of dried-up millponds, their broken dams in disrepair, gradually fade away.

Decline

Obsolete railways die hard because it is impossible to conceal the assets in their decline. Rusty rails and faded sheds are eyesores, and only as the rails are lifted does the futility of the scene diminish (Figure 18.5). Unwanted

Figure 18.5 THE VISIBILITY OF ABANDONMENT. Canadian National Railways line; photographed the week rails were lifted in 1987. Meaford, Grey County.

buildings may be demolished or removed only after protracted public hearings that other landowners do not require (Figure 18.6). Stations may be converted to houses, but thousands of kilometres of roadbed languish. It will take decades for grass and trees to recolonize the wasteland that was once the depot grounds and switching yard in Havelock, Palmerston, Thedford, and dozens more places. A generation will pass before the walls of the turntable pits in Port Rowan and Bobcaygeon collapse, and residents that never forgave the railway for abandoning them die off.[20] The concrete roundhouse at Madawaska, abandoned since 1937, may stand for ever.

The railways' continuing relevance elsewhere simply exacerbates the problem. From Thamesville to Bowmanville, Smithville, Beaverton, and Vankleek Hill, shiny tracks display full use at the regional scale, not local. Removal of unwanted trackside buildings surely restores the image of vitality and self-respect, but for whom? The railway line has become completely irrelevant to the life of numerous communities on the route.

Disused railway beds are long, narrow gravel pits, not little strips of arable

Figure 18.6 STATION RECYCLED TO NEW SITE. The abandoned King City railway station being removed in 1968. Highway 400, passing below, has assumed the arterial function originally held by Yonge Street (1796) and the Northern Railway (1853). York County.

land. A few abandonments in the 1930s were revived as motor roads at that time – the fourth concession of Russell Township, east of Ottawa, for example – but they are too narrow to be useful. Besides, rural Ontario does not need more local roads. If treated first as a quarry and then incorporated into farming, hundreds of kilometres of right-of-way may be productively obliterated and forgotten. This is the hope of many farmers through the strip of Huron County that the Canadian Pacific traversed from 1907 until 1988, bisecting dozens of farms. They are opposed by recreationists, who imagine bicycle paths or linear parks, and by municipal councillors pondering use by other utilities.[21] Until the last farmer has scratched away the embankment, or another use is found, the picture of dereliction will not be gone completely.

Between death and new life

The memory of eroded scraps is seldom honoured. In 1988 the Ontario Ministry of Works carried out substantial repairs to the central block of the Legislative Building at Queen's Park. For a few months a high-art dump in Etobicoke housed the worn bits and pieces that were replaced, but then they vanished.

Some such fragments do survive, however. In the Spencer Clark Collection at the Guild Inn in Scarborough,[22] in a garden setting, façades, porticos, columns, cornices, and other components of Toronto buildings demolished over the past half century pose for visitors. At Kingsmere, in Pontiac County, Quebec – that outlier of old Ontario – Mackenzie King did the same thing in the 1940s with some of his favourite Ottawa stones. Both men created cemeteries for old buildings, postponing rejuvenation until these follies themselves tumble to the ground.

Steam locomotive 2616, with an American builder's plate dated 1911, stands in the town of Haliburton on a piece of trackage barely more than its own length. It was one of the final cargoes transported by Canadian National Railways to Haliburton, in the early 1960s, and now is stranded by more than eighty kilometres of disused roadbed north from Lindsay. There, a defunct diesel locomotive and freight cars were positioned at the end of track about 1990, and they too have been cut off from a system cut still further back towards the Lake Ontario front. With no more than visual interest, such façades and inoperable machinery have little to live for. As with barn foundation walls or unused dams, they continue their decline towards oblivion. Museum exhibits are stabilized ruins that require perpetual intensive care.

An incalculable spread of materials lies somewhere between utility, decay, and resurrection. Items for which there is no immediate use pile up behind barns, and attics from Anderdon Township to Plantagenet Township are crammed with weary furniture. Some is blight, the result of neglect, misfortune, or incompetence. One is reminded of the fictional home of Mark Frank north of Brockville, `eroded by successive waves of alcoholism and fire, [its] hundred-yard driveway littered on either side with the dead vehicles and spare parts . . . – a cornucopia of rusting cars and trucks.'[23]

Country auctions, flea markets, and yard sales keep these objects stirred around in the landscape. Some climb back into use, some are sent far away for restoration and sale in pricy antique shops, and others reappear in next week's sale, pleading for another dollar from another sucker. More is stashed in public storage lockers – commercial pack-ratting for those whose ephemera have outrun the space at home.

Refuse is simply a temporary step on the road to renewal. At Ramey's Bend, a tranquil reach of the disused third Welland Canal (1880s) north of Port Colborne, lie the hulks of Great Lakes freighters. Dead ships plug a dead waterway, yet the scene itself is alive with scavengers salvaging parts for reuse. The steady stream of worn-out cars hauled into a wrecker's yard is balanced by truckloads of sorted parts going out for remanufacture. The auctioneer and house-wrecker are like microbes in compost, engaged in rejuvenation.

Heritage consciousness

Early in the 1980s, the town of Forest built a public library in the form of the 1914 railway station (with floor plan reversed) that had stood on the site until demolished in 1970, beside a railway line removed in 1987. It is accompanied by a full-scale reproduction of the portal to the St Clair River railway tunnel of 1908, more than one hundred kilometres away, used in a lying-down position as the motif for an outdoor amphitheatre. In 1995 the tunnel was replaced and closed up. While the evidence in Forest is ambiguous, there is little question that the past and the future somehow need each other.

Mississauga's city hall tells a similar tale. More than 400,000 residents own one of Canada's most striking creations of the 1980s building boom, described by the architects as a postmodern symbol of the rural society that the city has replaced (Figure 18.7).[24] The building appears to be made up of many components, just as on the farm, and brick pulls the scattered elements together. People come and go through a small rear door, while the front stands set well back; it is decidedly aloof, as so many rural Ontario housefronts are. The city hall faces southward, towards the lakefront, as public buildings in Ontario long have done. And just as the bell on the summer kitchen roof once rang out over the fields its summons to the dinner table, so today a slim clock tower, visible from every neighbourhood, draws the public eye to the centre of Canada's fastest-changing municipality. The medley consciously echoes rural Ontario.

Late in the twentieth century, the English-speaking population of British ancestry in Ontario is declining in numbers and in influence. Old Ontario is

Figure 18.7 AN ONTARIO IMAGE. Mississauga's city hall, 1987, is supposed to remind one of the Ontario farm. Until 1989 corn was being cultivated across the road in front. Peel County.

their Ontario, and for a few decades members of this ageing, generally well-to-do group have the means as well as the will to slow down, or at least to direct, the tumultuous rush towards the twenty-first century.

The heritage movement came together as widespread grassroots phenomenon in the 1960s to celebrate and promote the land's expression of nostalgic reflections. It invites citizens to manipulate the inevitable process of change in the landscape through conservation, preservation, and restoration of what exists, instead of letting the chips fall where they may. Keeping old buildings among newer ones and obsolete forms among functional is not artificial, however, because of the need for all forms to be occupied by modern, useful facilities if they are not to disappear entirely. 'Reproduction Ontario' is a landscape of time-honoured, familiar vistas occupied by modern, thriving households and businesses. It is old Ontario replicated in another time, the present, and is everywhere.

The Ontario Heritage Act, 1974, is the focal point of this process. Its roots extend back to the founding of the York Pioneer and Historical Society in the 1870s and of the Architectural Conservancy of Ontario in the 1930s. The Conservation Authorities Act, 1946, and the Planning Act, 1949, initiated the modern era of public participation. Eric Arthur's *The Early Buildings of Ontario*, published in 1938, continues to be a landmark in heritage literature. The first widely popular and influential publication on the subject of old buildings, MacRae and Adamson's *The Ancestral Roof*, appeared in 1963.

The Heritage Act enables citizens throughout the province to focus on ordinary buildings and sites personal to them.[25] It has had measurable influence in ensuring the survival of hundreds of structures, and through them of the little variations that have refuted arguments of Ontario's overall sameness. Unique, high-art buildings of national stature have always had their following from coast to coast. The Heritage Act has given supporters of vernacular buildings the opportunity for their own celebration too.

A firm strategy and commitment to the built heritage have been especially necessary on the fringes of the big cities. There the stakes are high, and the profile of the agricultural and village past is low. Owners and developers rarely have viewed a worn, old country store as an asset in their proposed suburban plans. Many of these people are recent immigrants with no loyalty to British roots and convinced that they will find a profitable future in a very different image.

After two decades, signs of the impact of the Heritage Act are everywhere. Plaques on individual buildings or entire neighbourhoods announce the role of the municipal Local Architectural Conservation Advisory Committee (LACAC) in guiding these structures through the redevelopment process. Nearly one hundred and fifty mucipalities in Ontario have passed by-laws establishing LACACs. Treelines are tended with care. Progressive developers hire heritage consultants to advise them on how to satisfy city hall while meeting investment goals. Demolition firms are supplemented by companies skilled in dismantling for reconstruction and others in moving buildings.

As pride in landscape takes hold, a true ethic for the built environment, like the land ethic for the natural setting, may become part of everyday consciousness.[26] Bolstered by the Environmental Assessment Act, 1977, and the revised Planning Act, 1980, LACACs have found that cases could be made for continued use of buildings of no apparent architectural merit and that they did not have to be the products of distinguished architects.[27] LACACs have resolved to set goals within the wider social and economic context and have established heritage districts to demonstrate the mixing of features great and small.[28]

Turning from a focus on the past to making statements about the future strikes responsive chords with politicians and developers. Passionate advocates have used droll wit and sound legal training to cajole disparate parties into agreeing that old and new features can coexist.[29] In Gravenhurst, for instance, the former CNR station stands actively in use as a veterinary hospital and a restaurant (called 'The Station'); a chain-link fence setting it off from busy mainline tracks signals how a conflict was resolved. Throughout the province, in thousands of thriving settings, one can see far back through time by way of buildings of several generations, with suitable alterations.

Figure 18.8 POSTMODERNISM. This mixture of materials and dramatic lines and shapes maintains Ontario's eclectic tradition. Storey-and-a-half near Guelph.

The spirit of 'reproduction Ontario' is being taken up privately, with varied interpretations (Figure 18.8). Freedom for personal expression is celebrated, and the educational role of the Heritage Act has fostered a widespread will to shepherd the current, dateable landscape along to future generations. Stewardship does not reject visual change and is true to the Ontario tradition of conservation and reuse.

In reproduction Ontario, vernacular construction has become a popular art form, maybe even high art. Future landscape students will have to be nimble to recognize late-twentieth-century components of earlier designs. Replication may be so well done as to hide itself and throw people's thoughts back to earlier periods.

The Ontario Archaeological and Historic Sites Board was established in 1953 to erect commemorative plaques throughout the province.[30] Gibraltar Point lighthouse (Figures 3.12), and two sites in Brockville (Figures 5.11 and 8.24), pictured in this book, show what these markers look like. There are hundreds more. Every one represents thousands of dollars of investment in research staff salaries, aluminum castings, and refreshments at unveiling ceremonies. Each helps to tie local interests into the wider picture of Ontario's history. Plaques are both a first and a last resort for heritage activity, sometimes prompting thoughts where no landscape clue ever existed and at other times preserving them after tangible evidence has faded away. The setting for the plaque enriches the reader´s appreciation of the subject.

Upper Canada Village and the Ontario Agricultural Museum are like `hands-on´ plaques. They maintain structures and records that have lost all utility save that of triggering memories and stimulating the intellect. The exposed water-wheel is one of many landscape elements of old Ontario incapable of surviving intact late in the twentieth century. Mature societies must support such cultural zoos, but to an even greater extent each country needs the participation of its citizens in keeping collective memory alive. In the best of all worlds, respect for the cultural landscape as a common resource and as part of the common wealth would be so strong that heritage legislation would not have to exist. We can only hope that reproduction Ontario and real Ontario are converging and might some day become indistinguishable.

Natural change

Constant reuse and adaptation in the built landscape have suppressed the purity of any one design. Throughout the twentieth century Ontarians have lived with the results of years of unsophisticated modification, which has shaped their heritage initiatives. Preservation and restoration have been con-tradictory to the step-by-step, future-oriented growth that prevailed throughout the nineteenth century. Preservation is most easily acknowledged in high-art structures, and routine maintenance of such places is actually routine resto-ration intended to keep faith with the design.

Redesigning a building defeats preservation but honours conservation. The Peterborough court-house of 1853 received a new façade in 1878, and ever since it has been remembered as an 1878 building.[31] Barrie´s town hall kept up appearances by going from Byzantine to Romanesque in 1856 and to Second Empire in 1877.[32] The survey system is perhaps the only component of landscape not to have undergone a facelift. Such a simple artefact has been neither abandoned nor adapted, only interpreted, and has come through to the present unscathed.

Signs of disorderly change were becoming evident by the end of the farm-making era in Ontario, and stewardship of the process of change dates from this time. Legislation in the 1880s commited residents to restoring the forests, by then reduced to one-quarter of southern Ontario, and woodland clearly was rebounding by the 1920s. Outdated military earthworks and stone fortifica-tions were falling into ruin by the 1860s, and stabilization of forts Wellington (at Prescott), Henry (at Kingston), York, Niagara, Malden (near Windsor), and Penetanguishene represented one of the earliest heritage projects undertaken in Ontario. (The elevated Gardiner Expressway, built about 1960, bends to avoid Fort York and thus demonstrates reverence for such sites even after generations of obsolescence.)

In the 1870s, the York Pioneer and Historical Society was formed to save the Scadding log house in Scarborough and move it to the Toronto Exhibition Grounds.[33] Though it seemed to be among the last of its type, in fact hundreds of log houses vanished beneath veneers at this time. Recent purchasers of country lots have been startled to find a log house preserved behind layers of stucco and brick. A chapter in Ontario's domestic construction has resurfaced after a century's eclipse.

The southern Ontario countryside became a faded and dated tapestry between the 1890s and the 1950s. In this stagnant period, alterations were more modest than in expansion days and marginalized structures sank away unnoticed. Innovation was suppressed; timbers in truss bridges along the Rideau Canal were completely replaced every twelve years, and all the while the structure remained the same.[34] Preservation and restoration grew to include smaller, and occasionally vernacular, buildings. Some lay beyond the cities, but the initiative and money came from non-rural people.

In the early 1930s, the Architectural Conservancy of Ontario (ACO) was formed to take on the Barnum house in Grafton, once described as 'a building with no history' (Figure 6.4).[35] The ACO showed that good looks were important too. The Barnum house became a focus for Loyalist-era heritage interest and still more meaningful when the St Lawrence Seaway flooded UEL land during the 1950s. Its restoration to an earlier age, and its conversion from a dwelling to a museum without its being moved set a style for institutionalized rejuvenation that has been honed ever since.

Old Ontario has been largely unselfconscious and oblivious of itself. Everyone who has lived on the land has shaped it, and only in recent decades have politicians and planners stepped in. City folks began offering puzzled farmers substantial amounts of money for run-down houses of little apparent value. Restoration and preservation became the fashion, indistinguishable from conservation. Much of this activity was undertaken with no knowledge of architectural history or of the cultural significance of artefacts, but with only the simple sincerity of people who believed that something old was something important.

Deterioration lays processes of change open for evaluation. It gives renovators a chance to replicate old ways, while insensitive rebuilding may well destroy all signs of them. The surcharge for taste in Ontario, however, has been low enough over the generations that keeping up to date has been achieved while maintaining much of the established countryside. Buildings that must have been looked upon a century ago as bizarre live on in the present as muted, aesthetic treats. Newcomers buy them, and artists paint them. Popular participation in the orderly process of landscape change continues to flourish.

We opened this study by gazing upon the Smith-Armstrong farm north of Brampton (Figure 1.4). This dynamic site has been kept fully up to date by generations of modern, pragmatic people. Cutting the trees along the lane,

Figure 18.9 WHICH TREE WILL GO ON LONGER? Palermo, Halton County.

replacing the barns, and demolishing the silos were sensible responses to pressing problems. We must assume that they were undertaken only after thoughtful consultation with family or business associates. Scattered disappearances from the countryside must be balanced against the continuing vitality of places such as the Smith-Armstrong house, most recently as an office building for a modern recreational enterprise. Fidelity to principles of order and common sense distinguishes the Ontario landscape, and these principles ensure the continued demonstration of all the chapters of its history far into the future.

For many generations, southern Ontario has been an idyllic middle ground – `the Garden´ – lying between the wilderness and the city, where mankind has sought to live since the beginning of time.[36] The first forest clearings, with temporary log shanties strewn over a tangled landscape, had the makings of little utopias with a dwelling-place at the centre. Some of these became schools or workshops; following the First World War some reverted to dwellings once more. Droves of people moved to the cities at the start of the twentieth century, and then a couple of generations later their successors started returning to the countryside. Some day it may be difficult to distinguish the twenty-first century from the nineteenth.

Expressions such as `unnostalgic permanence´ and `tradition-bound change´ suit the spirit of this orderly ebb and flow. I hope that readers have been visualizing their own examples while reading this book, for vernacular life repeats itself. The pictures used here could be replaced with different ones, generation upon generation, as personal to each reader as these are to me. Indeed, a good many of the examples shown no longer exist or have been so extensively modified as to tell other tales. The world of Headford United Church, for example, has been transformed from the rural scene of the 1960s (Figure 8.7) to suburban Markham in 1996.

However fragile the Garden may seem to be, it is nonetheless enduring. New fossils of historic Ontario are right now being laid down atop the bedding of the past two centuries. Far in the future some rockhound may come up with a fossilized diamond cross, or a team of archaeologists excavating a house site in South Crosby Township will speculate whether the building was a storey-and-a-half, and whether it was of veneered or solid brick. Someone will report that the streets of downtown Toronto filled up more than a metre above grade and will offer a social interpretation of the debris. Particular strata will be richer than others, the upper generally more varied, more complex, and less biodegradable than the lower. Beyond that, the landscape of southern Ontario's occupants over some seven generations will surely fade to a faint shadow (Figure 18.9). The Garden encroaches relentlessly and will have gone on without us.[37]

APPENDIX A
Structure and outside finish

If outside walling is:	Then the structure of the building will be:
Log or timber	... almost certainly *log or timber*. A *stone, brick, plank, timber frame, balloon frame*, or *concrete* structure is highly improbable in vernacular building. A load-bearing veneer is redundant, and a log wall socially gauche.
Stone	... almost certainly *stone*. It may possibly but not likely be *log or timber*, and it is not likely to be *brick, plank, timber frame, balloon frame*, or *concrete*. Stone is a difficult material to use decoratively.
Brick	... probably *brick, plank, timber frame*, or *balloon frame*. In a twentieth-century urban dwelling, it may be *concrete*. It may possibly but not likely be *log or timber*, and it may, rarely, be *stone*.
Board	... probably *timber frame* or *balloon frame*. A *log or timber* structure with successive layering is also common, and *plank* is functional but rarely occurs. *Stone* or *brick* is not likely, as neither offers functional or aesthetic advantages. *Concrete* is possible but rare.
Stucco	... very probably *log or timber* with successive layering. *Timber frame* and *balloon frame* are highly possible, but only with a rigid wall layer beneath. *Concrete* is also highly possible. *Plank* is common under stucco, but such structures are rare, and *stone* and *brick* are possible but also rare.
Sheeting*	... probably *plank, timber frame*, or *balloon frame*, or *log or timber* with successive layering. *Stone* is not likely, as it offers few advantages, and *concrete* is possible but occurs rarely.
Concrete	... almost certainly *concrete*. *Log or timber* is possible but rare, and *stone, brick, plank, timber frame*, and *balloon frame* are highly unlikely.

*Refers to asphalt, aluminum, or vinyl.

APPENDIX B
Halls

	Fraternal hall	School	Municipal hall	Church	Remarks
Plan					
Simple, without embellishments	Common	Common	Common (Fig. 8.9)	Common (Fig. 8.5)	Belfry may be missing from former school or former church; types not easily distinguished as to function.
Bellcote and/or porch	Common (Fig. 8.16)	Common (Figs. 3.3, 4,12, 8.18)	Common (Fig. 7.3)	Common (Fig. 5.8)	Normal features of church or school; schools may have paired entrances; porch may be an addition.
Recessed tower	Highly unlikely	Quite unlikely	Rare	Common (Fig. 8.10)	Belfry and porch may merge into incipient tower.
Free-standing tower	Almost inconceivable	Quite unlikely	Quite unlikely	Common (Fig. 8.7)	Tower an easy addition; likewise apse; steeples and spires atop towers are very ephemeral.
High art	Probably none	Probably no one-room versions	Common (Figs. 8.6, 8.8)	Common with transepts, apses, etc.	Hall-like shape is lost amid transepts, multiple classrooms, chambers, etc; tendency is to squareness.
Details					
Label, with date	LOL No.	SS No. USS No.	Various	CM, ME, PM, Wesleyan	Look for label stone above porch door; Anglican buildings may not be labelled.
Decoration	Rare; modest	Quite usual, but modest	Usual, modest to elaborate	Always; modest to elaborate	Date by styles same as houses; earlier dates possible for trend-setting structures.
Window head	Probably flat	Any shape but gothic	Rarely gothic	Any shape, esp. gothic	
Size	Small	One-room, mainly	Vary with authority	All	Smaller means older, except for Anglican churches.
Wall cover	Any, esp. wood	Brick; some stone	Any	Any	

(continued)

	Fraternal hall	School	Municipal hall	Church	Remarks
Roof pitch	Any	Any	Any	Any	Generally the flatter the pitch, the older the building.
Also to look for	Flag pole; closed shutters	Well; swing; two entrances	Flag pole; clock tower	Cemetery; spire; residence	

Disposal of surplus buildings

	Decay and demolition most likely	Housing	Housing or regional admin.	Before 1950, to other institutions; since 1950, to housing	Variations from appropriate detailing for the normal function are evidence that use has probably changed.

APPENDIX C
A fence typology

Fence type[1]	Material	Portable?	Land input	Labour input	Capital input	Fence needed?[2]	Durability[3]	Aesthetics[4]
Brush	Tree tops	Possibly	High	Low[5]	Low	Maybe	Short	Untidy
Pole, log	Tree trunks	Not likely	High	Low[5]	Low	Maybe	Moderate	Untidy
Rough boulder	Glacial debris	No	High	Low[5]	Low	Maybe	Long	Untidy
Snake rail	Split cedar; glacial debris	Yes	High	Moderate	Low	Yes[6]	Moderate	Attractive
Stump	Pine	Not likely	High	Low[5]	Low	Maybe	Long	Attractive
Dry stone	Fieldstone, river stone	No	Moderate	High	Low	Yes	Long	Handsome
Hedge	Hawthorn and other species	No	High	Moderate	Low	Yes	Moderate	Untidy, unless trimmed
Tripod[7]	Split cedar, wire	Yes	Low	Moderate	Moderate	Yes	Moderate	Attractive
Board	Plank, nails, wood posts	No	Low	High	High	Yes	Short	Inhibiting
Post and rail	Split cedar, wire, wood post	Possibly	Low	Moderate	Moderate	Yes	Moderate	Attractive
Barbed wire	Wire, staples, wood posts	No	Low	High	High	Yes	Short	Ugly
Box wire	Wire, staples, wood or metal posts	No	Low	High	High	Yes	Shortish	Utilitarian

[1] Roughly in historical sequence
[2] As opposed to the unintended side-effect from clearing land
[3] Of materials and configuration
[4] Author's personal opinion
[5] Low for fence making, but high for ground clearing
[6] But possibly with surplus materials
[7] Also known as Workman fence

Notes

1: Acknowledging landscape

1 Charles Dickens, *American Notes for General Circulation*, first pub. 1844, reprint (Harmondsworth: Penguin Books, 1972), 248; *Canadian Illustrated News*, 10 Jan. 1863, 97.
2 Karl Baedeker, *The Dominion of Canada* (Leipzig: Baedeker, 1894), 157.
3 John Kenneth Galbraith, *The Scotch* (Boston: Houghton-Mifflin, 1964), title to Chap. 1.
4 John Warkentin, `Southern Ontario: A View from the West,´ *Canadian Geographer*, 10 (1966), 157.
5 R.W. Chapman, *The Portrait of a Scholar, and Other Essays*, first pub. 1920, reprint (Freeport, NY: Books for the Libraries Press, 1968), 15.
6 William G. Hoskins, *Fieldwork in Local History* (London: Faber, 1967), 94.
7 Charles S. Buck, `The Origin and Character of the Early Architecture and Practical Arts of Ontario to 1850,´ MA thesis, University of Western Ontario, 1930, preface.
8 Diane I. Allengame, `Criteria for Preservation (of the) Smith-Armstrong House,´ unpublished paper, Town of Caledon Heritage Committee, Caledon East, Ont., 1982.
9 Carole Black, *Daddy´s Girl*, limited-edition reproduction of original watercolour painting, Carole Black Studios, Georgetown, Ont., 1988.
10 Donald W. Meinig, `Environmental Appreciation,´ *Western Historical Review*, 25 (1971), 11.
11 Buck, `Origin and Character,´ preface.

2: The evolving vernacular

1 John Mead Howells, *Lost Examples of Colonial Architecture: Buildings That Have Disappeared or Been So Altered as to Be Denatured*, first pub. 1931, reprint (New York: Dover, 1963).
2 Susan Walker and Dori Herod, *Exploring Niagara-on-the-Lake* (Toronto: Greey

de Pencier, 1977), 24–34; Peter J. Stokes and Robert Montgomery, *Old Niag-ara-on-the-Lake* (Toronto: University of Toronto Press, 1971), 5.

3 Roger L. Welsch, `Front Door, Back Door,´ *Natural History*, 88 no. 6 (June–July 1979), 81.

4 Henry Glassie, `Meaningful Things and Appropriate Myths: The Artifact´s Place in American Studies,´ in Robert B. St George, ed., *Material Life in America, 1600–1860* (Boston: Northeastern University Press, 1988), 82.

5 See, for example, John I. Rempel, *Building with Wood, and Other Aspects of Nineteenth-Century Building in Central Canada*, first pub. 1968, 2nd ed. (Toronto: University of Toronto Press, 1980), Chap. 8.

6 Orson S. Fowler, *A Home for All, or The Gravel Wall and Octagon Mode of Building* (New York: Fowlers and Wells, 1854), 80–1.

7 Eric Arthur, *The Early Buildings of Ontario* (Toronto: University of Toronto Press, 1938), 11.

8 *The Canadian Book of the Road*, 2nd ed. (New York: Reader´s Digest Corporation, 1980), 88.

9 R. Machin, `The Great Rebuilding: A Reassessment,´ *Past and Present*, 77 (1977), 55. See also Thomas C. Hubka, `In the Vernacular: Classifying American Folk and Popular Architecture,´ *The Forum: Bulletin of the Committee on Preservation*, 7 no. 2 (Dec. 1985), 1–2.

10 See `Suggested Reading,´ below, for an annotated review of a selection of the more important pattern books.

11 *Christian Guardian*, 9 March 1853, 86. The reference is to Guelph Wesleyan, reopened in December 1852, and at that time getting a gallery.

12 John Ruskin, *The Seven Lamps of Architecture*, first pub. 1851, rev. ed. (London: George Allen, 1906), 358.

13 Marion MacRae and Anthony Adamson, *Hallowed Walls: Church Architecture of Upper Canada* (Toronto: Clarke Irwin, 1975), 153.

14 Interview, M. Maxwell, Paisley, Sept. 1972.

15 Thomas F. McIlwraith, `Altered Buildings: Another Way of Looking at the Ontario Landscape,´ *Ontario History*, 75 (1983), cover.

16 *Illustrated Atlas of Grey County* (1880), 14. `Troughs´ are hollow logs.

17 Interview, George Grant, Paisley, Sept. 1973.

18 Rempel, *Building with Wood*, 43.

19 A schematic diagram of alternatives is laid out in Appendix A.

20 *Report on Agriculture* (Toronto: Ontario Agricultural Commission, 1881), question 18.

21 George W. Duncan, `Insulbrick as an Important Architectural Treatment,´ *Ontario Historical Society Bulletin*, 59 (Autumn 1988), 5.

22 C.P. Dwyer, *The Immigrant Builder* (Philadelphia: Claxton, Remsen and Haffelfinger, 1872), 74. Such is the case with old Clarkson United Church, on Lakeshore Road in Mississauga, converted to retail use in the 1950s.

23 Anna Jameson, *Winter Studies and Summer Rambles in Canada*, first pub. 1838, reprint (Toronto: McClelland and Stewart, 1972).

24 John I. Rempel Papers; Acc. 2070; Archives of Ontario. Verschoyle B. Blake and Ralph Greenhill, *Rural Ontario* (Toronto: University of Toronto Press, 1969), plate 28.

25 Susanna Moodie, *Life in the Clearings vs the Bush*, first pub. 1853, reprint (Toronto: Macmillan, 1959), 19.

26 Ruskin, *Seven Lamps*, Chap. 2; Ronald W. Brunskill and Alec Clifton-Taylor, *English Brickworks* (London: Ward Lock, 1977), 45; Eric Arthur and Thomas Ritchie, *Iron: Cast and Wrought Iron in Canada from the Seventeenth Century to the Present* (Toronto: University of Toronto Press, 1982), 166–7.

27 Mathematical tiles are panels that may be hooked onto board siding. A longstanding theory that they are the direct result of a heavy tax on brick in Britain between 1784 and 1833 is now generally discounted. See Ronald W. Brunskill, *Brick Building in Britain* (London: Victor Gollancz, 1990), 64–8.

28 *Financial Post*, 24 May 1989, 10, reporting on the activity of Joe Ghiz, at that time premier of Prince Edward Island.

29 Sibylle Moholy-Nagy, *Native Genius in Anonymous Architecture in North America* (New York: Schocken Books, 1957), 24; John Mactaggart, *Three Years in Canada, an Account of the Actual State of the Country in 1826–27–28* (London: Colburn, 1829), 197–8.

30 William A. Foster and D.G. Carter, *Farm Buildings* (New York: Wiley, 1922), 74. John L. Shawver, *Plank Frame Barn Construction* (New York: David Williams and Company, 1904), 10, puts the saving at 40 to 60 per cent.

31 Ruskin, *Seven Lamps*, 339.

32 Russell Lynes, *The Domesticated Americans* (New York: Harper and Row, 1957), 86.

33 Ralph Waldo Emerson, 'Nature' (1836); reprinted in Robert E. Spiller, ed., *Five Essays on Man and Nature* (New York: Appleton-Century Crofts, 1954), 3.

34 Amos Rapoport, *House Form and Culture* (Englewood Cliffs, NJ: Prentice-Hall, 1969), 67.

35 Henry Glassie, *Passing the Time in Ballymenone: Culture and History of an Ulster Community* (Philadelphia: University of Pennsylvania Press, 1982), 338.

36 David McClung, 'Mennonite Two-Door Houses of Rainham and South Cayuga Townships, Haldimand County,' in Julia Beck and Alec Keefer, eds., *Vernacular Architecture in Ontario* (Toronto: Architectural Conservancy of Ontario, 1993), 49–54.

37 Peter Ennals and Deryck Holdsworth, 'The Cultural Landscape of the Maritime Provinces' in Douglas Day, ed., *Geographical Perspectives on the Maritime Provinces* (Halifax: St Mary's University, 1988), 1–15.

38 Brunskill and Clifton-Taylor, *English Brickworks*, 43.

39 Charles S. Buck, 'The Origin and Character of the Early Architecture and Prac-

tical Arts of Ontario to 1850,' MA thesis, University of Western Ontario, 1930, 440–1.

3: Natural and human history

1 C.P. Dwyer, *The Immigrant Builder* (Philadelphia: Claxton, Remsen and Haffel-finger, 1872), 13. The comments of Edwin van Cortlandt, 'Of the Woods of the Ottawa,' *Canadian Journal* (Dec. 1853), 115, mix nautical and domestic needs. See also John I. Rempel, *Building with Wood, and Other Aspects of Nineteenth-Century Building in Central Canada*, first pub. 1968, 2nd ed. (Toronto: University of Toronto Press, 1980), and Donald C. Peattie, *A Natural History of Trees* (New York: Houghton Mifflin, 1950). Brenda Lee-Whiting, *Harvest of Stones: The German Settlement in Renfrew County* (Toronto: University of Toronto Press, 1985), is helpful on furniture woods. The problems of establishing pre-settlement vegetation patterns are addressed in Conrad E. Heidenreich, 'A Procedure for Mapping the Vegetation of Northern Simcoe County from the Ontario Land Survey,' in R. Louis Gentilcore and Kate Donkin, eds., *Land Surveys of Southern Ontario: An Introduction and Index to the Field Notebooks of the Ontario Land Surveyors, 1784–1859*, Cartographica Monograph No. 8 (Toronto: York University, 1973), 104–13.
2 Christopher A. Andreae, Cox and Willoughby Properties, unpublished, Historica Research Limited, London, 1989.
3 *Seventh Census of Canada, 1931*, Vol. 5 (Ottawa: Patenaude, 1935), Table 52.
4 Walter A. Kenyon, *Mounds of Sacred Earth: Burial Mounds of Ontario* (Toronto: Royal Ontario Museum, 1986); J.V. Wright, 'Cosmology,' in R. Cole Harris and Geoffrey J. Matthews, eds., *Historical Atlas of Canada: Vol. I, From the Beginning to 1800* (Toronto: University of Toronto Press, 1987), Plate 15. Conrad E. Heidenreich, *Huronia: A History and Geography of the Huron Indians, 1600–1650* (Toronto: McClelland and Stewart, 1971), provides a wider base for consideration of pre-European settlement.
5 The politics of land alienation is recorded in Lillian Gates, *Land Policies of Upper Canada* (Toronto: University of Toronto Press, 1968); its geography is sensitively treated in Andrew F. Burghardt, 'The Settling of Southern Ontario: An Appreciation of the Work of Carl Schott,' *Canadian Geographer*, 25 (1981), 76–93.
6 See, for example, *View from the Summit of the Ridge above Nicholl's Tavern, Penetanguishene Road*, water-colour painting by G.R. Dartnell, 1836, Royal Ontario Museum, Toronto, Acc. No. 952–87–8; reproduced in Thomas F. McIlwraith, 'Transportation in the Landscape of Early Upper Canada,' in David Wood, ed., *Perspectives on Landscape and Settlement in Early Upper Canada*, (Toronto: McClelland and Stewart, 1975), 54.
7 J. David Wood, Peter Ennals, and Thomas F. McIlwraith, 'A New Agriculture: Upper Canada to 1851,' in R. Louis Gentilcore and Geoffrey J. Matthews, eds.,

Historical Atlas of Canada: Vol. II, The Land Transformed, 1800–1891 (Toronto: University of Toronto Press, 1993), Plate 14; R. Cole Harris, Pauline Roulston, and Chris deFreitas, 'The Settlement of Mono Township,' *Canadian Geographer*, 19 (1975), 12.

8 On the tree as enemy, see Michael Dixon, 'Forests of the Mind,' *Forest Scene* (March 1981), 4, and Arthur R.M. Lower, *Great Britain's Woodyard: British America and the Timber Trade, 1763–1867* (Montreal: McGill-Queen's University Press, 1973), 31–3.

9 R.S. Dorney and D.W. Hoffman, 'Development of Landscape Planning Concepts and Management Strategies for an Urbanizing Agricultural Region,' *Landscape Planning*, 6 (1979), 154.

10 Elora *Backwoodsman*, 25 Aug. 1853.

11 F.E. Graef et al., *The House: A Pocket Manual of Rural Architecture* (New York: Fowler and Wells, 1859), 56.

12 John Harland, 'Report on the State of Agriculture in the County of Wellington, 1852,' *Journals and Transactions of the Board of Agriculture of Upper Canada*, 1 (1856), 218.

13 *Census of the Canadas, 1851–52*, Vol. 2 (Quebec: Lovell and Lamoureux, 1855), 430; *Census of Canada, 1880–81*, Vol. 1 (Ottawa: Maclear, Roger and Co., 1885), 2.

14 Brian Coffey, 'Building Materials in Early Ontario: The Example of Augusta Township,' *Canadian Geographer*, 32 (1988), 154–5.

15 *Report on Agriculture* (Toronto: Ontario Agricultural Commission, 1881), based on questions 1 and 3.

16 *Colonial Advocate*, 29 July 1824.

17 George Ley to Crown Lands Department, Petition, 10 Jan. 1857; RG1, Township Papers, Hamilton Township, Archives of Ontario.

18 Toronto *Globe*, 26 Sept. 1879, 7 Feb. 1880. Kenneth Kelly, 'Damaged and Efficient Landscapes in Rural and Southern Ontario, 1880–1900,' *Ontario History*, 66 (1974), 1–14.

19 See, for example, the 7th Concession of Fitzroy Township, complete with what could be a telephone line on poles, in *Illustrated Historical Atlas of the County of Carleton* (Toronto: H. Belden and Company, 1879), 17.

20 Elizabeth Bloomfield, 'Building Industrial Communities: Berlin and Waterloo to 1915,' in David F. Walker, ed., *Manufacturing in Kitchener-Waterloo* (Waterloo: University of Waterloo Press, 1987), 5–33.

21 Joseph Schull, *Ontario since 1867* (Toronto: McClelland and Stewart, 1978), 71, with reference to the 1890s.

22 Montreal, 10 Sept. 1888, Friedrich Engels, in Karl Marx and Friedrich Engels, *Letters to Americans, 1848–1895: A Selection* (New York: International, 1953), 203.

23 Eric Arthur, *The Early Buildings of Ontario* (Toronto: University of Toronto Press, 1938); Charles S. Buck, 'The Origin and Character of the Early Architec-

ture and Practical Arts of Ontario to 1850,' MA thesis, University of Western Ontario, 1930; Paul Duval, *A.J. Casson, His Life and Works: A Tribute* (Toronto: Cerebrus / Prentice-Hall, 1980); Charles W. Jefferys, 'The Visual Reconstruction of History,' *Canadian Historical Review*, 17 (1936), 249–65; Thoreau MacDonald, *House and Barn* (Toronto: D.M. Press, c. 1965); Robert Stacey, 'Salvage for Us These Fragments: C.W. Jefferys and Ontario's Historic Architecture,' *Ontario History*, 70 (1978), 147–70; Harry Symons, *Fences* (Toronto: Ryerson Press, 1958). The photographs of C.P. Meredith, taken about 1925, are in the National Picture Division, National Archives of Canada. Regarding Meredith and his work, see C.P. Meredith Papers, MG 29 B49, National Archives of Canada.

24 Harold D. Kalman, 'Canada's Main Streets,' in Deryck W. Holdsworth, ed., *Reviving Main Street* (Toronto: University of Toronto Press, 1985), 3–29.

25 'City Trying to Find Solution to the Domination of Garages,' *Mississauga News*, 18 May 1988.

26 *New Planning for Ontario* (Toronto: Ontario Royal Commission on Planning and Development Reform, 1993), 25.

27 *London Free Press*, 11 June 1949, sec. 9, 13.

4: Surveys and place names

1 The side road and concession road numbers usually correspond to the lot and concession on the side closer to the corner of the township from which the numbering begins.

2 William G. Dean and Geoffrey J. Matthews, *Economic Atlas of Ontario* (Toronto: University of Toronto Press, 1969), Plate 99. Maps in the illustrated county atlases of the 1870s and 1880s give full detail for each township in the province. For a full discussion of this helpful source see Edward Phelps, 'The County Atlases of Ontario,' in Barbara Farrell and Aileen Desbarats, eds., *Explorations in the History of Canadian Mapping* (Ottawa: Association of Canadian Map Libraries and Archives, 1988), 163–77. Topographic maps straddle township boundaries, drawing attention to discontinuities.

3 D.W. Smith, Surveyor General, York, to William Chewett, 2 March 1797; *Letters Written*, Surveys and Mapping Branch, Ontario Department of Lands and Forests (now Ministry of the Environment), cited in R. Louis Gentilcore and C. Grant Head, *Ontario History in Maps* (Toronto: University of Toronto Press, 1984), 58.

4 William Hutton, 'Letters on the Prospects of Agricultural Settlers in Upper Canada,' *British Agricultural Magazine* (April 1835), 105–6. These polite remarks are sufficiently plausible to pass general scrutiny but are not entirely correct. What Hutton reported happening to broken fronts and gores in his own region did not apply elsewhere, as a rule; his reference to a county road betrays his Irish terminology, applied years before the term 'county' came into use in Canada. Interview, D.W. Lambden, Guelph, Sept. 1993.

5 J.G. Chewett and Thomas Ridout, Deputy Surveyors General, York, to Reuben Sherwood, Deputy Surveyor, Elizabethtown, 7 Feb. 1807, regarding Pittsburg Township, near Kingston.

6 Dean and Matthews, *Atlas*, Plate 99; W.F. Weaver, *Crown Surveys in Ontario* (Toronto: Ontario Department of Lands and Forests, 1962).

7 R. Louis Gentilcore and Kate Donkin, *Land Surveys of Southern Ontario: An Introduction and Index to the Field Notebooks of the Ontario Land Surveyors, 1784–1859*, Cartographica Monograph No. 8 (Toronto: York University, 1973), 4–10.

8 This boundary in the survey is frequently misnamed 'the blind line', but no road allowance was provided at this point.

9 John R. Stilgoe, *Common Landscapes of America, 1580 to 1845* (New Haven, Conn.: Yale University Press, 1982), 55.

10 Sally McMurry, 'Progressive Farm Families and Their Houses, 1830–1855: A Study in Independent Design,' *Agricultural History*, 58 (1984), 336–7, 340–1. Illustrated county atlases display many such examples of the 1870s and 1880s.

11 W.F. Munro, *The Backwoods of Ontario* (London: n.p., 1881), 48. See also the coloured land-use map folded in with 'Land Use in the Saugeen Valley, 1976,' in J.D. McCuaig and Edward W. Manning, eds., *Agricultural Land-Use Change in Canada* (Ottawa: Lands Directorate, 1982). The woods stand out as long narrow strips, as they do also in an air photograph of northern Lambton County in Thomas F. McIlwraith, 'The Ontario Country Road as a Cultural Resource,' *Canadian Geographer*, 39 (1995), 327.

12 Fernand Braudel, *The Identity of France*, first pub. in French 1986, trans. Sian Reynolds 1988 (London: Fontana Press, 1989), 51.

13 Any short deviation from an allowance is, strictly speaking, a given road or an expropriation. Normally the specification of the line or crossroad of which it is a part prevails.

14 Province of Canada, 19–20 Victoria, cap. 62 (1856), 'An Act to Vest a Certain Road Allowance in the Township of Stamford in the Township Council.' The inadequate road passed in front of lots 128 to 120, on one side, and 129 to 136, on the other.

15 These densities are similar to those in upstate New York and southern Michigan, which had gridded landscapes without road allowances, and in New England and Quebec farm regions, where the road systems were entirely determined by physical features.

16 *Fourth Census of Canada, 1901*, Vol. 2 (Ottawa: Dawson, 1904), 2.

17 David Delisle, 'An Analysis of the Layout of Agricultural Holdings in Four Townships of Eastern Ontario,' MA thesis, University of Toronto, 1968, 63. Regarding farm vehicles on public roads, see Sylvia Crowe, *Tomorrow's Landscape* (London: Architectural Press, 1956), 104.

18 Partible inheritance requires subdividing the land equally among inheritors, which is socially egalitarian but economically destructive. Primogeniture (the opposite) deeds all land to the eldest son, an economically conservative but so-

cially divisive action; it was abolished in Canada West (Ontario) in 1856. See David Gagan, *Hopeful Travellers: Families, Land and Social Change in Mid-Victorian Peel County, Canada West* (Toronto: University of Toronto Press, 1981), 51–2.

19 Shirley Bentley, `The McCutcheons of Erin Township,´ BA thesis, Department of Geography, University of Toronto, 1985.

20 Marwyn Samuels, `The Biography of Landscape: Cause and Culpability,´ in Donald W. Meinig, ed., *The Interpretation of Ordinary Landscapes* (New York: Oxford University Press, 1979), 64; Wilbur Zelinsky, `Classical Town Names in the United States: The Historical Geography of an American Idea,´ *Geographical Review*, 57 (1967), 463–95. For the Ontario situation, see John N. Jackson, *Names across Niagara* (St Catharines: Vanwell Publishing Limited, 1989), and, more generally, Michael B. Smart, *Principles of Geographic Naming* (Toronto: Ontario Ministry of Natural Resources, Ontario Geographical Names Board, 1975), and Revised Statutes of Ontario, 1970, cap. 314.

21 J.V. Wright and R. Fecteau, `Iroquoian Agricultural Settlement,´ in R. Cole Harris and Geoffrey J. Matthews, eds., *Historical Atlas of Canada: Vol. I, From the Beginning to 1800* (Toronto: University of Toronto Press, 1987), Plate 12.

22 Peter Arnell and Ted Bickford, eds., *Mississauga City Hall: A Canadian Competition* (New York: Rizzoli International Publications, 1984)

23 J. George Hodgins, *The School House: Its Architecture, External and Internal Arrangements* (Toronto: Copp, Clark and Company, 1876), 21.

24 Ibid., 83.

25 *Illustrated Annual Register of Rural Affairs* 4 (1866), as quoted in Rodney Fox, `A Landscape in Transition,´ *Landscape*, 8 no. 3 (1959), 3.

26 *Illustrated Historical Atlas of the County of Simcoe* (Toronto: H. Belden and Company, 1881), 30–1. The townships are Mono, Adjala, Tecumseth, West Gwillimbury, Innisfil, Essa, Tosorontio, and Mulmer.

27 Tim Davis, `Rural America Enters the Space Age,´ *Journal of Popular Culture*, 21 no. 2 (1987), 117–42.

5: Building materials and arts

1 Arthur R.M. Lower, *Great Britain´s Woodyard: British America and the Timber Trade, 1763–1867* (Montreal: McGill-Queen´s University Press, 1973), 30.

2 John I. Rempel Papers; Acc. 2070, Nos. 7 and 9, Archives of Ontario. Eric Arthur and Dudley Witney, *The Barn* (Toronto: McClelland and Stewart, 1972), 72.

3 John I. Rempel, *Building with Wood, and Other Aspects of Nineteenth-Century Building in Central Canada*, first pub. 1968, 2nd ed. (Toronto: University of Toronto Press, 1980), 48–50. Measured example is from Scarborough. See also Brian Coffey, `From Shanty to House: Log Construction in Nineteenth Century Ontario,´ *Material Culture*, 16 (1984), 61–75.

4 Brian Coffey, 'Building Materials in Early Ontario: The Example of Augusta Township,' *Canadian Geographer*, 32 (1988), 156, a study in the Brockville region.

5 Interview, Herbert Walker, Medonte, Sept. 1971.

6 Thomas Ritchie, 'The Use of Planks in Wall Construction,' *APT Bulletin*, 6 no. 3 (1974), 26.

7 Rempel, *Building with Wood*, 173–88; John I. Rempel Papers; Acc. 2070, no. 8, Archives of Ontario; John Fitchen, *Building Construction before Mechanization* (Cambridge, Mass.: MIT Press, 1986), 137.

8 Martha Ann Kidd and Louis Taylor, *Historical Sketches of Peterborough* (Peterborough: Broadview Press, 1988), 50, 52, 54, 56, 94, 116. The house pictured on page 94 was built by a lumber merchant.

9 Jan L. Lewandowski, 'The Plank Framed House in Northeastern Vermont,' *Vermont Heritage*, 53 no. 2 (1985), 106.

10 Rempel, *Building with Wood*, 72; William H. Tishler, 'Stovewood Construction in the Upper Midwest and Canada: A Regional Vernacular Architectural Tradition,' in Camille Wells, ed., *Perspectives in Vernacular Architecture* (Annapolis, Md.: Vernacular Architecture Forum, 1982), 125–36.

11 Thomas Ritchie, ed., *Canada Builds, 1867–1967* (Toronto: University of Toronto Press, 1967), 158–9.

12 Residents of Caledon Township to John Colborne, Lieutenant-Governor, petition, 7 Feb. 1833, Miscellaneous Collections, 1833, no. 2, MU 2106, Archives of Ontario.

13 Walker Field, 'A Reexamination into the Invention of the Balloon Frame,' *Journal of the American Society of Architectural Historians*, 2 no. 4 (Oct. 1942), 6–8. Field draws substantially from George E. Woodward, 'Balloon Framing,' *Illustrated Annual Register of Rural Affairs for 1861, 1862, and 1863* (Albany: Luther Tucker and Son, 1869), 151–66.

14 Lewandowski, 'Plank House,' 119; Lee H. Nelson, *Nail Chronology, as an Aid to Dating Old Buildings* (Nashville, Tenn.: American Association for State and Local History, 1968). North America's first wire-nail machine was installed in Montreal in 1870; Ritchie, *Canada Builds*, 171.

15 William Dunlop, *Statistical Sketches of Upper Canada for the Use of Emigrants*, first pub. 1832, edited reprint (Toronto: McClelland and Stewart, 1967), 131.

16 Woodward, 'Balloon Framing,' 158.

17 Ritchie, *Canada Builds*, 171.

18 For an example of a church built in this fashion, see Charles S. Buck, 'The Origin and Character of the Early Architecture and Practical Arts of Ontario to 1850,' MA thesis, University of Western Ontario, 1930, 242.

19 J. George Hodgins, *The School House: Its Architecture, External and Internal Arrangements* (Toronto: Province of Canada Department of Public Instruction, 1857), 41. Hodgins recommends a minimum of 10 ft (3.3 m) height, and preferably 4 to 4.5 m (12 to 14 ft).

20 Interview, B. Madill, Hurontario Street, Mississauga, Feb. 1988.

21 For an example of clapboard, see Figure 11.2, below.

22 Rempel, *Building with Wood*, 115.

23 *Census of the Canadas, 1851–52*, Vol. 2 (Quebec: Lovell and Lamoureux, 1855), 430. *Census of Canada, 1890–91*, Vol. 1 (Ottawa: Dawson, 1893), 36.

24 Willet G. Miller, *Limestones of Ontario*, Ontario Sessional Papers, Vol. 13, pt. 2 (Toronto: Ontario Bureau of Mines, 1904), 14.

25 Charles Jones Correspondence, 9 Nov. 1808, MG 24 B7, National Archives of Canada.

26 Ronald W. Brunskill and Alec Clifton-Taylor, *English Brickworks* (London: Ward Lock, 1977), 43.

27 Allen G. Noble, *Wood, Brick and Stone: The North American Settlement Landscape* (Amherst: University of Massachusetts Press, 1984), 45–51; Charles F.J. Whebell, 'Pre-Confederation Houses in Norfolk County, Ontario,' *Ontario History*, 58 (1966), 233.

28 Augustus Welby Pugin, *An Apology for the Revival of Christian Architecture in England*, first pub. 1843, reprint (Oxford: St Barnabas Press, 1969); Marion MacRae and Anthony Adamson, *Cornerstones of Order: Courthouses and Town Halls in Ontario, 1784–1914* (Toronto: Clarke Irwin, 1985), 122–55.

29 Kathy Saul, 'The Life and Works of William and Hugh Saul,' *Papers and Proceedings*, Lennox and Addington Historical Society, 16 (1978), 114–32. The gothic theme is explored more fully in chapter 8, below.

30 Arthur and Witney, *Barn*, 98–9; Whebell, 'Houses in Norfolk,' 234; Barbara A. Humphreys, 'The Architectural Heritage of the Rideau Corridor,' *Canadian Historic Sites*, 10 (1974), 22.

31 Buck, 'Early Architecture,' 352.

32 Martin Weaver, 'Romancing the Stone: The Revitalization of the Canadian Building Stone Industry,' *Canadian Heritage*, 10 (Oct.–Nov. 1984), 45–6. Thomas Ritchie, 'Roman Stone and Other Artificial Decorative Stones,' *APT Bulletin*, 10 no. 1 (1978), 20–34.

33 *Seventh Census of Canada*, 1931, Vol. 5 (Ottawa: Patenaude, 1935), 951, 957.

34 Miller, *Limestones*, 15.

35 Mandel Sprachman, 'A City of "Delicious Morsels,"' *Globe and Mail*, 26 April 1986, 6, with reference to Toronto and making unspecified attribution to John Ruskin.

36 B. Napier Simpson, Jr., 'Mud Houses in York County,' *York Pioneer and Historical Society, Annual Report 1952*, 16.

37 'Unburnt Brick Houses,' *British American Cultivator*, 2, old series (1843), 40.

38 Ritchie, *Canada Builds*, 209; Rempel, *Building with Wood*, 274–82.

39 Heinrich Ries, *Clays: Their Occurrence, Properties, and Uses* (New York: Wiley, 1908), 197.

40 Clay with 5 to 7 per cent ferric oxide heated to 2000°F yields hard red brick. The addition of lime produces cream or yellow brick. Clay with alumina produces white, pale yellow, or pale buff brick, the more iron the yellower. Ries,

Clays, 197; Ronald W. Brunskill, *Brick Building in Britain* (London: Victor Gollancz, 1990), 40–1. Shale can be blasted to regain plasticity for making brick; slate cannot.

41 MacRae and Adamson, *Cornerstones*, 249.

42 Thomas Ritchie, `Early Brick Masonry along the St Lawrence in Ontario,´ *Journal, Royal Architectural Institute of Canada*, 37 (1960), 119–21; Ries, *Clays*, 221.

43 Ritchie, `Early Brick,´ 118.

44 Brunskill and Clifton-Taylor, *English Brickworks*, 81.

45 Charles Jones, Brockville, to Jonas Jones, Toronto, 23 April 1838; Charles Jones Letterbooks, vol. 3, MU 3187, Archives of Ontario.

46 John Weaver and Peter de Lottinville, `The Conflagration and the City: Disaster and Progress in British North America during the Nineteenth Century,´ *Histoire sociale / Social History*, 13 (1980), 442. See, for example, City of Belleville by-law no. 17, 1884, and Barrie *Northern Advance*, 25 May 1871.

47 A.J. Van Tassel and D.W. Bluestone, Mechanization in the Brick Industry, typescript, Philadelphia, 1939, 6–7.

48 *Census of the Canadas, 1860–61*, Vol. 2 (Quebec: Foote, 1864), 318; *Census of Canada, 1890–91*, Vol. 1 (Ottawa: Dawson, 1893), 36.

49 Ontario Bureau of Industries, *Report for 1897*, Ontario Sessional Papers, Report 32, part 1, 61 Victoria 1898, 1899 (Toronto, 1899), 30. Climatic conditions have been used to explain employment of brick in Ontario; Miller, *Limestones*, 13.

50 C.P. Dwyer, *The Immigrant Builder* (Philadelphia: Claxton, Remsen and Haffelfinger, 1872), 77; J. George Hodgins, *The School House: Its Architecture, External and Internal Arrangements* (Toronto: Copp, Clark and Company, 1876), 83; Thomas Ritchie, `Notes on the History of Hollow Masonry Walls,´ *APT Bulletin*, 5 no. 4 (1973), 40–9.

51 Buck, `Early Architecture,´ 147–58.

52 Interview, Oliver Seiler, Paisley, Sept. 1972.

53 Walter R. Jaggard, *Brickwork and Its Construction.* (London: Oxford University Press, 1929), 118–20; Brunskill and Clifton-Taylor, *English Brickworks*, 144.

54 *Journal of Education*, 23 no. 2 (Feb. 1870), 20. A course is a row, or layer, of bricks. See the gingerbread section in chapter 7, below, for further discussion.

55 R. Louis Gentilcore and C. Grant Head, *Ontario History in Maps* (Toronto: University of Toronto Press, 1984), 113.

56 Andrew Jackson Downing, *The Architecture of Country Houses, including Designs for Cottages, Farm Houses, and Villas*, (New York: Appleton, 1850).

57 Howard Levine, `Re-birth of the Red and White,´ in Julia Beck and Alec Keefer, eds., *Vernacular Architecture in Ontario*, (Toronto: Architectural Conservancy of Ontario, 1993), 89–93.

58 Miller, *Limestones*, 17.

59 Ronald Raeburn and Pauline Raeburn, `Lime Kilns and Remnants of Pioneer Technology,´ *Canadian Geographical Journal*, 86 no. 1 (1973), 14–7.

60 `Unburnt Brick Houses,´ 21.

61 Brunskill and Clifton-Taylor, *English Brickworks*, 43.

62 Dwyer, *Immigrant Builder*, 99; Orson S. Fowler, *A Home for All, or The Gravel Wall and Octagon Mode of Building* (New York: Fowlers and Wells, 1854).

63 *Report on Agriculture* (Toronto: Ontario Agricultural Commission, 1881), 220.

64 Interview, Lorne Joyce, Port Credit, Oct. 1973.

65 U.S. production of Portland cement rose from 8.5 to 88 million barrels between 1900 and 1914; George Perazich, S.T. Wood, and H. Schimmel, *Mechanization in the Cement Industry* (Washington, DC: Works Projects Administration, 1939), 7.

66 Miller, *Limestones*, 14. See also *Canadian Architect and Builder*, 17 (Feb. 1904), 25.

67 Ann Gillespie, `A Study of the Relationship between Boyd Brothers´ Concrete Block Manufacturing Company and Its Setting, the Village of Osgoode, Ontario,´ in Richard A. Jarrell and Arnold Roos, eds., *Critical Issues in the History of Canadian Science, Technology and Medicine* (Ottawa: HSTC Publications, 1983), 229–43.

68 Rempel, *Building with Wood*, 366–9; Nelson, *Nail Chronology*.

69 `Church Architecture,´ *Ontario Farmer*, 1 (Toronto: Hunter, Rose and Co, 1869), 226–8.

70 *Around and about Hamilton, 1785–1985: A Pictorial History of the Hamilton-Wentworth Region* (Hamilton: Head-of-the-Lake Historical Society, 1985), 40.

71 Richard Anderson, `Garbage Disposal in the Greater Toronto Area: A Preliminary Historical Geography,´ *Operational Geographer*, 11 no. 1 (March, 1993), 7–13.

72 The Pedlar Metal Roofing Company, *Catalogue*. (Oshawa: Pedlar, 1899), Pamphlet Collection, 1899, no. 55, Archives of Ontario. Pedlar made its first installations about 1861.

73 This episode occurred in Toronto, December 1989, in the author´s presence.

6: Houses

1 *Census of Canada, 1991*, Cat. No. 93–304 (Ottawa: Statistics Canada, 1992), 60ff.

2 Henry Glassie, *Passing the Time in Ballymenone: Culture and History of an Ulster Community* (Philadelphia: University of Pennsylvania Press, 1982), 338.

3 Stephen W. Johnson, *Rural Economy* (New Brunswick, NJ: I. Riley and Company, 1806), 91.

4 William E. Bell, *Carpentry Made Easy*, 2nd ed. (Philadelphia: Ferguson Brothers and Company, 1857), 56. The plate is the structural timber member running along the top of a wall.

5 Glassie, *Ballymenone*, 399–400.

6 John Howison, *Sketches of Upper Canada, Domestic, Local and Characteristic* (Edinburgh: Oliver and Boys, 1821), 27.

7 *Palliser's Model Homes*, first pub. 1878, reprint (Watkins Glen, NY: American Life Foundation, 1977), 8–9.

8 Henry W. Cleaveland, William Backus, and S.D. Backus, *American Village Homes* (New York: Appleton, 1856), 98.

9 Verschoyle B. Blake and Ralph Greenhill, *Rural Ontario* (Toronto: University of Toronto Press, 1969), 41.

10 Canadian Inventory of Historic Building; unpublished field notes, 1972–74. See 'Suggested Reading,' below, for more detail.

11 Mary K. Cullen, 'Highlights of Domestic Building in Pre-Confederation Quebec and Ontario as Seen through Travel Literature from 1763 to 1860,' *APT Bulletin*, 13 no. 1 (1981), 27–8.

12 Architects and Builders Edition, *Scientific American*, 1887, 1888; cited in Martha Ann Kidd and Louis Taylor, *Historical Sketches of Peterborough* (Peterborough: Broadview Press, 1988), 54.

13 'Return of the rise and progress of a settlement of Loyalist [sic] on the west side of the River Niagara, 18th April 1784,' Sir Frederick Haldimand, unpublished papers and correspondence, 1758–1784, vol. 21765, p. 388, British Museum. Niagara-on-the-Lake was known simply as Niagara at the time.

14 Jane Errington and George Rawlyk, 'The Loyalist-Federalist Alliance of Upper Canada,' *American Review of Canadian Studies*, 14 (1984), 169–70; Eric Arthur, *Small Houses of the Late 18th and Early 19th Century in Ontario* (Toronto: University of Toronto, Department of University Extension, c. 1926); Eric Arthur, 'Early Architecture in Ontario,' *Ontario Historical Society Papers and Records*, 28 (1932), 150–4.

15 There is also a British classical tradition, associated principally with administrative buildings; see chapter 8, below.

16 Eric Arthur, *The Early Buildings of Ontario* (Toronto: University of Toronto Press, 1938), 11. The most recent renovation of the Barnum House was completed in 1991; Ontario Historical Society, *OHS Bulletin*, no. 74 (Sept.–Oct. 1991), 8.

17 Marion MacRae and Anthony Adamson, *Cornerstones of Order: Courthouses and Town Halls in Ontario, 1784–1914*, (Toronto: Clarke Irwin, 1985), 37.

18 Marion MacRae and Anthony Adamson, *The Ancestral Roof: Domestic Architecture of Upper Canada* (Toronto: Clarke Irwin, 1963), 226; Ralph Greenhill, Ken Macpherson, and Douglas Richardson, *Ontario Towns* (Ottawa: Oberon Press, 1974), unpaginated.

19 Blake and Greenhill, *Rural Ontario*, 25, popularized this idea, but the thought was not new. 'Fashion ... is sometimes the result of so prosaic a cause as taxes. Queen Anne [reigned 1702–14] laid a tax on all two-story [sic] houses in the colonies, and the most loyal subject was justified in planning his house-walls to avoid an unnecessary expenditure.' Jane D. Shelton, *The Salt Box House: Eighteenth-Century Life in a New England Hill Town* (New York: Scribners, 1929), 23.

20 Upper Canada, 47 George III, cap. 7 (1807), `An Act [regarding] Assessment and Rates.´ Slight modifications occurred in 1811.

21 Blake and Greenhill, *Rural Ontario*, 25.

22 Province of Canada, 16 Victoria, cap. 182 (1853), `An Act to Amend and Consolidate the Assessment Laws of Upper Canada.´ Thereafter, rates were based on the value of all real property, not just the house.

23 F.E. Graef et. al., *The House: A Pocket Manual of Rural Architecture* (New York: Fowler and Wells, 1859), 57.

24 See Thomas C. Hubka, *Big House, Little House, Back House, Barn: The Connected Farm Buildings of New England* (Hanover, NH: University Press of New England, 1985), 49, for the New England experience. Eric Arthur and Dudley Witney, *The Barn* (Toronto: McClelland and Stewart, 1972), 111, demonstrates the predominance of T-junctions. See also R. Machin, `The Great Rebuilding: A Reassessment,´ *Past and Present*, 77 (1977).

25 Johnson, *Rural Economy*, 119.

26 `The Site of Paradise: A Settler's Guide to Becoming a Farmer in Early Upper Canada,´ 1833 letter, ed. Terence A. Crowley, reprinted in *Canadian Papers in Rural History*, 6 (1988), 272. Reference is to the Guelph area.

27 The advantage of double houses is expressed in *Canada Farmer's Sun*, 20 June 1893.

28 Glenn J. Lockwood, *Montague: A Social History of an Irish Ontario Township, 1783–1980* (Smiths Falls, Ont.: Township of Montague, 1980), 267. Kidd and Taylor, *Peterborough*, 90. The Local Architectural Conservation Advisory Committee of York Region has identified one such building on Yonge Street, Richmond Hill; interview, David and Janet Fayle, Sault Ste Marie, 1988.

29 This procedure is reported in *Illustrated Annual Register of Rural Affairs*, 3 (1869), 24, for example.

30 A dormer (as in `dormitory´) differs from a gable, being recessed and cut high into the roof; it is not part of the wall structure. See Thomas F. McIlwraith, `Altered Buildings: Another Way of Looking at the Ontario Landscape,´ *Ontario History*, 75 (1983), 118; John Penoyre and Jane Penoyre, *Houses in the Landscape: A Regional Study of Vernacular Building Styles in England and Wales* (London: Faber and Faber, 1978), 35–49.

31 Augustus Welby Pugin, *An Apology for the Revival of Christian Architecture in England*, first pub. 1843, reprint (Oxford: St Barnabas Press, 1969), 39.

32 A full discussion of gothicism in Ontario appears in chapter 8, below.

33 Nicholas Hill, *Historic Streetscapes of Huron County* (London: Middlesex Printing Company, 1981), 51; Charles S. Buck, `The Origin and Character of the Early Architecture and Practical Arts of Ontario to 1850,´ MA thesis, University of Western Ontario, 1930, photograph 35.

34 *Canada Farmer*, 15 April 1865. It has been reproduced in Greenhill, Macpherson, and Richardson, *Ontario Towns*, unpaginated.

35 *Canada Farmer's Sun*, 13 June 1893.

36 Lynne DiStefano, 'The Ontario Cottage: "Perfect of Its Kind,"' in Julia Beck and Alec Keefer, eds., *Vernacular Architecture in Ontario* (Toronto: Architectural Conservancy of Ontario, 1993), 45–8.

7: Revealing details

1 John Mactaggart, *Three Years in Canada, an Account of the Actual State of the Country in 1826–27–28*, Vol. 1 (London: Colburn, 1829), 308.
2 Cole Harris, 'The Simplification of Europe Overseas,' *Annals, Association of American Geographers*, 67 (1977), 469–83.
3 For a list of references on pattern books, see 'Suggested Reading,' below.
4 William Hay, 'Architecture for the Meridian of Canada,' *Anglo-American Magazine*, 2 (March 1853), 253.
5 Augustus Welby Pugin, *An Apology for the Revival of Christian Architecture in England*, first pub. 1843, reprint (Oxford: St Barnabas Press, 1969), 3.
6 Margaret S. Angus, 'William Coverdale,' *Dictionary of Canadian Biography*, 9 (1976), 164–5.
7 See the following paintings, reproduced in Alfred J. Casson, *My Favourite Watercolours* (New York: Cerebrus, Prentice-Hall, 1982): *Saturday Afternoon*, 1927, 39; *Early Summer, Norval*, 1928, 43; *Country Store*, 1930, 71; *Markham*, 1935, 91; *Village of Mount Albert*, 1938, 107; *York Mills*, 1947, 111.
8 See Solon Robinson, *Facts for Farmers and the Family Circle*, Vol. 1 (New York: A.J. Johnson, 1869), opposite 275, for one example of these fictional stereotypes.
9 Catharine Parr Traill, *The Backwoods of Canada*, first pub. 1838, reprint (Toronto: McClelland and Stewart, 1966), 142. See Pamela West, 'The Rise and Fall of the American Porch,' *Landscape*, 20 no. 2 (1976), 42–7, for a bit of porch nostalgia.
10 *British American Cultivator*, 2, old series (1843), 21, 40. Wooden dummies are visible in the wall in Figure 7.2, below.
11 Antony Pacey, 'A History of Window Glass Manufacture in Canada,' *APT Bulletin*, 13 no. 3 (1981), 34.
12 Mary K. Cullen, 'Highlights of Domestic Building in Pre-Confederation Quebec and Ontario as Seen through Travel Literature from 1763 to 1860,' *APT Bulletin*, 13 no. 1 (1981), 25, citing Alfred Domett, *Canadian Journal* (c. 1840), reprint (London: University of Western Ontario, 1955), 46, with reference to the 1830s.
13 Lewis F. Allen, *Farm Houses, Cottages and Outbuildings* (New York: Orange, Judd and Company, 1852), 75.
14 John G. Waite and Diana S. Waite, 'Stovemakers of Troy, New York,' *Antiques*, 103 no.1 (1973), 137; John Weaver, *Hamilton: An Illustrated History* (Toronto: Lorimer, 1982), 26. See Thomas C. Hubka, *Big House, Little House, Back House, Barn: The Connected Farm Buildings of New England* (Hanover, NH: Uni-

versity Press of New England, 1985), 123–5, on the need for stoves in mixed farming.

15 Marilyn G. Miller, *Straight Lines in Curved Space: Colonization Roads in Eastern Ontario* (Toronto: Ontario Ministry of Culture and Recreation, 1978), 60.

16 See also Robert M. Styran and Robert R. Taylor, *The Welland Canals: The Growth of Mr Merritt's Ditch* (Erin, Ont.: Boston Mills Press, 1988), 93.

17 Wood-burning central furnaces began to appear in the 1880s. Waite and Waite, 'Stovemakers,' 137.

18 Interview, Herbert Walker, Medonte Township, Sept. 1971.

19 John I. Rempel, *Building with Wood, and Other Aspects of Nineteenth-Century Building in Central Canada*, first pub. 1968, 2nd ed. (Toronto: University of Toronto Press, 1980), Chap. 10.

20 Many types of gingerbread trim are illustrated in Amos J. Bicknell and William T. Comstock, *Victorian Architecture: Two Pattern Books*, first pub. 1873, reprint, with introduction by John Maass (Watkins Glen, NY: American Life Foundation, 1977), Plate 35.

21 Anita C. Markler, 'Coloured Brick in Yorkville,' *Journal of Canadian Art History*, 4 no. 2 (1977–8), 98–110. Yorkville was three kilometres north of Lake Ontario on Yonge Street and has long since been absorbed into Toronto. See also Thomas Ritchie, 'Notes on Dichromatic Brickwork in Ontario,' *APT Bulletin*, 11 no. 2 (1979), 60–75.

22 *Canada Farmer*, 15 April 1865, 116; illustrated in Ralph Greenhill, Ken Macpherson, and Douglas Richardson, *Ontario Towns* (Ottawa: Oberon Press, 1974), unpaginated.

23 *Elgin, Middlesex and Oxford Directory* (1883–4), 65.

24 Nancy Z. Tausky and Lynne D. DiStefano, *Victorian Architecture in London and Southwestern Ontario: Symbols of Aspiration* (Toronto: University of Toronto Press, 1986), 372. The arts and crafts movement was at its root.

8: Community buildings

1 Marion MacRae and Anthony Adamson, *Cornerstones of Order: Courthouses and Town Halls in Ontario, 1784–1914* (Toronto: Clarke Irwin, 1985), 19.

2 Nancy Z. Tausky and Lynne D. DiStefano, *Victorian Architecture in London and Southwestern Ontario: Symbols of Aspiration* (Toronto: University of Toronto Press, 1986), 381.

3 A schematic diagram of details to watch for in identifying halls is laid out in Appendix B.

4 Marion MacRae and Anthony Adamson, *Hallowed Walls: Church Architecture of Upper Canada* (Toronto: Clarke Irwin, 1975), 223–5; MacRae and Adamson, *Cornerstones*, passim.

5 Upper Canada, 11 George IV, cap. 36 (1830), 'An Act to Make Valid Certain Marriages Heretofore Contracted and to Provide for the Future Solemnization

of Matrimony,' and Upper Canada, 1 William IV, cap. 1 (1831), extended the authority to all Protestant clergy.

6 MacRae and Adamson, *Hallowed Walls*, passim; Harold D. Kalman, 'The Development of Religious Architecture in Ontario,' in Harold D. Kalman, ed., *The Conservation of Ontario Churches: A Programme for Funding Religious Properties of Architectural and Historic Significance* (Toronto: Ontario Ministry of Culture and Recreation, 1977), 103–13.

7 'Upper Canada, 1842,' *Census of Canada, 1870–71*, Vol. 4 (Ottawa: Taylor, 1876), 135.

8 T.A. Davidson, *A New History of the County of Grey* (Owen Sound: Grey County Historical Society, 1972), 242.

9 W.F. Munro, *The Backwoods Life: An Interesting Story of Pioneer Days in Melancthon Township* (Shelburne, Ont.: Free Press, 1910), 48, near Hornings Mills, Dufferin County. 'Noo Connexion' refers to Methodist New Connection.

10 Napanee *Standard*, 18 June 1881.

11 Martha Ann Kidd and Louis Taylor, *Historical Sketches of Peterborough* (Peterborough: Broadview Press, 1988), 32.

12 In the 1860s the Cosmopolitan burying ground was legally severed from the Anglican ground, but the two cemeteries remain not obviously separate. Interview, Thompson Adamson, Mississauga, June 1980.

13 William Westfall, *Two Worlds: The Protestant Culture of Nineteenth-Century Ontario* (Montreal: McGill-Queen's University Press, 1989), 111. The United Church of England and Ireland (Anglican) and the Church of Scotland (Presbyterian) were also constituents of the established church.

14 Ibid., 77, 127–8, 141.

15 Ibid., 100.

16 *Census of the Canadas, 1851–52*, Vol. 2 (Quebec: Lovell and Lamoureux, 1855), 431; *Census of Canada, 1880–81*, Vol. 2 (Ottawa: Maclear, Roger and Co, 1885), 434.

17 John Webster Grant, *A Profusion of Spires: Religion in Nineteenth-Century Ontario* (Toronto: University of Toronto Press, 1988).

18 Fred A. Dahms, 'How Ontario's Guelph District Developed,' *Canadian Geographical Journal*, 94 no. 1 (Feb.–March 1977), 55.

19 Augustus Welby Pugin, *An Apology for the Revival of Christian Architecture in England*, first pub. 1843, reprint (Oxford: St Barnabas Press, 1969), frontispiece, 25–31. See also MacRae and Adamson, *Hallowed Walls*, 145–6, and Westfall, *Two Worlds*, Fig. 16.

20 Pugin, *Revival of Christian Architecture*, 2.

21 All dated 1843, by John G. Howard. MacRae and Adamson, *Hallowed Walls*, 99–104.

22 Westfall, *Two Worlds*, 67–8, 86.

23 George Gilbert Scott, *Remarks on Secular and Domestic Architecture, Present and Future* (London: Murray, 1856), 30.

24 For a sampling, see 'The Gables of Burlington,' poster published by Burlington Local Architectural Conservation Advisory Committee, 1989. Three of twenty-five front gables have gothic windows.

25 Historic plaques on site.

26 The architects Lloyd and Pierce built throughout western Ontario. Huron Diocese (London) Records, Archives of the Anglican Church, Toronto.

27 *Canadian Methodist Magazine*, 1 (1875), 18.

28 Westfall, *Two Worlds*, 153.

29 John Squair, *The Townships of Darlington and Clarke* (Toronto: University of Toronto Press, 1927), 238.

30 'Two Mono Churches Officially Closed,' *Orangeville Banner*, 3 Aug. 1977.

31 Hay Bay Methodist Church, 1925 (photograph), C.P. Meredith Collection, PA26810, National Archives of Canada.

32 Cecil J. Houston and William J. Smyth, *The Sash Canada Wore: A Historical Geography of the Orange Order in Canada* (Toronto: University of Toronto Press, 1980).

33 Ibid., 39.

34 Ibid., 90, 133.

35 *Illustrated Historical Atlas of the County of Middlesex* (Toronto: H.R. Page and Company, 1878), 36.

36 Hodgins Papers, MU1375–1381, Archives of Ontario.

37 Province of Canada, 9 Victoria, cap. 20 (1846), based on Egerton Ryerson's inquiry into the province's educational needs, is the key legislation.

38 J. George Hodgins, ed., *Historical and Other Papers and Documents Illustrative of the Educational System of Ontario, 1792–1872*, Vol. 3 (Toronto: Ontario Department of Education, 1911–12), 15. Province of Canada, 13–14 Victoria, cap. 48 (1850), 'Common School Act,' established full public financing for primary schools and gave the public access to school libraries.

39 J. George Hodgins, *The School House: Its Architecture, External and Internal Arrangements* (Toronto: Province of Canada Department of Public Instruction, 1857), iii.

40 Hodgins, *Educational System*, Vol. 2, 145.

41 Ontario, 34 Victoria, cap. 33 (1871).

42 J. George Hodgins, *The School House: Its Architecture, External and Internal Arrangements* (Toronto: Copp, Clark and Company, 1876), 76.

43 *Illustrated Historical Atlas of the County of Halton* (Toronto: Walker and Miles, 1877), 54.

44 Hodgins, *School House* (1876), 10.

45 Ibid., 21.

46 Hodgins, *School House* (1857), 38, 40.

47 Hodgins, *School House* (1876), 21–2.

48 Ontario, 37 Victoria, cap. 27 (1874), 'High School Act.' R.D. Gidney and W.P.J. Miller, *Inventing Secondary Education: The Rise of the High School in Nineteenth-Century Ontario* (Montreal: McGill-Queen's University Press, 1990).

49 Ontario, 9 Edward VII, cap. 90 (1909), 'Continuation Schools Act.' Sessional Papers, document no. 17, Report of the Department of Education for 1921 (Toronto: King's Printer, 1922), 95.

50 Lillian C. Gray, 'Rural Education in Ontario,' *Canadian Forum*, 26 (1946), 155–7.

51 Ibid., 155.

52 *Report of the Minister of Education, Ontario, for 1923* (Toronto: King's Printer, 1924), 39–40.

53 The province reorganized 1,423 school sections, covering some 25 per cent of southern Ontario, into 248 township areas. Gray, 'Rural Education,' 155.

54 There were 491 school buses registered in Ontario in 1945; Sessional Paper no. 32, Annual Report of the Department of Highways, Ontario, for 1946–47, 112.

55 Anne Logan, *School's Out!* (Erin, Ont.: Boston Mills Press, 1987), a picture book on conversions. See also May Thielgaard Watts, *Reading the Landscape of America* (New York: Macmillan, 1975), Chap. 7, 'Tree Rings in a Country Schoolyard.'

56 'The Little Red School House,' *Canadian Magazine*, 9 Aug. 1969.

57 Dana H. Johnson, *For the Privileged Few: The Private and Specialist Schools of Ontario, 1800–1930*, Research Bulletin No. 215 (Ottawa: Parks Canada, 1984).

58 Province of Canada, 22 Victoria, cap. 65 (1859). Further, twelve households could request a separate Protestant school or separate 'coloureds' school. Hodgins, *Educational System*, Vol. 3, 15.

59 Lorne Bruce, 'Public Libraries in Ontario, 1882–1920,' *Ontario History*, 77 (1985), 124.

60 Tausky and DiStefano, *Victorian Architecture*, 69–77.

61 Ontario Sessional Papers, no. 3 (1894), 220.

62 Hamilton Association, *75th Anniversary Meeting, April 29, 1932* (Hamilton: Hamilton Association for the Advancement of Literature, Science and Art, 1932).

63 Ontario, 45 Victoria, cap. 22 (1882), 'Free Libraries Act.' Ontario, 58 Victoria, cap. 45 (1895), 'Public Libraries Act.' Eric Bow, 'The Public Library Movement in 19th Century Ontario,' *Ontario Library Review*, 66 (1982), 1–16.

64 Margaret Beckman, *The Best Gift: A Record of the Carnegie Libraries in Ontario* (Toronto: Ontario Heritage Foundation and Dundurn Press, 1984), 10.

65 Province of Canada, 12 Victoria, cap. 81 (1849).

66 MacRae and Adamson, *Cornerstones*, 229.

67 Deryck W. Holdsworth, 'Architectural Expressions of the Canadian National State,' *Canadian Geographer*, 30 (1986), 169.

68 MacRae and Adamson, *Cornerstones*, 12.

69 J.F. Thompson, *A Century of Masonry in Simcoe County* (Waterford, Ont.: n.p., 1904), no page.

70 MacRae and Adamson, *Cornerstones*, 25, 64, 143, 197, 221.

71 Tausky and DiStefano, *Victorian Architecture*, chap. 1.

72 John J.-G. Blumenson, *Ontario Architecture: A Guide to Styles and Building Terms* (Toronto: Fitzhenry and Whiteside, 1989), opposite 109.

73 Christopher Thomas, `Architectural Image for the Dominion: Scott, Fuller and the Stratford Post Office,´ *Journal of Canadian Art History*, 3 nos. 1 and 2 (1976), 83–94; Christopher Thomas, `Thomas Fuller,´ *Dictionary of Canadian Biography*, 12 (Toronto: University of Toronto Press, 1990), 343–6.

74 Liz Armstrong, `Keeping Posted,´ *Canadian Heritage*, 14 no. 1 (spring 1988), 14–9.

75 *La Rochefoucault-Liancourt´s Travels in Canada, 1795*, first pub. 1795, reprint as 13th Report of the Bureau of Archives for the Province of Ontario (Toronto, 1917), 38–9.

76 W.H. Bartlett, `Port Hope,´ in *Canadian Scenery, Illustrated*, Vol. 2, N.P. Willis and W.H. Bartlett (London: James S. Virtue, c. 1840), opposite 38.

9: Barns

1 *The Plough, the Loom and the Anvil*, 2 (Nov. 1849), 302.

2 *BT Barn Book* (Fergus, Ont.: Beatty Brothers, 1918), 11.

3 Thomas F. McIlwraith, `The Diamond Cross: An Enigmatic Symbol in the Ontario Landscape,´ *Pioneer America*, 13 (1981), 32–9.

4 In Niagara´s first year half the barns had these dimensions. `Return of the rise and progress of a settlement of Loyalist [sic] on the west side of the River Niagara, 18th April 1784,´ Sir Frederick Haldimand, unpublished papers and correspondence, 1758–1784, vol 21765, p. 388, British Museum.

5 Cunningham Geike, ed., *Life in the Woods* (London: Routledge, Warner and Routledge, 1864), 63.

6 Mary K. Cullen, `Highlights of Domestic Building in Pre-Confederation Quebec and Ontario as Seen through Travel Literature from 1763 to 1860,´ *APT Bulletin*, 13 no. 1 (1981), 26.

7 *BT Barn Book*, 62; Ronald W. Brunskill, *Illustrated Handbook of Vernacular Architecture*, 2nd ed. (London: Faber and Faber, 1978), 140–1.

8 Clarence Danhof, *Change in Agriculture: The Northern United States, 1820–1870* (Cambridge, Mass.: Harvard University Press, 1969), 221–50.

9 United States of America, Senate Document no. 1589, hearings (1874–5), 4.

10 *Illustrated Annual Register of Rural Affairs*, 7 (1889), 159.

11 Interview, Herbert Walker, Medonte, Sept. 1971.

12 William A. Foster and D.G. Carter, *Farm Buildings* (New York: Wiley, 1922), 93.

13 Byron D. Halsted, *Barn Plans and Outbuildings*, first pub. 1881, rev. ed. 1903, reprint (Brattleboro, Vt.: Stephen Greene Press, 1977), 1–8.

14 C.P. Dwyer, *The Immigrant Builder* (Philadelphia: Claxton, Remsen and Haffelfinger, 1872), ix.

15 Halsted, *Barn Plans*, 12.

16 See, for example,*Canada Farmer*, 1 (1864), 77.

17 Foster and Carter, *Farm Buildings*, 58.

18 *BT Barn Book*, 2.

19 Interview, Chester Teeple, Greenock Township, Bruce County, Sept. 1973.

20 `Practical Enlargement of Old Barns,´ in Halsted, *Barn Plans*, 55–6.

21 Interview, Deight Potts, Paisley, Sept. 1973.

22 Foster and Carter, *Farm Buildings*, 61–2.

23 Charles Klamkin, *Barns: Their History, Preservation and Restoration* (New York: Hawthorn Books, 1973), 54.

24 John L. Shawver, *Plank Frame Barn Construction* (New York: David Williams and Company, 1904), 5.

25 John I. Rempel, *Building with Wood, and Other Aspects of Nineteenth-Century Building in Central Canada*, first pub. 1968, 2nd ed. (Toronto: University of Toronto Press, 1980), 205; Halsted, *Barn Plans*, 27; Richard Rawson, *Old Barn Plans* (Toronto: Beaverbooks, 1979), 9–15.

26 Shawver, *Barn Construction*, 6.

27 Ibid. See Figure 5.5 and illustration in *Beatty Barn Book* (Toronto: Beatty Brothers, 1930), 336.

28 Ontario Bureau of Industries, *Report for 1897*, Ontario Sessional Papers, Report 32, part 1, 61 Victoria, 1898 (Toronto, 1899), 15. See also Allen G. Noble, `The Diffusion of Silos,´ *Landscape*, 25 no 1 (1981), 11–4.

29 John C. Woolley, *Farm Buildings* (New York: McGraw-Hill, 1946), 15; *BT Barn Book*, 59.

30 Woolley, *Farm Buildings*, 227.

31 *Farming Opportunities in Ontario* (Toronto: Ontario Department of Agriculture, 1909).

32 *BT Barn Book*, 3.

33 Foster and Carter, *Farm Buildings*, 57. J.H. Sanders, *Practical Hints about Barn Building* (Chicago: J.H. Sanders Publishing Company, 1892), 8.

34 *BT Barn Book*, 64.

35 Mary M. Foley, `The American Barn,´ *Architectural Forum*, 50 (Aug. 1951), 170–8, is an early reference.

10: Fences

1 Harry Symons, *Fences* (Toronto: Ryerson Press, 1958), xxiii-xxiv.

2 Catharine Parr Traill, *The Backwoods of Canada*, first pub. 1836, reprint (Toronto: McClelland and Stewart, 1966), 66.

3 James Strachan, *A Visit to the Province of Upper Canada in 1819* (Aberdeen: J. Strachan, 1820), 65.

4 Jeffrey L. Brown, `Earthworks and Industrial Archaeology,´ *Industrial Archaeology*, 6 (1980), 1–8. These machines were a sideline of the farm-machinery and railway-construction industries.

5 Samuel Strickland, *Twenty-Seven Years in Canada West*, Vol. 1 (London: R. Bentley, 1853), 20.

6 See Appendix C for a typology of fence types. Two relevant texts from the nineteenth century are Henry M. Smith, ed., *The Fence: A Compilation of Facts, Figures and Opinions*. (Worcester, Mass.: Noyes, Snow and Company, 1879), and `Fences and Fence-Making,´ *Rural Affairs for 1858–59–60* (Albany, NY, 1860), 271–7.

7 Cecil J. Houston and William J. Smyth, *Irish Emigration and Canadian Settlement: Patterns, Links, and Letters* (Toronto: University of Toronto Press, 1990), 133.

8 William Hutton, `Letters on the Prospects of Agricultural Settlers in Upper Canada,´ *British Agricultural Magazine* (April 1835), 111, writing about Hastings County; cited in Houston and Smyth, *Irish Emigration*, 133.

9 William Hosmer, Feeding Hills, Massachusetts, diary entry for 10 April 1849; Baker Library, Harvard University, Cambridge, Mass.

10 A.F. Scott, `Agricultural Report for the County of Peel, 1853,´ *Journal and Transactions of the Board of Agriculture for Upper Canada*, 1 (1856), 357.

11 Municipal survey no. 507. Norval, Concession 10, Esquesing Township, Halton County.

12 Scott, `Agricultural Report,´ 357.

13 Glenn J. Lockwood, *Montague: A Social History of an Irish Ontario Township, 1783-1980* (Smiths Falls, Ont.: Township of Montague, 1980), 239. Interview, Gerry Shain, Oakville, May 1986, regarding upgrading of Middle Road, Trafalgar Township, in the 1920s.

14 Brantford, Norfolk and Port Burwell Railway, Tillsonburg, 1878, RG 30, box 12584, file no. 2, National Archives of Canada. Fence rails twelve feet (almost four metres) long and four inches (ten centimetres) thick; `worm´ means swath.

15 Interview, James McClure, Chesley, Oct. 1974.

16 Ontario, 31 Victoria, cap. 41 (1868), `An Act to incorporate The Toronto and Nipissing Railway Company,´ cited in Lindsay *Expositor*, 23 Dec. 1869.

17 *Canada Farmers´ Sun*, 13 June 1893.

18 *Illustrated Annual Register of Rural Affairs*, 2 (1860), 120–1.

19 Ibid., 136.

20 Ontario Bureau of Industries, *Report for 1897*, Ontario Sessional Papers, Report 32, part 1, 61 Victoria, 1898 (Toronto, 1899), 28–30; M.A.R. Kelley, *Farm Fences*, Bulletin No. 1832 (Washington, DC: United States Department of Agriculture, 1940), 8.

21 Ontario and Quebec Railway, Inspection, July 1884, RG 46, Vol. 690, no. 2997, National Archives of Canada.

22 Advertisement in *The Railway and Shipping World*, 1 (1898), 118.

23 John C. Woolley, *Farm Buildings* (New York: McGraw-Hill, 1946), 52–4; *Rural Affairs*, 136.

24 Kelley, *Farm Fences*, 21.

25 Ontario Bureau of Industries, *Report for 1897*, 29.

11: **Power and mills**

1 Charles S. Buck, 'The Origin and Character of the Early Architecture and Practical Arts of Ontario to 1850,' MA thesis, University of Western Ontario, 1930, 576; William Canniff, *The Settlement of Upper Canada* (Toronto: Dudley and Burns, 1869), 216.

2 *Christian Guardian*, 19 March 1856, 94, cited in William Westfall, *Two Worlds: The Protestant Culture of Nineteenth-Century Ontario* (Montreal: McGill-Queen's University Press, 1989), 142.

3 Ontario Bureau of Industries, *Report for 1897*, Ontario Sessional Papers, Report 32, part 1, 61 Victoria, 1898, (Toronto, 1899), 15.

4 The most useful source on Ontario water-powered milling is Felicity L. Leung, *Grist and Flour Mills in Ontario: From Millstones to Rollers, 1780s-1880s*, Historical and Archaeology Series No. 53 (Ottawa: National Parks Service, 1981). Oliver Evans, *The Young Mill-wright and Miller's Guide ... with a Description of an Improved Merchant Flour Mill*, 14th ed. (Philadelphia: Blanchard, 1853), was the standard work in the United States and Canada during the nineteenth century. Popular treatments include David Macaulay, *Mill* (New York: Houghton Mifflin, 1983), and Carol Priamo, *Mills of Canada* (Toronto: McGraw-Hill Ryerson, 1976).

5 John L. Ladell, *They Left Their Mark: Surveyors and Their Role in the Settlement of Ontario* (Toronto: Dundurn Press, 1993), 80.

6 Ontario, 36 Victoria, cap. 40 (1873), 'An Act for the improvement of water privileges.'

7 G. Brockitt Abrey, Provincial Land Surveyor, Milton, to William Fraser, Esq., Esquesing, 30 Oct. 1863, Ontario, Department of Lands and Forests (now Ministry of the Environment), document 53750; photocopy in possession of author. Concerns a branch of the Credit River near Norval.

8 James Leffel, *The Construction of Mill Dams* (Springfield, O.: James Leffel and Company, 1874), 25.

9 Leung, *Grist and Flour Mills*, 47–50.

10 Ibid., 47–50.

11 Ibid., 83.

12 R. Peter Gillis, 'Rivers of Sawdust: The Battle over Industrial Pollution in Canada, 1865–1903,' *Journal of Canadian Studies*, 21 (1986), 84–103.

13 'Page's Portable Saw Mill,' *British American Cultivator*, 2 (1843), 2, 19.

14 Leung, *Grist and Flour Mills*, 32–4, 146.

15 *The Flour and Grist Milling Industry in Canada, 1921* (Ottawa: Dominion Bureau of Statistics, 1923). The Goldie-McCulloch firm of Galt patented its porcelain roller process in 1883; Leung, *Grist and Flour Mills*, 209.

16 Dianne Newell, `Belt and Line-Shafting Transmission of Power,´ in Dianne Newell and Ralph Greenhill, eds., *Survivals: Aspects of Industrial Archaeology in Ontario.* (Erin, Ont.: Boston Mills Press, 1989), 109–11. William Greey and J.G. Greey, *Toronto Mill Furnishing Works: Illustrated General Catalogue of Mill Machinery and Supplies* (Toronto: W. and J.G. Greey, 1888).

17 Theodore Z. Penn, `The Development of the Leather Belt Main Drive,´ *Industrial Archaeology,* 7 (1981), 6; A.B. McCullough, `Technology and Textile Mill Architecture in Canada,´ *Material History Bulletin,* 30 (1989), 26.

18 Leung, *Grist and Flour Mills,* 43–7.

19 Interview, James McClure, Chesley, 1974.

20 *Colonial Advocate,* 27 May 1824.

21 Joseph Dart, `The Grain Elevators of Buffalo,´ *Buffalo Historical Society Publications,* 1 (1879), 391–404; Thomas Ritchie, ed., *Canada Builds, 1867–1967* (Toronto: University of Toronto Press, 1967), 166.

22 Displays at Ontario Agricultural Museum, Milton, trace the history of farm traction thoroughly.

23 Elizabeth Bloomfield, `Building Industrial Communities: Berlin and Waterloo to 1915,´ in David F. Walker, ed., *Manufacturing in Kitchener-Waterloo* (Waterloo: University of Waterloo Press, 1987), 5–33; Richard Tatley, Industries and Industrialists of Merrickville, 1792–1979, Park Canada Ms. No. 423, c. 1981.

24 Ralph Greenhill, `Hamilton Pumphouse,´ in Newell and Greenhill, eds., *Survivals,* 69–84.

25 John Weaver, `The Location of Manufacturing Enterprises: The Case of Hamilton´s Attraction of Foundries, 1830–1890,´ in Richard A. Jarrell and Arnold Roos, eds., *Critical Issues in the History of Canadian Science, Technology and Medicine* (Ottawa: HSTC Publications, 1983), 197–217.

26 Christopher Tunnard and Henry Hope Reed, *American Skyline* (New York: New American Library, 1956), 30–1.

27 Augustus Bridle, `Trip over a Gas Producer Plant,´ *Engineering Record* (1904), cited in Bloomfield, *Berlin and Waterloo,* 33.

28 F.H. Baddeley, `Report on Marmora Iron Works and Local Geology,´ first pub. 1828, reprint, *APT Bulletin,* 5 no. 3, (1973), 21–3. See also Arthur D. Dunn, `The Marmora Iron Works, 1820–24,´ *Anthropological Journal of Canada,* 18 (1980), 2–7.

29 Joseph D. Lindsey, `Water and Blood: The Georgian Foundry, Hydraulic Technology, and the Rise and Fall of a Family Firm in Small Town Ontario,´ *Ontario History,* 75 (1983), 244–65.

30 Mark Fram, *Ontario Hydro, Ontario Heritage: A Study of Strategies for the Conservation of the Heritage of Ontario Hydro* (Toronto: Ontario Ministry of Culture and Recreation, 1980).

31 Ibid., 24–5, 34–5.

12: Graves and monuments

1 Jacalyn Duffin, *Langstaff: A Nineteenth-Century Medical Life* (Toronto: University of Toronto Press, 1993).

2 Interview, George Grant, Paisley, Sept. 1973.

3 Stephen Leacock, 'The Place of History in Canadian Education,' *Canadian Historical Association Report* (1925), 33.

4 Gravestone of Richard Hallowell (1837–1867), Shiloh Church, Clarke Township, Durham County, courtesy of Gerald Hallowell. Another one of many variations of this well-used verse: 'Pause a moment passerby. / Where you are now, there once was I. / Where I am now there shall you be. / Prepare in death to follow me,' on which stone were scribbled the lines: 'To follow you I am not bent / Until I know which way you went.' Related in William N. Parker, 'The Magic of Property,' *Agricultural History*, 54 (1980), 489.

5 Carl Arfwedson, *The United States and Canada in 1832*, Vol. 1 (London: Bentley, 1834), 211, 213, referring to the opening of Mount Auburn Cemetery in Boston in 1831.

6 Carole Hanks, *Early Ontario Gravestones* (Toronto: McGraw-Hill Ryerson, 1974).

7 W. Harrison, 'Detection of Graves and Underground Objects by Dowsing,' *New Horizons*, 1 (1974), 155. I was among the little group of people that witnessed this activity.

8 *Bylaws, Rules and Regulations of the Ontario Union Cemetery Company* (Oshawa: Luke and Larke, 1875), 3.

9 Revised Statutes of Ontario, 1980, cap. 4, 'The Cemeteries Act.' Sections 44 to 61 deal with cemetery restoration.

10 'Cemetery Board Cleans up Mono's Pioneer Cemeteries,' *Orangeville Banner*, 3 Aug. 1977.

11 Darrell Norris and Anne Krogh, 'Cemetery Marker Origins: A Key to Market Evolution,' in Darrell Norris and Victor Konrad, eds., *Visible Landscapes* (Quebec: Canadian Association of Geographers, 1976), 14.

12 Bowmanville, *Canadian Statesman*, 24 March 1869.

13 W.C. Miller, *Vignettes of Early St. Thomas* (St Thomas: Sutherland Press, 1967), 183; Barbara Rotundo, 'Monumental Bronze: A Representative American Company,' in Richard E. Meyer, ed., *Cemeteries and Gravemarkers: Voices of American Culture* (Ann Arbor, Mich.: UMI Reserach Press, 1989), 263–92. White Bronze was a subsidiary of a Connecticut company.

14 *Elgin, Middlesex and Oxford Directory* (1883–4), 65.

15 Another metal marker, much more localized, is the subject of an essay by Nancy-Lou Patterson, 'The Iron Cross and the Tree of Life: German Alsatian Gravemarkers in Waterloo Region and Bruce County Roman Catholic Cemeteries,' *Ontario History*, 68 (1976), 1–16.

16 In the gravestone inscriptions that appear on the following pages, punctuation

has been inserted and upper and lower cases standardized for ease of understanding.

17 See, for example, Basil Cottle, *The Penguin Dictionary of Surnames* (London:
Penguin Books, 1967).

18 Fingal, Elgin County.

19 Donald H. Akenson, *The Irish in Ontario* (Montreal: McGill-Queen's University
Press, 1984), 9.

20 Port Hope, Lindsay and Beaverton Railway, later a component of Canadian National Railways. Douro, Peterborough County.

21 A.W. Currie, *The Grand Trunk Railway of Canada* (Toronto: University of Toronto Press, 1957), 173.

22 Charles Godfrey, *The Cholera Epidemics in Upper Canada, 1832–1866* (Toronto:
Seccombe House, 1968), 50–4.

23 Centennial UEL Church, near Adolphustown, Lennox and Addington County.

24 Ebenezer United Church, Nassagaweya Township, Halton County.

25 Robert Shipley, *To Mark Our Place: A History of Canadian War Memorials* (Toronto: NC Press, 1987), 25–31.

13: Farms

1 John Harland, 'Report on the State of Agriculture in the County of Wellington,
1852,' *Journals and Transactions of the Board of Agriculture of Upper Canada,* 1
(1856), 218.

2 'Farm Buildings,' *Genesee Farmer,* 9 (12 Jan. 1839), 12, cited in Sally McMurry,
'Progressive Farm Families and Their Houses, 1830–1855: A Study in Independent Design,' *Agricultural History,* 58 (1984), 337.

3 'Laying out Farms,' *Illustrated Annual Register of Rural Affairs,* 1 (1858), 105–8,
233–8.

4 Thomas F. McIlwraith, 'The Ontario Country Road as a Cultural Resource,'
Canadian Geographer, 39 (1995), 330.

5 For example, interview with occupant of west half, Lot 13, Concession 5, Toronto Township, Aug. 1971.

6 Ronald Blythe, *Akenfield: Portrait of an English Village* (Harmondsworth: Penguin Books, 1969), 20.

7 *BT Barn Book* (Fergus, Ont.: Beatty Brothers, 1918), 11.

8 John Harland, 'Report on the State of Agriculture in the County of Wellington,
1852,' *Journals and Transactions of the Board of Agriculture of Upper Canada,* 1
(1856), 218. *New England Farmer,* 7 (19 Sept. 1828), 69, cited in McMurry,
'Progressive Farm Families,' 336.

9 Frank Waugh, *Rural Improvement* (New York: Orange Judd, 1914), 143. The figures: centrality within the farm 30 per cent, convenience to the countryside 20
per cent, water-supply 15 per cent, outlook 15 per cent, drainage 10 per cent,
and wind shelter 10 per cent.

10 Michael Troughton, `Farmsteads as Heritage Features in the Ontario Rural Landscape,´ in Julia Beck and Alec Keefer, eds., *Vernacular Architecture in Ontario* (Toronto: Architectural Conservancy of Ontario, 1993), 21–6.

11 William Dunlop, *Statistical Sketches of Upper Canada for the Use of Emigrants*, first pub. 1832, edited reprint (Toronto: McClelland and Stewart, 1967), 130–1.

12 W.F. Munro, *The Backwoods Life: An Interesting Story of Pioneer Days in Melancthon Township* (Shelburne, Ont.: Free Press, 1910), 37.

13 Amos Rapoport, *House Form and Culture* (Englewood Cliffs, NJ: Prentice-Hall, 1969), 67.

14 Roger L. Welsch, `Front Door, Back Door,´ *Natural History*, 88 no. 6 (June–July 1979), 81. The subject of prospect and refuge is thoroughly explored by Jay Appleton, `Prospect and Refuge in the Landscape of Britain and Australia,´ in I. Douglas, ed., *Geographical Essays in Honour of Gilbert J. Butland* (Armidale, Australia: University of New England Press, 1975), 1–20.

15 On tenantry, see William Marr, `Tenant vs Owner Occupied Farms in York County, Ontario, 1871,´ *Canadian Papers in Rural History* 4 (1984), 50–71.

16 *Report [on] Standards for Inexpensive Houses* (Toronto: Ontario Housing Committee, 1919), 62–6.

17 C.P. Dwyer, *The Immigrant Builder* (Philadelphia: Claxton, Remsen and Haffelfinger, 1872), ix.

18 *The Plough, the Loom and the Anvil*, 2 (Nov. 1849), 300–2.

19 J. Hammond, *The Farmer´s and Mechanic´s Practical Architect and Guide in Rural Economy* (Boston: J.P. Jewett, 1858), 150.

20 Interview, Chester Teeple, Paisley, Sept. 1973. John C. Woolley, *Farm Buildings* (New York: McGraw-Hill, 1946), 40–1.

21 R. Riley, `Square to the Road, Hogs to the East,´ *Places*, 2 (1985), 72.

22 E.F. Johnston, `Windbreaks on the Farm,´ *Your Forests*, 14 no. 1 (spring 1981), 5.

23 `R.A.´ of Bowmanville, reporting in Toronto *Globe*, 20 Sept. 1879. Fourteen barns burned in one electrical storm.

24 `Itinerant Rod Erectors,´ *Rural Affairs*, 2 (1860), 112–4.

25 See, for example, strolling on the lawn of Richard Kidd, Carp, and croquet on the lawn of G. Learmonth of Fitzroy Harbour; *Illustrated Historical Atlas of the County of Carleton* (Toronto: H. Belden and Company, 1879), 42.

26 Humphrey Repton, *Sketches and Hints on Landscape Gardening*, first pub. 1794, partial reprint, *APT Bulletin*, 8 1976), 80. See also Thomas J. Schlereth, `Vegetation as Historical Data: A Historian´s Use of Plants and Natural Material Culture Evidence,´ in Thomas J. Schlereth, ed., *Artifacts and the American Past* (Nashville, Tenn.: American Association for State and Local History, 1980), 147–59.

27 Ralph Krueger, `The Geography of the Orchard Industry in Canada,´ *Geographical Bulletin*, 7 (1965), 46. From 1931 and 1961, farms with more than twenty-five trees fell from 53,000 to 8,000.

28 Willet G. Miller, *Limestones of Ontario*, Ontario Sessional Papers, Vol. 13, pt. 2 (Toronto: Ontario Bureau of Mines, 1904), 14.

29 Revised Statutes of Ontario 1990, Aggregate Resources Act, Ch. A8, pt. 2, on rehabilitation.

30 Alice Munro, `Walker Brothers Cowboy,´ in *Dance of the Happy Shades* (Toronto: Ryerson Press, 1968), 7.

31 Ontario, 14–15 Elizabeth II, cap. 161 (1966).

14: Roadsides

1 Wellington County Journals and Proceedings, Bylaw no. 177, 4 Oct. 1870. Province of Canada, 29 Victoria, cap. 40 (1866), `An Act to Prevent the Spreading of Canada Thistles.´ See also George H. Clark, *Farm Weeds of Canada*, 2nd ed. (Ottawa: Canada Department of Agriculture, 1909).

2 *Roadsides for Wildlife* (St Paul: Minnesota Department of Natural Resources and Minnesota Department of Highways, 1976).

3 Ontario, 36 Victoria, cap. 38 (1873), `Ontario Drainage Act´; and Ontario, 36 Victoria, cap. 39 (1873), `Ontario Municipal Drainage Aid Act.´ The Ontario Agricultural Museum, Milton, has a fine display of the principles and artefacts of underdrainage.

4 Provincial aid to drainage, Revised Statutes of Ontario, 1914, caps. 42–4, vol. 1, 579–92.

5 For text and maps showing the extent of poor drainage in western Ontario, see Elizabeth A. Snell, *Wetland Distribution and Conversion in Southern Ontario*, Working Paper 48 (Ottawa: Environment Canada, Inland Waters and Lands Directorate, Dec. 1987), Figs. 3 and 4.

6 Burton W. Potter, *The Road and the Roadside* (Boston: Little, Brown and Company, 1886), Chap. 8; John A. Ramsden, `Reforestry,´ *Minutes of the Municipal Good Roads Convention* (Toronto: W.S. Johnston and Co., 1900), 14. Quotation is taken from preamble to Ontario, 46 Victoria, cap. 26 (1883).

7 *Canada Farmers´ Sun*, 7 Feb. 1893.

8 A.W. Campbell, *Report of the Provincial Instructor in Roadmaking for 1896*, Ontario Sessional Papers, 60 Victoria, no. 24, (Toronto, 1897), 38.

9 W.F. Munro, *The Backwoods of Ontario* (London, 1881), 48; Campbell, *Roadmaking*, 38.

10 Wellington County Journal and Proceedings, 81st sess., 5 June 1877, 88th sess., 17 June 1879, and 90th sess., 29 Jan. 29, 1880.

11 Ontario, 44 Victoria, cap. 26 (1881), `An Act Respecting Snow Fences.´

12 Ontario, 44 Victoria, cap. 26 (1881), sec. 1; and its amendment, Ontario, 49 Victoria, cap. 40 (1886).

13 Ontario, 49 Victoria, cap 40 (1886), sec. 2. Confirmed in Revised Statutes of Ontario, 1897, cap. 240, and revised in 2 George V, cap. 52 (1912), `Snow Fences Act.´ Law still in effect, up to Revised Statutes of Ontario, 1960, cap.

376. Campbell, *Roadmaking*, 38. Ontario Bureau of Industries, *Report for 1897*, Ontario Sessional Papers, Report 32, part 1, 61 Victoria, 1898 (Toronto, 1899), 30. The rate in North Gower Township was 10 cents per rod (about five metres), Carleton County, 1890.

14 Ramsden, 'Reforestry,' 14.

15 Ontario, 34 Victoria, cap. 31 (1871–2); Ontario, 46 Victoria, cap. 26 (1883), 'An Act to Encourage the Planting and Growing of Trees,' sec. 3 and 4; sustained through 3–4 George V, cap. 53 (1913), to Revised Statutes of Ontario, 1937, cap. 292.

16 The number of motor cars in Ontario rose from 100,000 in 1918 to 500,000 in 1930. Ontario Department of Highways, *Annual Report for 1941–42* (Toronto 1943).

17 Interview, Gordon Cochrane, Ivy, Simcoe County, Dec. 1988.

18 Specimen exhibited at Ontario Agricultural Museum, Milton.

19 E.F. Johnston, 'Windbreaks on the Farm,' *Your Forests*, 14 no. 1 (spring 1981), 5.

20 *Trees and Roads: A Report on the Opportunities for Preserving Roadside Trees* (Toronto: Conservation Council of Ontario, 1970).

21 'Touchons du bois,' *Actualité* (Oct. 1986), 172.

22 W.F. Munro, *The Backwoods Life: An Interesting Story of Pioneer Days in Melancthon Township* (Shelburne, Ont.: Free Press, 1910), 48.

23 In 1849, 1,131 schools were on leased land, and 1,842 on owned land; J. George Hodgins, ed., *Historical and Other Papers and Documents Illustrative of the Educational System of Ontario, 1792–1872*, Vol. 5 (Toronto: Ontario Department of Education, 1911–12), 86.

24 J. George Hodgins, *The School House: Its Architecture, External and Internal Arrangements* (Toronto: Province of Canada Department of Public Instruction, 1857), 35, 38.

25 Province of Canada, 19–20 Victoria, cap. 61 (1856), 'An Act to Authorize . . . Chatham . . . to dispose of the land now set apart for a cemetery.'

26 Ontario, 37 Victoria, cap. 28, sec. 46 (1874). 'An Act to Amend and Consolidate the Public School Law.'

27 Interview, Ralph Krueger, Collingwood Township, 1991.

28 Robert E. Summerby-Murray, 'The Centralization of Power: An Historical Geography of Roads, Railways and Manufacturing in Wellington County, Ontario, 1849–1930,' PhD thesis, University of Toronto, 1992, 195–7.

29 Charles S. Buck, 'Clay Mixed by Open Hooves Provided London's Bricks,' *London Free Press*, 4 Dec. 1948.

30 Charles S. Buck, 'The Origin and Character of the Early Architecture and Practical Arts of Ontario to 1850,' MA thesis, University of Western Ontario, 1930, 958. See also Willet G. Miller, *Limestones of Ontario'*. Ontario Sessional Papers, Vol. 13, pt. 2 (Toronto: Ontario Bureau of Mines, 1904), 28.

31 See, for example, engraving of the Quance sawmill, Binbrook Township, Went-

worth County, c. 1880; *Illustrated Historical Atlas of the County of Wentworth* (Toronto: Page and Smith, 1875), 14.

32 Hodgins, *Educational System*, Vol. 1, 29.

33 Carol Priamo, *The General Store* (Toronto: McGraw-Hill Ryerson, 1978); Margaret McBurney and Mary Byers, *Tavern in the Town: Early Inns and Taverns of Ontario* (Toronto: University of Toronto Press, 1987).

34 *Illustrated Historical Atlas of the County of Lambton* (Toronto: H. Belden and Company, 1880), 12.

35 John Kenneth Galbraith, *The Scotch* (Boston: Houghton-Mifflin, 1964), 107.

15: Transport systems

1 Interview, Oliver Seiler, Paisley, Sept. 1972.

2 'Report on Highway Improvements,' Ontario Sessional Papers, 1912, no. 14, 15, with pictures of a road camp in Lanark County.

3 Thomas F. McIlwraith, 'The Ontario Country Road as a Cultural Resource,' *Canadian Geographer*, 39 (1995), 330.

4 John C. Van Nostrand, 'The Queen Elizabeth Way: Public Utility vs Public Space,' *Urban History Review*, 12 no. 2 (1983), 1–24.

5 Michelle Greenwald, Alan Levitt, and Elaine Peebles, *The Welland Canals: Historic Resource Analysis and Preservation Alternatives* (Toronto: Ontario Ministry of Culture and Recreation, 1979).

6 Christopher A. Andreae, *Archaeological Excavation of Lock 24, First Welland Canal* (London, Ont.: Historica Research Ltd., 1988). After study, the site was reinterred and marked with a small recreational park and a plaque.

7 For pictures and description of many Grand Trunk structures, see Ralph Greenhill, 'Early Grand Trunk Railway Bridges and Stations,' in Dianne Newell and Ralph Greenhill, eds., *Survivals: Aspects of Industrial Archaeology in Ontario* (Erin, Ont.: Boston Mills Press, 1989), 46–68.

8 Frederick W. Cumberland, 'Some Notes of a Visit to the Works of the Grand Trunk Railway, West of Toronto, February, 1855,' *Canadian Journal*, 3 (May 1855), 225.

9 *Census of Canada, 1870–71*, Vol. 3 (Ottawa: Taylor, 1876), Tables 31, 35, 36.

10 Thomas F. McIlwraith, 'The Adequacy of Rural Roads in the Era before Railways: an Illustration from Upper Canada,' *Canadian Geographer*, 14 (1970), 355–6.

11 'The road network of the Ottoman Empire, object of much admiration in Europe, consisted of narrow paved tracks, one metre wide, for horsemen, on either side of which flocks and pedestrians had beaten out footpaths ten times the width.' Fernand Braudel, *The Mediterranean and the Mediterranean World in the Age of Philip II*, first pub. 1949, trans. Sian Reynolds, 1972 (New York: Harper and Row, 1972), 284. Gunter's chain was invented in 1620 by Edmund Gunter (1581–1626), an English mathematician.

12 A.W. Campbell, *Report of the Provincial Instructor in Roadmaking for 1896*, Ontario Sessional Papers, 60 Victoria, no. 24 (Toronto, 1897), 25. The roadbed was to be twenty-four feet (about seven metres) wide. The Guelph and Arthur Road Company was designed with a roadbed fifteen feet (about five metres) wide; minutes, 10 Feb. 1848, MG 24 E11, National Archives of Canada. Cited in Robert E. Summerby-Murray, 'The Centralization of Power: An Historical Geography of Roads, Railways and Manufacturing in Wellington County, Ontario, 1849–1930,' PhD thesis, University of Toronto, 1992, 149. A contract on the Brantford, Norfolk and Port Burwell Railway in 1878 allowed twenty-four feet (about seven metres) for a farm crossing; RG 30, box 12584, file no. 2, National Archives of Canada. A few townships laid out before 1800 had allowances of forty feet (about thirteen metres); William G. Dean and Geoffrey J. Matthews, *Economic Atlas of Ontario* (Toronto: University of Toronto Press, 1969), Plate 99.

13 John J. Mannion, *Irish Settlements in Eastern Canada: A Study of Cultural Transfer and Adaptation* (Toronto: University of Toronto Press, 1974), 78.

14 Horses need smooth, dry roads if they are to work more efficiently than oxen; *Ontario Farmer*, 1 (1869), 17.

15 Summerby-Murray, 'Roads, Railways and Manufacturing,' 184. Ontario, 1 Edward VII, cap. 32 (1901), 'An Act for the Improvement of Public Highways.' See also Ontario, 55 Victoria, cap. 42 (1892), 'An Act to Consolidate the Acts Respecting Municipal Institutions,' with its provision for assisting the construction of bridges over one hundred feet (about thirty-two metres) in length.

16 Ontario, 5 George V, cap. 16 (1915), 'Highway Improvement Act,' and cap. 17 (1915), 'Ontario Highways Act.'

17 *Seventh Census of Canada*, 1931, Vol. 8 (Ottawa: Patenaude, 1936), xxvii. One-quarter of the rest of the roads were earth, three-quarters gravel.

18 *London Free Press*, 11 June 1949, 9th sec., 8.

19 *Statements, Reports and Accounts of the Grand Trunk Railway of Canada* (Toronto, 1857), 12. The substantialness of the 'British system' was praised by Cumberland, 'Some Notes.'

20 T.C. Clarke, CE, 'Report on the Action of Ice upon the Bridge at Rice Lake,' *Canadian Journal*, 3 (1854–5), 249; A.W. Currie, *The Grand Trunk Railway of Canada* (Toronto: University of Toronto Press, 1957), 284–6.

21 Winston M. Cosgrove, *Wolfe Island Past and Present* (Kingston: privately printed, 1973), 21.

22 The Toronto Suburban Railway (from Toronto Junction to Guelph) ran from 1917 to 1931 only. John F. Due, *The Intercity Electric Railway Industry in Canada* (Toronto: University of Toronto Press, 1966), 85–7. There is a picture of Kelly's bridge over the unbuilt Newmarket canal in David J. Cuming, *Discovering Heritage Bridges on Ontario's Roads* (Erin, Ont.: Boston Mills Press, 1983), 84.

23 Mark Fram, 'The Customary Shores: Tracing and Conserving the Material Past

in Its Historic Contexts on the Rideau, Quinte, Trent, Simcoe, and Severn Waterways,´ in Mark Fram and John Weiler, eds., *Continuity with Change: Planning for the Conservation of Ontario´s Man-made Heritage* (Toronto: Ontario Ministry of Culture and Recreation, 1981), 33–103. See also W. George Richardson,
Bridges over the Trent-Severn Waterway 1826–1978, Parks Canada, ms. no.
328, 1978.

24 McIlwraith, ´Ontario Country Road,´ 324.

25 Ontario and Quebec Railway papers, 1884, RG 46, Vol. 686, no. 2271, National Archives of Canada.

26 Dianne Newell, ´The Rideau Canal,´ in Dianne Newell and Ralph Greenhill,
eds. *Survivals: Aspects of Industrial Archaeology in Ontario* (Erin, Ont.: Boston
Mills Press, 1989), 40–3. See also Robert Passfield, Historic Bridges on the Rideau Waterway System, Parks Canada, ms. no. 212, 1976.

27 William Kilbourn, *The Elements Combined: A History of the Steel Company of
Canada* (Toronto: Clarke, Irwin and Company, 1960), 45–50.

28 ´Proceedings of the 4th Annual Convention of Eastern Ontario Good Roads
Association,´ 28–29 June 1905 (Brockville: n.p., 1906), 28.

29 Canada´s first reinforced-concrete truss bridge was built on Etobicoke Creek
near Long Branch in 1909 and is still used by pedestrians. It is a rare type.
Phyllis Rose, ´Bridges,´ in Norman Ball, ed., *Building Canada* (Toronto: University of Toronto Press, 1988), 20–1.

30 Ibid., 20.

31 Ibid., 11.

32 Robert M. Stamp, *Riding the Radials: Toronto´s Suburban Electric Streetcar Lines*
(Erin, Ont.: Boston Mills Press, 1989), 72–7.

33 Province of Canada, Legislative Assembly, Appendix no. 13, 1856; Greenhill,
´Grand Trunk Bridges and Stations.´

16: Townscapes

1 Alice Munro, ´The Flat Roads,´ in *Lives of Girls and Women* (Toronto: McGraw-
Hill Ryerson, 1971), 5.

2 *Brantford Courier*, 7 June 1862; Barrie *Northern Advance*, 25 May 1871.

3 On 14 January 1881, six stores burned; 12 August 1883, a ´big fire;´ 19 March
1889, three frame stores burned; 7 July 1889, three frame stores burned; 25
Jan. 1892, three stores and one hotel burned; March 1907, Trout Block
burned; and 5 Oct. 1907, town hall burned. Other fires consumed a frame
woollen mill (1903), a factory (1907), and an elevator (1913). Floods damaged
buildings in 1884 and 1912. T.A. Davidson, *A New History of the County of
Grey* (Owen Sound: Grey County Historical Society, 1972), passim. A map of
the extent of major fires in 1864, 1865, 1872, 1887, and 1902 in Rogues Hollow appears in Tom Cruickshank and Peter Stokes, *Rogues´ Hollow: The Story*

of the Village of Newburgh, Ontario, through Its Buildings (Toronto: Architectural Conservancy of Ontario, 1983), 28.

4 John Weaver and Peter de Lottinville, 'The Conflagration and the City: Disaster and Progress in British North America during the Nineteenth Century,' *Histoire sociale / Social History*, 13 (1980), 421.

5 S.J. Brown, 'Irish Immigrants to Mono Built Town's Jackson Block,' Orangeville *Banner*, 3 Aug. 1974.

6 Barrie *Northern Advance*, 25 May 1871.

7 Town of Belleville, Bylaw no. 17, in effect in 1869, as reported in *Directory of County of Hastings* (Belleville: Intelligencer Office, 1869).

8 Willet G. Miller, *Limestones of Ontario*, Ontario Sessional Papers, Vol. 13, pt. 2 (Toronto: Ontario Bureau of Mines, 1904), 16.

9 Albert E. Berry, 'Developments in Canadian Water Works Practice, 1850–1940,' *Water and Sewage* (Dec. 1940), 10.

10 *Illustrated Historical Atlas of the County of Halton* (Toronto: Walker and Miles, 1877), 59.

11 *Peterborough Examiner*, 15 Jan. 1880, cited in Martha Ann Kidd and Louis Taylor, *Historical Sketches of Peterborough* (Peterborough: Broadview Press, 1988), 76.

12 William Westfall and Malcolm Thurlby, 'Church Architecture and Urban Space: The Development of Ecclesiastical Forms in Nineteenth Century Ontario,' in David Keane and Colin Read, ed., *Old Ontario: Essays in Honour of J.M.S. Careless* (Toronto: Dundurn Press, 1990), 139. Dundas Street United Church, Woodstock, is a good example.

13 J.B. Jackson, 'Landscape as Theatre,' *Landscape*, 23 no. 1 (1979), 3–7; reprinted in J.B. Jackson, ed., *The Necessity for Ruins* (Amherst: University of Massachusetts Press, 1980), 67–75.

14 Christina Cameron and Janet Wright, *Second Empire Style in Canadian Architecture*, Canadian Historic Sites, Occasional Papers in Archaeology and History, No. 24 (Ottawa: Parks Canada, 1980), 17.

15 Richard Cartwright, writing to Isaac Todd, c. 1800, cited in John I. Rempel, *Building with Wood, and Other Aspects of Nineteenth-Century Building in Central Canada*, first pub. 1968, 2nd ed. (Toronto: University of Toronto Press, 1980), 12.

16 Richard B. Splane, *Social Welfare in Ontario, 1791–1893* (Toronto: University of Toronto Press, 1965), 157.

17 For a chronology of Ontario legislation dating from Upper Canada, 11 George IV, cap. 20 (1830), and construction of asylums, with pictures, see T.J.W. Burgess, 'A Historical Sketch of Our Canadian Institutions for the Insane,' *Transactions of the Royal Society of Canada*, sec. 4 (1898), 14–47.

18 John Kenneth Galbraith, *The Scotch* (Boston: Houghton-Mifflin, 1964).

19 Thomas F. McIlwraith, 'Digging Out and Filling In: Making Land on the Toronto Waterfront in the 1850s,' *Urban History Review*, 20, no. 1 (1991), 16–22.

20 Alfred Brunel to Sandford Fleming, Toronto, 17 April 1863, in Sandford Fleming, *Memorial of the People of Red River to the British and Canadian Governments* ... [regarding] ... *a Great Terrestrial Road from Canada to British Columbia* (Quebec: Hunter, Rose and Co, 1863), 36.

21 Deryck W. Holdsworth, ed., *Reviving Main Street* (Toronto: University of Toronto Press, 1985).

22 Fred A. Dahms, `The Process of Urbanization in the Countryside: A Study of Huron and Bruce Counties, 1891–1981,´ *Urban History Review*, 12 no. 3 (1984), 1–18.

23 Reproduced in Paul Duval, *A.J. Casson, His Life and Works: A Tribute* (Toronto: Cerebrus / Prentice-Hall, 1980), unpaginated.

17: Boundaries

1 J. Russell Whitaker, `Peninsular Ontario: A Primary Regional Division of Canada,´ *Scottish Geographical Magazine*, 54 (1938), 263–84. Leeds and Lanark counties form the eastern limit for his maps.

2 Arthur R.M. Lower, `Ontario – Does It Exist?´ *Ontario History*, 60 (1968), 65–9. See also William Goulding, `Upper Canada, Where Are You?´ *Ontario History*, 63 (1971), 155–9, and William H. Magee, `A Pallid Picture: The Image of Ontario in Modern Literature,´ *Ontario History*, 58 (1966), 225–33.

3 Robert M. Styran and Robert R. Taylor, *The Welland Canals: The Growth of Mr Merritt´s Ditch* (Erin, Ont.: Boston Mills Press, 1988); Vrenia Ivanoffski and Sandra Campbell, eds., *Exploring Our Heritage: The Ottawa Valley Experience* (Arnprior: Arnprior and District Historical Society, 1980).

4 Mary Byers and Margaret McBurney, *The Governor´s Road: Early Buildings and Owners from Mississauga to London* (Toronto: University of Toronto Press, 1982); Mark Fram, `The Customary Shores: Tracing and Conserving the Material Past in Its Historic Contexts on the Rideau, Quinte, Trent, Simcoe, and Severn Waterways,´ in Mark Fram and John Weiler, eds., *Continuity with Change: Planning for the Conservation of Ontario´s Man-made Heritage* (Toronto: Ontario Ministry of Culture and Recreation, 1981), 33–103.

5 J. Gordon Nelson and Pauline C. O´Neill, eds., *The Grand River as a Heritage River*, Occasional Paper No. 9 (Waterloo, Ont.: University of Waterloo Heritage Resources Centre, 1989). The Grand has been nominated as a heritage river under the terms of the Canadian Heritage Rivers Program.

6 Thomas F. McIlwraith, `Ontario´s Beautiful Credit River Valley,´ *Canadian Geographical Journal*, 92 no. 3 (1977), 10–19.

7 William G. Hoskins, *The Making of the English Landscape*, first pub. 1955, 2nd ed. (Harmondsworth: Penguin Books, 1970), 298.

8 John R. Stilgoe, *Common Landscapes of America, 1580 to 1845* (New Haven, Conn.: Yale University Press, 1982), 29.

9 Howard Levine, `Re-birth of the Red and White,´ in Julia Beck and Alec Kee-

fer, eds., *Vernacular Architecture in Ontario* (Toronto: Architectural Conservancy of Ontario, 1993), 89–93.

10 Matt Cohen, *The Disinherited* (Toronto: McClelland and Stewart, 1974), 166.

11 Dan Needles, *Letters from Wingfield Farm* (Toronto: Key-Porter Books, 1989).

12 *Fifth Census of Canada, 1911*, Vol. 4 (Ottawa: Taché, 1914), x; *Census of Canada, 1991*, Cat. No. 93–348 (Ottawa: Statistics Canada, 1992), 4.

13 Mary K. Cullen, 'Highlights of Domestic Building in Pre-Confederation Quebec and Ontario as Seen through Travel Literature from 1763 to 1860,' *APT Bulletin*, 13 no. 1 (1981), 28, citing Basil Hall and William Dunlop.

14 Peter Ennals, 'Nineteenth Century Barns in Southern Ontario,' *Canadian Geographer*, 16 (1972), 256–70.

15 Sam Sheldon, 'Ontario Flue-Cured Tobacco Industry: The Southern United States Legacy,' *American Review of Canadian Studies*, 18 no. 2 (1988), 196.

16 David McClung, 'Mennonite Two-Door Houses of Rainham and South Cayuga Townships, Haldimand County,' in Julia Beck and Alec Keefer, ed., *Vernacular Architecture in Ontario* (Toronto: Architectural Conservancy of Ontario, 1993), 49–54.

17 Sheila Staats, 'The Six Nations Council House: Historic Building at Ohsweken,' *Ontario History*, 85 (1993), 215, 218.

18 Interview, Tom Hill, Brantford, Sept. 1993.

19 Peter Ennals and Deryck Holdsworth, 'Vernacular Architecture and the Cultural Landscape of the Maritime Provinces: A Reconnaissance,' *Acadiensis*, 10 (1981), 87.

20 Karl Marx and Friedrich Engels, *Letters to Americans, 1848–1895: A Selection* (New York: International, 1953), 204.

21 Patrick McGreevy, 'The End of America, the Beginning of Canada,' *Canadian Geographer*, 32 (1988), 307–18; Peirce F. Lewis, 'Common Houses: Cultural Spoor,' *Landscape*, 19 no. 2 (1975), 17; Percy E. Nobbs, 'Canadian Architecture,' *Canada and Its Provinces*, 12 (1914), 671.

22 Elizabeth G. Hitchcock, *Jonathan Goldsmith: Pioneer Master Builder in the Western Reserve* (Cleveland, O.: Western Reserve Historical Society, 1980).

23 Allen G. Noble, 'Evolution and Classification of Nineteenth Century Housing in Ohio,' *Journal of Geography*, 74 (1975), 285–302; Allen G. Noble, *Wood, Brick and Stone: The North American Settlement Landscape* (Amherst: University of Massachusetts Press, 1984), 52–3; Fred B. Kniffen, 'Folk Housing, Key to Diffusion,' *Annals, Association of American Geographers*, 55 (1965), 553–5.

24 Marion MacRae and Anthony Adamson, *Hallowed Walls: Church Architecture of Upper Canada* (Toronto: Clarke Irwin, 1975), 70.

25 Donald G. Cartwright, 'Institutions on the Frontier: French-Canadian Settlement in Eastern Ontario in the Nineteenth Century,' *Canadian Geographer*, 21 (1977), 1–21.

26 Sibylle Moholy-Nagy, *Native Genius in Anonymous Architecture in North America* (New York: Schocken Books, 1957), 171.

27 John Clarke and Karl Skof, `Social Dimensions of an Ontario County, 1851–1852,´ in David Knight, ed., *Our Geographic Mosaic* (Ottawa: Carleton University Press, 1985), 112.

28 R. John Corby, `The Alligator Steam Warping Tug: A Canadian Contribution to the Development of Technology in the Forest Industry,´ *Industrial Archaeology*, 3 (1977), 15–42.

29 Ron Brown, *Ghost Towns of Canada* (Toronto: Cannonbooks, 1987), 28–57.

30 Glenn Wright, `Railway School Cars and Education,´ *Archivist*, 12 no. 3 (May–June 1985), 3–4. The railway school car in which the Slomon family taught between the 1930s and 1950s has been preserved as a small museum in their home town of Clinton.

31 Brenda Lee-Whiting, *Harvest of Stones: The German Settlement in Renfrew County* (Toronto: University of Toronto Press, 1985); Marilyn G. Miller, *Straight Lines in Curved Space: Colonization Roads in Eastern Ontario* (Toronto: Ontario Ministry of Culture and Recreation, 1978).

32 See Maggie Siggins, *Revenge of the Land* (Toronto: McClelland and Stewart, 1991), for case histories of Ontarians drawn to the prairies in this period.

33 Brown, *Ghost Towns*, 29–37.

34 John Scott, `Pontiac County Talks Secession from Quebec,´ *Globe and Mail*, 19 May 1971. The subject has been raised repeatedly in the 1990s.

35 Pauline Frost, `Cultural Landscapes of the Rouge River Valley, Quebec,´ *Cahiers de géographie de Québec*, 28 (1969), 88.

18: Decay and renewal

1 CPR bought rails, bridge girders, and locomotives in both Britain and Saxony from 1880 until 1903 or later. Voucher collection, CPR Corporate Archives, Montreal.

2 Augustus Welby Pugin, *An Apology for the Revival of Christian Architecture in England*, first pub. 1843, reprint (Oxford: St Barnabas Press, 1969), 5.

3 `Preservation of Heritage Takes Work, Meeting Told,´ *Mississauga News*, 5 June 1988.

4 Charles S. Buck, `On Millstones,´ *London Free Press*, 5 April 1952.

5 Richard Anderson, `Garbage Disposal in the Greater Toronto Area: A Preliminary Historical Geography,´ *Operational Geographer*, 11 no. 1 (March, 1993), 7–13.

6 Sydney Mines area of Cape Breton Island, during 1980s. Hugh Millward, `Mining and Landscape Modification on the Sydney Coalfield,´ in Douglas Day, ed., *Geographical Perspectives on the Maritime Provinces* (Halifax: St Mary´s University, 1988), 90.

7 For illustrations of the Rideau Canal see the Burrowes collection of water-colour paintings in the Archives of Ontario. On the Welland Canal, see John N.

Jackson, *The Four Welland Canals* (St Catharines: Vanwell Publishing Limited, 1988).

8   William Kingsford, *The Canadian Canals: Their History and Cost* (Toronto: Rollo and Adam, 1865), 35. On the contribution of Burrowes to our understanding of the cultural landscape, see Brian S. Osborne, `The Artist as Historical Commentator: Thomas Burrowes and the Rideau Canal,´ *Archivaria* 17 (1983–4), 41–59.

9   Jeffrey L. Brown, `Earthworks and Industrial Archaeology,´ *Industrial Archaeology*, 6 (1980), 1–8.

10 William A. Parks, *Report on the Building and Ornamental Stones of Canada, 1912–1917*, Vol. 1 (Ottawa: Canada Bureau of Mines, 1912), 216; M.B. Baker, *The Clays and Bricks of Ontario*, Ontario Sessional Papers, Vol. 15, pt. 2 (Toronto: Ontario Bureau of Mines, 1906), 12.

11 Parks, *Building and Ornamental Stones*, 242.

12 For a fine series of photographs illustrating this process, see Michael Barnes, *Link with a Lonely Land: The Temiskaming and Northern Ontario Railway* (Erin, Ont.: Boston Mills Press, 1985), 75.

13 Charles S. Buck, `The Origin and Character of the Early Architecture and Practical Arts of Ontario to 1850,´ MA thesis, University of Western Ontario, 1930, 932. These are called `French drains.´ There is a comprehensive exhibit of drainage technology at the Ontario Agricultural Museum, Milton.

14 Aggregate Resources Act, Revised Statutes of Ontario, 1980, cap. A.8, especially sec. 47–56.

15 Petition, 3 April 1856. *Journal of the Legislative Assembly*, Province of Canada, 5th Parliament, 2nd Session, 1856, 234–5.

16 Interview, Lorne Joyce, Port Credit, Oct. 1973.

17 Interview, Jerry Shain, Oakville, May 1986.

18 Interview, Tim Orpwood, Trow Engineering, Toronto, Oct. 1989.

19 The Canadian Pacific line betwen Guelph and Goderich is such a case; see Brad Cundiff, `Rails to Trails,´ *Seasons*, 31 no. 3 (1991), 24–7, 39.

20 Jacques Dalibard, `Getting on the Right Track: A Two-pronged Solution for Redundant Stations,´ *Canadian Heritage*, 10 (Feb.–March 1984), 2–4; Marc Denhez, `Railway Blues: Stations are Coming Down in a Legal Vacuum,´ *Canadian Heritage*, no. 41 (Aug.–Sept. 1983), 15, 24. The geography of decline in secondary railway lines is shown in Gerald T. Bloomfield, `The Railway Life Cycle in Southwestern Ontario: The Contraction Phase, 1923–1990,´ *Operational Geographer*, 9 no. 2 (1991), 3–9.

21 Cundiff, `Rails to Trails.´

22 *The Spencer Clark Collection of Historic Architecture* (Scarborough, Ont.: Guild Inn, 1982).

23 Matt Cohen, *The Sweet Second Summer of Kitty Malone* (Toronto: McClelland and Stewart, 1979), 42.

24 Peter Arnell and Ted Bickford, eds., *Mississauga City Hall: A Canadian Competition* (New York: Rizzoli International Publications, 1984).

25 The Ontario Heritage Act, Revised Statutes of Ontario, 1990, cap. O.18. Conservation occurs under archaeological, architectural, and historical criteria, for both individual structures and districts.

26 J.B. Jackson, 'By Way of Conclusion: How to Study the Landscape,' in J.B. Jackson, ed., *The Necessity for Ruins* (Amherst: University of Massachusetts Press, 1980), 113–14, 120. On the land ethic, see Aldo Leopold, *A Sand County Almanac* (San Francisco: Sierra Club, 1949).

27 Paul Berton, 'Developer Agrees to Save Free Reformed Church,' *London Free Press*, 31 March 1989.

28 Bill Thomson, 'Meadowvale Village: The Interrelationships between Heritage Conservation and City Planning,' *Plan Canada*, 25 (1985), 10–20. Support for this integrative approach comes most recently from the report of the commission headed by John Sewell, *New Planning for Ontario* (Toronto: Ontario Royal Commission on Planning and Development Reform, 1993).

29 See, particularly, Denhez, 'Stations,' and his frequent essays in *Heritage Canada* magazine in the early 1980s.

30 Ontario, 1 Elizabeth II, cap. 4 (1953).

31 Martha Ann Kidd and Louis Taylor, *Historical Sketches of Peterborough* (Peterborough: Broadview Press, 1988), 38–9.

32 Marion MacRae and Anthony Adamson, *Hallowed Walls: Church Architecture of Upper Canada* (Toronto: Clarke Irwin, 1975), 222–8.

33 John I. Rempel, *Building with Wood, and Other Aspects of Nineteenth-Century Building in Central Canada*, first pub. 1968, 2nd ed. (Toronto: University of Toronto Press, 1980), 71.

34 Robert W. Passfield, 'Swing Bridges on the Rideau Canal,' *Industrial Archeology*, 2 (1976), 61.

35 Anthony Adamson, address to Local Architectural Conservation Advisory Committee (LACAC) conference, Sault Ste Marie, June 1988.

36 Leo Marx, *The Machine in the Garden* (New York: Oxford University Press, 1964).

37 Lorna Crozier, *The Garden Going On without Us* (Toronto: McClelland and Stewart, 1985).

Suggested reading

Landscape

It has been said that sight is a faculty but that seeing is an art that must be cultivated and kept finely honed through persistent field observation. The periodical *Landscape*, of which J.B. Jackson has been the founder (in 1951) and moving spirit, most fully sustains this principle. In *Close-Up* (1973), Clay likewise urges people to open their eyes. Weitzman (1976), Lewis (1983), and the contributors to Meinig's *The Interpretation of Ordinary Landscapes* (1979) are among other helpful sources in a wide literature.

Henry Glassie (1985) explores the borderlands between high art and the vernacular in an outstanding essay that draws attention to the readability of vernacular forms. Glassie has written widely and thoughtfully; for his creative work in seeking the structure and grammar of the built-up land he has been called 'the Noam Chomsky of landscape' (Peirce Lewis, in a guest lecture, University of Toronto, 16 October 1983). In *The Past Is a Foreign Country* (1985), Lowenthal treats us to the subject of the ability to remember through landscape, the root of all heritage conservation activity.

Timothy Dwight's deliberate manner of pausing to look and talk, and Henry David Thoreau's penchant for walking, stirred Stilgoe to undertake his seminal book on ordinary landscapes as 'a self-paced searching after details and wholes' (Dwight, 1821, and Thoreau, 1863, both cited in Stilgoe, 1982, 28). Watts's delightful study (1957) sensitively mixes natural and cultural ecology and is a fine companion for landscape wanderers.

Several generations of architects and architectural historians have helped landscape observers to strike off on their own. Architects' books identifying building styles and their history, illustrated with engravings and photographs, have been basic fare since the days of A.W. Pugin (1843) and John Ruskin (1851). W.G. Hoskins's *The Making of the English Landscape* (1955) set the modern standard for the narration of landscape. The writings of Arthur (c. 1926) and MacRae and Adamson's *The Ancestral Roof* (1963) started the explorations of the Ontario branch of this great human enterprise.

A chapter in Harris and Warkentin, *Canada before Confederation* (1974), introduces pre-Confederation Ontario geographically; my own paper (1987) puts it in a wider,

North American context. Schull (1978) covers the period since Confederation. In Gentilcore and Head (1984) appear important maps of provincial development, and fine thematic essays. Wood (1975) and a theme issue of *American Review of Canadian Studies* (Vol. 14 no. 3, 1984) contain helpful essays. The quarterly *Ontario History* has had a steady increase in the number of papers concerned with the human landscape in recent years; studies on special topics include Gilmour (1972, corporate consolidation), Ladell (1993, land surveying), McCalla and George (1986, economic development), Nelles (1975, resource development), and Spelt (1975, urban systems).

Glacial landforms, and the bedrock, soils, and vegetation associated with them, are dealt with in Chapman and Putnam (1951); the revised edition (1984) adds detail about the Precambrian Shield. Sadler (1987) discusses processes in natural history; Peattie (1950) has written a social history of trees. Gillard and Tooke (1975) provide one of a number of regional studies, in this case of the Niagara Escarpment. A special fiftieth-anniversary reflection on the founding of the Federation of Ontario Naturalists covers various aspects of awareness of the physical and cultural landscapes; *Seasons*, 21 no. 4 (1981).

Blake and Greenhill (1969) and Greenhill, Macpherson, and Richardson (1974) continue to provide, after a quarter-century, the best-illustrated introduction to the ordinary Ontario countryside. Rickard's drawings (1977) cover a broad range of landscape detail with sensitivity and interest. MacRae and Adamson have written perceptive and delightfully readable books on churches (1975) and administrative buildings (1985). Eric Arthur and Dudley Witney, *The Barn* (1972), is a standard work that reaches well beyond Ontario to make comparisons with barns in the adjacent American states and Quebec.

A century ago landscape enthusiasts would have relied almost entirely on the series of illustrated historical atlases of individual counties – folio volumes filled with large engravings of houses and other buildings, as well as farm scenes and streetscapes. Detailed township maps show all farm lots and are useful for identifying the road systems and layouts of villages. These volumes were published in the 1870s and 1880s and cover practically all counties. See Edward Phelps, 'The County Atlases of Ontario,' in Barbara Farrell and Aileen Desbarats, eds., *Explorations in the History of Canadian Mapping* (Ottawa: Association of Canadian Map Libraries and Archives, 1988), 163–77.

Leung (1981) has provided the standard piece on milling in Ontario. Duval (1980) has given us access to the rural Ontario of Alfred J. Casson, more generally known for his northern landscapes. Casson painted from the 1920s to the 1980s. Leitch's celebration of Simcoe County (1967) is a fine example of the many Ontario regional books, while Fram and Weiler (1981) cleverly relate artefacts to broad landscape themes. Buck's (1930) rural-landscape fieldwork in Elgin County during the 1920s was a half-century ahead of its time and is a rich source of questioning and insight.

Ontario's land-oriented literature is an entertaining way to become acquainted with the varied landscape. Robertson Davies and Alice Munro freely give of their Ontario small-town roots as settings for their novels and short stories. One effortlessly arrives centre-stage in Renfrew County through *What's Bred in the Bone* (Davies, 1985), or in Huron County by way of `Walker Brothers Cowboy' (Munro, 1968). Sherwood Fox's *The Bruce Beckons* (1952), focused northwest of London, and Kenneth M. Wells's *By Jumping Cat Bridge* (c. 1954), set near Medonte, ooze Ontario in a year-round cycle of little things such as squeaky, snow-packed roads in February and fields of rasping crickets in August. Dan Needles's *Letters from Wingfield Farm* (1989) and Theatre Passe Muraille's *The Farm Show* (Johns and Thompson, 1976) are entertaining introductions to the modern rural scene, geared to city folks of the 1980s and 1990s seeking refuge in the country. Keith (1992) is a recent overview with a substantial landscape slant.

Pattern books

`Pattern book' is a comprehensive term for the hundreds of illustrated treatises on buildings and the land published throughout the nineteenth century. Most originated in the United States, and many found their way into libraries in Canada. They offer a distinctive mixture of writing on architecture, building technology, aesthetics, domestic science, agricultural economics, and social mores. The case studies tend to be from New England, New York, and Ohio, but a great many have a universality that makes them applicable to Ontario. All provide first-hand insights into the look of the land.

What follows is a list of the more useful pattern books for the study of Ontario, listed in chronological order.

Lafever, Minard. *The Modern Builder's Guide*. 1833. Reprint. New York: Dover
  Publications, 1969. Classical-revival architecture.
Hall, T. *A Series of Select and Original Modern Designs for Dwelling Houses*. Balti-
  more: John Murphy, 1840. Regency and classical-revival architecture.
Downing, Andrew Jackson. *The Architecture of Country Houses, including Designs for
  Cottages, Farm Houses, and Villas*. New York: Appleton, 1850. Fashionable country
  living; earth tones.
Bullock, John. *The American Cottage Builder*. New York: Stringer and Townsend,
  1854. Rebuilding.
Bell, William E. *Carpentry Made Easy*. 2nd ed. Philadelphia: Ferguson Brothers and
  Company, 1857. Timber framing. Further editions appeared until at least 1890.
Hammond, J. *The Farmer's and Mechanic's Practical Architect and Guide in Rural
  Economy*. Boston: J.P. Jewett, 1858. Broadly informative on vernacular matters.
Graef, F.E., et. al. *The House: A Pocket Manual of Rural Architecture*. New York:
  Fowler and Wells, 1859. The meaning of a house; thoughtful and vernacular.
Wheeler, Gervase. *Rural Houses*. New York: George E. Woodward, 1868. Plumbing,
  education.

Bicknell, Amos J. *Bicknell's Village Builder and Supplement.* 1872. Reprint. Watkins Glen, NY: American Life Foundation, 1976. Second Empire and Italianate architecture.

Dwyer, C.P. *The Immigrant Builder.* Philadelphia: Claxton, Remsen and Haffelfinger, 1872. The best vernacular building handbook.

Bicknell, Amos J., and Comstock, William T. *Victorian Architecture: Two Pattern Books.* 1873. Reprint, with introduction by John Maass. Watkins Glen, NY: American Life Foundation, 1977. House as social symbol.

A Cabinet of Quintissential Books. Watkins Glen, NY: American Life Foundation, 1981. Introduction by John Maass. This volume contains one-paragraph summaries of twenty pattern books reprinted by the American Life Foundation. Some have new introductions by Maass.

The spread of American pattern books into Canada might be traceable through the history of holdings at the University of Western Ontario (London), the University of Guelph, or the Metropolitan Toronto Reference Library. See also Tausky and DiStefano (1986), 69-77.

Canadian Inventory of Historic Building

The Canadian Inventory of Historic Building (CIHB) is a field study, undertaken during the 1970s by non-professional volunteers working within townships and villages throughout the province. Their task was to identify, describe, and classify buildings (excluding barns) apparently dating from before 1914. They used a variant of a check-off recording procedure devised in England by Brunskill (1978).

From the CIHB survey of about 300 houses in the Bay of Quinte region, recorded between 1972 and 1974, the following generalizations are possible. Almost all buildings are of unknown structure, and one cannot rely on outside-wall material to indicate what the structure is. Roof-pitch steepens as the nineteenth century progressed. Cambered (arched) bricks mounted vertically over window openings and doorways are characteristic of the 1870s and 1880s. Decorative trim of all sorts was being applied most commonly from the 1860s to the 1890s. Many new school buildings were put up in the 1870s.

The CIHB project was daunting, and the listing of buildings in itself is a major achievement. Refinements of the evidence have occurred, stimulated particularly by studies of individual buildings made by Local Architectural Conservation Advisory Committees (LACACs). The CIHB's records are deposited in the National Archives, Ottawa. For an evaluation of the project see Brian Coffey, 'The Canadian Inventory of Historic Buildings as a Basis for Housetype Classification: an Example from Southern Ontario,' *Canadian Geographer*, 28 (1984), 83-9.

Selected bibliography

Adamson, Anthony, and Willard, John. *The Gaiety of Gables*. Toronto: McClelland and Stewart, 1974.

Angus, James T.A. *Respectable Ditch: A History of the Trent-Severn Waterway, 1833–1920*. Montreal: McGill-Queen's University Press, 1988.

Angus, Margaret S. *The Old Stones of Kingston: Its Buildings before 1867*. Toronto: University of Toronto Press, 1966.

Appleton, Jay. *The Experience of Landscape*. London: John Wiley and Sons, 1975.

Armstrong, Fred, ed. *Aspects of Nineteenth Century Ontario*. Toronto: University of Toronto Press, 1974.

Arthur, Eric. *The Early Buildings of Ontario*. Toronto: University of Toronto Press, 1938.

– *Small Houses of the Late 18th and Early 19th Century in Ontario*. Toronto: University of Toronto, Department of University Extension, c. 1926.

Arthur, Eric, with Otto, Stephen A. *Toronto, No Mean City*. 3rd ed. Toronto: University of Toronto Press, 1986.

Arthur, Eric, and Ritchie, Thomas. *Iron: Cast and Wrought Iron in Canada from the Seventeenth Century to the Present*. Toronto: University of Toronto Press, 1982.

Arthur, Eric, and Witney, Dudley. *The Barn*. Toronto: McClelland and Stewart, 1972.

Ball, Norman R., ed. *Building Canada: A History of Public Works*. Toronto: University of Toronto Press, 1988.

Blake, Verschoyle B., and Greenhill, Ralph. *Rural Ontario*. Toronto: University of Toronto Press, 1969.

Blumenson, John J.-G. *Ontario Architecture: A Guide to Styles and Building Terms*. Toronto: Fitzhenry and Whiteside, 1990.

Blythe, Ronald. *Akenfield: Portrait of an English Village*. Harmondsworth: Penguin Books, 1969.

Bothwell, Robert. *A Short History of Ontario*. Toronto: Hurtig, 1986.

Bourcier, Paul G. `In Excellent Order: A Gentleman Farmer Views His Fences.´ *Agricultural History*, 58 (1984), 546–64.

Brosseau, Mathilde. *Gothic Revival in Canadian Architecture*. Ottawa: Parks Canada, 1980.

Brunskill, Ronald W. *Illustrated Handbook of Vernacular Architecture,* 2nd ed. London: Faber and Faber, 1978.

Brunskill, Ronald W. and Clifton-Taylor, Alec. *English Brickworks.* London: Ward Lock, 1977.

Buck, Charles S., `The Origin and Character of the Early Architecture and Practical Arts of Ontario to 1850.´ MA thesis, University of Western Ontario, 1930.

Bucovetsky, Joseph, and Greenwald, Michelle. *Townsend Traces: Heritage Conservation in Townsend New Town.* Toronto: Ontario Ministry of Culture and Recreation, 1976.

Byers, Mary, Kennedy, Jan, and McBurney, Margaret. *Rural Roots: Pre-Confederation Buildings of the York Region of Ontario.* Toronto: University of Toronto Press, 1977.

Byers, Mary, and McBurney, Margaret. *The Governor's Road: Early Buildings and Owners from Mississauga to London.* Toronto: University of Toronto Press, 1982.

Cameron, Christina, and Wright, Janet. *Second Empire Style in Canadian Architecture.* Canadian Historic Sites, Occasional Papers in Archaeology and History, no. 24. Ottawa: Parks Canada, 1980.

Casson, Alfred J. *My Favourite Watercolours.* New York: Cerebrus, Prentice-Hall, 1982.

Chapman, Lyman J., and Putnam, Donald F. *The Physiography of Southern Ontario.* 3rd ed. Toronto: University of Toronto Press, 1984.

Clay, Grady. *Close-Up: How to Read the American City.* New York: Praeger, 1973.

Countryside Planning: A Pilot Study of Huron County. Toronto: Ontario Ministry of Housing, 1976.

Cullen, Mary K. `Highlights of Domestic Building in Pre-Confederation Quebec and Ontario as Seen through Travel Literature from 1763 to 1860.´ *APT Bulletin,* 13 no. 1 (1981), 16–34.

Cuming, David J. *Discovering Heritage Bridges on Ontario's Roads.* Erin, Ont.: Boston Mills Press, 1983.

Davies, Robertson. *What's Bred in the Bone.* Toronto: Macmillan, 1985.

Denhez, Marc. *Heritage Fights Back.* Toronto: Fitzhenry and Whiteside, 1978.

Duval, Paul. *A.J. Casson, His Life and Works: A Tribute.* Toronto: Cerebrus, Prentice-Hall, 1980.

Ennals, Peter. `Nineteenth Century Barns in Southern Ontario.´ *Canadian Geographer,* 16 (1972), 256–70.

Evans, E. Estyn. *The Personality of Ireland: Habitat, Heritage, and History.* 2nd ed. Belfast: Blackstaff Press, 1981.

Evoy, Donald. `The Twelve: The Discovery of a Ghostscape.´ BA thesis, Department of Geography, Erindale Campus, University of Toronto, 1989.

Fox, W. Sherwood. *The Bruce Beckons: The Story of Lake Huron's Great Peninsula.* Toronto: University of Toronto Press, 1952.

Fox, William, Brooks, Bill, and Tyrwhitt, Janice. *The Mill.* Toronto: McClelland and Stewart, 1976.

Fram, Mark. *Ontario Hydro, Ontario Heritage: A Study of Strategies for the Conserva-*

tion of the Heritage of Ontario Hydro. Toronto: Ontario Ministry of Culture and Recreation, 1980.

Fram, Mark, and Weiler, John, eds. *Continuity with Change: Planning for the Conservation of Ontario's Man-made Heritage*. Toronto: Ontario Ministry of Culture and Recreation, 1981.

Galbraith, John Kenneth. *The Scotch*. Boston: Houghton-Mifflin, 1964.

Gentilcore, R. Louis. 'Lines on the Land: Crown Surveys and Settlement in Upper Canada,' *Ontario History* 61 (1969), 57–73.

Gentilcore, R. Louis, and Head, C. Grant. *Ontario History in Maps*. Toronto: University of Toronto Press, 1984.

Gillard, William, and Tooke, Thomas. *The Niagara Escarpment, from Tobermory to Niagara Falls*. Toronto: University of Toronto Press, 1975.

Gilmour, James M. *Spatial Evolution of Manufacturing: Southern Ontario, 1851–1891*. Toronto: University of Toronto Press, 1972.

Glassie, Henry. 'Artifact and Culture, Architecture and Society.' In Simon J. Bronner, ed., *American Culture and Folklife*, 47–62. Ann Arbor: University of Michigan Press, 1985.

– *Folk Housing in Middle Virginia.: A Structural Analysis of Historic Artifacts*. Knoxville: University of Tennessee Press, 1975.

– *Passing the Time in Ballymenone: Culture and History of an Ulster Community*. Philadelphia: University of Pennsylvania Press, 1982.

– 'The Variation of Concepts within Tradition: Barn Building in Otsego County, New York.' In H.J. Walker and W.G. Haag, eds., *Man and Cultural Heritage*, 177–235. Baton Rouge: Louisiana State University Press, 1974.

Gowans, Alan. *Building Canada: An Architectural History of Canadian Life*. New York: Oxford University Press, 1967.

Greenhill, Ralph, Macpherson, Ken, and Richardson, Douglas. *Ontario Towns*. Ottawa: Oberon Press, 1974.

Harris, Cole. 'The Simplification of Europe Overseas.' *Annals Association of American Geographics*, 67 (1977), 496–830.

Harris, R. Cole, and Warkentin, John. 'Ontario.' In R. Cole Harris and John Warkentin, eds., *Canada before Confederation*, 110–68. New York: Oxford University Press, 1974.

Holdsworth, Deryck W., ed. *Reviving Main Street*. Toronto: University of Toronto Press, 1985.

Hoskins, William G. *The Making of the English Landscape*. 2nd ed. Harmondsworth: Penguin Books, 1970.

Houston, Cecil J., and Smyth, William J. *The Sash Canada Wore: A Historical Geography of the Orange Order in Canada*. Toronto: University of Toronto Press, 1980.

Hubka, Thomas C. *Big House, Little House, Back House, Barn: The Connected Farm Buildings of New England*. Hanover, NH: University Press of New England, 1985.

Jackson, J. B. *Discovering the Vernacular Landscape*. New Haven: Yale University Press, 1984.

– *The Necessity for Ruins*. Amherst: University of Massachusetts Press, 1980.

Johns, Ted, and Thompson, Paul. *The Farm Show*. Toronto: Theatre Passe Muraille, Coach House Press, 1976.

Kalman, Harold, ed. *The Conservation of Ontario Churches*. Toronto: Ontario Ministry of Culture and Recreation, 1977.

Keith, W.J. *Literary Images of Ontario*. Toronto: University of Toronto Press, 1992.

Kelly, Kenneth. 'The Artificial Drainage of Land in Nineteenth-Century Southern Ontario.' *Canadian Geographer*, 19 (1975), 279–98.

Kidd, Martha Ann, and Taylor, Louis. *Historical Sketches of Peterborough*. Peterborough: Broadview Press, 1988.

Ladell, John L. *They Left Their Mark: Surveyors and Their Role in the Settlement of Ontario*. Toronto: Dundurn Press, 1993.

Ladell, John L., and Ladell, Monica. *Inheritance: Ontario's Century Farms, Past and Present*. Toronto: Macmillan, 1979.

Lee-Whiting, Brenda. *Harvest of Stones: The German Settlement in Renfrew County*. Toronto: University of Toronto Press, 1985.

Leitch, Adelaide. *The Visible Past: The Pictorial History of Simcoe County*. Toronto: Ryerson Press and County of Simcoe, 1967.

Leung, Felicity L. *Grist and Flour Mills in Ontario: From Millstones to Rollers, 1780s-1880s*. Historical and Archaeology Series, no. 53. Ottawa: National Parks Service, 1981.

Lewis, Peirce F. 'Axioms for Reading the Landscape.' In Donald W. Meinig, ed., *The Interpretation of Ordinary Landscapes*, 11–32. New York: Oxford University Press, 1979.

– 'Learning from Looking: Geographic and Other Writing about the American Cultural Landscape,' *American Quarterly*, 35 (1983), 242–61.

Lockwood, Glenn J. *Montague: A Social History of an Irish Ontario Township, 1783–1980*. Smiths Falls, Ont.: Township of Montague, 1980.

Lowenthal, David. *The Past Is a Foreign Country*. New York: Cambridge University Press, 1985.

MacGillivray, Royce. *The Mind of Ontario*. Belleville, Ont.: Mika, 1985.

McAlester, Virginia, and McAlester, Lee. *A Field Guide to American Houses*. New York: Knopf, 1984.

McCalla, Douglas, and George, Peter. 'Measurement, Myth and Reality: Reflections on the Economic History of Nineteenth Century Ontario.' *Journal of Canadian Studies*, 21 (1986), 71–86.

McIlwraith, Thomas F. 'Altered Buildings: Another Way of Looking at the Ontario Landscape.' *Ontario History*, 75 (1983), 110–34.

– 'British North America, 1763–1867.' In Robert D. Mitchell and Paul A. Groves, eds., *North America: The Historical Geography of a Changing Continent*, 218–52. Totowa, NJ: Rowman and Littlefield, 1987.

– 'The Fourth of Trafalgar.' In Donald Janelle, ed., *Geographic Snapshots of North America*, 333–6. New York: Methuen, 1992.

– 'The Ontario Country Road as a Cultural Resource.' *Canadian Geographer,* 39 (1995), 324–35.

MacRae, Marion, and Adamson, Anthony. *The Ancestral Roof: Domestic Architecture of Upper Canada.* Toronto: Clarke Irwin, 1963.

– *Cornerstones of Order: Courthouses and Town Halls in Ontario, 1784–1914.* Toronto: Clarke Irwin, 1985.

– *Hallowed Walls: Church Architecture of Upper Canada.* Toronto: Clarke Irwin, 1975.

Martin, Virgil. *Changing Landscapes in Southern Ontario.* Erin, Ont.: Boston Mills Press, 1989.

Meinig, Donald W., ed. *The Interpretation of Ordinary Landscapes.* New York: Oxford University Press, 1979.

Miller, Marilyn G. *Straight Lines in Curved Space: Colonization Roads in Eastern Ontario.* Toronto: Ontario Ministry of Culture and Recreation, 1978.

Munro, Alice. *Dance of the Happy Shades.* Toronto: Ryerson Press, 1968.

– *Lives of Girls and Women.* Toronto: McGraw-Hill Ryerson, 1971.

Munroe [*sic*], Alice. 'The Edge of Town,' *Queen's Quarterly,* 62 (1955), 368–80.

Needles, Dan. *Letters from Wingfield Farm.* Toronto: Key-Porter Books, 1989.

Nelles, H.V. *The Politics of Development.* Toronto: Macmillan, 1975.

Newell, Dianne, and Greenhill, Ralph, eds. *Survivals: Aspects of Industrial Archaeology in Ont..* Erin, Ontario: Boston Mills Press, 1989.

Norris, Darrell A. 'Ontario Fences and the American Scene.' *American Review of Canadian Studies,* 12 no. 2 (1982), 37–50.

Norris, Darrell A., and Konrad, Victor. 'Time, Context and House Type Validation: Euphrasia Township, Ontario.' *Canadian Papers in Rural History,* 3 (1982), 50–83.

Otto, Steven A. *Maitland: 'A Very Neat Village Indeed.'* Erin, Ont.: Boston Mils Press, 1985.

Peattie, Donald C. *A Natural History of Trees.* New York: Houghton Mifflin, 1950.

Pugin, Augustus Welby. *An Apology for the Revival of Christian Architecture in England.* First published 1843. Reprint Oxford: St Barnabas Press, 1969.

Rempel, John I. *Building with Wood, and Other Aspects of Nineteenth-Century Building in Central Canada.* 2nd ed. Toronto: University of Toronto Press, 1980.

Rickard, George P. *Sketching Rambles in Ontario: A Collection of Pen-and-ink Drawings.* 2 vols. London: George Rickard Studios, 1977.

Ritchie, Thomas, ed. *Canada Builds, 1867–1967.* Toronto: University of Toronto Press, 1967.

Ruskin, John. *The Seven Lamps of Architecture.* First published 1851. Reprint London: George Allen, 1906.

Sadler, Doug. *Reading Nature's Clues: A Guide to the Wild.* Peterborough, Ont.: Broadview Press, 1987.

Schlereth, Thomas J., ed. *Artifacts and the American Past.* Nashville, Tenn.: American Association for State and Local History, 1980.

Schull, Joseph. *Ontario since 1867.* Toronto: McClelland and Stewart, 1978.

Spelt, Jacob. *The Urban Development in South Central Ontario.* First published 1955. Reprint Toronto: McClelland and Stewart, 1975.

Stilgoe, John R. *Common Landscapes of America, 1580 to 1845.* New Haven, Conn.: Yale University Press, 1982.

Symons, Harry. *Fences.* Toronto: Ryerson Press, 1958.

Tausky, Nancy Z., and DiStefano, Lynne D. *Victorian Architecture in London and Southwestern Ontario: Symbols of Aspiration.* Toronto: University of Toronto Press, 1986.

Thorean, Henry David. `Walking.´ First pub. 1862 in *Atlantic Monthly.* Reprinted in Lily Owen, ed., *Works of Henry David Thoreau,* 369–414. New York: Avenel Books, 1981.

Watts, May Theilgaard. *Reading the Landscape of America.* New York: Macmillan, 1975.

Weitzman, David. *Underfoot: An Everyday Guide to Exploring the American Past.* New York: Scribner´s, 1976.

Wells, Kenneth M. *By Jumping Cat Bridge.* Toronto: William Heinemann Limited, 1956.

Westfall, William. *Two Worlds: The Protestant Culture of Nineteenth-Century Ontario.* Montreal: McGill-Queen´s University Press, 1989.

Wood, J. David, ed. *Perspectives on Landscape and Settlement in Nineteenth Century Ontario.* Toronto: McClelland and Stewart, 1975.

Zube, Ervin H., and Zube, Margaret J., eds. *Changing Rural Landscapes.* Amherst: University of Massachusetts, 1977.

Illustration credits

All photographs, unless otherwise specified below, were taken by the author, between 1963 and 1995.

Archives of Ontario: Figures 1.1 (S5422), 7.1 (S16349), 11.1 (S7903), 13.4 (13281-153), 15.3 (S11947), 15.7 (16607-1-48, no. 27), and 18.3 (Burrowes Collection, no. 38).

Beatty Barn Book (Fergus, Ont.: Beatty Brothers, 1930): Figure 5.5.

Cartography Laboratory, University of Toronto: Figures 4.2, 4.4, 4.6, 4.10, 5.16, 8.11, 10.2, 11.3, and 14.4.

Cartography Laboratory, University of Toronto, and Donald Evoy: Figures 1.3, 2.2, 3.10, 4.3, 4.11, 6.2, 6.6, 6.11, and 9.5.

Donald Evoy: Figure 19.1.

Mark Fram: Figure 11.14.

Gunter Gad: Figure 11.6.

Globe and Mail: Figure 18.6 (Fred Ross, 2 March 1968, 5).

Toronto Mill Furnishing Works: Illustrated General Catalogue of Mill Machinery and Supplies (Toronto: W. and J.G. Greey, 1888): Figure 11.5.

Illustrated Historical Atlas of the County of Northumberland and Durham (Toronto: H. Belden and Company, 1878): Figure 12.3.

Metropolitan Toronto Reference Library: Figure 5.13 (Salmon Collection, S1-662).

National Archives of Canada: C.P. Meredith Collection: Figures 5.6 (PA26966), 6.4 (PA26873), and 6.10 (PA26823).

Darrell Norris: Figure 5.7.

Simcoe County Archives, Barrie: Figure 16.4.

Index